Working Couples Caring for Children and Aging Parents

Effects on Work and Well-Being

SERIES IN APPLIED PSYCHOLOGY

Edwin A. Fleishman, George Mason University,
Jeanette N. Cleveland, Pennsylvania State University
Series Editors

Heinz Schuler, James L. Farr, and Mike Smith
Personnel Selection and Assessment: Individual and Organizational Perspectives

John W. Senders and Neville P. Moray
Human Error: Cause, Prediction, and Reduction

Frank J. Smith
Organizational Surveys: The Diagnosis and Betterment of Organizations Through Their Members

George C. Thornton III and Rose Mueller-Hanson
Developing Organizational Simulations: A Guide for Practitioners and Students

George C. Thornton III and Deborah Rupp
Assessment Centers in Human Resource Management: Strategies for Prediction, Diagnosis, and Development

Yoav Vardi and Ely Weitz
Misbehavior in Organizations: Theory, Research and Management

Patricia Voydanoff
Work, Family and Community

**For more information on LEA titles, please contact
Lawrence Erlbaum Associates, Publishers, at www.erlbaum.com**

Working Couples Caring for Children and Aging Parents

Effects on Work and Well-Being

by

Margaret B. Neal, PhD
Institute on Aging, Portland State University

and

Leslie B. Hammer, PhD
Department of Psychology, Portland State University

2007

LAWRENCE ERLBAUM ASSOCIATES, PUBLISHERS

Mahwah, New Jersey   London

Lawrence Erlbaum Associates, Inc., Publishers
10 Industrial Avenue
Mahwah, New Jersey 07430
www.erlbaum.com

Cover design by Kathryn Houghtaling Lacey

Library of Congress Cataloging-in-Publication Data

Neal, Margaret B.
Working couples caring for children and aging parents : effects on work-family fit, well-being, and work / by Margaret B. Neal and Leslie B. Hammer.

p. cm.

Includes bibliographical references and index.
ISBN 978-0-8058-4603-4 — 0-8058-4603-4 (cloth)
ISBN 978-0-8058-4604-1 — 0-8058-4604-2 (pbk.)

1. Work and family—United States. 2. Sandwich generation—United States. 3. Dual-career families—United States. I. Hammer, Leslie B. II. Title.
HD4904.25.N44   2006
306.8740973—dc22

2006029720
CIP

Printed in the United States of America
10 9 8 7 6 5 4 3 2 1

This book is dedicated to all working couples caring for children and aging parents everywhere, and especially to those who so generously agreed to share their experiences with us by participating in our research.

We dedicate it, as well, to our own husbands, parents, children and grandchildren: David Leckey and Lee Spector; Rosemary and Maurice Neal, Barbara and Charles Hammer, and Marjorie and Harry Spector; Erin, Jamien, Christian, Sharon, Cole and Lola Leckey, and Joshua and Benjamin Spector.

MBN and LBH
Let us take care of the children,
for they have a long way to go.
Let us take care of the elders,
for they have come a long way.
Let us take care of those in between,
for they are doing the work.
—*Traditional African Prayer*

Contents

III: Effecting Change: Where Do We Go from Here?

Series Foreword

Series Editors

Jeanette N. Cleveland
Pennsylvania State University

Edwin A. Fleishman
George Mason University

There is a compelling need for innovative approaches to the solution of many pressing problems involving human relationships in today's society. Such approaches are more likely to be successful when they are based on sound research and applications. This Series in Applied Psychology offers publications that emphasize state-of-the-art research and its application to important issues of human behavior in a variety of social settings. The objective is to bridge both academic and applied interests.

The rapidly aging population within the United States is described as "one of the most important social phenomena of the next half century" (Preston & Martin, 1994, p. 3). As Baby Boomers approach age 60, the U.S. workforce will begin to lose millions of highly skilled and experienced workers during the next decade due to retirement. This, coupled with the drop in birthrates following the Baby Boomers, could lead to labor shortages of younger entrants into the workforce. At the same time, managing family responsibilities while maintaining a job is another critical workforce issue. The participation rates of women with children, especially young children, have increased. Within an aging society, increasing numbers of workers will take on multiple caregiving responsibilities. The resulting demographic shift and lengthening life span places tremendous burden on working couples who must care for both children and their aging parents.

Margaret B. Neal and Leslie B. Hammer have skillfully integrated two of the most significant workforce trends: aging society and work–family caregiving. Workers who take care of family members at both ends of the life span—children and elders—are called the "sandwiched generation." Because of a confluence of demographic shifts, this generation is increasing with its unique set of work, family stress, and health issues. This book is based on one of the first longitudinal studies of working couples who are caring for both children and parents.

The goal of the research and book is multifaceted: (1) to provide a profile of dual-earner couples who provide care for both children and aging parents, (2) to determine the prevalence of these couples, and (3) to understand the effect of being sandwiched at work and for well-being. Research on work and family issues has historically focused on how *individuals* navigate among the various life domains. In addition to expanding the caregiver role to include aging parents as well as children, the authors incorporate a neglected unit of analysis in this book: namely, dual-earner *couples*.

From the first chapter, the sandwiched generation is identified, defined, and placed within a larger historical context of more traditional research on work and family. Neglected research areas within work and family are presented, highlighting the dearth of information or understanding of work and family concerns involving the care of elderly persons. One such neglected area is simply tracking family-care arrangements using U.S. census data or other large-scale surveys. Therefore, one first step reported in the book is the telephone screening of more than 33,000 U.S. households. On the basis of these calls, between 9% and 13% of households with a telephone and with one or more persons aged 30 through 60 are composed of dual-earner, sandwiched-generation couples. This is a conservative estimate using a fairly narrow definition of *sandwiched generation*. Although these proportions are modest, there are several reasons why this population is important, including the aging of the American population and workforce, the delay in and reduced childbearing and the increase in the age of parents with young children, rising health care costs, increasing numbers of families in which both parents work and care for children/elders, and because of increasing evidence that work–family demands affect the health and well-being of individuals and the productivity of organizations.

Three chapters provide a rich backdrop and introduction to the longitudinal research study and results. A historical review of work and family initiatives (or lack thereof) within the United States is presented, including an interesting documentation of the parallels between U.S. demographic trends and the availability of work–family initiatives. In addition, another chapter is devoted to the range of caregiving options available in other countries facing similar demographic shift and caregiving pressures. A third chapter prior to the introduction of the research study itself provides a review of the theoretical perspectives underlying the relationships and dynamics between our work and family lives.

Six chapters describe the rich, year-long longitudinal data on 309 couples at Time 1 and 234 couples at Time 2 who provide care for both their children and their parents. Results are reported for both wives and husbands and at the couple level on such important outcomes as absenteeism, depression, and work-to-family and family-to-work conflict as well as positive spillover, or facilitation. A model of coping strategies is presented based on past research on stress and coping and on the qualitative advice from couples. This is followed by a discussion of findings on couple coping strategies and their effects on work and well-being. Again, Neal and Hammer are able to discuss not only results from wives and husbands separately but also the stress or coping strategy of one spouse and the effects on the other spouse, or crossover.

In addition to individual- and couple-level coping strategies, the perceived benefits associated with workplace supports are assessed. The supports include more formal support or organizational policies such as flexible work arrangements, services such as resource and referral systems about dependent-care options, and benefits such as child care. Informal supports include the degree to which an organization is perceived to have a family-friendly or positive work–family culture. As Neal and Hammer point out, the number of formal work and family programs offered by organizations has increased over the years. However, there are few studies that document the extent of program utilization or program effectiveness in reducing work–family conflict.

Changes in work and family roles are presented separately in the chapter describing findings from the longitudinal data. Longitudinal data were obtained to assess the changes that occurred in role demands and role quality. In addition, Neal and Hammer assessed how these changes affected the outcomes of interest in the study, specifically, work–family fit, well-being, and work-related outcomes. The final chapter in the book provides an overview of the major findings and recommendations for future research. In addition, the authors discuss their findings, highlighting their implications for couples within the sandwiched generation, for employers and managers, for family-care practitioners, and for policymakers.

Foreword

In an aging society with an aging workforce, increasing numbers of workers will assume multiple caregiving responsibilities. Perhaps none will bear the burden more than those dual-earner couples who simultaneously care for children and aging parents. Characterized as the "sandwiched generation," their experiences have not yet been fully described or understood—until now. In this important book, *Working Couples Caring for Children and Aging Parents,* by Margaret B. Neal and Leslie B. Hammer, we see analyzed, for the first time, the issues faced by as many as 1 in 10 of all American households. We gain insight into the typical sandwiched couple, learning that these dual earners are most apt to be in their 40s and to work for pay over 85 hours a week, while caring for two children and two aging parents. The care of the parents alone adds the equivalent of over 2 full workdays a week to their responsibilities. Yet, as Hammer and Neal reveal, shouldering these caregiving responsibilities also yields some very positive consequences on the couples' health and well being.

The Alfred P. Sloan Foundation is pleased to have provided the support for the research that informed this book, as well as for its writing. This support is part of a larger effort begun by Sloan over a decade ago. In 1994, the foundation launched a major grant-making initiative that has had as one of its primary goals the support of basic research on working families at all stages of their lives. Over these past 11 years, the foundation has funded six Centers on Working Families, one Workplace Center, and one Center on Older Workers, in addition to nearly 200 other research projects that have examined issues faced by working families. Our research has focused on working families at all stages of the life span: from child bearing to child rearing to aging and retirement. By providing the only source of sustained funding for researchers in sociology, psychology, anthropology, political science, labor economics, and industrial relations to conduct interdisci-

plinary research on issues faced by working families, the Sloan Foundation has played a vital role in developing a new field scholarship focused
on the intersection of working families and the workplace. But this research has revealed a fundamental structural problem that will not be un-
familiar to many readers.

Many of Sloan's research investigations have identified a basic mismatch between the needs and priorities of working families and the way
that work is organized into full-time, full-year arrangements, with few to
no opportunities for time off. While the demographics of the American
workforce have changed dramatically over the last 30 years, the American
workplace is organized in very much the same way it was when the
workforce consisted almost entirely of male breadwinners. It is not surprising, therefore, that much of the Sloan-supported research, including
the important work in this volume, reveals that significant percentages of
working Americans, at all stages of their lives, want more flexibility at
work. And that flexibility provides a basic way of correcting the workplace–workforce mismatch.

The sandwiched couples of today, while facing dual responsibilities for
aging parents and children, will likely be the older workers of tomorrow
who will have caregiving responsibilities for aging spouses and grandchildren. As this timely book suggests, it is incumbent upon us to understand
the issues that these workers face and to identify what they need to be able
to fulfill their work and family responsibilities. One certain arena for
change is the workplace. We must face the challenge of ensuring that the
workplace of today fits the aging workforce of tomorrow. And there is no
better way to start than by identifying and understanding the needs of today's workers as they care for their family members, regardless of their
ages and circumstances.

—*Kathleen Christensen*
Alfred P. Sloan Foundation
New York City
May 30, 2006

Preface

This book is the culmination of one of the first comprehensive national studies of working, "sandwiched-generation" couples, that is, dual-earner couples caring both for children and aging parents. The study was funded by the Alfred P. Sloan Foundation for the purpose of identifying, understanding, and ultimately improving the interrelationships between work and family roles over time and their impact on work–family fit, well-being, and work among middle- and upper-income working, sandwiched couples from across the United States. Early findings of the research have been highlighted in *Time Magazine, Businessweek Online, Seattle Weekly,* the *Chicago Tribune,* MSNBC.com, and on the *NBC Nightly News.*

DISTINGUISHING FEATURES OF THE BOOK

This book focuses on a unique group of working couples: the *sandwiched generation,* that is, those caring both for dependent children and for aging parents. Because of this focus alone, the book is very different from existing ones on work and family issues. Moreover, we present data from *both members of couples.* Typically, information is collected from just one "representative" member; dyadic data provide a more complete picture of the family and also enable direct examination of the effects of one member's attitudes and behaviors on the other's. In addition, because we gathered data at two points in time, we can address *change over time* in caregiving responsibilities and the effects of those changes on individuals' work–family fit, well-being, and work. The vast majority of existing work–family research is based on cross-sectional data only. Another distinctive feature of the book is our focus on the *positive, as well as negative, aspects* of combining work and family; previous research has neglected the positive outcomes.

Finally, the *quantitative* findings are supplemented with *qualitative* data. The data gathered through this mixed-methods approach are extremely rich in depth and breadth. Quotations from focus group, survey, and telephone interview participants are presented to contextualize the findings presented and to illustrate particular points.

We, the authors, have an extensive history of collaborating together on projects, including the study on which the book is based. In addition, we represent multiple disciplines (i.e., industrial/organizational psychology, gerontology, urban studies, and sociology) and methodologies (quantitative and qualitative). Previous organizational research pertaining to work–family issues has lacked a gerontological focus, prior gerontological research has lacked an organizational perspective, and previous work–family research has only rarely integrated mixed methods (qualitative and quantitative data).

This book offers important information to managers; policymakers; academics; family-care practitioners; and working, sandwiched couples themselves. We expect that it will be of particular interest to these couples; human resource, employee assistance, and work/life professionals; corporate and public policymakers; and researchers, teachers, and students in the disciplines of industrial/organizational psychology, gerontology, sociology, family studies, health psychology, occupational health psychology and public health. We hope that individuals in other nations, as well as the United States, will find the book useful. Although methodologically rigorous, we have written the book so as to be accessible by nonresearchers and researchers alike. We believe that all those who are interested in the interface between individuals' work and family lives will find something of value here, particularly those who are concerned with elder care as well as child-care related issues.

BACKGROUND AND APPROACH

This 3-year study, initiated in 1997, involved the collection of longitudinal qualitative and quantitative data. The project began with focus groups held locally, in Portland, Oregon, with a sample of working couples caring for children and aging parents. Our goal was to learn about the role responsibilities of these couples and the coping strategies, workplace accommodations, and workplace supports they used. We then identified a national sample of such couples using telephone screening and surveyed them by mail; 309 couples (618 individuals) meeting the study criteria for participation completed the survey. We resurveyed the same couples by mail 1 year later to assess changes in their work and family characteristics and outcomes. Both members of 234 of the couples responded to second wave of the mailed survey. At the conclusion of the project, we reconvened two focus groups to discuss role changes that had occurred. We also conducted telephone interviews with individuals whose outcomes had improved the most and others whose outcomes had deteriorated the most over the year between the surveys, to learn in greater detail about what factors had contributed to these changes.

The majority of the findings presented in this book are based on the first wave of survey data. This has allowed us to highlight the characteristics of working, sandwiched couples and describe the relationships between these characteristics and individuals' work–family fit, well-being, and work outcomes in a straightforward way. Furthermore, we did not expect changes in the outcomes to occur beyond those due to changes in the roles occupied (spouse, parent, caregiver to an aging parent, and worker). One chapter (chap. 10), however, is devoted to examining these changes over time in characteristics and their effects on changes in individuals' outcomes.

To facilitate examination of similarities and differences between husbands and wives, and for purposes of understanding the family system, we collected data from both members of the couple. Although there are statistical techniques that enable examination of couples as the unit of analysis, it was our belief that we could most clearly depict the lives of working, sandwiched couples by focusing on individuals as the unit of analysis, comparing husbands and wives with respect to their role characteristics and outcomes and by examining the effects of one spouse's attitudes and behaviors on the other's. Thus, throughout the book we have highlighted similarities and differences between husbands and wives and included sections on spousal crossover effects within the relevant chapters.

ORGANIZATION OF THE BOOK

The book has three parts: Introduction, Findings From a National Study, and Effecting Change: Where Do We Go From Here? Beginning each chapter and throughout the book, as appropriate, quotations from study participants are included to illustrate the issues and challenges faced by dual-earner couples caring for children and aging parents and the strategies they have adopted to help them manage their work and family lives.

In Part 1, chapter 1 establishes the context for the book, describing the population of study—dual-earner couples in the sandwiched generation—and its prevalence, trends affecting prevalence, and why this group is of interest. Chapter 2 provides a general review of employer and governmental policies affecting work and family life in the United States, describing the history of employer-based provision of supports for working families in the United States, the range of available employer and governmental supports, and factors affecting both the provision and the use of supports. Chapter 3 describes current work and family initiatives in countries other than the United States. Chapter 4 provides an overview of key theoretical perspectives on the work and family interface and describes our book's conceptual framework.

Part 2 (chaps. 5–10) constitutes the bulk of the book. In it, we present the findings from our national study of working couples caring for children and aging parents. In chapter 5, we briefly describe the study's research methods and then detail the personal, family, and work-related characteristics of participants in the survey. In chapter 6, we describe our findings concerning the relationships between participants' role characteristics and outcomes pertaining to work–family fit, well-being, and work. We examine both positive and negative outcomes of working and having multiple family caregiving roles and identify the factors that predict those outcomes. Chapter 7 presents the development of our model of coping strategies used by working, sandwiched couples and the corresponding measure used for the analyses described in chapter 8 concerning the effects of work–family coping strategies on work–family fit, well-being, and work. In chapter 9, we examine the workplace supports that are used and desired by working sandwiched couples, and then the effects of use of supports. In addition to the effects of role characteristics (chap. 6), coping strategies used (chap. 8), and workplace supports used (chap. 9) on *individuals*, in each of those chapters, we also present findings from dyadic analyses, that is, *couple, or crossover*, effects. *Longitudinal* analyses are then presented in chapter 10, focusing on changes in work and family roles that occur over time and how these changes affect work–family fit, well-being, and work.

Part 3 consists of the book's final chapter: chapter 11, in which we summarize the key findings from the study and offer recommendations for working, sandwiched couples themselves, employers, policymakers, practitioners, and researchers.

Acknowledgments

We began the research project upon which the book is based in January 1997. The project and the book would not have been possible without the support, both financial and emotional, from numerous sources. We are grateful to Kathleen Christensen (Program Officer) and the Alfred P. Sloan Foundation for their support. Without the initial enthusiasm of Kathleen for our project, it never would have happened. And without the funding from the Sloan Foundation, we would not have had the resources to undertake such a significant national study. We thank the Department of Psychology for providing the space needed to carry out this large project and the Institute on Aging for administrative support throughout. In addition, we thank Portland State University for providing general support and resources to us.

We are deeply indebted to the many graduate and undergraduate students who played critical roles in our research over the past 8 years and without whom we would not have been able to carry out the study. Foremost are Jo Isgrigg and Krista Brockwood, who served as Project Managers, and who applied their excellent organizational skills to make sure that the day-to-day logistics of the project kept running smoothly. In addition, we thank the following students who participated in various aspects of the project, many of whom have now moved into their own careers: Ishrat Ara, Kathleen Bonn, Paula Carder, Suzanne Caubet, Cari Colton, Jennifer Cullen, Alan DeLaTorre, Terry Hammond, Ginger Hanson, Yueng Hsiang Huang, Jeffrey Johnson, Daniel Kaung, Erin Leckey, Jost Lottes, Nisreen Pedhiwala, Angela Rickard, Khatera Sahibzada, Margarita Shafiro, and Kathleen Sullivan.

We are truly grateful to many colleagues who so willingly provided support and consultation during the various phases of our research project. They include Marie Beaudet, Vern Bengtson, Todd Bodner, Berit Ingersoll-Dayton,

Keith Kaufman, Elizabeth Kutza, Cynthia Mohr, David Morgan, Jason Newsom, Ellen Skinner, Robert Sinclair, Aloen Townsend, Donald Truxillo, Donna Wagner, and IOR and Psychology faculty, staff and students.

We would also like to acknowledge the early assistance of two consultants on our project, Rosalind Barnett and Richard Schulz, as well as that provided by colleagues who served as discussants on symposia based on the findings of our study and who offered extremely valuable feedback on the papers: Anne Martin-Matthews, Carolyn Rosenthal, and Mary Ann Parris Stephens.

We thank Jamien Leckey for assistance with child care during our focus groups and Ellie Justice, Director of the Portland State University Helen Gordon Child Development Center, for the use of space during our focus groups.

We are grateful to Anne Duffy, our editor at Lawrence Erlbaum Associates, and Jeanette Cleveland and Edwin Fleishman, the Applied Psychology series editors, for their continued support and encouragement throughout the book-writing process. They continually reinforced our work by stating and restating the importance of our contributions. We are grateful, as well, to four reviewers who provided important substantive comments that improved the final book manuscript: Tammy Allen, Ann Crouter, Donna Wagner, and Mina Westman.

We also thank those individuals in our community of friends who have provided informal support in so many countless ways. These people include, but are not limited to, Monica Brenner and Susan Greenberg, friends of Leslie's, and Maria Talbott, friend of Margaret's.

For their support and patience throughout this 9-year process we cannot thank our families enough, including our spouses (Margaret's husband David Leckey and Leslie's husband Lee Spector), parents (Rosemary and Maurice Neal, Barbara and Charles Hammer, and Marjorie and Harry Spector), and children (Erin, Jamien, Christian, and Sharon Leckey, and Joshua and Benjamin Spector). During this time, between the two of us, we have experienced the birth of two children (Joshua, now 9 years old, and Benjamin now 6 years old), two grandchildren (Cole, nearly 3 years old, and Lola, born May 29, 2006), the relocation of both sets of parents to Portland (Margaret's early in the project, Leslie's at the end of the project), the loss of three cats, and the addition of three cats. Indeed, we have felt sandwiched ourselves from time to time.

We have come to appreciate even more the value of a family systems approach to thinking about the intersection between work and care, due to the increased responsibility assumed by our respective husbands as our work and family care demands grew in substance and complexity. In fact, each of our spouses were gratified to learn of one of the key findings of the study, the importance of spousal role quality to well-being.

Finally, and especially, we express our deepest gratitude to all of the couples who took the time out of their very busy lives to participate in and contribute to our study.

—*MBN and LBH*

List of Figures

PART

I

INTRODUCTION

1

The Sandwiched Generation: Introduction

I have a wonderful place to work. I just wish they would let me go to my appointments ... They let me most of the time, but they have an attitude about it ... It is hard to be "The All" for everyone: wife, mother, career lady, and help out my parents.

... Between my health and the stress of my father-in-law, then trying to sell the home, and raise three kids, and work full time, it's just taken a toll on our marriage.

Maintaining a job while managing family responsibilities has become a major issue for much of today's workforce, and some workers are caring for family members at both ends of the life span: children and elders. These employees are members of a unique and understudied group called *the sandwiched generation* (e.g., D. A. Miller, 1981; Nichols & Junk, 1997). A survey of IBM's workforce conducted in 1986 found that 6% of employees were caring both for elders and for children; 5 years later, this figure had jumped to 11%, although estimates have varied from 6% to 40% depending on workforce demographics (i.e., age, gender, marital status; Durity, 1991). Although no more recent statistics on employees caring both for children and elders could be located, the Families and Work Institute's National Study of the Changing Workforce found that the percentage of employees who reported having elder-care responsibilities within the previous year increased from 25% in 1997 (Bond, Galinsky, & Swanberg, 1998) to 35% in 2002 (Bond, Thompson, Galinsky, & Prottas, 2003). Thus, it appears that the numbers of sandwiched employees may well be on the rise.

Several social and demographic trends have contributed to the phenomenon of working, sandwiched-generation caregivers in the United States, including delayed childbearing (Casper & Bianchi, 2002), the aging of the American population, the aging of the American workforce, an increasing number of women in the workforce, decreases in family size and changes in family composition, and rising health care costs (Neal & Wagner, 2002).

In this book, we present findings from our Alfred P. Sloan Foundation-funded national, longitudinal study of working couples caring both for dependent children and aging parents. Because of their multiple family roles as spouses, parents, and caregivers to their own aging parents, these workers are likely to be among the most stressed with respect to their family obligations, and this stress is likely to extend to the work setting. Furthermore, this work stress is likely to have a more profound impact on family life, compared with workers who have fewer family obligations.

Our purpose for the research we present here is to provide a profile of dual-earner couples caring both for children and aging parents, to determine the prevalence of these couples, and to understand the effects of being sandwiched on work and well-being. In addition, we felt that, given the complexity of their lives, much could be learned from these couples regarding how they manage their work and family responsibilities and the coping strategies and workplace supports that are most effective in helping couples best integrate work and family. This information can then be used by sandwiched couples themselves and by practitioners and policy-makers to design programs to best meet the needs of working couples caring for children and aging parents.

In particular, we describe how the working couples in our study best achieve "fit" between their work lives and their family lives, along with well-being and positive work outcomes. On the basis of these findings, we provide suggestions for practice and policy for human resources personnel; employee assistance programs; work-life professionals; and working, sandwiched couples themselves. There is a growing need for researchers and practitioners alike to recognize that employees may care not only for children but also for aging parents or other relatives. Because the responsibility of maintaining a job and caring for family members of all ages can, at times, be overwhelming, and can affect both the health of workers and organizations' bottom lines, it is in all of our interests to identify ways to help people and their employers deal effectively with both work and family responsibilities.

In this first chapter, we discuss some neglected areas of research within the existing work–family literature. We then define the group of individuals about whom this book is written—that is, couples who are simultaneously working, caring for children, and caring for aging parents—and we discuss their prevalence. We provide the rationale for studying this group of people and note the important social and demographic influences that led us to conduct our study. Finally, we review the limited existing literature on working, sandwiched couples.

Before proceeding, it is important to note that although we refer to the work–family interface in this book, this is due to our focus on working, sandwiched-generation couples, who, by definition, are attempting to manage their work and *family* lives. We recognize that, as Lewis, Rapoport, and Gambles (2003) and others have frequently noted, to have the greatest relevance and impact, work–family research and practice must shift to a broader focus on work and *life*, rather than work and family, to include examination of the full range of nonwork aspects of employees' lives, regardless of their family situations. Nonetheless, we use the term *work–family* because of the specific focus of our book, on working couples caring for children and aging parents.

We discuss two other terms that we use in this book as well: *elder care* and *parent care*. We agree with Martin-Matthews (1996, cited in Martin-Matthews, 1999) that the term *elder care* is potentially pejorative and implies inappropriate parallels to child care. Several factors, in fact, distinguish child care from elder care, including "the trajectory and duration of care, the presumption of dependency of the care receiver, the role of reciprocity, the autonomous decision making of the care receiver, and the potential involvement of formal community services" (Martin-Matthews & Campbell, 1995, cited in Martin-Matthews, 1999, p. 24). Thus, the two are qualitatively different. Because these terms are commonly used in the gerontological and organizational literatures, and because we could identify no other reasonably concise terms to use in their stead, we reluctantly use them here.

BACKGROUND ON THE STUDY OF WORK AND FAMILY AND THE SANDWICHED GENERATION

The relationship between work and nonwork activities has been recognized for more than 100 years, with interest in work and family issues being traced to the work of Engels in 1844 (Wilensky, 1960). Studies of this relationship have been initiated by child and marriage specialists, clinical psychologists, family sociologists, demographers, vocational psychologists, industrial and organizational psychologists, gerontologists, and specialists in organizational behavior and human resources management. Because the intersection of work and family has been examined from many different theoretical and philosophical perspectives, there have been inconsistencies in conceptual frameworks and even in which factors are viewed as antecedents and which are seen as consequences. Furthermore, the existing research has been subject to design and sampling limitations. For example, most research has been cross-sectional in nature, looking at the situation at just one point in time. Also, much of the existing research has failed to include men, culturally diverse populations, and/or individuals in a wide variety of occupations.

Prior research also has neglected to examine the effects of combining work and family roles on dual-earner *couples*, focusing instead on individuals (Barnett, 1998; Hammer, Allen, & Grigsby, 1997; Rosenthal, Martin-Matthews, & Matthews, 1996), despite the growing number of such couples in the workforce (Zedeck, 1992). Very few studies have examined the larger family context—for example, by gathering data from both members of couples. The limited research of this nature that has been conducted, however, has demonstrated that one spouse's stress and strain in his or her various roles can cross over and affect the stress and strain of the other spouse in his or her various roles (Hammer et al., 1997; Parasuraman, Greenhaus, & Granrose, 1992; Westman, 2001). Studying both members of the couple contributes to improved understanding of the family system and the ways in which it affects the work system and vice versa.

Another area that has been neglected in the work–family research literature, although not in the gerontological literature, is the study of employees who are caring informally for aging parents and other elders or adults with disabilities. The U.S. population is aging at a rapid rate because of an increase in life expectancy and a decline in the birth rate. Thus, the number of individuals caring for elders is increasing. It is often the case that these individuals with elder-care responsibilities have other role commitments as well (e.g., spouse, employee, and/or parent; Neal, Chapman, Ingersoll-Dayton, & Emlen, 1993; Penning, 1998). For example, in their study of 9,573 employees in 33 different companies, Neal et al. (1993) found that 42% of the employees who were caring for elders (including aging parents or other relatives or friends) were also caring for children. Using data from the Informal Caregivers Survey, Stone and Short (1990) found that 34% ($N = 1003$) of all caregivers to disabled elderly persons (i.e., elders who were limited in one or more activities of daily living) had children younger than 18 years, and a similar percentage, 33% ($N = 491$) of employed caregivers to disabled elderly persons had children younger than 18 years. These individuals with dual caregiving roles have been dubbed the *sandwich* or *sandwiched generation* (Durity, 1991; Fernandez, 1990; D. A. Miller, 1981; Nichols & Junk, 1997; Rosenthal et al., 1996; Spillman & Pezzin, 2000), in that they are sandwiched between the needs of their children and their parents, and often, their jobs.

THE PREVALENCE OF INDIVIDUALS CARING FOR CHILDREN AND CARING FOR PARENTS IN THE UNITED STATES

Although, as Rosenthal et al. (1996) noted, being sandwiched between caring for children and aging parents is not a typical situation, the issue has practical significance, and individuals, employers, and the general community must be more informed about the needs of this important demographic group in order to craft supports that will be as responsive as possible. In this section, we provide the latest prevalence estimates available of members of the sandwiched generation in the United States. We follow with prevalence estimates of sandwiched-generation individuals in other countries.

Available estimates of the prevalence of adults with caregiving responsibilities for both children and aging parents vary considerably. In general, existing estimates are based on surveys exclusively of employees (e.g., Neal et al., 1993); studies of caregivers to elders regardless of employment status (e.g., Stone & Short, 1990); or surveys of households, again regardless of the employment status of the householders (e.g., National Alliance for Caregiving/AARP, 2004).

The U.S. decennial census details the characteristics of households and does not include family care arrangements that occur outside of the household, as is the case with most sandwiched couples, whose aging parents tend to live on their own or in a care facility; thus, no estimates concerning sandwiched individuals or households are available based on census data.

Prevalence estimates of individuals in the sandwiched generation vary greatly depending on a number of factors. These include the population that is under study and thus sampled (e.g., the entire adult population, only women, only people of a certain age, only employees, only caregivers to elders), the age criterion for "elder" (e.g., 50, 60, 65, or no age criterion), the relationship to the elder (e.g., parent only, any older relative, any elder regardless of relationship), the operational definition used for what constitutes *elder care* (Gorey, Rice, & Brice, 1992; Wagner & Neal, 1994), the age criterion for either the caregiver or the child (Nichols & Junk, 1997; Spitze & Logan, 1990; Ward & Spitze, 1998), or the operational definition of *child care* (e.g., Raphael & Schlesinger, 1993; U.S. Bureau of the Census, 1996).

For example, some studies have used a very narrow definition of *elder care*, including only the provision of the most intensive forms of care, such as nursing care or hands-on assistance with personal activities of daily living (ADLs; e.g., help with dressing, bathing, and eating; e.g., Stone, Cafferata, & Sangl, 1987). Other studies have used broader definitions that include providing instrumental support (e.g., shopping, transportation), as well as personal Activities of daily living assistance. Still others include, as well, the provision of emotional support (e.g., calling regularly to check on or visit with the elder). Other studies, such as our own, have stipulated a minimum amount of time spent weekly in caregiving. Some studies (like ours) include care only of parents and not other elders, whereas others include caregivers of grandparents, aunts or uncles, or even friends and neighbors (e.g., Neal et al., 1993). Finally, other studies have determined prevalence rates of the sandwiched generation based on the age of the caregiver. For example, Nichols and Junk (1997) received mailed survey responses from 1,466 randomly sampled individuals between the ages of 40 and 65 in four states and found that 15% had responsibility both for aging parents and financially dependent children (no age specified). Alternatively, an AARP study (2001) categorized all individuals between the ages of 45 and 55 as being in the sandwiched generation, based solely on their age, regardless of any type of caregiving responsibilities. That study found that among individuals in that age group, more than 20% were providing care to their parents or other older adults.

Other estimates of the prevalence of sandwiched-generation caregivers, too, include in their definitions those who are providing financial support to children, regardless of the children's age, such as children in college (U.S. Bureau of the Census, 1996) or those who have adult children living at home (e.g., Raphael & Schlesinger, 1993). Ward and Spitze (1998) were interested in care to all living children, regardless of age or financial obligations. They analyzed a sample of 2,129 married men and women from the National Survey of Families and Households and arrived at a higher estimate than that of Nichols and Junk (1997). Specifically, they found that nearly 20% of the respondents in their 40s and 50s were *providing* help to both children and parents, although almost 50% reported *having* both children and a living parent (Ward & Spitze, 1998) and thus were viewed as having the possibility of finding themselves with both parent-care and child-care responsibilities at some point in the future.

A National Alliance for Caregiving and AARP study (2004) surveyed 6,139 adults by telephone and estimated that 21% of the U.S. adult population, and 21% of U.S. households, provide unpaid care to another adult aged 18 or older; unpaid care was defined as helping with one or more of 13 tasks that caregivers commonly perform. A total of 16% of the adult population, and 17% of U.S. households, were estimated to provide unpaid care to another adult aged 50 or older. Among caregivers of persons aged 18 and over, 48% worked full time, and another 11% worked part time. A total of 37% of caregivers of persons aged 18 and over also had children under the age of 18 living in their households. Marks (2001) analyzed data from the National Survey of Families and Households and estimated that more than one in seven U.S. adults reported caring for ill or disabled relatives or friends within or outside their household during the previous year. No estimates are provided pertaining to multiple caregiving responsibilities. Nonetheless, as she concluded, the prevalence of caregiving over the life span suggests that it is both a public and a private concern.

Finally, some studies have derived their estimates on the basis of samples composed exclusively of employees (see Gorey et al., 1992, and Wagner & Neal, 1994, for reviews). For example, Neal et al. (1993) studied a sample of employees and found that 9% had both child-care and elder-care responsibilities. The estimates reported by Durity (1991), noted earlier, also were based on samples of employees and ranged from 6% to 40%. The considerable variation in estimates may be attributed to differing workforce demographics of the organizations (i.e., age, gender, marital status; Durity, 1991). Another problem with basing estimates of prevalence of caregiving on surveys of employees is that such surveys may yield overestimates. This is because employees with caregiving responsibilities may be more likely than those not involved in family care to respond to surveys conducted to learn more about employees' work–family situations (Gorey et al., 1992).

THE PREVALENCE OF WORKING, SANDWICHED COUPLES: FINDINGS FROM OUR STUDY

As a part of the national study of working, sandwiched-generation couples that is the subject of this book, we were interested in estimating the prevalence specifically of *dual-earner couples* caring both for children and aging parents in the United States. In deriving this estimate of working, sandwiched couples, we set relatively stringent criteria for being sandwiched while working: couples (one member or both) were required to provide a minimum of 3 hours per week of care to an aging parent, stepparent, or parent-in-law; have a child aged 18 or under living in the household at least 3 days per week; and have been together for at least 1 year. In addition, both members of the couple had to be engaged in paid employment, with one member working at least 35 hours per week and the other at least 20 hours per week. A final criterion was that the couple's annual gross household income was $40,000 or higher; this requirement was set because of the specific interest of the study's funder, the Alfred P. Sloan Foundation, in middle- and upper income couples.

Thus, our estimate is based on a definition of *sandwiched* that is fairly stringent in that it pertains only to couples, stipulates a specific age of the child (18 or under), a minimum number of days per week that the child is in the household (3 days), a specific relationship with the elder (a parent or parent-in-law), a minimum amount of time spent by at least one member of the couple in providing care to the aging parent (3 hours/week), a minimum amount of time that the couple has been together (at least 1 year), a minimum level of employment (one member working full time and the other at least half time), and a minimum level of household income ($40,000/year or higher). In other words, single parents, people who were caring for adult children, those who were caring for elders other than parents, those who were working less than half time, and those with low incomes were not enumerated in this estimate.

To derive the estimate, we made more than 33,000 telephone screening calls to households across the United States. (See Appendix A for details about the study's methods.) *The first key finding of our study that we report here, then, concerns the prevalence of working, sandwiched couples:* On the basis of the screening calls, we conclude that *between 9% and 13% of American households with a telephone and with one or more persons aged 30 to 60 are composed of dual-earner, sandwiched-generation couples.*

PREVALENCE OF THE SANDWICHED GENERATION OUTSIDE OF THE UNITED STATES

There are few studies of the prevalence of sandwiched-generation caregiving in countries other than the United States. One such study was conducted in the Netherlands by Dautzenberg, Diederiks, Philipsen, and Stevens (1998). These researchers identified women who were sandwiched between the care of their children, parents, and sometimes grandchildren, but who were not necessarily employed. Using a random probability sample, the researchers approached, by telephone, 1,207 women between the ages of 40 and 54 in the Limburg province. A total of 933 women agreed to participate in the survey. Parent care was measured in terms of times per week helped, with *intense care* being defined as care provided more than four times per week. A total of 29% of the respondents between the ages of 40 and 54 reported caring both for children and aging parents, with 15% of the 29% indicating that they were caring for grandchildren as well.

A second study, which was based on a Canadian national probability study of both women and men between the ages of 35 and 54 who had living parents, was conducted by Rosenthal et al. (1996). These researchers found that an estimated 4% to 8% of respondents helped parents on a monthly basis or more, had children in the household, and held a job.

A third study also focused on Canadians. Specifically, on the basis of her research on parent care in the province of British Columbia, Penning (1998) estimated that of those who provided parent care, 45% had children, and 27% had children, a spouse, and a job.

PROBLEMS IN ESTIMATING THE PREVALENCE OF SANDWICHED-GENERATION CAREGIVERS

As can be seen from the preceding review of existing estimates, and from the criteria we specified for deriving our own estimates, prevalence rates of sandwiched-generation caregivers are heavily dependent on how this group is identified and defined. As a result, rates are inconsistent across studies.

A number of issues are apparent concerning the preceding estimates of the prevalence of sandwiched-generation caregiving. First, estimates of sandwiched individuals that are derived from a sample that already meets one of the criteria (e.g., they are known to be involved in elder care, or are employed) will yield higher prevalence rates than those based on the population as a whole. Second, the age span of the population studied will greatly affect the prevalence estimates; for example, prevalence rates for 30- to 40-year-olds, most of whose parents are still relatively young, will likely be smaller than those for 40- to 50-year-olds. Third, when studies cast their nets broadly with respect to the definitions used of *elder care* or *child care,* higher prevalence rates will be yielded. For example, when elder care is defined as the provision of emotional care as well as instrumental care, estimates will be higher than when it is defined only as the provision of instrumental care or, even more narrowly, as the provision of personal care. This is true as well with respect to level of responsibility for care (e.g., when secondary caregivers to elders are included as well as primary caregivers, or when child care is defined merely on the basis of having a child in the household, regardless of degree of responsibility assumed for the care of the child). Similarly, when children of any age are considered in estimates, prevalence rates obviously will be higher than when only minor children are considered, and when care to elders other than parents is included, estimates will be higher. Finally, prevalence estimates of sandwiched-generation caregivers that include only people who are engaged in paid work will, of course, be lower than those who include caregivers regardless of their employment status.

WHY WE SHOULD CARE: THE SANDWICHED GENERATION AS A FAMILY, COMMUNITY, AND CORPORATE CONCERN

Despite the disparities in study findings concerning the prevalence of sandwiched caregiving, it is clear that a significant number of people are working, caring for children, and caring for aging parents. Despite this, few systems are in place to help these individuals.

A number of factors are fueling interest in people in this situation on the part of public policymakers, employers, and researchers. In the United States, these include (a) the aging of the population, the aging of the work-force, and the increased care needs of an older population; (b) delayed and reduced childbearing, the resulting increase in the age of parents of young children, and the decrease in the number of siblings available to share in the care of aging parents; (c) an increasing number of women, the tradi-tional caregivers of both children and elders, who have entered or re-turned to the labor force and the related increase in the number of families where both the husband and the wife are working (i.e., dual-earner cou-ples); (d) an increase in multigenerational households; (e) rising health care costs and the increased pressures on families to provide care; and (f) growing documentation of the dynamic interplay between work and fam-ily demands and the effects on individuals' health and well-being as well as on organizations' bottom lines in the form of absenteeism, turnover, and overall market performance (Arthur, 2003; Eby, Casper, Lockwood, Bordeaux, & Brinley, 2005; Hammer, Cullen, Neal, Sinclair, & Shafiro, 2005; Neal et al., 1993). These various factors are detailed in the sections that follow.

The American Population is Aging, the Workforce is Aging, and People Are Delaying Childbearing

The population in the United States that is 65 and older is growing rapidly, and the aging of the "baby boomers" will accelerate this growth (Federal In-teragency Forum on Aging-Related Statistics, 2000). For most of the 20th century, except during the 1990s, the 65+ population grew faster than the to-tal population and the under age 65 population (U.S. Census Bureau, 2005). With increased longevity, a growing number of people can expect to be pro-viding informal, unpaid care to their aging parents in the future. In 2003, there were nearly 36 million Americans over the age of 65, representing over 12% of the American population (Federal Interagency Forum on Aging-Re-lated Statistics, 2004). By 2030, persons aged 65 or older are projected to com-prise nearly 20% of the U.S. population (Federal Interagency Forum on Aging-Related Statistics, 2004). By 2030, the number of older Americans will outnumber children under the age of 18 (Bronfenbrenner, McClelland, Wethington, Moen, & Ceci, 1996). Among the older population, persons 85 years of age and above (who have the highest care needs) showed the largest percentage increase between 1990 and 2000, growing by 38% (U.S. Census Bureau, 2001b). After 2030, this oldest-old population is expected to grow rapidly as the Baby Boomers begin to turn 85 (U.S. Census, 2005).

As the population ages, the median age of the workforce is rising and will continue to do so, also contributing to the possibility that workers will be faced with parent-care demands in addition to their responsibilities for dependent children (Rosenthal et al., 1996). For example, in 2002, 44% of the U.S. civilian workforce was age 45 or older, and it is expected that this group will comprise 53% of the workforce by the year 2050 (National Research Council & Institute of Medicine, 2004). Middle-aged and older workers are those who are most likely to have aging parents in need of care. In 2002, the National Study of the Changing Workforce found that 35% of workers indicated that they had provided care for someone who was aged 65 or older in the past year (Bond et al., 2003); this is compared to 25% in 1997 (Bond et al., 1998). Contributing to this trend are reductions in early retirement and increases in postretirement work. A Committee for Economic Development (1999) survey of Baby Boomers found that 70% intend to work at least part-time after retirement, and similar studies commissioned by AARP in 1998 and 2004 found an even higher percentage. Specifically, the AARP survey conducted in 1998 revealed that 80% of Boomers planned to work in some capacity during their retirement years (Roper Starch Worldwide, 1999), and the 2003 survey had comparable results, with 79% reporting they planned to continue working (RoperASW & Zapolsky, 2004). Boomers' reasons for planning to continue to work had changed, however, with fewer Boomers planning to work for enjoyment and more planning to work for needed income (RoperASW & Zapolsky, 2004).

Simultaneously, the U.S. population has shown a trend toward delayed childbearing (Casper & Bianchi, 2002). This leads to couples having children later in life and during the time that their parents begin to need assistance. As the average age of the workforce increases, aging parents live longer, and people delay childbearing (Casper & Bianchi, 2002), the phenomenon of being sandwiched between the care of aging parents and the care of children will continue to be a factor for significant numbers of employees and their work organizations.

More Women Are in the Workforce

Today, women comprise about 59% of the workforce, compared to about 43% in 1970 (U.S. Department of Labor, Bureau of Labor Statistics, 2005a). This increase has led to a number of changes in the family, including a redistribution of traditional gender role responsibilities, increases in the number of dual-earner couples (Offermann & Gowing, 1990), and an increase in the interdependency between work and family (e.g., Barnett, 1998). Just over 75% of women between the ages of 25 and 54 are in the labor force today (U.S. Department of Labor, Bureau of Labor Statistics, 2005a). As female labor participation has grown, so too has concern for the groups traditionally cared for by women—elders as well as children.

There Are More Multigenerational Households

In addition to the aging of the population and the increased number of women in the workplace, a number of grandparents are raising grandchildren (U.S. Census Bureau, 2003). Among the 45- to 55-year-olds examined in the AARP (2001) study noted earlier, nearly 17% were living in multigenerational households (e.g., grandparents, parents, and grandchildren). It should be noted that multigenerational households may include a subset of those who are in the sandwiched generation if the oldest generation in the household is receiving some type of care (Casper & Bianchi, 2002). Of all the households in which both grandparents and grandchildren live, however, approximately four-fifths are headed by the grandparents, not the adult children, and thus generally are not considered to be part of the sandwiched generation (Casper & Bianchi, 2002).

Increased Health Care Costs Are Leading to Greater Reliance on Informal Caregiving

With health care costs skyrocketing, there is increased reliance on family and friends to provide informal care to substitute for formal health care services, especially with respect to care for elders (Wagner, 2000). Older adults who, in the past, remained in the hospital for most of their recovery period from an illness or accident today are sent home after considerably fewer days and with less formal support. Family members or other informal supports, rather than trained personnel, are left to manage the care and to perform sometimes very complicated health care tasks, frequently with little or no training (Wagner, 2000).

There Is Increased Recognition of the Dynamic Interplay Between Work and Family Responsibilities

Managing both work life and family life has become a major issue for much of today's workforce. Research demonstrates that work–family conflict is related to negative individual outcomes such as decreased mental health, increased stress, and strain both on and off the job (e.g., Hammer, Cullen, et al., 2005). In addition, work–family conflicts are related to negative work outcomes such as increased absenteeism (Neal et al., 1993), decreased job satisfaction, and increased turnover (e.g., Eby et al., 2005). In chapter 4, we summarize the results of research that has shown a variety of positive and negative effects both and organizations that are associated with combining work and family for individuals. There is a need to identify ways to help individuals and couples having multiple work and family responsibilities minimize the negative and maximize the positive effects of combining work and family. Little research to date, however, exists on workers caring both for children and aging parents. In the following review, we focus on the few studies that have examined this population.

PREVIOUS RESEARCH: WORK AND WELL-BEING OUTCOMES EXPERIENCED BY WORKERS CARING FOR CHILDREN AND AGING PARENTS

Little research exists specifically concerning workers caring for children and aging parents, or sandwiched-generation caregivers. In this section, we review this limited research. Both work-related and well-being outcomes of being sandwiched have been observed, with most of the work outcomes focusing on absenteeism and most of the well-being outcomes centering around generalized experiences of stress, depression, or role satisfaction. By studying working caregivers, researchers are able to more broadly examine the competing role demands that individuals face and the potential for workplace policy and culture to influence how individuals experience their multiple roles. It is important to note, however, that such research does not allow examination of individuals who have permanently or temporarily exited the work role because of excessive stress from their work and family role demands. Thus, any negative outcomes found may actually be minimized in much of the existing research.

Work Outcomes

Only a few studies have examined the work-related effects of having both child- and elder-care responsibilities. For example, as described below, Buffardi, Smith, O'Brien, and Erdwins (1999) found that negative work attitudes (i.e., decreased job satisfaction) were associated with being in the sandwiched generation based on a study of federal employees conducted by the U.S. Office of Personnel Management. Neal and colleagues (1993) found that employees occupying multiple caregiving roles tended to experience higher levels of absenteeism than did employees occupying only one caregiving role. The findings of Fernandez (1990) were similar, although only for women.

More specifically, Buffardi et al. (1999) examined the impact of child-care and elder-care responsibilities on various aspects of job satisfaction and work–family balance. Federal employees ($N = 20,015$) in dual-income households completed a 184-item questionnaire covering a wide range of personnel topics, including employee dependent-care responsibilities and job satisfaction. Of these individuals, 8% had only elder-care responsibility, 33% had only child-care responsibility, and 3.6% had both child- and elder-care responsibilities. The results showed that individuals with elder-care responsibilities were significantly less satisfied with their organizational support, pay, leave benefits, and work–family balance than those without such obligations.

Neal and colleagues (1993) conducted a study to simultaneously assess the effects of various types of caregiving responsibilities (child, adult, and elder). Employees from 33 businesses and agencies in the Portland, Oregon, metropolitan area were surveyed concerning their informal caregiving responsibilities. Of the 9,573 respondents, 46% of participants reported having child-care responsibilities. Of those individuals, just over 23% were also providing care to an elder and/or to a disabled adult. A total of 23% of the 9,573 were providing elder care; of those, 42% also had children in the household, and another 0.7% were caring for an adult with a disability as well as an elder. Just under 4% (3.7%) of all respondents were providing care to an adult with a disability; 60% of these individuals also had caregiving responsibilities for elders and/or children. Employees with caregiving responsibilities of any kind (child, adult, or elder) experienced more absenteeism and stress than did employees with no caregiving responsibilities. This higher level of absenteeism and stress suggests a need for assistance in balancing their work and family roles. Moreover, the need was shown to be especially great for employees caring for multiple types of dependents (specifically, those providing all three kinds of care simultaneously or care for children and disabled adults), as these employees experienced the most problems (Chapman, Ingersoll-Dayton, & Neal, 1994; Neal et al., 1993).

Fernandez (1990), in some of the earliest research on working, sandwiched caregivers, surveyed 26,000 employees across 30 companies involved in telecommunications, finance, and real estate. Although only 2.4% to 3.3% of the survey participants had both child- and elder-care responsibilities, Fernandez found that women who worked and were sandwiched were more likely to miss work than those who were not sandwiched. No significant differences were found for men.

Well-Being Outcomes

Consistent with much of the caregiving literature (e.g., Brody, 1981), Ward and Spitze (1998) found that women were more likely than men to report helping children, parents, and both children and parents. They also found that the quality of relations with children and parents who were provided care was related to overall marital happiness. This examination of the effect of caregiving on marital happiness relates to the broader question of whether multiple concurrent roles serve to enhance or reduce caregiver stress and well-being. The answer to this question is complex, as evidenced by the results of several studies based on employee populations. For example, in their sample of 9,573 employees, Neal et al. (1993) found that employees occupying multiple caregiving roles almost always experienced more stress than employees occupying only one caregiving role. These results were similar to those of Fredriksen-Goldsen and Scharlach (2001), who compared sandwiched employees to those caring only for children and those caring for adults among a sample of 2,000 employees from a technology research firm. Likewise, in some of the earliest research on working, sandwiched caregivers, Fernandez (1990) found that workers with both child- and elder-care responsibilities had higher stress levels and greater stress-related health problems than employees who were not sandwiched (i.e., those with only elder-care or only child-care responsibilities or those with no family care responsibilities at all).

Additional effects on well-being have been observed in other studies of the sandwiched generation. For example, using data from the National Survey of Families and Households, Voydanoff and Donnelly (1999) showed that among a sample of couples caring both for adolescent children and aging parents, the number of hours spent providing parent care was significantly related to depression for women. No relationship was found for men, however.

Loomis and Booth (1995) questioned whether multigenerational caregiving responsibilities (i.e., caring for at least one child and at least one parent/parent-in-law) really have an adverse effect on caregivers' well-being. Their study, which was part of a 12-year longitudinal project titled "Marital Instability Over the Life Course," used a national sample of 2,033 married persons between the ages of 16 and 55. The results indicated that taking on multigenerational caregiving responsibilities did not significantly affect a variety of measures of well-being, including caregivers' marital quality, psychological well-being, financial resources, or satisfaction with leisure time. However, respondents who took on multigenerational caregiving responsibilities were more likely to think that the division of labor in the household had become unfair. These results were consistent for both men and women, regardless of the number of hours worked in paid employment.

Stephens and Townsend (1997) examined role rewards and stressors for 296 women who were occupying roles as mothers, wives, employees, and primary caregivers to an ill or disabled parent or parent-in-law. They found that stress in the roles of mother, wife, and employee exacerbated the effects of stress in the parent-care role with respect to psychological well-being indexes of depression and life satisfaction. They also found that rewards in the employee role buffered the effects of parent-care stress. These findings underscore the complex relationships that often exist between women's multiple role expectations and their psychological well-being and point to the importance of examining role quality.

Penning (1998) studied 1,789 Canadian caregivers to aging parents to examine the relationship between concurrent multiple roles (as a caregiver to a parent, a spouse, a parent, and/or an employee) and perceived stress as well as emotional health. She found that 45% of the caregivers to parents also were parents themselves with at least one child living at home. It is interesting that she found that among male caregivers to parents, those who were parents themselves reported lower stress than those who were not parents themselves. However, male caregivers to parents who also held roles both as a paid employee and as a parent reported poorer emotional health than male caregivers to parents who did not also occupy these two other roles. In contrast, female caregivers to parents who also held roles as a parent and a paid employee were less likely to report poor emotional health than were female caregivers to parents who were not also a parent and an employee. These results indicate different relationships for men and women between multiple role occupancy and well-being.

Finally, K. A. Christensen, Stephens, and Townsend (1998) attempted to explain the differences observed in well-being among caregivers who were occupying multiple roles by using the notion of *mastery*, that is, one's belief that one is able to influence/control life events and is competent in managing these events. Their study involved a sample of 296 women who were married and employed and also served as caregivers to an impaired parent and to a child living at home. The researchers found that feelings of mastery in the roles of wife, mother, and caregiver to a parent were related to psychological well-being and that the more roles in which women experienced higher levels of mastery, the greater their satisfaction with life. These findings suggest that feelings of mastery in roles may be a means by which well-being is achieved.

In sum, the limited research to date has demonstrated higher levels of stress and absenteeism among workers caring both for children and aging parents, or those in the sandwiched generation (e.g., Fernandez, 1990; Neal et al., 1993). At the same time, there is evidence that this stress can be buffered by the beneficial effects of multiple roles (e.g., Stephens, Franks, & Townsend, 1994).

Finally, and importantly, it should be noted that although there is some previous research on the sandwiched generation, ours is the first national study of dual-earner couples in the sandwiched generation. Moreover, we were able to examine role changes and the effects of those changes. Thus, the study we present in this book is unique in its ability to represent and examine over time the work and family experiences of couples who work, care for children, and care for aging parents.

SUMMARY

In this first chapter, we have demonstrated that there are many different ways of defining the sandwiched generation, and we have provided our operational definition of this demographic group. We have discussed issues related to their prevalence, and we have presented the first key finding from the study that is the subject of book, which is that 9% and 13% of U.S. households with heads of household between the ages of 30 and 60 are composed of dual-earner sandwiched couples. We also have discussed the importance of studying sandwiched-generation caregivers as a family, community, and corporate concern. Finally, we reviewed the small amount of existing literature on individuals who work and care both for children and for aging parents and described how our study makes a contribution to this field.

There is a need for more integrated research that examines the work and family role characteristics of people who are working, caring for children, and caring for aging parents. In addition, there is a need for research that includes both men and women and that approaches the work–family interface from the perspective of both members, not just one member, of the couple. Moreover, it is important to study the benefits, as well as the costs, of combining work and family. Finally, it is important to examine the effects of changes in roles on work–family fit, well-being, and work. The study that constitutes the focus of this book attempts to address these gaps in previous research.

First, though, in the remainder of Part 1, to further set the context for our study, we review current government and employer work–family policies, benefits, and services that exist in the United States (chap. 2), and in other nations (chap. 3), to support working caregivers. In chapter 4, we identify key theoretical frameworks for conceptualizing the work–family interface among sandwiched generation couples and review the more general work–family research.

2

Employer and Governmental Initiatives Affecting Work and Family Life in the United States

In this chapter, we describe organizational and governmental initiatives in the United States that may assist employees who have responsibilities for the care of children, elders, or other family members. In particular, we chronicle the history of employer and governmental responses to employees' family care responsibilities in the United States. We then describe the range, prevalence and utilization of workplace-based supports in the United States.

HISTORY AND EVOLUTION OF EMPLOYER AND GOVERNMENTAL RESPONSES IN THE UNITED STATES

Employee benefits, as provided in the United States, have two primary purposes. The first is to provide income security by ensuring against loss of income should the wage earner die, become disabled, or voluntarily retire. The second is to raise the standard of living through the provision of certain vital services, such as medical care. As a result, the economy as a whole is improved (Employee Benefit Research Institute [EBRI], 1990; Kossek & Ozeki, 1999; Piacentini & Cerino, 1990).

In the United States, the employee benefit system is a partnership among employers, individuals, and the government (Kossek & Ozeki, 1999; Piacentini & Cerino, 1990). Many employment-based benefits are offered voluntarily by employers; others are mandated by the government. This chapter highlights employers' voluntary responses to their employees' family-related needs, although government-mandated benefits, where relevant, are also indicated. Additional key U.S. governmental initiatives also are described.

Employee benefits programs have existed in the United States since colonial times. Early programs addressed employees' retirement and health care needs. Examples include the military retirement program for Plymouth colony settlers (established in 1636), a profit-sharing plan for Gallatin Glassworks employees (initiated in 1797), and a private employer pension plan for American Express Company employees (implemented in 1875; EBRI, 1990; Piacentini & Cerino, 1990). Benefits that are specifically family oriented date back to the Industrial Revolution, when women (and children) began to work outside the home in the first factories and mills (Kamerman, 1983; Morgan & Tucker, 1991). It was during this time, in 1825, that Robert Owen, an English businessman, established the first employer-sponsored child-care center in the United States, in New Harmony, Indiana (Morgan & Tucker, 1991).

In the late 1800s, the presence of women and children in the workforce caused disruption in family life, resulting in high employee turnover, labor militancy, and the threat of government interference. It was then that welfare capitalism and voluntary social welfare agencies, such as charity organization societies and settlement houses, emerged in the United States. These responses were modeled after the social insurance provisions, the kindergarten movement, and related measures in Germany, as well as the creches in France for the children of factory workers (Kamerman, 1983; Morgan & Tucker, 1991). Examples include a preschool for the children of working parents in Philadelphia during the Civil War; the kindergartens that were open to children ages 2 and over and operated by settlement houses and charitable groups in the 1890s; and day nurseries such as that opened by the Ewa Sugar Company for plantation workers' children in Honolulu, Hawaii, in 1897 (Morgan & Tucker, 1991).

About 1900, however, child labor was outlawed, and initiatives encouraging mothers to stay at home to nurture and educate their children began to be advanced (Morgan & Tucker, 1991). "Mothers' pensions," which provided small pensions to single mothers and mothers married to men who were disabled, ill, or imprisoned, were introduced about the time of World War I. Because these pensions were often inadequate and not universally available, however, many mothers preferred to work. A few companies responded, such as the Kellogg Company, in Battle Creek, Michigan, which operated a child-care center from 1924 to 1932 (Morgan & Tucker, 1991).

Overall, "company welfarism" in the United States peaked in the prosperous 1920s; then the Great Depression hit in the 1930s (Kamerman, 1983), and not only could companies no longer afford extras such as family supports, but the pressure to provide them was gone, as the supply of labor outstripped demand. Furthering the decrease in corporate welfarism was government intervention, through the New Deal legislation (Kamerman, 1983); once government social programs were more widely available, the need for corporate involvement was reduced.

At the same time, federal government involvement resulted in expansions in health insurance and retirement benefits (Wiatrowski, 1990). Some of these increases were mandated; others were implemented voluntarily by employers as a result of tax incentives (Piacentini & Cerino, 1990). For example, in 1921, the federal tax code began providing tax incentives to employers sponsoring pension plans. In 1935, in response to the Depression, the federal government mandated basic retirement income protection under the Social Security Act. In 1939, tax incentives were established for employers providing compensation to employees for injuries or sickness. Later, in 1954, such incentives were created for employers sponsoring health plans (EBRI, 1990; Piacentini & Cerino, 1990).

The advent of World War II changed the employee benefits scene once again (Wiatrowski, 1990). Men left to serve in the military, and the need for production increased; thus came, as Morgan and Tucker (1991) noted, "another surge of employer interest in family concerns, and an intriguing lapse in the popular disapproval of working mothers" (p. 22). The government made available some funding for communities to provide child-care services, and some businesses, in response to problems with absenteeism due to child-care problems, created their own child-care centers (Morgan & Tucker, 1991). Kaiser Industries' parental supports at two shipbuilding plants in Oregon in 1944 were exemplary even by today's standards: two child-care centers providing 24-hour care for more than 1,000 children, infirmaries for ill children, work schedule flexibility, take-home meals, a mending service, an errand service, and a service that arranged for and transported children to medical and dental appointments (Morgan & Tucker, 1991).

After the end of World War II, social disapproval of working mothers recommenced. Some women left their jobs, federal support for child care was eliminated, and child-care centers associated with war industry companies closed (Morgan & Tucker, 1991). Employee benefits plans, however, grew rapidly because of four factors. First, wage controls that permitted benefits plans, but not wage increases, were instituted. Second, a ruling concerning the 1947 Labor Management Relations Act allowed pensions to be included as a collective bargaining issue. Third, a 1949 report by the Steel Industry Fact Finding Board asserted that employers had a social as well as an economic obligation to provide social insurance and pensions to workers. Fourth, wages were once again frozen during the Korean War, permitting increases only in benefits (Kamerman, 1983, citing Koludrubetz, 1974; Wiatrowski, 1990).

A few child-care centers survived the 1940s and 1950s, and in the 1960s, the federal government's Great Society programs and the War on Poverty sparked public interest in child-care programs, especially for the children of low-income parents (Morgan & Tucker, 1991). For example, the Project Head Start program, begun in 1965, emphasized early childhood education, with a goal of reducing poverty, similar to the first American child-care center (Morgan & Tucker, 1991).

During this same time, the problems of elderly persons, especially those with low incomes, also came into focus. In 1965, health insurance for elderly and disabled individuals became a federally mandated benefit through the Medicare program (EBRI, 1990; Piacentini & Cerino, 1990). The Older Americans Act was also passed, resulting in a number of government-funded services for elderly persons, including senior centers, meal sites, homemaker and home health services, and adult day care (Hooyman & Kiyak, 2005).

The 1970s and 1980s saw gradual increases in employer efforts to assist working parents and seemed to be "about to swell into a flood" in the 1990s (Morgan & Tucker, 1991, p. 25). Moreover, in the mid-1980s, American employers began to introduce elder-care programming to their array of work–family programs, fashioned after the child-care resource and referral services (Wagner, 2000). Spurring this interest were the demographic and social changes described in chapter 1, including the aging of the American population, especially the growing numbers of very old Americans, who are those most likely to need care; the entrance of increasing numbers of women into the paid labor force; the trend toward smaller families; and the rising number of divorces and remarriages, with the result that adult children may have responsibility for a greater number of parents, including stepparents and parents-in-law.

The Travelers Insurance Companies, particularly aware of these trends due to the nature of their business, were the first to survey their employees to learn about the extent, nature, and effects of their informal elder-care responsibilities (Travelers Insurance Companies, 1985). IBM also conducted an internal survey to gauge the extent of elder care among its employees, first in 1988, then in 1993 (Childs, 1993). The first workplace elder-care program was begun in 1986 by Hallmark Cards; called "Family Care Choices," it was a resource center modeled after child-care resource and referral programs designed to link workers with services in the community (Wagner, 2003). Similar programs were initiated in 1987 by Herman Miller, an office furniture manufacturer, and in 1988 by IBM (Wagner, 2003). These programs were developed more as a "proactive response to undeniable demographic trends" than as a result of employee demand (Kossek, DeMarr, Backman, & Kollar, 1993, p. 634).

As Wagner (2003) noted, other key events in the development of workplace elder care programs were the following: in 1988, the New York City Department on Aging began the first public–private partnership to provide workplace elder-care referral services to employees of Phillip Morris, American Express, and J.P. Morgan; in 1990, AT&T and two labor unions, the Communications Workers of America and the International Brotherhood of Electrical Workers, created the Family Care Development Fund and national elder-care referral program; in 1991, the *Wall Street Journal* began its "Work and Family" column as a regular feature; and in 1992, the American Business Collaborative was established to enhance the quality and availability of child care and elder care (see abcdependentcare.com).

Finally, also during this time, the United States and some state governments stepped in with legislation aimed at assisting family caregivers. In particular, as described below, in 1993, the federal Family and Medical Leave Act was passed by Congress. Several states also passed family leave legislation with additional benefits, generally applying to more employees (e.g., to those working for organizations with 25 or more employees, rather than 50; Martocchio, 2003). None of this leave, however, was mandated to be paid leave. This changed for employees in the state of California, when that state enacted the first Paid Family Leave Law in the United States (Dube & Kaplan, 2002).

Another key piece of federal legislation is the National Family Caregiver Support Program, which was passed by Congress in 2000 as an amendment to the Older Americans Act. The law stipulates that states provide to caregivers of adults aged 60 and over several direct services: information about available services; assistance in gaining access to supportive services; individual and group counseling; as well as caregiver training, respite care, and supplemental services to elders complement the services provided by caregivers. Under this legislation, states are required to give consideration to the economic need of recipients (Feinberg, Newman, & Steenberg, 2002). Feinberg and Newman (2004), however, found that implementation of the program has varied greatly by state, with policy choices made regarding developing or expanding caregiver-support services influenced by "state officials' views of whether or not family caregivers should be considered legitimate consumers of services in their own right" (p. 767).

Other family-friendly provisions appear in the federal tax code, including dependent-care assistance plans (DCAPs) and the federal dependent-care tax credit. These legislative initiatives are described in the next section.

In sum, although examples of employment-based work–family supports existed in the United States even in colonial times, employer concern typically has been manifest only during periods of history when women were needed in the workplace, such as during the two world wars, when women were recruited to fill jobs left by men serving in the military. During those times, employers viewed the provision of family supports (i.e., child-care programs) as a strategy to attract and retain needed workers. For most of the 19th and 20th centuries, however, managing the intersection of work and family was seen as the sole responsibility of the workers themselves. In the late 1970s and 1980s, as increasing numbers of women began to enter and remain in the workforce, this began to change. The prevailing belief that family life and family responsibilities could and should be left at home was challenged by the realities facing workers as they struggled to manage their work and family obligations. Increasing awareness of the demographic and social changes affecting the workforce created a shift in the philosophy of both employers and employees regarding the appropriateness of employer involvement in the family-related aspects of employees' lives (Neal, 1999) and spurred the development of work and family supports, particularly those related to child care.

Today, U.S. employers have implemented a wide variety of supports that may assist employees who have family responsibilities. We describe this array of supports in the next section.

TYPES OF WORKPLACE-BASED SUPPORTS IN THE UNITED STATES FOR EMPLOYEES WITH FAMILY RESPONSIBILITIES

In this section, we provide an overview of the range of workplace-based supports that U.S. employers have implemented that can be of assistance to employees with family responsibilities. Some supports are targeted specifically to employees with families; others are intended for other groups, or for the entire workforce, but may be helpful to working caregivers nonetheless. Employers' primary motivation in implementing these supports has been to lessen employees' work–family conflict and thereby improve worker productivity.

Because an exhaustive presentation of workplace support programs for working caregivers is beyond the scope of this book, readers may wish to consult the work–family sourcebook that we have developed for employers (Neal & Hammer, 2001; see http://www.sandwich.pdx.edu). This sourcebook details the various supports and their possible advantages and disadvantages; it also includes information concerning how to conduct a needs assessment. Fredriksen-Goldsen and Scharlach (2001); Lechner and Creedon (1994); Neal et al. (1993); Scharlach, Lowe, and Schneider (1991); Wagner, Creedon, Sasala, and Neal. (1989), and several studies by the Families and Work Institute also have provided extensive examinations of the range of supports available, including Bond, Galinsky, and Swanberg (1998); Bond, Thompson, Galinsky, and Prottas (2003);

Galinsky and Bond (1998); Galinsky, Friedman, and Hernandez (1991); and Shore (1998).

Several possible frameworks exist for depicting the types of supports offered to date by U.S. employers. The framework we use, developed by Neal et al. (1993), consists of three major categories, as shown in Fig. 2.1. These categories include (a) policies concerning work schedule, place, and leave, (b) benefits, and (c) services. In general, these three categories of employer support options involve different levels of employer involvement and investment. Policies usually represent the least amount of employer involvement in the lives of employees, whereas services require the most employer involvement. Benefits and paid-leave policies typically are the most costly responses, although the costs associated with certain work–family services, such as an on-site child- or adult day-care center, are quite substantial, and some benefits involve only administrative costs.

Policies provide guidelines, either formal or informal, for dealing with certain situations, such as the ways in which employees' work and leave schedules are handled (Ontario Women's Directorate, 1990). They can be supportive of employees with caregiving responsibilities, although they usually are not designed exclusively for these employees. Policies generally involve no direct compensation or cash benefit.

Benefits are forms of compensation, direct or indirect, that provide protection against loss of earnings; payment of medical expenses associated with illness, injury, or other health care needs, or paid released time for vacations or personal needs. Benefits may also include full or partial payment for other services, such as legal, educational, or dependent-care services (Kamerman & Kingston, 1982).

Services are programs that are provided directly by or through the employer to address specific employee needs. Services are a tangible form of help but are not direct compensation. These services can be organized into broad categories that, again, vary in the level of employer involvement and investment (Neal et al., 2001).

Policies

Flexibility in the structure of work is viewed as one of the most important types of support that employers can provide for employees who have dependent-care responsibilities. Time to deal with family issues is seen by employees as a crucial need (Byars & Rue, 2004). Policies that increase work flexibility include those that increase flexibility in the work schedule and place of work; provide options for paid or unpaid leave; and provide mechanisms or provisions for the implementation, creation, and review of workplace-based supports.

Policies	Benefits	Services
Flexible work schedules	*Flexible benefits plans*	*Education on caregiving*
• Compressed work weeks	• Cafeteria plans	• Corporate libraries
• Flextime	• Flexible spending accounts	• Newsletters and guidebooks
• Cross-trained employees	• Dependent-care assistance plans	• Educational seminars
Reduced work hours	*Tax benefits*	• Caregiving fairs
• Part-time employment	• Earned income credit	• Internet access
• Job-sharing	• Dependent-care tax credits	• Voluntary reduce time (V-time)
• Phased retirement	Insurance	*Resources on caregiving*
• Phase-in schedule after leave	• Health insurance	• Dependent-care information and referral
Options for leave	• Dental insurance	• Case management
• Sick leave (days, hours)	• Disability insurance	• Support groups
• Family leave (paid or unpaid)	• Life insurance	• Peer support
• Personal leave (earned time)	• Long-term care insurance	• Wellness programs
• Vacation leave		*Direct services*
		• On-site child-care center and/or program
Where work is done		• Adult day-care center
• Telecommuting		• Child/adult day-care consortium
Relocation		• Subsidies, vouchers, discounts for child/elder care, including respite
• Relocation policies		• sick and emergency care
Management sensitivity		• Before/after-school, summer/vacation care
• Management training in work/life issues		*Employee assistance programs*
		• Substance-abuse treatment
		• Stress management
		• Consumer counseling
		• Crisis intervention
		• Bereavement counseling
		• Personal and family counseling
		• Community involvement
		• Stimulating care-related resources

Figure 2.1.   Workplace-based supports use to family caregivers. From *Balancing Work and Caregiving for Children, Adults, and Elders*, by M. Neal, N. Chapman, B. Ingersoll-Dayton, and A. Emlen, 1993. Copyright 1993 by Sage. Adapted with permission.

Flexibility in Work Schedule

Since the late 1970s, there has been a growing trend in the implementation of alternative work schedules in U.S. organizations (Bond et al., 2003; Grover & Crooker, 1995; Olmsted & Smith, 1989). This has occurred in response to both employee and organizational needs (see Pierce, Newstrom, Dunham, & Barber, 1989, for a comprehensive review of alternative work schedules).

One type of alternative work schedule involves reducing the number of hours worked. Specifically, employers may allow employees to work part time (i.e., defined by the U.S. Department of Labor as less than 35 hours of work per week; Olmsted & Smith, 1989; Rosin & Korabik, 2002). Some employers have even established alternative career paths for professionals who work part time (Morgan & Tucker, 1991; Schwartz, 1989).

Another option is job sharing. *Job sharing* is a variation of part-time employment in which a single full-time job is shared by two (or more) individuals. Two types of job sharing have been identified: (a) job splitting/vertical and (b) job pairing/horizontal job sharing (Byars & Rue, 2004; Pierce et al., 1989). In *job splitting*, two individuals with complementary skills share one job, but the tasks performed and levels of responsibility assumed by each person differ. In *job pairing*, the two individuals take equal responsibility for all job tasks.

A third option is flexible work hours, or *flextime*. Variable start and stop times characterize jobs offered on a flexible work hours basis. Although employees are given some discretion in arranging their daily schedules, constraints are imposed by employers through the use of bandwidths (i.e., the organization's daily span of operating hours) and core times (i.e., management-imposed times when employees are required to be on the job; Baltes, Briggs, Huff, Wright, & Neuman, 1999; Kossek & Ozeki, 1999; Olmsted & Smith, 1989; Thomas & Ganster, 1995).

A fourth option is *compressed work weeks*. This form of alternative work schedule involves a reduction in the number of days per week in which full-time work is performed, without a corresponding reduction in the number of weekly hours. Many variations of this theme exist (e.g., 10 hours/day, 4 days/week; 12 hours/day, 3 days/week).

Flexibility in Place of Work

Another policy that increases work flexibility involves the place of work. Specifically, some employers have flexplace or telecommuting policies that allow employees to work from home or at some other site besides the main office or job site (K. E. Christensen & Staines, 1990; Hill, Miller, Weiner, & Colihan, 1998).

Leave Options

Most U.S. employers offer their employees some form of paid sick or vacation leave. However, personal sick leave is often used (legitimately or not) for the care of sick children or elders, which leaves employees with less paid time off to take care of themselves when they are ill (Health Action Forum of Greater Boston, 1989). In addition, some employers have implemented, either voluntarily or as mandated by the U.S. or state government, family leave options for the birth or adoption of a child or for the care of an ill or disabled family member (K. E. Christensen & Staines, 1990; Martocchio, 2003). Nonetheless, whereas in 1986, 70% of employees working in medium and large private establishments were provided some paid sick leave, and 25% were offered paid personal leave, in 1997, these numbers had fallen to only 56% and 20%, respectively (Heymann, 2000, citing the U.S. Department of Labor, Bureau of Labor Statistics). Only 50% of individuals working for small private employers were offered paid sick leave, and only 14% were offered paid personal leave, in 1996 (Heymann, 2000, citing the U.S. Department of Labor, Bureau of Labor Statistics).

For employers with 50 or more employees, offering unpaid leave is mandated by the federal Family and Medical Leave Act (FMLA) of 1993. The FMLA allows an employee to take up to 12 weeks of unpaid leave, with a guarantee of being able to return to his or her same or similar job at the same pay and benefits. The time taken off, however, generally is unpaid. Thus, it is not universally available to U.S. employees: those who work for small employers, who feel they cannot afford to take time off without compensation, or who fear that the progress of their careers will be jeopardized, may not be able to use this leave (Allen, 2001; C. A. Thompson, Beauvais, & Lyness, 1999). Moreover, there is evidence that firms do not always comply with the FMLA (Scharlach, Sansom, & Stanger, 1995).

As noted earlier, an exception exists in the state of California, which has mandated that family leave be paid. Specifically, California employees who work for employers having 50 or more employees may receive up to 6 weeks of paid leave per year to care for a new child or an ill family member. This benefit is financed through the State Disability Insurance system and covers all workers who have a State Disability Insurance deduction taken from their paychecks. The benefit replaces up to 55% of wages, up to a maximum of $728 per week (in 2004). Also, employers are required to hold the job for an employee who goes on paid family leave (Family Caregiver Alliance, 2003). To access the benefit, employees apply to a state-administered, employee-funded insurance fund. The estimated average cost is $27 per year (http://www.paidfamilyleave.org).

Relocation Policies

Some employers have implemented relocation policies that are family friendly. These include minimizing the transfer of employees; helping employees' spouses find a job in their new location; allowing spouses to work for the same company (Kingston, 1990); and, on occasion, providing relocation assistance for employees' relatives when employees are reluctant to transfer because of elder-care concerns (Flynn, 1994).[1]

Policy Development and Implementation

Work and Family Task Forces. Because employees' needs are ever changing, the development of family care policies, as well as benefits and services, must be a continuous, dynamic, problem-solving process. Given this, some employers have established work and family task forces (Haupt, 1992; Lechner & Creedon, 1994). Several years ago, for example, Barr Laboratories created a joint labor–management committee on work and family issues (Bureau of National Affairs, 1988).

Management Training. Finally, to increase managers' compliance with formal family-responsive policies that are in place, as well as to enhance informal response by supervisors to employees' family care situations; some employers have implemented training for managers. This training is designed to increase managers' sensitivity to the needs of employees who have caregiving responsibilities and to improve their awareness of the organization's formal policies as well as informal ways in which employees' needs can be met through supervisor flexibility and responsiveness (Friedman & Johnson, 1997; Lechner & Creedon, 1994; C. A. Thompson et al., 1999).

Benefits

U.S. employers are required by federal law to provide certain employee benefits; in addition, most employees are eligible for other benefits that their employer has chosen voluntarily to offer. Examples of mandatory benefits include Social Security retirement (a lifetime annuity), Social Security disability (for individuals who are disabled and unable to work), Medicare Part A (hospitalization for elderly persons), workers' compensa-

---

[1]The 27th Atlas Van Lines Survey of Corporation Relocation Policies found that, among the 183 companies surveyed, 6.8% reported they would move an elderly relative who would be living with the transferee in the new location, and 1.7% would relocate elderly relatives who would be living separately from the transferee (Flynn, 1994).

tion (for workers who become disabled), and unemployment insurance (for workers who are temporarily unemployed; Byars & Rue, 2004).

Most U.S. employers' benefits packages voluntarily include health insurance; life insurance; participation in a pension plan and/or profit sharing; paid time off for holidays, vacations, and sick leave; and short-term disability. Additional benefits, such as for dental care, vision care, dependent care, long-term disability, and liability insurance, are also sometimes offered (Byars & Rue, 2004).

Benefits may be offered through a *standard* (or *traditional*), a *flexible* (or *cafeteria*), or a *life cycle* (or *life span*) plan. A standard plan is composed of an identical set of benefits for all employees in a given company; alternatively, a cafeteria, or flexible benefits, plan permits employees to select from among several possible benefits or cash. In a flexible plan, the employer pays a major portion of the costs of the benefits by establishing a *flexible benefit allowance* of a certain dollar amount. This allowance is large enough to cover the full cost of those benefits (called *basic* or *core benefits*) that the employer feels all employees should have, such as medical insurance and death benefits. Remaining benefits dollars can then be used to purchase additional benefits, or they may be taken in cash (Martocchio, 2003; Neal et al., 1993; U.S. Department of Labor, Office of the Secretary, Women's Bureau, n.d.). The life span approach involves developing options that fit the various life cycle stages of employees (e.g., new worker, marriage, pregnancy and adoption, childrearing, divorce, elder care, retirement, death) and explaining to employees that benefits not applicable to them now may well be useful to them in the future (Martinez, 1993; Vanderkolk & Young, 1991). A similar approach is the life cycle allowance, in which a company designates a fixed amount of money that can be used by the employee for dependent-care expenses at any time over his or her career, such as to fund purchase of a home, college tuition, long-term care, financial planning, and/or legal services (Grant, 1992).

Flexible benefits and life span plans are considered more family responsive in that they recognize that individual employees' benefits needs will differ depending on the employee's age, salary, and family status. In addition, as discussed below, they are seen as more equitable.

Flexible Spending Accounts

Flexible spending accounts are accounts in which employees can allocate their own pre-tax dollars, credits, or flexible-benefits dollars given to them by their employer to pay for certain expenses (e.g., medical, dental, legal, dependent care) that are not covered under the standard benefits package. Dependent-care assistance plans (DCAPs) are flexible-spending accounts created by the U.S. government to provide tax relief specifically to employees who have dependent-care responsibilities and who must purchase dependent care or related services in order to be gainfully employed. DCAPS allow employees to set aside pre-tax dollars for dependent care expenses. Employees take pre-tax payroll deductions, up to $5,000 per year, to pay for dependent-care expenses that are work-related (U.S. Department of the Treasury, Internal Revenue Service, 2005). DCAPs may or may not involve direct employer contributions, but they are available only when set up by employers for their employees (Canan & Mitchell, 1991).

Dependent Care Tax Credit

Although not technically an employee benefit, a federal tax credit for employment-related expenses incurred is available to individuals who have dependent-care responsibilities. Dependent care-related expenditures are made throughout the year, records are kept, and then a percentage of the expenses incurred can be deducted from the amount of income taxes owed, up to $3,000 ($6,000 for two or more dependents; U.S. Department of the Treasury, Internal Revenue Service, 2005). The percentage varies depending on the income of the employee and his or her spouse and is a maximum of 35% of these expenses per dependent. The majority of states also have state dependent-care tax credits, most of which are tied to the federal tax credit (Martocchio, 2003). Although employers have no direct role in the provision or implementation of these credits, they can actively publicize their availability (Neal et al., 1993).

Long-Term Care Insurance

Long-term care refers to the health care, personal care, and social services needed by persons of any age who have physical or mental limitations and who have lost or never acquired some degree of functional capacity (Byars & Rue, 2004). The only federal program that finances long-term care extending beyond a few months is Medicaid, which is available only to low-income individuals. As a result, individuals pay privately for needed care until their financial reserves are completely depleted. Although private long-term care insurance policies exist, because of cost and lack of awareness of their availability, few individuals possess them. To address this need, some employers have begun offering group long-term care insurance for employees, their spouses, and sometimes their parents and parents-in-law, and/or retirees and their spouses (Martocchio, 2003; Neal et al., 1993; Scharlach et al., 1991; U.S. Department of Labor, Office of the Secretary, Women's Bureau, n.d.). The benefit typically consists of the opportunity to purchase a long-term care insurance policy at reduced, group rates and includes no employer subsidy (Caldwell, 1992; Neal et al., 1993).

Services

Education and Instructional Materials

The provision of education and instructional materials is often the first step that U.S. companies take to directly address employees' family-care needs (Kossek & Ozeki, 1999). Employers may establish a library with print, audio, and videotaped materials on the premises, distribute newsletters and guidebooks, provide educational seminars on the aging process and caregiving concerns, and/or offer caregiving fairs where local providers of service set up tables or booths and employees may obtain information at one time in one place (Neal et al., 1993; Scharlach et al., 1991). They may also make available computers so that employees can access information electronically through company intranets or the Internet (Kuzmits, 1998).

Resource and Referral and Case Management

Resource (or *information*) and *referral* (or *assistance*) is the second type of direct service that some U.S. employers offer their caregiving employees. Information and referral services help employed caregivers to clarify issues and determine appropriate responses, including identifying actions the family can take as well as locating specific services that are available and potentially helpful. Typically, employees call a telephone number and receive personalized consultation over the telephone, a follow-up call, and possibly a handbook with more detailed information. Information and referral services are relatively inexpensive and are frequently the second step that organizations make after providing educational materials and seminars to employees with dependent-care responsibilities (Friedman & Johnson, 1999). Employers generally provide this service through a contractor, such as a specialized information and referral services vendor or an employee assistance program (EAP; Lechner & Creedon, 1994; Neal et al., 1993).

For employees with children, the typical service generally involves providing a list of child-care providers or facilities, along with questions employees should ask to determine the quality of care provided. The problems associated with elder care, however, are often more complex than those associated with child care, because elder care may involve care at home; care in a transitional living setting; care by visiting nurses; legal issues, such as financial planning and living wills; intergenerational communications; and the delicate balancing of family dynamics (Barnett & Hyde, 2001; Haupt, 1992; Martin-Matthews, 1996, cited in Martin-Matthews, 1999). When the elder needing care lives in another locality or state, acquiring and providing the necessary information about available resources can be especially difficult and time consuming (Barnett & Hyde, 2001).

In addition to employer-sponsored resource and referral services, the Eldercare Locator, a government-sponsored referral service, is available. This service was established by the National Association of Area Agencies on Aging with funding through the federal government's Older Americans Act. It is a service that is universally available to all caregivers (employed or not). By dialing a toll-free telephone number (1-800-677-1116), callers are referred to the appropriate state or local source of information services for older people living in a given community in the U.S. ("Eldercare Referrals for Employees," 1994; see http://www.eldercare.gov/Eldercare/Public/Home.asp).

Case, or care, management is a more intensive and individualized form of resource and referral that is offered by some employers. With case management, a detailed needs assessment is performed, a care plan is developed with several care options, and regular follow-up is provided. (See Ingersoll-Dayton, Chapman, & Neal, 1990, for a description of a workplace-based, elder-care demonstration program.)

Individual Counseling/Support Groups

A third type of direct support sometimes provided by U.S. employers to working caregivers is individual counseling or support group assistance. This service is intended specifically for employees who need help coping with their family responsibilities. Help in managing the emotional and psychological consequences of caregiving can be needed as much as specific information regarding the caregiving process (Lambert, 2000; Rosin & Korabik, 2002). Professional counseling generally is offered to employees through an EAP either within or external to the organization, or through a health and wellness program (U.S. Department of Labor, Office of the Secretary, Women's Bureau, n.d.).

Support groups have also been established directly by some U.S. employers or through EAPs. In such groups, employees with similar kinds of work–family issues get together and talk, generally with facilitation provided by a professional counselor. Also, a few employers have attempted to institutionalize the support that one employed caregiver can offer to another, such as through establishing a peer counseling or mentoring program (Ingersoll-Dayton et al., 1990).

Some employers have created a "work–family coordinator" position, hiring either from among their internal human resource staff or externally, from among individuals with child- and/or elder-care expertise and professional credentials in social work, counseling, or a related field (Lechner

& Creedon, 1994; Martinez, 1993). As Lechner and Creedon (1994) noted, such a coordinator "presents a highly visible symbol of corporate commitment to family support programs" (p. 101).

Direct Services

A few U.S. companies help employees to deal with their dependent-care needs by providing direct services for the care recipients (e.g., elders or children), such as on-site or near-site day-care facilities or by offering subsidies, vouchers, or discounts for such services provided in the community. Corporate child-care centers are much more common than are adult day-care centers. Respite care, which involves care by a substitute caregiver to assist an elder (or a child with special needs) when the employee needs to take a break on evenings or weekends, is another direct service that has been provided directly or subsidized by an employer (Friedman & Johnson, 1997; Scharlach et al., 1991; Wagner & Hunt, 1994).

Other direct services may include take-home dinners from the company's cafeteria (for example, as offered by the SAS Institute and Steelcase); employee convenience centers that will do grocery shopping, rent videos, and drop off/pick up dry cleaning for employees while they work (for example, as at Riverside Methodist Hospital in Columbus, Ohio) or do dry cleaning, laundry, and shoe repair on site (as at Massachusetts Mutual Life Insurance); and provision of door-to-door transportation in employee-driven vans (Morgan & Tucker, 1991). The benefit consists of the time and travel costs saved; employees pay for the actual services.

Community resource development is another way that some U.S. employers have provided family-care services. These employers have determined that the best way to help their employees is to contribute funds to expand the supply and improve the quality of elder and child care services in the local community. Community resource development contributions may be made individually or in partnership with other employers. An example of a large private sector collaborative is the American Business Collaboration for Quality Dependent Care (ABC). The ABC is a group of leading corporations ("Champions") that joined together in 1992 to increase access of their employees to quality dependent care programs and services (see http://www.abcdependentcare.com). Current ABC Champions include Abbott Laboratories, Deloitte, ExxonMobil, General Electric, IBM, Johnson & Johnson, PriceWaterhouseCoopers, and Texas Instruments. As of 2002, the ABC Champions had committed $136 million in total funding for innovative programs, training, and research related to child and elder care in more than 65 communities where their employees live and work. Consortia of small businesses also have been formed to provide some economies of scale in offering elder (or child) care benefits and services to employees (Lechner & Creedon, 1994).

PREVALENCE AND UTILIZATION OF FAMILY-SUPPORTIVE POLICIES, BENEFITS, AND SERVICES PREVALENCE OF SUPPORTS IN THE UNITED STATES

Although a wide range of policies, benefits, and services to assist employees with family responsibilities has been provided by U.S. employers, it is important to consider how widely such initiatives have actually been implemented. Fifteen years ago, U.S. authors began lamenting the fact that businesses in the United States had made only modest progress in instituting family-friendly practices. For example, Kingston (1990) cited the fact that family-friendly initiatives still were "news," and Aldous (1990) made a similar observation. In 1994, E. Davis and Krouze stated that "The United States consistently falls behind other industrialized countries in its treatment of family-related issues" (p. 20). More than a decade later, as discussed in the next chapter, the United States continues to lag behind.

To date, U.S. employers have directed much more attention toward employees' child-care concerns than their elder-care needs, although even the attention to child care is limited compared with the efforts in other industrialized nations, as we will detail shortly. Only in the past few years has the phrase *dependent-care benefits* begun to include attention to elder-care concerns, and inclusion is far from universal. For example, in the *Fundamentals of Employee Benefit Programs* handbook published in 1990 by the Employee Benefit Research Institute, the chapter on dependent care made no mention of elder care, and the term *elder care* was not included in the index. Even in the chapter "Emerging Benefits," the paragraph on dependent care discussed only child-care benefits. Elder-care benefits were similarly omitted from the *EBRI Databook on Employee Benefits* by Piacentini and Cerino (1990). Fifteen years later, despite Friedman's (1986) speculation that, given the aging of the population, elder care would become "the new, pioneering benefit of the 1990s" (p. 51), both Martocchio's (2003) reference guide on employee benefits for human resource professionals and the benefits chapters in Byars and Rue's (2004) volume, *Human Resource Management*, provide merely a mention of elder care.

Nonetheless, according to the National Study of the Changing Workforce[2] surveys conducted in 1997 and 2002 (Bond et al., 2003), al-

---

[2]The National Study of the Changing Workforce is conducted every 5 years (first in 1992, then 1997, then 2002) by the Families and Work Institute with a sample of about 3,500 wage and salaried employees and self-employed workers in the civilian labor force residing in the contiguous 48 states and living in a noninstitutional residence. A regionally stratified unclustered random probability sample generated by random-digit-dial methods is used (Bond et al., 2003).

though work-life supports on the job—both specific benefit entitlements and less formal policies and practices—increased somewhat between 1992 and 2002, one work-life program that grew significantly was elder-care resource and referral services. Specifically, 24% of employees reported having access to this work-life benefit in 2002, compared with 11% in 1992. In fact, Bond et al. (2003) noted that "although much has been made of employers offering child care services to their employees," they found no change in the proportion of employers (10%) offering employer sponsored/operated child care centers between 1992 and 2002. Moreover, they found that very few parents (about 0.2%) used employer-sponsored/-operated child care center as their main arrangement for their youngest preschool child. Similarly, they found no evidence that employees in 2002 with children under age 13 had more access to child-care resource and referral services through their employers than they did in 1992 (18%; Bond et al., 2003).

Another way to examine prevalence of benefits is to study companies rather than employees. The Families and Work Institute's 1998 Business Work-Life Survey (Galinsky & Bond, 1998) and their corresponding 2005 National Study of Employers (Bond, Galinsky, Kim, & Brownfield, 2005) are the two most comprehensive studies of employer work-life benefits, practices, and supports to date. The 1998 survey examined a representative sample of 1,057 companies with 100 or more employees, whereas the 2005 study was redesigned to include a nationally representative sample of 1,092 employers with 50 or more employees. It should be noted that these samples are not directly comparable because of the differences in the size of companies. The Families and Work Institute is planning to repeat the 2005 survey in 2007, which will provide for more direct comparisons.

In the 1998 study, about 84% of the employers were for profit, and 16% were not for profit, whereas in the 2005 study, 66% were for profit and 34% were not for profit. Furthermore, although 100% of the companies included in the 1998 survey had 100 or more employees, only 49% of those included in the 2005 survey had 100 or more employees. Within the 2005 report, analyses were conducted to compare the 1998 and 2005 findings by restricting the 2005 survey findings to companies with 100 or more employees. Of these comparisons, only two were statistically significantly different; employers were more likely to allow employees to change their starting and quitting time daily and less likely to approve the use of a compressed work week in 2005 compared with 1998.

With respect to leaves, the studies found that the median amount of leave for maternity, paternity, adoption/foster care, and care of seriously ill children was 12 weeks in both 2005 and 1998. About 54% (2005; 53% in 1998) of companies offered at least some replacement pay during maternity leave, compared to only about 13% (in both 2005 and 1998) for paternity leave or adoption/foster care leave.

The most common forms of child-care assistance reported in the 2005 study were low- or no-cost options such as DCAPS (45%), although 34% of companies offered access to information to locate child care in the community. Only 7% provided child care at or near the worksite; similarly, 3% provided financial support of local child care. Once again, when these data were adjusted and compared to the 1998 data, no significant differences were found.

A somewhat smaller number of companies offered access to elder-care resource and referral services compared to child care. However, of those companies with 100 or more employees, 34% reported the provision of elder-care information and resources in 2005, compared with 23% in 1998. This difference is statistically significant and indicates a positive trend in U.S. employers with 100-plus employees in terms of their responsiveness to the growing numbers of employees providing elder-care assistance. In addition 5% of employers provided direct financial support for local elder-care programs in both 2005 and 1998.

When company representatives were asked about the supportiveness of the supervisors and the culture in 2005, 63% responded "very true" to a statement concerning whether supervisors were encouraged to be supportive of employees with family problems, and 76% felt it was "very true" that men and women were equally supported when they needed to attend to family matters. About 48% of companies reported that they provided training to supervisors with respect to responding to employees' work–family needs. There were no comparisons reported with the 1998 data; however, the percentages reported are very similar.

Personal health insurance for full-time employees was widely covered (by 98% and 97%, respectively, of companies in 2005 and 1998), as was coverage that included family members (95% and 94%, respectively). About 12% covered all of the premium for family members in 1998, but the comparison with 2005 employers with 100 or more employees shows that just 7% covered all of the premium for family members. It is not surprising that, with the increase in health care costs and corresponding decreases in employer support of health coverage, this difference is statistically significant. The data do demonstrate however, that more employers are covering health insurance for unmarried partners in 2005 (21%) compared to the 1998 (14%). About 38% in 2005, compared to 33% in 1998, provided health insurance for part-time employees, and this difference is not statistically significant.

Finally, compared to 1998, fewer companies reported the provision of a defined benefit pension plan (41% in 2005 compared to 48% in 1998) or contributed to employee retirement plans (81% in 2005 compared to 91% in

1998). These differences are significant and indicate a disturbing trend among companies in providing less and less support for employee retirement.

More recently, in 2003, the Society for Human Resource Management (SHRM; the world's largest organization of human resource professionals, with more than 170,000 members) found that 20% of companies were providing elder-care referral services, 15% were providing elder-care leave, 3% were providing emergency elder care, 2% were subsidizing elder care, and 1% were paying for elder care or had an on-site elder-care center. This report was based on an online survey of 3,000 randomly selected SHRM members, 584 of whom responded. A William M. Mercer, Inc., survey of 55 large companies employing a total of 1.5 million workers found that 43 (78%) of the companies offered elder-care referral services (see http:// www.mercerhr.com).

This latter survey, in particular, illustrates the need to exercise caution when viewing findings related to the prevalence of work-life supports when organizations are studied. This is because much of the data available and widely reported pertain to major, or large, firms, that is, firms having at least 500 employees, yet in 2003 only about half (49.3%) of U.S. aid employees worked for firms of this size (U.S. Census Bureau, 2006). Currently, family-responsive supports are much more likely to be offered by large organizations; the many workers employed by smaller organizations often do not have access to this assistance (Allen, 2001; Grandey, 2001; Hughes & Galinsky, 1988; Kamerman, 1983).

Moreover, the types of supports offered by small and large employers differ. For example, Raabe (1990, citing Hayghe, 1988) noted that larger employers offer more direct family support services, whereas smaller ones are more likely to offer flexible leave and alternate work patterns. Such forms of support are more feasible for small employers to provide than direct services such as day care centers, for example, which require a certain number of users to be economically viable. For instance, the SHRM (2003) survey found that employees of smaller companies (fewer than 100 employees) were much more likely to be allowed to bring their children to work in an emergency (39%) than were employees of companies with 500 or more employees (21%). In contrast, larger employers were much more likely than smaller employees to offer child-care referral (27% vs. 12%) as well as on-site child care (10% vs. 1%). Similarly, with respect to elder care, the SHRM study found that resource and referral services were provided by 31% of large companies but by only 15% of small companies and that 6% of large companies subsidized elder care, compared to no small and medium-sized companies.

Finally, not all policies, benefits, and services are available equally to all employees of a given organization (Grandey, 2001). For example, research has consistently shown that even within a single company, employees in certain positions experience greater work schedule flexibility than those in other positions (Grandey, 2001). As corporate employee relations manager Anne Kinney stated, "We offer very generous family benefits at Sprint, but flextime for operators isn't an option. We have to run a business" (Fierman, 1994, p. 66).

USE OF WORKPLACE SUPPORTS IN THE UNITED STATES

Even after family care benefits and services have been made available, they often are not used as extensively as expected or are sometimes used by those not expected to use them (Fierman, 1994; Wagner & Hunt, 1994). Employees attending elder care informational seminars, for example, often include "pre-caregivers" (Garrison & Jelin, 1990; Ingersoll-Dayton et al., 1990). Also, only 1% to 4% of the workforce has been found to use available elder care programs (Barr et al., 1992; Ingersoll-Dayton et al., 1990; SHRM, 2003; Wagner & Hunt, 1994), although between 7% and 12% of the workforce was estimated to have current elder-care responsibilities in 1992 (Gorey, Rice, & Brice, 1992), and 17% in 2002 (Bond et al., 2003). A study by the National Alliance for Caregiving in collaboration with AARP (2004) estimated the prevalence of unpaid caregiving at 21% of the U.S. population aged 18 or older, with 59% of those caregivers being employed full or part time.

Wagner and Hunt (1994) explored the reasons for the relative lack of use specifically of elder-care supports. They found that use is related both to the type of caregiving situation in which an employee is involved and the work-related burdens of the caregiving experience. They concluded that although some employees who have elder-care responsibilities may remain resistant to workplace services for a variety of reasons, improved management training and other activities that heighten employees' comfort level in revealing their caregiving situations could increase service use. Another factor found to limit the use of elder-care services has been that options implemented by employers have not always been perceived as desirable or useful, often because programs were adopted without conducting a needs assessment (Kossek et al., 1993; Solomon, 1994) or because of a lack of training of service providers (Gorey, Brice, & Rice, 1990).

Employees may not use work-life supports for other reasons as well. For example, employees sometimes feel penalized, such as through loss of seniority or resentment from coworkers, when they use work schedule flexibility and leave policies (Grandey, 2001). Others may feel that despite the presence of work-life programs, a company's true commitment is to productivity over employee and family well-being, such as when working long hours and "face time" are seen as signs of employee dedication (Fredriksen-Goldsen & Scharlach, 2001, citing Gonyea, 1997).

Nonetheless, the traditional 40-hour, full-time work schedule in U.S. organizations is becoming a myth. For example, the percentage of workers on flexible work schedules rose from 12.4 in 1985 to 15.0 in 1991, and to 27.5 in 2004 (U.S. Department of Labor, Bureau of Labor Statistics, 2005b). This increase in the number of workers on alternative work schedules in U.S. organizations has been attributed to a variety of social, demographic, and economic factors, including (a) greater emphasis on leisure time; (b) changes in the composition of the workforce to include a proportionately larger representation of women, minorities, and the elderly—groups that may be particularly amenable to alternative work schedules; (c) a shift toward the service industry, where atypical patterns of work are more common; and (d) skill obsolescence, which may be combated by providing employees with flexibility to pursue educational and retraining opportunities while remaining on the job (Hammer & Barbera, 1997).

With respect to available governmental initiatives related to work and family, regulatory restrictions limit the usefulness of many such policies. For example, with DCAPS, only expenses incurred directly as a result of the employee's working can be reimbursed. Also, care must be provided by someone other than an employee's dependent (e.g., child or nonemployed spouse), and receipts or invoices indicating the care provider's name, place of business, and Social Security or tax identification number must be submitted. Any funds that have been set aside for use in a DCAP but that remain in the account at the end of the year are forfeited, yet estimating the amount of money that should be allocated to such an account is difficult, especially for employees caring for dependent elders, whose needs for assistance fluctuate. Also, although not problematic for most employees with children, the requirement that the dependent spend 8 hours a day in the employee's home has made DCAPs less useful for employees with elder-care responsibilities, most of whom do not share a household with the elder whom they are assisting (Byars & Rue, 2004; Neal et al., 1993).

With respect to DCAPs and the dependent-care tax credit, although they can be used simultaneously, the same expenditures cannot be claimed twice. Also, the tax credit tends to be most helpful for persons with lower annual incomes. Similar to the DCAP, the tax credit has received limited use for elder care, in large part because of the restrictive regulations that govern its use (Meeker & Campbell, 1986; Neal et al., 1993; Neal et al., 2001).

Finally, the unpaid nature of the leave provided for in the 1993 federal Family and Medical Leave Act limits the usefulness of this leave. Many employees simply cannot afford to take time off without pay.

BARRIERS TO THE WIDESPREAD IMPLEMENTATION
OF FAMILY-CARE SUPPORTS IN THE UNITED STATES

Back in 1990, Kingston argued that the incentives for U.S. employers to respond to employees' work–family conflict might not be as strong as they once appeared to be. For example, he rightly noted that predicted labor shortages might have been overstated; that job growth would occur in jobs that were low paying, required little experience, and had few benefits; and that the economic benefits of family-friendly policies and practices had yet to be demonstrated. Aldous (1990) concurred:

> Few businesses see it as in their self interest to institute family benefits. There is little solid research that would indicate they pay off in profitability. More surprising, however, is the lack of evidence showing how benefits ease the lives of employees with families. The few who receive them and their relatively advantaged status may account for this situation. (p. 365)

Today, the situation has changed to some degree, as the costs to employers of not addressing employees' dependent-care needs have begun to be documented, family-friendly benefits are more widely available (Bond et al., 2003; SHRM, 2003), and the effects of use of supports have been researched in greater detail. For example, in a study for the Metropolitan Life Insurance Company, Coberly and Hunt (1995) examined workers at one company and estimated that each person who provided personal care cost the company $3,142 a year (e.g., in time lost from work, medical benefits, employee assistance costs, replacement costs for those who quit), or $5.5 million, assuming 2% of the company's workforce was providing personal care. This would be an underestimate given the narrow focus on personal care. It was concluded, then, that the economic costs of lost productivity to employers as a result specifically of employees' elder care duties ranged from $11.4 to $29.0 billion a year (MetLife & National Alliance for Caregiving, 1997). On the basis of findings from the National Alliance for Caregiving and AARP study in 2004, these figures were updated, with the total estimated cost to U.S. employers for full-time employees with caregiving responsibilities ranging from $17.1 to $33.6 billion (MetLife Mature Market Institute & National Alliance for Caregiving, 2006).

Moreover, most studies of the effects of use of support have found positive outcomes associated with the use of supports. Flexible work schedules, for instance, have been linked to increased performance (Kossek & Ozeki, 1999), increased job satisfaction (Scandura & Lankau, 1997), and reduced work–family conflict (e.g., K. E. Christensen & Staines, 1990). Hill et al. (1998) found positive effects of telecommuting on flexibility and productivity. Grover and Crooker (1995) found that use of dependent-care benefits reduces intentions to quit and improves organizational commitment. Rothausen, Gonzales, Clarke, and O'Dell (1998) found a relationship between the use of on-site child care and satisfaction with organizational support.

Although additional research examining the effectiveness of family-responsive supports is needed, these and other studies have strengthened the business case in favor of providing work-life supports. As Fernandez (1990) pointed out, "Companies look only at the cost and not at the return on the dollars spent" (p. 188), and these returns typically are very favorable for companies. Companies will fare best, however, if they direct their supports according to actual need based on studies of their own workforces (Neal et al., 1993).

A second barrier to the implementation of family-care supports is employer concern about equity and fears of backlash (Fredriksen-Goldsen & Scharlach, 2001; Grandey, 2001; Rothausen et al., 1998). Family-friendly backlash occurs when policies, benefits, or services are available to employees with dependent-care responsibilities but are not balanced with other types of policies, benefits, and services made available to employees without dependent-care responsibilities or those with alternative arrangements (e.g., stay-at-home spouses). Employers fear that some groups of employees (e.g., those with family responsibilities) will be seen as favored, or as receiving extra benefits, when supports such as elder- or child-care benefits are offered (Grandey, 2001; Rothausen et al., 1998). Likewise, if employees believe that they have differential access to such family-friendly policies, they may feel unfairly treated, resulting in negative backlash feelings against those who do have access. This situation ultimately may result in feelings of inequity and resentment experienced by employees without dependents (Grandey, 2001).

Similarly, when employees perceive that they will be treated or thought of in a negative way for making use of family-friendly supports, they may tend to not make use of such supports. Thus, backlash can result in diminished use of supports. Ultimately, how people respond to organizational family-friendly supports depends on their philosophical perspective. Specifically, if people believe that everyone should be treated in the same way, instead of believing that people with specific needs should be given benefits, then perceptions of inequity and backlash are likely to occur. For example, childless workers may feel that their benefit allocation is used to subsidize benefits for workers with children (Kossek & Nichol, 1992; Rothausen et al., 1998). On the other hand, if people believe that benefits should be distributed on the basis of need, then backlash is less likely to occur.

Organizations are making attempts to diminish the negative effects of backlash by reframing family-friendly initiatives as *work-life* initiatives, with the hope that this term will be seen as more inclusive (Fredriksen-Goldsen & Scharlach, 2001). Furthermore, offering cafeteria-style benefit plans that allow employees to chose benefits that they need helps reduce the negative effects of backlash. Finally, introducing benefits that are attractive to employees without dependent-care responsibilities, such as health club memberships and concierge services, to offset more family-oriented benefits, may help to reduce the negative effects of work–family backlash.

A third barrier to the implementation of family-friendly supports is the lack of universal agreement that it is even appropriate for employers to attempt to address employees' family needs. Some employers maintain that the traditional division between an employee's work life and his or her family life is a real and important one to maintain. Others may fear creating a culture of entitlement, whereby employees would become overly dependent on employers to meet their personal or family needs (Frederiksen-Goldsen & Scharlach, 2001).

Fourth, corporate management is not always unified in its dedication or willingness to support employees with family responsibilities. For example, although the top management may be committed to the establishment of work-life programs (an element argued to be crucial for successful implementation; Axel, 1985; Galinsky & Stein, 1990), middle managers often become barriers to supports such as flexible work hours and time off (Grandey, 2001; Martinez, 1993). Primary reasons may be that often, no incentives for adhering to family-sensitive policies are offered, and in fact managers may be penalized if the standards for evaluating their performance do not take into account short-term productivity shortfalls that can result when employees are allowed to take time off when necessary to perform their family-care duties (New York Business Group on Health, 1986).

Finally, other barriers include a lack of community resources to address employees' dependent-care needs (Liebig, 1993), and, specifically for elder care, lack of employee demand (Creedon & Tiven, 1989; Lambert, 2000; Rosin & Korabik, 2002; Wagner & Hunt, 1994). This latter concern has emerged in part because of low rates of utilization by employees of the elder-care benefits and services offered by their employers, some reasons for which were outlined earlier in this chapter.

CHARACTERISTICS OF FAMILY-SUPPORTIVE EMPLOYERS

The 1998 Business Work-Life Survey found that the most common organizational characteristics of companies that provided work-life support were (a) type of industry (finance/insurance/real estate services are the most generous, and wholesale and retail are the least); (b) size, with larger companies (1,000 employees) most likely to provide supports than smaller (an exception was that smaller companies were more likely to provide wage replacement for paternity leave); and (c) having a higher proportion of top executive positions filled by women. Having a larger percentage of women in the workforce was a fourth factor that was associated with the provision of more supports, but having a smaller percentage was associated with more company investment in more costly options, such as paid leave and health insurance. Additional factors included (a) hourly employees as a percentage of the workforce, with companies having larger proportions of these employees less likely to provide many forms of assistance, and (b) the percentage of part-time employees, with companies having larger proportions of part-time employees being more likely to offer flexible work arrangements but less likely to offer health care benefits. Other factors included unionization, with companies with large proportions of unionized workers being less likely to provide part-time options, gradual return to work after childbirth, and flexibility to move between part- and full-time work; however, leave options were more prevalent, as were health benefits. Finally, having more sites was associated with having a number of types of work-life assistance (Galinsky & Bond, 1998).

The Society for Human Resource Management study (SHRM, 2003) investigated the types of family supports offered by different industries. With regard to compressed work weeks, for instance, there were significant differences between government and health (52% and 45%, respectively, offered this benefit) and durable goods manufacturing (15% offered the benefit). Similarly, 50% of high-tech companies offered domestic partner benefits, whereas only 11% of durable goods manufacturers offered this benefit. About 50% of insurance companies offered telecommuting, but only 6% of durable goods manufacturers did. With regard to child care, 27% of educational services offered on-site child care, compared to only 2% of durable goods and service industries. No significant relationships by industry type were found for elder-care referral services, but 38% of insurance companies and only 12% of educational services offered such services. Only government agencies provided on-site elder care (4%); no other industries were found to provide this service.

A 1985 Conference Board study of 93 corporate human resource professionals for major U.S. corporations (generally employing 10,000 employees or more) looked at the question of why some industries are more likely to offer family-supportive benefits than others. The study involved conducting interviews to identify factors contributing to family friendliness on the part of an organization. The companies that participated represented a mix of industries and were known to have experience with innovative programs. The findings indicated that family responsiveness was likely to be greatest when two or more of the following characteristics were met: (a) the company was in a high-tech or scientific industry; (b) the company had a relatively young workforce (this would be true for child-care benefits, in particular); (c) the company had a high proportion of female employees; (d) the company was located in a "progressive" community; (e) the company was nonunion, or largely nonunion (and thus lacked constraints due to institutionalized and sometimes antagonistic relationships between labor and management); (f) the company was close to its founders' (generally paternalistic) traditions; and (g) the company made products for or offers services to the consumer market (because employees themselves were potential customers, and family-responsive efforts could be seen as enhancing the corporate image and, ultimately, profitability; Axel, 1985).

With regard specifically to elder-care policies, benefits, and services, there is some indication that personal experience with elder care on the part of top managers has positively influenced employers' responses. For example, a study of employers who were pioneers in the offering of group long-term care insurance to employees revealed personal experience with elder care to be a motivating factor (Neal, 1990). Also, second only to a desire to know more about their employees' child-care needs, personal experience with elder care was a major catalyst in employers' agreement to participate in a survey of employees in 33 organizations concerning their informal caregiving duties for children, adults, and elders (Ebert & Neal, 1988). Similarly, after his review of survey data from chief executive officers and corporate managers concerning their perspectives on elder care, Creedon (1995) noted that "the more senior executives seem more aware of the impact of elder care than do managers" (p. 103), which is probably due to their greater likelihood of having personally experienced elder-care concerns.

Gender composition of the workforce may also influence employers' responses to their employees' family responsibilities. For example, probably because the majority of caregivers to elders are women (Stone, Cafferata, & Sangl, 1987), Tennstedt and Gonyea (1994) found that employers with large female employee populations had higher elder-care prevalence rates than employers with predominantly male employee populations. Specifically, between two companies, the rate of employee caregiving among the company with a 75% male workforce was 4%, whereas that among the company with a 60% female workforce was 13%. Similarly, in an exploratory study of 66 employers, Liebig (1993) found that large employers with higher proportions of female workers and female managers were more likely to have elder-care programs. The same phenomenon occurs with respect to child-care programs. As Morgan and Tucker (1991) noted, many companies feel they have no choice but to respond to the rapid growth in numbers of women in their workforces by implementing family-friendly supports.

A final dimension is the great diversity among companies regarding their level of commitment to family-responsive supports. Galinsky and Stein (1990) identified stages in the development of such supports. For example, they distinguished between companies in the early stages of identifying employee needs and developing responsive programs ("Stage 1 organizations") and those that had established a comprehensive approach to employees' dependent care needs ("Stage 2 organizations"). Features that contributed to the process of organizational change from Stage 1 to Stage 2 included a corporate culture in which a commitment to helping employees balance work and family responsibilities is seen as legitimate; support from the head of the organization; training of management to be sensitive to workers' needs; assignment of responsibility for coordinating dependent-care programs; and regular review and modification, as appropriate, of the company's policies. IBM was offered as an example of a company that moved from a Stage 1 to a Stage 2 organization. The company began by addressing its employees' child-care concerns through establishment of a child-care information and referral service. Later, a similar referral program for elder-care concerns was added. Then, flextime policies were instituted (Galinsky & Stein, 1990).

SUMMARY

The United States has a history of workplace-based work–family supports that have broadened and narrowed in scope over time, depending on demographic, social, political, and economic factors. In general, supports for working caregivers have been provided more by employers than by the government, although some governmental policies and benefits exist.

U.S. responses to employees' elder-care responsibilities, in particular, are relatively recent and have emerged as a result of the growing numbers of elders in the population, the aging of the labor force, the entrance of women (elders' primary caregivers) into the workforce, and other related trends that have contributed to recognition of the intertwinement of work and family life. Although a profusion of types of employer responses exists, implementation of many of the supports has not been widespread and has been most common among large employers.

In the next chapter, we discuss the supports provided to working caregivers in other countries, both to provide some basis for comparison and to see what might be learned from other nations' experiences.

3

A Brief Overview of Supports Provided to Working Caregivers in Countries Other Than the United States

The United States stands apart not only from developed but also developing nations with respect to the limited amount of responsibility assumed by the government for the social welfare of its citizenry. This is especially true in regard to children. For example, the United States is one of only two United Nations member countries, out of 193 member countries worldwide, that have not ratified the International Convention on the Rights of the Child; the other country is Somalia (M. F. Davis & Powell, 2003). Article 18 of the International Convention on the Rights of the Child stipulates that although parents have the primary responsibility for the upbringing and the development of their children, the state has an obligation to assist parents, especially when parents are working (M. F. Davis & Powell, 2003).

Other examples of the limited social welfare responsibility assumed by the U.S. government include policies restricting eligibility to government programs, low funding levels of programs such as the Childcare and Development Fund and the Head Start Program, minimal assistance provided to middle- and upper income families, and the lack of significant assistance to low-income families through the U.S. government's dependent-care tax credit (M. F. Davis & Powell, 2003). In addition, the utility of the federal Family and Medical Leave Act is limited because many employees cannot afford to take unpaid family leave and because the act fails to address the lack of availability or quality of child care. As noted by M. F. Davis and Powell (2003):

These deficiencies, though great in themselves, are even more glaring when compared to the wide range of options, such as universal childcare and paid parental leaves, available to parents in other countries around the globe. Quite simply, the United States has yet to make a commitment to U.S. families by enacting policies that adequately address the care of children. (p. 711)

The United States is also the only industrialized nation in the world without some form of national health insurance (OECD, 2004). Instead, health insurance generally is made available through employers; part-time employees and contract workers are typically excluded from employer health care programs (Kaiser Family Foundation & Health Research and Educational Trust, 2003). Smaller employers are increasingly less likely to offer health insurance to employees because of the cost (Gabel et al., 2001). Even employees who do have health insurance generally must share the costs of health care services, and the costs of the copayments that must be made by employees are increasing; moreover, certain services are excluded altogether from coverage (Freudenheim, 2003; Gabel et al., 2001).

The U.S. government does provide health insurance to most persons aged 65 and older through its Medicare program; however, coverage is inadequate for prescription drugs, long-term care, regular preventative care, and other services. This can lead to staggering out-of-pocket costs, even with supplementary insurance (Snyder, Rice, & Kitchman, 2003). In addition, getting reimbursement for expenses can be a complex and time-consuming process. This creates another problem for working caregivers, who often must help their aging parents directly with health and long-term-care expenses and assist them in interpreting and managing payments and reimbursements (Hoffman, 2000).

In this chapter, we provide examples of the types of options available to working caregivers of children and/or aging parents in countries other than the United States. Few publications exist that take an international approach to examining work and family issues (for exceptions, see the edited books by Lechner & Neal, 1999, and Poelmans, 2005). Therefore, here we attempt to represent in a brief and coherent fashion the various workplace and government supports provided to working couples in other countries.

One way to understand national differences in the degree of governmental support provided to working caregivers is offered by Esping-Andersen's (1990, 1999) discussion of the social foundations of postindustrial economies. As Esping-Andersen noted, the countries of western Europe, North America, and Japan vary with respect to the systems that are responsible for the welfare of their citizens. In some countries, the responsibility falls primarily on the state; in others, the market; and in still others, the family.

In particular, Esping-Andersen (1999) depicted three types of welfare regimes: (a) social-democratic, (b) liberal, and (c) conservative/corporatistic. An example of the *social-democratic* welfare regime is Sweden. As den Dulk (2005) described, "The Swedish government takes responsibility for a broad range of social issues including public work-family arrangements such as public day care and advanced statutory leaves" (pp. 221–222). Social-democratic welfare regimes treat men and women as equals and advocate the labor market participation of both women and men (den Dulk, 2005). Other nations that can be classified as social-democratic welfare regimes are the remaining Nordic countries, including Norway, Denmark, and Finland (den Dulk, 2005; Esping-Andersen, 1999).

A *liberal* welfare state regime is characterized by the belief that the marketplace is self-regulating; intervention by the state occurs only in dire circumstances, usually in the form of limited and short-term assistance (Esping-Andersen, 1990, 1999). The government and employers are not bound to provide care; instead, liberal welfare regimes are characterized by market involvement in the facilitation of families being able to care for their kin. Examples of liberal welfare states include the Anglo-Saxon countries of the United States, Canada, Australia, New Zealand, and the United Kingdom (den Dulk, 2005; Esping-Andersen, 1999).

The *conservative/corporatistic* welfare state regime provides financial compensation when market outcomes are unacceptable to society (Esping-Andersen, 1999). These regimes look first to the family as the main provider of welfare for its kin; "the role of the family is more important than in the social-democratic regime, and externalization of care is limited" (den Dulk, 2005, p. 222). Examples of conservative/corporatistic welfare state regimes include the continental European countries of Austria, Belgium, France, Germany, Spain, Italy, The Netherlands, and Japan (den Dulk, 2005; Esping, 1999).

Most industrialized nations of the world are some form of welfare state (Esping-Andersen, 1999). Depending on the type of welfare state represented, they differ accordingly with respect to their work–family arrangements. For instance, Anglo-Saxon countries such as the United States, Australia, and the United Kingdom are liberal welfare states characterized by minimal governmental intervention, whereas in social-democratic regimes like Denmark, Germany, and Sweden, the government assumes considerable caregiving responsibility. In liberal welfare states the expectation is that working caregivers should rely on their own resources for managing their work and family responsibilities (den Dulk, 2005). In social-democratic welfare states, responsibility for addressing the needs of workers and their families is understood to be both a private (family) and public (government) responsibility. Social-democratic welfare states do not expect employers to assist their employees in managing family care responsibilities (Andersson, 1999; Reichert & Naegele, 1999), whereas in liberal welfare states employers may elect to offer some assistance (den Dulk, 2005).

These distinctions by Esping-Andersen and den Dulk are helpful, then, in understanding the differences in various countries' approaches to work and family issues and the supports available. At the same time, it is important to note that family structure is changing globally. The nuclear family is no longer the bedrock of family structure; increasingly, the extended family and the state (and/or market) are partners in the care of kin (Bengtson, Lowenstein, Putney, & Gans, 2003; Litwak, Silverstein, Bengtson, & Hirst, 2003). Litwak et al. (2003) cited evidence that, despite fears on the part of some to the contrary, the emergence of organizations, state, or market programs to manage family tasks has not resulted in the abdication of family responsibility. Instead, they argued, "To understand the role of the family in modern society, theorists should consider the partnership role between formal organizations and networks of supportive primary groups" (Litwak et al., 2003, p. 50).

What follows are examples of types of responses by countries other than the United States to the needs of working caregivers. Our review is not intended to be comprehensive but rather merely illustrative of the supports available elsewhere.

OTHER COUNTRIES' CHILD CARE POLICIES AND PROGRAMS

As M. F. Davis and Powell (2003) noted, "As a practical matter, parents, particularly mothers, cannot work without access to adequate childcare" (p. 693). In Europe and Japan, the norm is subsidized, and in many cases, fully paid maternity leave, and sometimes paid paternity leave, is offered (M. F. Davis & Powell, 2003; Fukuda, 1993). There also are financial supports for parents who seek child-care services outside the home. In addition, expanded access to early childhood education is provided at age 1 in Denmark, Finland, and Sweden and at age 2 in France (M. F. Davis & Powell, 2003, Kamerman, 1991).

The following are some examples of child-care policies and programs that are offered in other countries. Unless otherwise noted, the information provided is derived from that presented by M. F. Davis and Powell (2003) in their review article. In addition to type of social welfare regime, there is another factor driving the child-care policies and programs in some countries. Specifically, some countries, such as Japan and many countries in the European Union, have a very low (below-replacement) fertility rate, thus compelling these governments to make having children, and having a greater number of children, more attractive.

Australia

The Australian government provides a variety of child-care programs, including child-care centers, family day care, occasional care services, outside school hours care services, vacation-care services, play group associations, multifunctional children's services (multipurpose centers that offer the preceding type of care), and in-home care services for families in which the parent or child has an illness or disability. The costs of these services are state funded up to $144.63 per week per child for low- and middle-income families. Regardless of family income and type of program, up to 50 hours of care per week are funded when both parents are working, studying, or looking for work, and 20 hours of care otherwise.

Together, both parents are allowed 52 weeks of unpaid leave, shared sequentially by either parent, to care for a newborn or newly adopted child. Employees of the government itself are allowed 12 weeks of paid maternity leave, and some larger private companies also offer some paid maternity leave to employees. In addition, for low- and middle-income families, the government pays a maternity allowance of $851.44, regardless of the work status of the mother prior to childbirth and, at 18 months, an additional $208 for immunization costs.

Finland

Each child under the age of 7 has a right to local government-provided day care, regardless of the family's financial or employment status. Options include family day-care centers, open day-care centers (where parents can visit along with their child), and 'round-the-clock care (for the children of parents who do shift work). Parents of children under the age of 3 are entitled to take unpaid child-care leave and to receive a child home care allowance for the period of this leave. In addition, approximately one half of necessary child-care expenses are covered by various child allowance programs. Both parents are eligible to take paid parental leave (263 days total, with the first 105 days for the mother, 6-30 days for the father, and the remainder for either parent), and parents of young children may work reduced hours.

France

The French government has "one of the most coherent and deliberate family policies of industrialized countries, and certainly one of the most generous" (M. F. Davis & Powell, 2003, p. 702). Payroll taxes paid by both employees and employers finance day care and preschools operated by the Ministry of Education. Preschools are attended, with no tuition charge, by 95% of children aged 3 to 5. For children under the age of 3, parents pay 25% of the day-care center costs.

For first and second children, paid maternity leave of 16 weeks at 84% of a basic daily wage is provided; for subsequent children, the paid leave increases to 26 weeks. Paid paternity leave of 2 weeks may be taken during the 15 days before or after the child's birth or adoption. Additional unpaid leave with job protection is available to either parent during the child's first 3 years and may be combined with part-time employment or education and training. Up to 5 days a year of paid leave to care for a sick child under age 16 is provided to all working parents. A variety of tax and other benefits are available as well, including a child-care tax credit and a cash family allowance to families with two or more children. Low-income families are eligible for a flat-rate parental allowance payable either from the 4th month of pregnancy to the 3rd month after birth, or paid from age 3 months to 3 years.

Sweden

By federal law, municipalities must provide all requesting families with slots in preschool child care or after-school leisure time centers. "Already in the 1960s, Sweden developed supportive policies for working parents. As a result, the fact that the majority of people combine work with caring responsibilities is taken for granted in the Swedish context" (den Dulk, 2005, p. 222). Parents pay a fee, capped, based on income. As of January 1, 2003, universal preschool for children aged 4 to 5 was provided at no charge for at least 525 hours per year. Paid parental leave of 18 months at 80% of salary (with 1 month reserved for the father), and paid time off to care for ill children (up to age 12 or, for handicapped children, age 21), up to 60 days per year at 80% salary, also are provided. Child care is subsidized, with parents paying, on average, 13% of the total costs and the central and local governments funding the remainder. Fees for preschool and school-aged child care are fixed at 1% to 3% of parental income.

Mexico

Mexico, which is not considered an industrialized nation, has developed programs to assist employees with small children, including the establishment of government-mandated and employer-funded child care. In addition, there is a government program that allows unemployed caregivers to request priority placement over unemployed persons without caregiving duties. The same program also allows unemployed caregivers to participate in job training (Bialik, 1999).

OTHER COUNTRIES' SUPPORTS FOR WORKERS CARING INFORMALLY FOR ELDERS

Unlike the attention to workers' needs for child care, awareness of and responses to workers' caregiving responsibilities specifically for elders tends to be limited in other countries, as it is in the United States. This is despite the fact that, as Lechner (1999) concluded, "Throughout the world the combining of work with informal care to elders is a fairly common phenomenon that will become even more so in the future" (p. 214).

Even in those countries where supports are provided by the government or by employers, they typically are recent and are not targeted specifically to employed caregivers of elders but to all employees or to elders themselves. Moreover, where family-focused supports are not universal, public sector employees and those employed by large corporations generally have more supports than other workers (Lechner, 1999). Workplace practices also often involve informal rather than formal arrangements between employees and their supervisors, making them more tenuous (Martin-Matthews, 1999; Neal & Wagner, 2002). Finally, even when formal supports are available, many employees do not use them. For example, researchers from the United States (Lechner & Neal, 1999; Wagner & Hunt, 1994), Canada (Martin-Matthews, 1999), Britain (Phillips, 1999) and Germany (Reichert & Naegele, 1999) have suggested that some employed caregivers are reluctant to use workplace benefits because they fear such action would jeopardize their jobs, they have to negotiate with unsympathetic supervisors for the benefits, they are not aware of the benefits and how to use them, they do not identify themselves as caregivers, and/or because they simply do not expect assistance from others with their caregiving responsibilities (Lechner, 1999). Yeandle, Wigfield, Crompton, and Dennet (2002) found that in companies in the United Kingdom, "Awareness of policies varies by organisation ... Despite written formal company policy, implementation often takes place on an informal, flexible basis and is determined by reciprocity between managers and employees" (p. 17).

With that said, employees in the most developed countries typically are better off than those in developing countries. Countries such as Mexico, Brazil, and Uganda, for example, generally have very limited family-care supports, and many employees are struggling with their own economic insecurity due to unemployment or employment in the informal sector, where low wages predominate and benefits and job security are nonexistent (Lechner, 1999). Moreover, these countries are undergoing steady urbanization (i.e., movement from rural to urban areas), with people moving to the cities finding it difficult to care for elders who remain in the rural areas because of the substantial distances and limited means of transportation (Lechner, 1999).

The following is a summary of some supports made available to working caregivers of elders in other nations throughout the world. Much of the information presented is derived from various chapters contained in a book edited by Lechner and Neal (1999) on international perspectives on work and elder care, supplemented by additional sources as noted.

Australia

One in five households in Australia, or 2.3 million Australians, are providing "regular and sustained care and assistance, without payment other than government income support, to a person with disability or who is aging" (National Alliance for Caregiving, 2005). Because of such a large need, the Australian government has responded with various programs, including a National Respite for Carers Program, the Home and Community Care Act, and a Carer Recognition Policy. The stated purpose of this latter policy (Queensland Government, 2003) is:

> to raise awareness of the role carers play in our community and to provide a basis for the Government to work with them and their representatives to develop practical action for now and in the future. Anticipated changes in the population during the next decade will see the role of carers becoming increasingly important. (p. 3)

Canada

Canada has a number of universally accessible social programs, including a national medical insurance program established in 1972. Medical and hospital care are free, although the strong medical and institutional focus within the health care system contributes to an expensive system of care and delays in access to health services. Moreover, programs and policies are in flux because of cost-cutting concerns (Martin-Matthews, 1999).

A policy of family reunification in immigration in Canada has resulted in an increase in the number of elders from ethnocultural minorities, with 17% of elderly Canadians born outside of Canada (Martin-Matthews, 1999). At the same time, there is legal recognition of the statutory obligations of adult children to support a parent who can prove need and who has cared for or provided support for the child. These filial obligation laws are rarely used and are seldom effective when the required support is not given willingly (Snell, 1990, cited in Martin-Matthews, 1999), although there are instances in which the courts have ordered adult children to provide monthly support to their parents (Martin-Matthews, 1999).

Some provincial governments in Canada have programs in which financial compensation is provided for family members who care for elders (e.g., the Nova Scotia Home Life Support Program). In general, however, these programs have quite restricted eligibility guidelines (Martin-Matthews, 1999).

With regard to workplace-based initiatives, meeting individual needs generally is seen by employers as the responsibility of the employee. Also, many Canadian employers feel that their social obligations to the employees are met through the corporate taxes that they pay. Increasingly, though, Canadian corporations are recognizing potential value in the provision of family-supportive programs. The few private sector initiatives that have been introduced closely parallel those of the United States. They include child-care and elder-care information services, handbooks concerning how to apply for and manage flexible work arrangements, "supportive manager" training, job share registries, work and family newsletters, compressed workweeks, flexible work arrangements, regular part-time employment, telecommuting, leave programs, and flexible benefits.

By and large, Canadian leave programs have been created through labor legislation by the federal government. Until recently, leaves were typically for only a few days and were unpaid, except for those related to the birth or adoption of a child (Martin-Matthews, 1999). Effective in January 2004, however, the Canadian federal government amended its Employment Insurance Act and the Canada Labour Code in the Budget Implementation Act of 2003 (Bill C-28) to introduce a compassionate-care leave program providing 6 weeks of benefits for individuals caring for a seriously ill or dying immediate family member (Hayward, Davies, Robb, Denton, & Auton, 2004). Other relevant federal government support for working caregivers comes through the Canada Pension Plan, which has a dropout provision for people who must leave the workforce temporarily to care for an ailing spouse or those who are forced to retire early to provide care (Hayward et al., 2004). The Canadian tax system does not offer any direct tax relief or benefits for people who care for an infirm spouse (Hayward et al., 2004).

In Canada, many of the private sector initiatives with respect to work–family integration have come from major financial institutions, which are highly competitive and have predominantly female labor forces. An exception is the federal government, which, as an employer, has implemented work-at-home options (Martin-Matthews, 1999). Most workplace work–family practices in Canada, however, involve informal rather than formal arrangements between managers and employees. In general, managers perceive elder care to be a less acceptable reason than child care for making special workplace arrangements (Martin-Matthews, 1999). In time, workplace-based initiatives may become more common in Canada, given the increasing legal recognition of the statutory obligations of adult children to elderly parents, together with limits and cutbacks being placed on health and social welfare spending (Martin-Matthews, 1999).

Germany

In Germany, employers see managing work and family care responsibilities as a private family matter, with the responsibility to support employed caregivers falling within the public, not corporate, domain (Reichert & Naegele, 1999). Only very large, international companies, such as Bayer, Mercedes Benz, IBM, and Siemens, have programs and policies to support employees with caregiving duties. The supports available consist of a career break for up to 12 months with a guaranteed return to the same job (Mercedes Benz and Siemens), paid (Bayer only) or unpaid leave from the job for 2 to 3 years, or flexible work hours and part-time work (Bayer, Mercedes Benz, IBM, and Siemens; Reichert & Naegele, 1999).

No community services directly support employed caregivers of elders in Germany, although the establishment of day- and short-term care centers and other community services, as influenced by the implementation of Long-Term Care Insurance in 1994, has helped indirectly. Instead, social policy focuses on the older dependent person rather than on the caregiver, although the needs of caregivers are recognized to some extent in the Long-Term Care Insurance Law that was implemented as a fifth pillar of the Social Security System (the other pillars are Health, Unemployment, Pension, and Accident Insurance). This is mandatory insurance that covers the entire population. All those who are (compulsorily or voluntarily) insured under the statutory sickness insurance, including pensioners, are obliged to make compulsory contributions to long-term care insurance. The insured person pays 50% of the contribution, and the employer (or pension insurance funds) pays the other 50%. To reduce the impact on employers, one of Germany's paid public holidays was abolished (Reichert & Naegele, 1999).

The provisions of the Long-Term Care Insurance program allow persons entitled to and in need of care to choose between receiving professional care services or benefits in cash, which they can use to pay informal caregivers (generally family). Both types of benefits are potentially useful to employed caregivers, enabling them to stay in the workforce if care is provided professionally, or to be compensated to some extent for income lost due to a reduction of working hours. If the informal caregiver is not employed at all or is employed less than 30 hours a week and is providing care for at least 14 hours a week, Long-Term Care Insurance also pays contributions to the pension funds on behalf of the caregiver. This insurance program has led to an expansion of services to support home care, including day or night care; short-term care (up to 4 weeks/year); home modification funds for persons with disabilities; and funds for aids and appliances, such as wheelchairs (Reichert & Naegele, 1999). On the downside, however, the program may cause some caregivers to quit their jobs entirely, thus losing some of the benefits of working, such as social contacts and support and having their own income; also, those out of work for a long period of time may later find it difficult to find suitable work. Important to note, as well, is the requirement of 1 year of service work for young men who refuse to serve in the German army; this "free" care is a key means by which the country has been able to provide the Long-Term Care Insurance (Birg, 2001).

A second relevant government initiative in Germany is the "2. Equality Law," which urges public employers to allow highly qualified employees and those with executive functions to choose part-time work or take a career break because of family reasons. These options, however, are seldom used by employees (Reichert & Naegele, 1999). Finally, it is noteworthy that although the government requires that German parents be given paid leave from work for up to 10 days per year to look after a sick child under the age of 12, no such provision exists for the care of older family members (Reichert & Naegele, 1999).

United Kingdom

Very few policies have been developed that specifically target employed caregivers of elders, but these caregivers are indirect beneficiaries of child-care policies implemented in the workplace. When employers *are* responsive to the needs of caregivers, they typically have developed a range of flexible policies, such as flextime, part-time work, telecommuting, or job sharing. Telecommuting, especially, has become more popular in recent years. Sabbatical programs are offered by a few employers. The Royal Bank of Scotland, for instance, offers a "Career Break" program, which allows employees to take up to three breaks totaling a maximum of 5 years (Phillips, 1999). The provision of services by employers is relatively uncommon in the United Kingdom, and the services that do exist tend to involve rather limited employer involvement, such as the provision of elder-care guides or sponsored access to a telephone hotline. A very few employers with a long-established philanthropic history, however, offer respite care or on-site facilities. Although these programs have been established, carers often do not understand what they are (e.g., carer's leave) or, if they do, whether the programs or policies are available for their particular situation (Phillips, Bernard, & Chittenden, 2002).

The United Kingdom remains a heavily unionized country; thus, the support of the trade unions is vital to any workplace initiative. The unions generally have been supportive of the caregiving needs of employees, monitoring their situations and lobbying for improvements in community care. In negotiations, unions tend to focus on benefits available to all employees, however, such as flexible working conditions.

Similarly, although few of the services of the National Health Service and local social services specifically target employed caregivers of elders, caregivers often benefit from initiatives aimed at the elderly care recipient, such as day care, respite care, home care, and home health care, even though these services are more readily available to elders living alone. Payment for nursing home care is based on level of income, and often even those caregivers who secure placement face additional costs associated with related services. In 1995, legislation aimed at supporting caregivers was introduced (the Carers Act), recognizing the needs of caregivers separately from care recipients. This legislation, however, applies only to caregivers who provide more than 20 hours of care per week and thus does little to alleviate the needs of the majority of caregivers (Phillips, 1999).

Japan

Because of low fertility and an aging population, the Japanese government (along with the governments of European countries) has implemented policy measures to "reconcile work and family responsibilities and to raise birth rates" (Fukuda, 1993, p. 31). Japan is one of the oldest and fastest aging countries in the world; an estimated 27% of the population will be aged 65+ in 2025 (Ishii-Kuntz, 1999). Consequently, elder care is and will continue to be a growing concern of policymakers, nonprofit organizations, and employers alike. For instance, in 2000, the government introduced and passed legislation that requires all persons aged 40 or older to buy into the country's Public Long-Term Care Insurance program (National Alliance for Caregiving, 2005). The government pays half of the premium of these policies, and the individual pays the other half. Such policy initiatives demonstrate the acknowledgment of country's future care needs as its society ages. Most care in Japan is provided by women, although in contrast to most other nations where this is also the case, cultural expectations are that daughters-in-law, in particular, not just wives and daughters, will serve as caregivers (Ishii-Kuntz, 1999).

The government seeks to support working caregivers of elders through a number of policies, as outlined by Ishii-Kuntz (1999). First, the Long-Term Leave law of 1999 allows employees to take a 3-month leave (at 25% pay) to care for a family member (child, spouse, parent, or parent-in-law) who needs constant attention. Although employees are protected from layoffs during this period, the leave can be taken only once, and the 25% salary replacement is insufficient to maintain the previous living standard. To combat these weaknesses, numerous amendments have been discussed to expand the legislation. Second, telecommuting has been promoted by the Ministry of Labor, and efforts have been made to increase the pool of workers who could fill vacancies created by the Long-Term Leave law.

Third, the government sponsors various direct services to support employed caregivers, such as counseling, seminars on combining work and caregiving, and the distribution of educational materials. Fourth, taxpayers can claim a flat deduction for each elderly dependent, and investments made to accommodate elders are tax deductible as well.

Finally, as noted by Koyano (2003), a new long-term care system enacted in 2000, called Insurance Against Care, "acknowledges social responsibility for long-term care ... [and] is a response to the changes in family life of seniors symbolized by the decrease of coresidence with adult children" (p. 281). Koyano argued that the importance of family care may be reduced by this new system of long-term care.

Japan is a highly collectivistic country, and the interdependence between employees and their employers is much greater than it is in Western countries. Japanese employees typically stay with their companies for life and define themselves as citizens of their corporation. Consequently, to be successful, caregiving initiatives must be embedded in the company culture. Although all companies are bound by the Long-Term Leave law, a number of major corporations now go beyond the 3-month provision and offer leaves of longer, or even unlimited, duration. In addition, other types of leave are available, including sick, vacation, personal, and medical leave. Corporations typically also consider care responsibilities when making relocation decisions, and flextime is widely available. Companies also offer benefits, although these tend to be geared toward the needs of retired employees (e.g., pensions, additional health insurance, etc.; Ishii-Kuntz, 1999).

Despite this relatively extensive array of support, however, economic downturns and the rapid growth of the older population are likely to create a need to reduce spending on elders and health care in the future, with a negative impact on caregivers (Ishii-Kuntz, 1999).

Sweden

Sweden presents an example of a European social welfare regime. Taxation of individuals is extensive, and the public sector is financier and provider of virtually all social services. Consequently, neither employers nor nonprofit organizations get involved in caregiving, which is seen as the responsibility of the family and the state (Andersson, 1999). In the mid-1980s, the government began to recognize that not all care was being provided formally, and local governments assumed responsibility for informal care. This initially involved educating informal caregivers about the availability of formal services, but a paid caregiver program and paid temporary work leaves soon followed. The paid caregiver program stipulates that if an elderly person is in need of family care, the local government must employ a family member, who must give up all or part of his or her regular work to be recognized as a paid caregiver. The salary of the family caregiver is dependent on the care needs of the elder and is paid an hourly rate, using the salary of a professional home helper as the basis for calculation. About 85% of the paid caregivers under this program are women; the average caregiver is between 50 and 65 years old. About 50% of caregivers work in a full- or part-time job in addition to their paid caregiving. Use of this provision grew initially but then declined, because of the marginal weight of informal care compared with formal care in a welfare state and because of the lack of nationwide criteria for qualification for the program (Andersson, 1999).

Sweden also has a paid leave-of-absence program that has been in effect since 1989. This policy allows employees to take paid time off work for the purpose of caring for an acutely ill family member. The leave is limited to 60 days in the lifetime of the sick individual, and the caregiver receives 75% of his or her usual salary (Andersson, 1999).

The government, through the Working Hours Act, also requires employers to provide employees the right to work part time or use flextime. However, companies do not provide policies, benefits, and services beyond what is required by the law or provided by the government (Andersson, 1999).

China

Finally, the situation of China is interesting to note. Despite currently being a nation with one of the youngest populations in the world, China is home to about 20% of the world's 60+ population (Chi, 1999). Because of rapidly declining fertility (as a result of China's one-child policy), it is estimated that about 31% of the Chinese population will be age 60 and over by 2040 (Chi, 1999).

In China, the traditional support system in old age is the family, and family caregiving is deeply rooted in the value system. For workers, however, the Chinese welfare system traditionally has been based on employment in state-owned enterprises. Workers are allocated to these companies, and companies then provide for all the social and economic needs of their employees, including housing, education, medical care, and social security. With the transition to a market economy, although some state-owned enterprises still operate in the traditional manner, many of the now increasingly common privately owned companies do not follow the traditional system. Thus, employer supports in China vary greatly (Chi, 1999).

A case study of the Guangzhou province, one of the pioneers in the transition to a market economy, found that state-owned companies represented a minority of companies but continued to employ the bulk of employees (Chi, 1999). In general, state-owned companies were found to offer better supports than privately owned companies, such as 3 months of sick or personal leave offered by state-owned companies, compared to only 1 week by private companies, with family leave care needs not qualifying an employee for a leave in the private companies. Similarly, although about 75% of Chinese workers are union members, unions in state-owned companies are generally much more successful in negotiating elder-care services and benefits than unions in individually owned companies (Chi, 1999).

SUMMARY

In this chapter, we have provided examples of family-friendly supports to working caregivers in countries throughout the world. These examples demonstrate that we have much to learn from each other. In particular, the United States lags far behind other industrialized nations with respect to government support of working caregivers to children and/or elders. Such governmental support is consistent with the type of welfare state regime that characterizes these countries. Other industrialized nations, both social-democratic and conservative regimes (Esping-Andersen, 1999), provide universal child care and paid family leave through their governments (M. F. Davis & Powell, 2003). In the United States, federally mandated family leave protects the employee's job (or guarantees a job of equivalent status and pay), but the employer is not required to pay the employee while she or he is on leave, except where state law mandates otherwise. Currently, only in the state of California are employers required to offer paid family leave (M. F. Davis & Powell, 2003). The governments of many countries other than the United States also provide pay to family caregivers of children and/or elders. In the United States, such payments are the exception rather than the rule (Lechner & Neal, 1999).

In the next chapter, we move to the central focus of this book: our own study of working couples in the United States who are caring simultaneously for dependent children and aging parents, also known as the *sandwiched-generation*. We provide a brief description of the study's methods and then describe in detail the characteristics of the husbands and wives who participated in the study and comprise members of the population of dual-earner couples in the sandwiched generation.

4

Theoretical Perspectives on the Work–Family Interface and Conceptual Framework for the Book

---

...We have sent our son to the grandparents after school where they could keep an eye on him and him on them plus he helped them with odd jobs ... That in turn helped us and made our parents feel better because they weren't bothering us ...

In chapter 1, we provided an overview of working couples caring for children and aging parents and identified some of the neglected areas of research within the field of work and family. We also highlighted what is known about the prevalence of the sandwiched generation as well as the social and demographic trends that led to our focus on this group of people. Before we detail the findings of our study, which provide an in-depth examination of sandwiched-generation couples and their complex work and family lives, it is important to include an overview of the existing work–family research and present our conceptual framework.

Previous research on the intersection between work and family has been criticized for not being sufficiently based in theory and for lacking interdisciplinary integration, such as among the fields of organizational behavior, human resources, and gerontology (Hammer, Colton, Caubet, & Brockwood, 2002; Kossek & Ozeki, 1998; Westman & Piotrkowski, 1999; Zedeck, 1992). In this chapter, we provide a broad overview of the two primary theories that have been used to better understand the relationships between work and family: (a) role theory and (b) systems theory. We integrate these theories and the available empirical work–family research to develop the conceptual model that forms the basis for our study.

In general, we are interested in the effects of being sandwiched on three general types of outcomes: (a) work–family fit (i.e., work–family conflict and work–family positive spillover), (b) well-being (i.e., depression, life satisfaction, overall health, and overall role performance), and (c) work (i.e., job satisfaction, absence due to dependent-care responsibilities, work accommodations used, and poor work performance due to caregiving responsibilities). These relationships are described in more detail later, after a review of role theory and systems theory.

ROLE THEORY

According to R. L. Kahn, Wolfe, Quinn, Snoek, and Rosenthal (1964), roles are based on expectations about appropriate behavior in a given position. *Role conflict* is the tension that results from conflicting role pressures. Role theory stipulates that *inter-role conflict*, a form of role conflict, occurs when individuals engage in multiple roles that are incompatible, such as work and family roles (D. Katz & Kahn, 1978). Thus, work–family conflict is a type of inter-role conflict that occurs when role demands stemming from one domain (work or family) are incompatible with role demands stemming from the other domain (family or work; Greenhaus & Beutell, 1985).

Work–family conflict consists of two broad dimensions: (a) work-to-family conflict (i.e., work interfering with family) and (b) family-to-work conflict (i.e., family interfering with work). These dimensions have been identified as distinct, reciprocal constructs that have independent antecedents and outcomes (Frone, Russell, & Cooper, 1992; Frone, Yardley, & Markel, 1997; Huang, Hammer, Neal, & Perrin, 2004). Therefore, the recent trend in research that examines work–family conflict has been to model these dimensions of work-to-family and family-to-work conflict separately to better understand their independent effects.

The conflict perspective of the work–family interface suggests that multiple roles inevitably create strain (Goode, 1960). This has been the basic premise behind most of the work–family literature (e.g., Beutell & Greenhaus, 1982; Chapman, Ingersoll-Dayton, & Neal, 1994; Frone et al., 1992; Goff, Mount, & Jamison, 1990; Hammer, Allen, & Grigsby, 1997; Loerch, Russell, & Rush, 1989; Stephens, Townsend, Martire, & Druley, 2001).

This work–family conflict perspective has garnered the majority of the attention from researchers, the media, and the public. There is increasing awareness, however, of the positive effects of combining work and family (e.g., Greenhaus & Powell, 2006). Thus, it is important to highlight the theoretical perspectives related to the benefits of combining work and family roles, in addition to the costs. These benefits have been referred to variously as *work–family enrichment* (Greenhaus & Powell, 2006), *work–family facilitation* (Wayne, Musisca, & Fleeson, 2004), and *work–family positive spillover* (Hammer, Cullen, Neal, Sinclair, & Shafiro, 2005).

Although theorists have recognized the potential benefits of combining work and family for some time (S. R. Marks, 1977; Sieber, 1974), little actual research has focused on these positive effects (for exceptions, see Baruch & Barnett, 1986a; Grzywacz & Marks, 2000a; Hammer, Cullen, et al., 2005; Kirchmeyer, 1992, 1993; N. L. Marshall & Barnett, 1993; Pavalko & Woodbury, 2000; Wayne et al., 2004). Regardless of the term used to describe these benefits, as Barnett and Hyde (2001) emphasized in their seminal work, the enhancing effects of combining work and family roles should not be overlooked.

One mechanism by which combining work and family can have beneficial effects is via positive spillover. *Positive spillover* between work and family roles refers to the occupation of one role resulting in perceived gains in the other role (Stephens, Franks, & Atienza, 1997). The term positive spillover reflects the general construct related to the benefits of combining work and family and encompasses other constructs referred to in the literature (e.g., work–family enrichment, work–family facilitation; see Hanson, Hammer, & Colton, in press). Similar to work–family conflict, two dimensions of positive spillover have been identified: (a) positive work-to-family spillover and (b) positive family-to-work spillover (Edwards & Rothbard, 1999; Grzywacz & Marks, 2000a; Stephens et al., 1997). In our study, then, we examined positive as well as negative outcomes of combining work and family roles and refer to these constructs together as indicators of *work–family fit*, as described later in this chapter.

In addition to work–family conflict and work–family positive spillover, the perceived quality of a role is important to consider in work–family research. A limitation of previous work–family research has been the failure to consider role quality as a factor in the relationship between role occupation and outcomes (Hammer et al., 2002). Exceptions include work by Stephens and colleagues (e.g., Stephens & Franks, 1994; Stephens et al., 1997; Stephens, Franks, & Townsend, 1994; Stephens & Townsend, 1997) and by Barnett and colleagues (e.g., Barnett & Hyde, 2001; Barnett, Marshall, Raudenbush, & Brennan, 1993; Barnett, Raudenbush, Brennan, Pleck, & Marshall, 1995). Froberg, Gjerdingen, and Preston (1986) argued similarly in their review of research concerning multiple-role occupation and health, stating that the quality of a role will influence the outcomes of role participation. Thus, in this present study we examined the effects of role quality, as well as role occupation, work–family conflict, and work–family positive spillover, experienced among sandwiched generation couples.

SYSTEMS THEORY

General systems theory provides a useful framework for understanding the dynamic relationships between work and family (Bronfenbrenner, 1977; Piotrkowski, 1979). It is only recently, however, that the systems approach been applied in this way (e.g., Grzywacz & Marks, 2000a; Hammer, Allen, & Grigsby, 2003; Shellenbarger & Hoffman, 1995; Westman, 2001). A *system* can be defined as "any two or more parts that are related, such that change in any one part changes all parts" (Hanson, 1995, p. 27). Thus, when a change is made in one part of a system, all other components of that system, as well as other neighboring and connected systems, also are affected. These changes create a ripple effect throughout the system and return to the point of origin, continuing the cycle.

Family systems theory, a subset of general systems theory, calls for examination of the effects of complex interactions among family members on individual behavior (Day, 1995). The premise is that we learn more about the family if we study the interactions among family members than if we simply study each family member individually. Family systems researchers have noted the effects of stress and strain of one family member on another (Cook, 1994; Hayden et al., 1998). Furthermore, research has demonstrated that the attitudes and behaviors of individuals within a family have effects on other family members' attitudes and behaviors (e.g., Hammer et al., 1997; Hammer et al., 2003; Hayden et al., 1998; Westman & Vinokur, 1998). These effects have been called *crossover effects* (Westman & Vinokur, 1998; Westman, Vinokur, Hamilton, & Roziner, 2004).

Crossover effects are the transmission of emotions, affect, or stress from one member of a dyad to another (e.g., Bolger, DeLongis, Kessler, & Wethington, 1989; Hammer et al., 1997; Jones & Fletcher, 1993; Westman & Etzion, 1995; Westman & Vinokur, 1998; Westman et al., 2004). The examination of crossover effects allows us to better understand how an employee's work–family experiences influence the work–family experiences of his or her spouse.

Systems theory provides a clear theoretical basis for the study of crossover effects (Bronfenbrenner, 1977), as it conceptualizes an individual in relation to the family system, the work system, and the work–family system. The crossover model contributes to the study of work and family issues by highlighting the importance of dyadic effects of partners' experiences.

Recent research on crossover effects has demonstrated, for example, that the work and family experiences of one member of a dyad are significant predictors of the work and family experiences of the other member (e.g., Hammer et al., 1997; Hammer et al., 2003; Westman, 2001; Westman & Etzion, 1995). Using this family systems perspective can enhance our understanding of the work–family interface.

It has been suggested that work–family researchers begin to consider the broader family system by, at a minimum, gathering data from both members of the couple rather than examining work and family attitudes and behaviors from the perspective of only one individual in the family (Hammer et al., 1997; Hammer et al., 2003; Zedeck & Mosier, 1990). Although a few researchers have approached the study of work and family from the perspective of couples, such as Moen and colleagues (2003) in their *Cornell Couples and Career Study*, and Sekaran (1986), the examination of couples is not the norm in work–family research. In our study, then, we gathered data from both members of the couple. Systems theory provides a framework for directing such research.

Our research, therefore, is based on both role theory and systems theory. We believe that the integration of these two theories in the study of the work–family interface will help to improve our knowledge, especially when working families are involved in multiple caregiving roles, such as caring for children and for aging parents. Role theory is central to our framework, leading us to examine both work and family role demands and resources that affect work–family fit, well-being, and work outcomes for working, sandwiched couples. To more fully capture the effects of these multiple roles, systems theory suggests that we gather data and examine responses from both members of working couples, realizing that the work and family attitudes and behaviors of individuals are intimately affected by those of their spouses or partners.

CONCEPTUAL FRAMEWORK

Our key interests in this book are to better understand working, sandwiched couples' work–family situations and to identify what factors predict both positive and negative outcomes. The conceptual framework guiding our work is based on the above-noted theories, on previous models of the work–family interface (Duxbury & Higgins, 1991, Frone et al., 1992; Greenhaus & Beutell, 1985), and on existing empirical work–family research (see Eby, Casper, Lockwood, Bordeaux, & Brinley, 2005, for an extensive review of the work–family literature). Our model adds to the work–family literature in four primary ways. First, with its focus on couples caring for both children and aging parents, our model integrates literature from organizational psychology, gerontology, sociology, social work, organizational behavior, and other related disciplines. Second, our model includes both work–family positive spillover and work–family conflict as outcomes, as opposed to the traditional focus only on conflict. Third, our model is based on both role theory and systems theory, extending current theorizing about the work–family interface to encompass the broader family systems theory perspective.

Fourth, our model includes an examination of the effects of role quality as well as role occupation.

The variables we examined in our study were selected on the basis of our theoretical orientation and on the empirical literature. We selected two objective role characteristics for each role (the child-care, parent-care, and work roles), along with that role's measure of role quality. The two objective role characteristics selected for each role were chosen for three reasons: (a) because of their common appearance as predictors in the work–family or gerontological literature, (b) their relative lack of intercorrelation (to avoid problems of multicolinearity, which would result in reduced ability to identify significant predictors of the outcomes), and (c) our desire to tap some dimension of intensity of role demands. Therefore, the objective characteristics we selected were as follows: for the child-care role, number of children aged 18 or under living at home and having a child with special needs; for the parent-care role, total number of parents, stepparents, or parents-in-laws helping and total number of activities of daily living (ADLs) with which the respondent helped; and, for the work role, number of hours worked per week and degree of flexibility in work schedule (e.g., Brennan, Rosenzweig, Ogilvie, Wuest, & Shindo, in press; Major, Klein, & Ehrhart, 2002; Neal et al., 1993). For the spouse/partner role, we could identify no consistent measures of objective role characteristics, so for that role we included only spousal role quality. For example, we considered including the number of years living together, but it was unclear whether fewer or more years together would be associated with greater role demands.

These variables are indicated with **boldface, *italic*** font when mentioned for the first time below, in the review of the literature. We describe here only the research pertaining to those variables that are part of our conceptual model and that are included in further analyses presented later in this book. Chapters 5 and 6 and Appendix A contain complete descriptive information on these variables. We note that there are other important objective role characteristics that could have been included in the model. In general, these variables either did not have as strong a conceptual basis for inclusion or they were interrelated with other variables in the model and thus could not be included. We briefly identify some of these additional variables at the end of this chapter, and in chapter 5 we provide basic descriptive information on several of them for the purpose of providing a broader description of dual-earner couples in the sandwiched generation.

Our conceptual model of the work–family interface among working, sandwiched couples is presented in Fig. 4.1. The components of our model include objective and/or subjective characteristics within the following roles: *personal* (i.e., education, income adequacy, negative affectivity), *spousal* (i.e., spousal role quality), *child care* (i.e., number of children aged

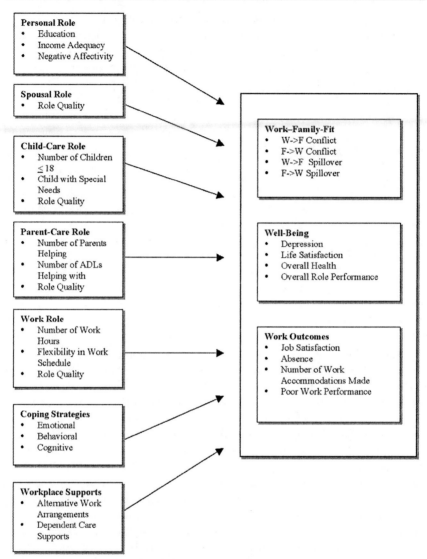

Note. ADL = activities of daily living; W = work; F = family.

Figure 4.1.   Conceptual framework.

18 or under, presence of a child with special needs, child-care role quality), *parent care* (i.e., number of parents helping, number of activities of daily living helping with, parent-care role quality), and *work* (i.e., number of hours worked per week, degree of flexibility in the work schedule to handle family responsibilities, job role quality).

In addition to these objective and subjective role characteristics, we also include two types of resources that are expected to affect couples' work–family fit, well-being, and work outcomes. These are *coping strategies* (i.e., emotional, behavioral, cognitive), and *workplace supports* (i.e., use of alternative work schedules, use of dependent-care supports).

Our model depicts the relationships between these role characteristics, coping strategies, and workplace supports and three sets of outcomes: (a) *work–family fit* (i.e., work-to-family and family-to-work conflict, and work-to-family and family-to-work positive spillover), (b) *well-being outcomes* (i.e., depression, life satisfaction, overall health, overall role performance), and (c) *work outcomes* (i.e., job satisfaction, absence from work due to dependent-care responsibilities, number of work accommodations made, and poor work performance due to caregiving responsibilities). In the following sections, we discuss these outcomes and briefly review the work–family literature relevant to them and the other components of our model.

The Outcomes of Interest

Work–Family Fit

The construct of "work–family fit" has never been clearly operationalized in the literature. Here we conceptualize it as a function of both work–family conflict and work–family positive spillover. Barnett (1998) was one of the first researchers to use the term *work–family fit*. She described it as consisting of a dynamic process of adjustment between work conditions and worker characteristics in which workers select strategies to meet their own needs as well as the needs of other people in their social system.

In our view, it is logical to think of work–family fit, instead, as comprising work–family conflict and work–family positive spillover; these are separate constructs that, together, reflect the degree to which work and family roles are integrated. It is possible to simultaneously experience a high level of positive spillover and a high level of conflict between work and family roles, experience a high level of one and a low level of the other, or experience low levels of both. By investigating both work–family positive spillover and work–family conflict as outcomes, our study encompasses a broader conceptualization of the work–family interface than has typified past research.

Work–Family Conflict.   As mentioned earlier, role theory suggests that conflict occurs when individuals engage in multiple roles that are incompatible (see D. Katz & Kahn, 1978), and work–family conflict is a form of inter-role conflict that occurs when engaging in one role (work or family) interferes with engaging in the other role (family or work; Greenhaus & Beutell, 1985). Netemeyer, Boles, and McMurrian (1996) conceptualized *work-to-family conflict* as a form of inter-role conflict in which the general time and strain demands created by one's job interfere with performing family-related responsibilities. Conversely, *family-to-work conflict* is a form of inter-role conflict in which the general time and strain demands created by the family interfere with the performance of work-related responsibilities. Work-to-family conflict and family-to-work conflict are each associated with unique antecedents and outcomes (e.g., Frone, Yardley, & Markel, 1997; Grzywacz & Marks, 2000b; Kinnunen & Mauno, 1998).

Work–family conflict can arise from pressures originating either in the individual's work or family domain (e.g., Frone et al., 1992; Greenhaus & Beutell, 1985). Previous research has demonstrated that lower levels of work–family conflict are related to many desirable individual and organizational outcomes, such as marital satisfaction (Kinnunen & Mauno, 1998), emotional well-being (Burke, 1988), and general life satisfaction (Adams, King, & King, 1996; Kossek & Ozeki, 1998; Loerch et al., 1989; Watkins & Subich, 1995).

Alternatively, studies have shown that work–family conflict is related to life stress (Greenhaus & Parasuraman, 2002), burnout (Burke, 1994; Kinnunen & Mauno, 1998), distress (Frone et al., 1992), psychological strain (Barling, MacEwen, Kelloway, & Higginbottom, 1994), alcohol use (Frone, Russell, & Cooper, 1997), depression, and other negative mental as well as physical health outcomes (Barnett & Rivers, 1996; Boles, Johnston, & Hair, 1997; Frone, 2000; Frone, Russell, & Cooper, 1992, 1997; Kinnunen & Mauno, 1998; Stephens et al., 1997; Thomas & Ganster, 1995). Work–family conflict also has been linked to decreased life satisfaction (Bedian, Burke, & Moffett, 1988; Kossek & Ozeki, 1998; Pleck, Staines, & Lang, 1980) and decreased family satisfaction (Higgins, Duxbury, & Irving, 1992). Finally, work–family conflict has been found to be associated with the work outcomes of intention to quit (Aryee, 1992; Burke, 1994), decreased job satisfaction (Aryee, 1992; Bedian et al., 1988; Boles et al., 1997; Burke, 1988; Kossek & Ozeki, 1998; Thomas & Ganster, 1995; Wiley, 1987), and absenteeism from work (Barling et al., 1994; Goff et al., 1990; Hammer et al., 2003; Hepburn & Barling, 1996; Kossek, 1990; Kossek & Nichol, 1992; MacEwen & Barling, 1994; Thomas & Ganster, 1995). As can be seen, work–family conflict is a variable that has been studied frequently in the work–family literature (Kossek & Lambert, 2005) and that has established relationships with both organizational and individual antecedents and outcomes.

Work–Family Positive Spillover. Positive spillover between work and family roles refers to the way in which the occupation of one role results in perceived gains in other roles (Stephens et al., 1997). Positive role spillover is related to various favorable physical and psychological health outcomes (Grzywacz, 2000; Williams & Alliger, 1994). Similar to work–family conflict, researchers conceptualize work–family *positive spillover as occurring from work to family* and from *family to work.* The two dimensions are independent and uniquely related to different antecedents and outcomes (Edwards & Rothbard, 2000; Grzywacz, 2000). For example, decision latitude at work has been positively related to work-to-family positive spillover (Grzywacz & Marks, 2000b). In the limited research to date, positive spillover has been shown to be associated with positive health, well-being, and work outcomes (e.g., Hammer, Cullen, et al., 2005; Kirchmeyer, 1992). These findings demonstrate the importance of viewing the combination of work and family roles as having potential positive effects on work, health, and well-being, as well as the already recognized negative effects.

Well-Being Outcomes

The well-being outcomes that we have included in our conceptual model for understanding and examining the work–family interface are *depression, life satisfaction, overall health,* and *overall role performance.* These are indicators of general well-being that have been used in much of the previous research on work–family role integration (e.g., Eby et al., 2005; Frone, 2000). The exception is *overall role performance,* which is a measure that we developed specifically for our study. This measure is a composite indicator of self-reported performance in the roles of worker, spouse, parent, caregiver to a parent or parent-in-law, and in taking care of one's own physical and mental health needs. Although not examined in previous research, to our knowledge, we believe that this measure helps to capture the essence of being sandwiched between various role responsibilities.

A number of studies have found a positive relationship between high levels of work and family role demands and *depression* (Frone, 2000; Frone et al., 1992, 1997; Kirchmeyer & Cohen, 1999; MacEwen & Barling, 1994; N. F. Marks, 1998; Vinokur, Pierce, & Buck, 1999). Similarly, previous research has found that high levels of work and family role demands are associated with lower levels of *life satisfaction* and poorer *overall health* (Aryee, 1992; Bedian et al., 1988; Judge, Boudreau, & Bretz, 1994; Pleck et al., 1980; Sekaran, 1983).

Work Outcomes

Work-related outcomes are varied, with some more feasible to assess than others. For example, obtaining accurate assessments of job performance has been a problem that has plagued both managers and researchers for some time. Problems inherent in objective performance indicators range from unreliability of measurements to biases due to market conditions and region. This "criterion problem" in the area of work and family was elaborated by Cleveland (2005), who suggested that organizations should expand their criteria for successful performance to include measures that extend to the work–family domain, such as divorce rates and child health outcomes.

Traditionally, attention has been given to more subjective indicators of workplace outcomes, and although such measures clearly have their own limitations, they are more easily obtained and are better reflections of employees' perceptions and experience of the workplace. The workplace outcomes included in our conceptual model, therefore, include self-reported job satisfaction, absence due to dependent-care responsibilities, number of work accommodations made in response to work and family demands, and reports of poorer work performance due to dependent-care responsibilities.

Job satisfaction is the affective reaction to one's work and is a frequently examined global outcome measure of how one feels about work (Kossek & Ozeki, 1998). Another often studied workplace outcome in both the child-care and elder-care literature is *absence, or absenteeism,* with work and family role demands being positively related to missing work (Boise & Neal, 1996; Goff et al., 1990; Neal, Chapman, Ingersoll-Dayton, Emden, & Boise, 1990; Youngblood & Chambers-Cook, 1984). In addition, excessive work and family role demands have been related to such absence-related behaviors as reporting late, leaving early, taking time off during the workday, spending time on the telephone while at work, or missing an entire day of work (Barling et al. 1994; Boise & Neal, 1996; Gignac, Kelloway, & Gottlieb, 1996; Hammer et al., 2003; Hepburn & Barling, 1996; Neal et al., 1993; Smith, Buffardi, & Holt, 1999). For example, Smith et al. (1999) compared employees with elder-care responsibilities to employees with no elder-care responsibilities on a number of work-related outcomes and found that the only significant difference was in the number of days missed from work. Respondents who were caring for elderly parents reported missing more full days of work than employees with no elder-care duties. Given research findings regarding differences in caregiving burden between men and women (e.g., Kramer & Kipnis, 1995; Neal, Ingersoll-Dayton, & Starrels, 1997), it is not surprising that some researchers have found gender differences in absenteeism, with female caregivers exhibiting higher levels of absenteeism than male caregivers (MacEwen & Barling, 1994).

Previous research, especially in the work and elder-care literature, has demonstrated that *making work accommodations* in response to dependent-care responsibilities, such as limiting travel or postponing a promotion, is a frequent result of engaging in multiple work and family roles (Neal et al., 1993; Pavalko & Artis, 1997). For example, Pavalko and Artis (1997) found that women who were providing care to an ill or disabled adult were more likely than noncaregivers to reduce their work hours over a 3-year period in response to their caregiving demands.

In one of the earliest studies of employees' elder-care responsibilities, a national survey of employees about to retire conducted by Retirement Advisors Inc. found that employees caring for elders were aware that their caregiving was negatively affecting their *performance at work* (Creedon, 1987). In addition, although other accounts of multiple work and family responsibilities negatively affecting job performance have been noted (e.g., Kossek & Ozeki, 1999; Netemeyer et al., 1996), there is a general lack of empirical research on this outcome variable because of the difficulty in objectively measuring performance at work and concerns about the reliability of self-reports of performance.

Predictors: Objective and Subjective Role Characteristics

In this section, we review the objective and subjective role characteristics that are included in our conceptual model of dual-earner couples in the sandwiched generation. The model incorporates the characteristics from multiple roles in a way that allows for determination of the relative impact of each of the roles as well as the relative impact of objective versus subjective role characteristics.

As mentioned earlier, we have incorporated role characteristics into our conceptual framework that include objective (i.e., number of children aged 18 or under, presence of children with special needs, number of aging parents being helped, number of activities of daily living helped with, number of hours worked, flexibility in work schedule) and subjective (i.e., spousal role quality, child-care role quality, parent-care role quality, job role quality) characteristics associated with the personal, spousal, child-care, parent-care, and work role characteristics. Objective role characteristics/demands are more easily quantified and based less on individual perception than are the subjective role characteristics. Subjective role characteristics are based on the respondent's perceptions of the quality of a particular role with respect to both its stressors and its rewards.

Few studies to date have included an examination of role quality, in addition to or instead of mere role occupation, in the context of multiple family roles. It was not until the mid-1980s that researchers, such as Barnett and Baruch (1985), began to take a role quality approach to studying the effects of multiple roles (Rickard, 2002). Two basic approaches have been taken to measuring role quality. The first is to create an overall measure, composed of the difference between the mean level of rewards and the mean level of concerns, or stressors, to indicate whether the role occupant experienced the role positively or negatively (Barnett & Baruch, 1985). The second is to examine the two components of role quality separately, by creating a composite rewards score and a composite stressors, or concerns, score (Aneshensel, Rutter, & Lachenbruch, 1991; Baruch & Barnett, 1986b; Stephens et al., 1997). In the interest of parsimony, we elected to use an overall measure of role quality in our multivariate analyses.

Personal Role Characteristics

The personal role characteristics that are components of our conceptual framework include education, income adequacy (i.e., ability to get along on one's income) and negative affectivity. Some research demonstrates that there tends to be a negative relationship between resources such as *education* and *income* and work–family conflict (e.g., Allen, 2001; Grzywacz, Almeida, & McDonald, 2002), although it has been speculated that such resources are positively related to work–family positive spillover (Wayne et al., 2004).

Financial distress, or economic instability, has been shown to have a significant negative effect on well-being (Probst, 2005; Westman et al., 2004). In their nationally representative study of work, family, and well-being, Miech and Shanahan (2000) found that individuals with lower levels of education (10–12 years) experience higher levels of depression than individuals with 16 or more years of education and also that the level of depression increases with age. These same researchers also found a negative relationship between income and depression and a positive relationship between economic strain and depression, much like the findings of V. W. Marshall, Clarke, and Ballantyne (2001). Frone, Russell, and Cooper (1992) demonstrated similar effects of education and income on well-being outcomes.

Negative affectivity, another personal characteristic identified as important in the literature, refers to a dispositional tendency to experience more negative events and see the world in a more negative light (Watson, Clark, & Carey, 1988). This disposition has been shown to be highly correlated with negative work attitudes (Chan, 2001) and with higher levels of depression (Watson et al., 1988). Although we used this characteristic as a measure of dispositional tendency in our research, we do want to note that some researchers argue that negative affectivity is not a disposition at all but rather a measure of general strain outcomes (e.g., Stone-Romero, 2005). Future research is needed to address these differing conceptualizations.

Spousal Role Characteristics

For reasons detailed earlier, the only spousal role characteristic in-cluded in our model is *spousal role quality.* Role quality, which typically is examined in the context of the roles of spouse, parent, caregiver to a parent, and/or worker, is composed of two distinct but related constructs: (a) role concerns (or stressors) and (b) role rewards (Barnett & Hyde, 2001). High role quality occurs when role concerns are low and role rewards are high. Stephens and Townsend (1997), who examined the effects of role quality on overall well-being in a sample of working, sandwiched-generation women, demonstrated that higher role quality was related to greater well-being. Furthermore, research has demonstrated that the perceived role quality experienced in one role can exacerbate or buffer the effects of stress from other roles (e.g., Stephens et al., 1994; Stephens & Townsend, 1997; Voydanoff & Donnelly, 1999). Westman et al. (2004) demonstrated that marital role quality (in this case, marital dissatisfaction) had significant crossover effects from husbands to wives, but not from wives to husbands. In general, previous research has found that marital role quality is related to higher levels of well-being as indicated by both physical and mental health (Barnett & Marshall, 1992; Barnett et al., 1995).

Child-Care Role Characteristics

The child-care role characteristics we examined include number of chil-dren aged 18 or younger, having a child with special needs, and child-care role quality. These variables have been related to work–family conflict, well-being, and work outcomes. For example, having younger children and *larger numbers of children* in the household have been linked to higher levels of work–family conflict (e.g., Beutell & Greenhaus, 1982; Goff et al., 1990; Hammer, Allen, & Grigsby, 1997; Pleck et al., 1980), higher levels of overall life stress (V. W. Marshall et al., 2001), higher levels of reported work role demands (S. Kahn, Long, & Peterson, 1989) and less personal and professional satisfaction (Amaro, Russo, & Johnson, 1987). In recent research on women with *children who have special needs,* Leiter, Krauss, Anderson, and Wells (2004) found that the more severe the health condi-tions of children with special needs, the more likely women were to reduce their work hours and to experience poor health. In a rare study on the ef-fects of children with mental health disorders on employed parents' role quality, Brennan et al. (in press) found that higher parental role quality and higher job role quality were related to having greater workplace flexibility, as expected. Finally, Barnett and colleagues found that higher *child-care role quality* is related to higher levels of physical health (Barnett & Marshall, 1993).

Parent-Care Role Characteristics

The parent-care role characteristics included in our model are the number of parents/in-laws a respondent is helping, the total number of personal and instrumental activities of daily living with which the respondent helps the parent, and parent-care role quality. A variety of impacts on work and well-being have been found to be associated with having caregiving responsibilities for aging parents or other ill or disabled adults (see Frederiksen-Goldsen & Scharlach, 2001, and Neal & Wagner, 2002, for reviews). For example, Pavalko and Woodbury (2000) found that the combination of work and caregiving for an ill or disabled person in the household is related to increased psychological distress among working women. Martire and Stephens (2003) reviewed considerable research indicating that the demands of parent care and employment frequently interfere with each other. More specifically, existing research has demonstrated that the *number of aging relatives in need of care* is positively related to work–family conflict (Neal et al., 1993; Scharlach, 1994). In addition, the extent to which help with *activities of daily living* is provided (including personal, instrumental, and/or eldercare management activities of daily living) has been found to be associated with work–family conflict (specifically, family-to-work), stress, personal costs, and job costs (Gottleib, Kelloway, & Fraboni, 1994). Other researchers, too, have found that caregivers who have the heaviest caregiving responsibilities, including those who care for family members with Alzheimer's disease, provide 40 or more hours of care per week, and assist with two or more activities of daily living, are more likely to experience physical strain (National Alliance for Caregiving/AARP, 1997; Scharlach et al., 1997), and be at risk for future health problems (Scharlach et al., 1997). Similarly, having more intensive caregiving responsibilities with respect to hours of care and types of help provided has been associated with high levels of family conflict, being forced to make accommodations at work because of family caregiving responsibilities, losing time at work (National Alliance for Caregiving/AARP, 1997), reducing work hours from full time to part time (Boaz & Muller, 1992), and decreased productivity (Scharlach, 1994). Stoller and Pugliesi (1989), too, found an association between providing more hours of care and higher levels of burden.

There are conflicting findings, as well, however. For example, in their study of middle-aged women from the Netherlands, Dautenzberg et al. (2000) found that many employed caregivers reported little impact of caregiving on absenteeism in the workplace and that only a small percentage of women made changes to their work schedules or used sick leave to care for their parents. They also found that being employed did not increase caregiver role strain.

Moreover, there is evidence of positive, as well as negative, effects of caregiving to elders, such as positive spillover from family to work (e.g., better interactions with customers, greater self-confidence, and increased feelings of competence; Martire & Stephens, 2003; Stephens et al., 1997) and higher levels of job satisfaction among caregivers who see their work as respite from their caregiving duties (Scharlach, 1994).

With respect to *parent-care role quality,* Stephens et al. (1997) examined the relationship between quality in the parent-care role, as measured by separate role satisfaction and role stress scales, and two measures of psychological well-being (i.e., positive affect and depression). Among their sample of 105 employed adult daughters caring for an ill or disabled parent, they found that parent-care role stress (along with job role stress) was positively related to depression, They found no relationship between parent-care role satisfaction and positive affect (although job role satisfaction was positively related to positive affect).

Martire, Stephens, and Atienza (1997), in their study of 118 employed women caring for an older impaired parent, found that satisfaction in the parent-care role is positively associated with physical health and with positive affect and negatively associated with depression. They found that parent-care role stress is associated with poorer physical health and with higher levels of depression.

In their study of the effects of role quality on psychological well-being among 296 women caring for ill or disabled parents or parents-in-law, Stephens and Townsend (1997) found that parent-care role stress is positively associated with depression. Although they found no direct relationship between parent-care role stress and life satisfaction, they did find a significant interaction effect with the child-care role: Specifically, greater parent-care role stress was associated with less life satisfaction for women with high child-care role stress.

Work Role Characteristics

The work characteristics included in our model, given their expected relationships with the work–family fit, well-being, and work outcomes, are number of hours worked per week, flexibility in work schedule to handle family responsibilities, and job role quality. Previous research has demonstrated that *number of work hours* is related to higher work–family conflict (Gutek, Searle, & Klepa, 1991; Jacobs & Gerson, 2004; Major et al., 2002; Shamir, 1983). Additionally, other research has demonstrated relationships between the number of hours worked and physical and psychological health outcomes, with working more hours being associated with negative outcomes (e.g., Bird & Fremont, 1991; Barnett et al., 1995). Furthermore, greater *flexibility in work schedule* has been linked to lower levels of work–family conflict (e.g., Bond, Thompson, Galinsky, & Prottas, 2003; Hammer et al., 1997). Finally, Barnett and colleagues have found positive relationships between *job role quality* and psychological and physical health (e.g., Barnett et al., 1995).

In addition to the objective and subjective role characteristics expected to have an impact on work–family fit, well-being, and work, we include both coping strategies and workplace supports as personal and organizational resources that can help improve these outcomes for working, sandwiched generation couples, as described next.

Resources: Coping Strategies

Substantial evidence demonstrates that the way in which we cope with stress in everyday life affects our physical and psychological well-being (Billings & Moos, 1981; Folkman & Lazarus, 1980) and that type of *coping strategy* used is an important factor in coping effectiveness (Billings & Moos, 1981; Folkman & Lazarus, 1980; Hall, 1972; Pearlin & Schooler, 1978). Folkman and Lazarus (1980) defined *coping* as "the cognitive and behavioral efforts made to master, tolerate, or reduce external and internal demands and conflicts ... [that] are made in response to stress appraisals" (p. 223). A subset of the stress-and-coping literature has focused specifically on the strategies used by individuals in response to work–family conflict in order to facilitate their management of both work and family roles (e.g., Amatea & Fong-Beyette, 1987; Behson, 2002; Hall, 1972; Kramer, 1993; Matsui, Ohsawa, & Onglatco, 1995; Pruchno, Burant, & Peters 1997; Wiersma, 1994).

Thus, we expect that work and family coping strategies play a significant role in individuals' experiences of work–family fit, well-being, and work. On the basis of a combination of both the qualitative and quantitative data we gathered as a part of our study, we developed a measure of coping strategies for managing work and family. These strategies and the measure are elaborated in chapters 7 and 8. Because the lives of individuals who are engaged in paid work and who are sandwiched between child- and parent-care responsibilities are so complex, it is important to understand which strategies are used by these couples, and their effects of work–family fit, well-being, and work; thus, we have included these resources in our conceptual model.

Resources: Workplace Supports

Neal, Chapman, Ingersoll-Dayton, and Emlen (1993) made a distinction among three general types of family-friendly workplace supports provided by organizations: (a) policies, such as flexible work arrangements;

(b) benefits, such as child-care subsidies; (c) and services, such as programs providing resource and referral information about dependent-care options. In this book, we use the term *workplace supports* to include all three types.

Research regarding the effects of family-friendly workplace supports on individuals' job-related attitudes and behaviors typically has focused on the perceived availability of workplace supports, actual utilization of formal workplace supports, and factors related to organizational adoption of such supports. The bulk of this research is concerned with the perceived availability of workplace supports. This research generally has demonstrated a positive relationship between availability of supports and attachment, such as organizational commitment and job satisfaction (e.g., K. E. Christensen & Staines, 1990; Grover & Crooker, 1995; Honeycutt & Rosen, 1997; Scandura & Lankau, 1997; Sinclair, Hannigan, & Tetrick, 1995; Thomas & Ganster, 1995; C. A. Thompson, Beauvis, & Lyness, 1999).

Although a number of studies have demonstrated positive effects of *use of alternative types of work schedules* in helping people to better balance their work and family demands (see Baltes, Briggs, Huff, Wright, & Neuman, 1999, and Pierce & Newstrom, 1983, for reviews), the findings are somewhat inconsistent (K. E. Christensen & Staines, 1990; Hammer & Barbera, 1997; Hammer, Neal, Newsom, Brockwood, & Colton, 2005). Additionally, research has revealed relationships between the utilization of *dependent-care supports* and decreased turnover, decreased absenteeism, and increased organizational commitment and satisfaction (e.g., Milkovich & Gomez, 1976; Youngblood & Chambers-Cook, 1984), as well as increased organizational citizenship behaviors (Lambert, 2000). Other studies, however, have found the utilization of on-site child care to be unrelated to work–family conflict, absenteeism (e.g., Goff et al., 1990), and performance (e.g., Kossek & Nichol, 1992; Milkovich & Gomez, 1976). These inconsistent effects of utilization of workplace supports may be due to such factors as variations in study samples, type of support, or length of time the support had been in place. Here we focus on the effects of utilization of workplace supports, which we conceptualize as resources that would help to improve work–family fit, well-being, and work outcomes for dual-earner couples in the sandwiched generation.

SUMMARY

In this chapter, we have provided an overview of two primary theories of the work–family interface: role theory and systems theory. These theories serve as explanatory mechanisms for the conceptual model that guides our research. We have presented our conceptual model and then reviewed relevant work–family research that supports the model.

In the remainder of the book, we describe the findings from our study of dual-earner couples in the sandwiched generation, with the goal of providing a clear analysis of factors that affect the work–family fit, well-being, and workplace outcomes experienced by working sandwiched individuals and couples. It is our hope that the information provided in this book will be useful, not only to theory development in the field of work and family but also to the improvement of workplace and public policies that assist working families.

FINDINGS FROM
A NATIONAL STUDY

CHAPTER

5

Who Are Working, "Sandwiched-Generation" Couples?

We have an adopted 16-year-old daughter who had a heart transplant 6/88—to whom I donated a kidney in Aug. 1997, who was diagnosed with lymphoma in Jan. 1998 ... [She spent] 6 weeks in [a] hospital that is 30 miles from our home. Mother came to live with us 2 weeks before [the] lymphoma [was] diagnosed. We do whatever is necessary to get by. My employer gave me the past week off with pay while]my] child was in ICU [the intensive care unit] on a vent. Work is a stable environment I want to go back to once [my] child is stable—but who suffers? At home I have mom, spouse and 2 bio[logical] children—and a 60 hr/wk management position. This is a very unusual year for us—but never more stressful.

I have a wonderful place to work. I just wish they would let me go to my appointments—make up the time later and do it with good grace. They let me most of the time, but they have an attitude about it. Which just adds to my guilt feelings. Like, no matter how much I do or when I do it, it still isn't right or good enough. It is hard to be The All for everyone. Wife, mother, career lady, and help out my parents. My husband owns his own business, and I have to start coming in on Saturdays to help with the book work. There goes my housework and baking day!!! Life is definitely a challenge and never dull!!!

In this chapter, we briefly outline the design of the study we conducted, and then we describe the couples who participated. As stated earlier, our purpose for the research, as a whole, was to understand the relationships between work and family role characteristics and work–family fit, well-being, and work-related outcomes for middle-income, dual-earner couples who are caring both for children and for aging parents, with the ultimate goal of identifying ways of assisting these couples to maximize positive and minimize negative outcomes.

ABOUT THE STUDY

The findings we report here and in the remainder of the book are based on a national study of dual-earner, sandwiched-generation couples. Appendix A details the study's methods, measures, and procedures. In brief, we conducted focus groups, mailed surveys, and telephone interviews over a 3-year period. First, to help in developing some of the questions for the mailed survey, we held several focus groups locally with working couples who were caring for children and for aging parents. Then we sent two mailed surveys, 1 year apart, to a national sample of such couples. After the two waves of the survey had been completed, we met again with a subset of our original focus group couples to discuss the findings. We also conducted telephone interviews with selected couples who had completed both waves of the survey and had either improved or declined in the year between the two surveys.

For the mailed survey, which was the main component of the study and which is the primary focus of this book, we used telephone screening to identify couples from across the United States who met the criteria for participation. These criteria were (a) the couple had been married or living together for a minimum of 1 year; (b) one person in the couple worked at least 35 hours per week, and the other worked at least 20 hours per week; (c) the couple had one or more children aged 18 or younger who lived with them at least 3 days a week; (d) combined, one or both members of the couple spent at least 3 hours per week caring for one or more aging parents or parents-in-law; and (e) both members of the couple were willing to participate in the study. Because of the specific interest of the study's funder, the Alfred P. Sloan Foundation, in middle- and upper income working families, the final study criterion was that the couple have a combined household income of $40,000 or greater.

Once we established, over the telephone, that a couple met the study's eligibility requirements, we described the project to the potential participant. If he or she indicated that the couple might be willing to consider participating, we obtained the couple's mailing address. We then mailed two survey packets (one for each member of the couple) and asked both members to complete and return their surveys separately. Only couples in which both members returned surveys were included in the study. As a token of appreciation, couples received a check for $40. One year later, we mailed these same couples survey packets that were virtually identical to the first packets and again sent couples a check for $40, once we received both members' completed surveys. Both members of 309 couples returned the first survey. Both members of 234 couples (76%) returned the second survey. Appendix A contains additional details about the methods and procedures we used. Although we provide brief descriptions of the survey questions and measures below, detailed descriptions are included in Appendix A. The survey instrument itself is presented in Appendix B.

CHARACTERISTICS OF WORKING, SANDWICHED COUPLES

To begin to understand the relationships between work and family roles and their impact on work–family fit, well-being, and work outcomes experienced by working couples caring for children and aging parents, it will help to know more about who these couples are in terms of their personal characteristics and their family and work situations. As we noted in chapter 1, little research exists on individuals holding these multiple roles, and no previous research has examined this phenomenon among couples.

In this chapter, which is based on the data from our first national mailed survey to such couples, we add to this literature, addressing two basic questions. First, what are the personal, family, and work characteristics of the men and women who comprise working couples caring both for children and aging parents? Second, how do men and women compare with respect to these characteristics? In chapter 6, we describe husbands and wives with respect to the outcomes measured in the study.

Here we examine a variety of individual, family, and work-related characteristics in each of the four roles: (a) spouse, (b) parent, (c) caregiver to an aging parent, and (d) worker. Because this study focuses on couples, and because virtually all (98.7%) of the respondents to our survey reported that they were married, as opposed to living together (1.3%), we refer to the male members of our couples as *husbands* and the female members as *wives*. Although the study's selection criteria did not exclude same-sex couples from participating, there were no same-sex couples in the sample.

In reporting the findings, we note the mean, or average, values for husbands and wives. Any differences that we describe between husbands and wives are statistically significant unless we say otherwise (i.e., paired *t* tests between husband–wife pairs reveal differences at the .05 level of significance or higher). The characteristics that we describe are based on the responses from the 309 couples (618 individuals) who completed the first wave of the mailed survey.

For less cumbersome reading, we generally report only one decimal place when we provide statistics in the narrative. Also, detailed tables containing the results from this chapter and all subsequent ones are presented not here, in the narrative, but in Appendix C. The tables are numbered first by chapter and then in order of discussion, to facilitate locating them. For example, Table 5.1 details the personal characteristics of the husbands and wives who participated in the study. Additional tables depict husbands' and wives' characteristics in the spousal role (Table 5.2), the child-care role (Table 5.3), the parent-care role (Table 5.4), and the work role (Table 5.5). Below we describe our sample of working, sandwiched-generation couples.

PERSONAL CHARACTERISTICS OF WORKING, SANDWICHED HUSBANDS AND WIVES

Demographic Characteristics

A total of 618 individuals comprising 309 couples participated in our national study by completing the first mailed survey. Nearly all respondents were White (95% of husbands and 94% of wives; see Table 5.1). It is clear that persons of color are underrepresented in our sample. This lack of diversity is a limitation of the study and should be kept in mind.

Husbands, on average, were 2 years older than wives, 43.5 compared to 41.5, and ranged from 30 to 60 years of age, compared to a range of 27 to 56 years for wives. On average, both husbands and wives had attended college for 2 to 3 years, although wives had somewhat more education (15.1 years compared to 14.7 for husbands). Although wives' and husbands' reports of their gross household income varied somewhat, the difference was not statistically significant: The mean household income reported by husbands was $73,204, with a median income of $65,000, compared to the mean income reported by wives of $69,880, and a median income of $60,000. Husbands, however, did rate the couple's ability to get along on their income somewhat more highly than did wives. On a scale from 1 (*can't make ends meet*) to 4 (*always have money left over*; Stewart & Archbold, 1996), husbands' mean rating was 2.8, compared to 2.7 for wives. As noted earlier, low-income couples were not included in this study given our primary funder's interests in middle- and upper income couples; thus, this limitation of the sample also must be kept in mind.

Negative Affectivity

Another personal characteristic of interest is negative affectivity, a measure of personality that has been demonstrated in previous research to be associated with many of the work and well-being outcomes of interest here (see chap. 4 for a brief review). Examples of items on the scale we used to measure this characteristic are "I see myself as someone who gets nervous easily," "worries a lot," and "is relaxed" (reverse coded; John, 1989). In our study, wives reported more negative affectivity than did husbands. with an average of 2.8 for wives compared to 2.5 for husbands, on a 7-item scale that ranged from 1 (*disagree strongly*) to 5 (*agree strongly*).

Family Involvement

A final personal characteristic is the extent to which participants were involved in their families. A sample item from the 4-item scale we used is "Most of my interests are centered around my family" (Frone & Rice, 1987). In addition to their spouse and their children, we asked respondents to include their parents and their spouse's parents in their definition of *family*. The wives in our study reported somewhat greater family involvement than did the husbands (an average of about 3.7 compared to 3.5 on a 4-item scale that ranged from 1 [low] to 4 [high]).

THE SPOUSAL ROLE

Years Together

The couples in our study had been together for an average of about 18 years (see Table 5.2). The length of time they had been married (or living together, for the 1.3% who were not married) ranged from 6 months[1] to 38 years. Wives and husbands did not differ with respect to previous marriages: About 17% of the wives and 18% of the husbands had been married before.

Spousal Role Quality

As discussed earlier, and as Barnett and Hyde (2001) noted, it is important to assess role quality as well as role occupation or participation. Thus, we included measures of role quality for each of the roles of interest. To assess spousal role quality, we asked respondents to indicate how *rewarding* nine different characteristics of the spousal role had been in the past month and how *concerned* they had been about eight different role characteristics on a scale that ranged from 1 (*not at all*) to 4 (*very*; adapted from Barnett, Marshall, Raudenbush, & Brennan, 1993). For example, one question asked "How rewarding has it been having a spouse or partner who is easy to get along with?" Another asked "How concerned have you been about poor communication with your spouse or partner?"

Both husbands and wives reported relatively high spousal role rewards, although husbands reported greater spousal role rewards than did

---

[1]Couples were considered eligible for the study if at least one of the two members reported that the couple had lived together for1 year or more.

their wives: 3.4 compared to just under 3.3 on a scale that ranged from 1 (*not at all rewarding*) to 4 (*very rewarding*). As might be expected from these findings, wives reported higher role concerns, or stressors, than did their husbands, although the level of stressors reported was fairly low relative to that of rewards: The husbands' mean score was 1.7, compared to just over 1.8 for wives on a scale that ranged from 1 (*not at all concerned*) to 4 (*very concerned*). To compute overall role quality (the measure that we use in the analyses in subsequent chapters), we subtracted mean role stressors from mean role rewards. Thus, a positive number indicates that rewards outweigh stressors or concerns. With respect to overall role quality, then, husbands' spousal role quality was higher than wives': 1.7 compared to about 1.4 (there are slight discrepancies due to rounding).

THE CHILD-CARE, OR PARENTING, ROLE

Number and Ages of Children

The couples in this study had from one to five children aged 18 or younger living with them, with an average of two children at home (see Table 5.3). The youngest child averaged about 10 years of age, according to both husbands and wives. Between 8% and 9% of couples (the difference in husbands' and wives' reports was not statistically significant) had children from a prior relationship living with them, and over one quarter (27%) had additional children who did not live with them (e.g., they were away at college, were living independently, or were living with another parent). More wives (17%) than husbands (12%) reported having a child in the household who had special needs (e.g., due to physical disabilities, poor physical health, substance abuse, emotional or behavioral problems, or learning disabilities).

Satisfaction With Child-Care Arrangements

Husbands and wives were reasonably satisfied with the child-care arrangements they had made for their youngest child (or, for couples with special-needs children, for the child with special needs). On a scale composed of 7 items with responses ranging from 1 (low) to 5 (high), both husbands and wives reported an average satisfaction level of about 4.

Responsibility for Child Care

Concerning who assumed responsibility for child care, wives reported taking the most responsibility. Their husbands' responses, too, indicated that this was the case. The survey item asked "Would you say that: (1) you are the person who takes most responsibility for seeing to the care of the children in your household, (2) you and your spouse or partner share this responsibility equally, or (3) your spouse or partner takes on the most responsibility?" Responses were recoded as 1 = *low/spouse mostly*, 2 = *equal*, and 3 = *high responsibility/self mostly*. The mean for wives was 2.5, compared to 1.6 for husbands.

Child-Care Role Quality

To determine the quality of their child-care role, we asked respondents to indicate how rewarding each of 8 parental role characteristics had been in the past month and how much of a concern 13 different parental role characteristics had been, on a scale that ranged from 1 (*not at all*) to 4 (*very*; adapted from Barnett et al., 1993). For example, one question asked respondents how stressful problems in communicating with their child(ren) had been in the past month. Another asked how rewarding it had been, in the past month, to see "your relationship with your child(ren) mature and grow." Wives reported slightly higher parenting rewards (M = 3.6) than did husbands (M = 3.6) but also higher stress associated with parenting (wives' mean was 1.9, compared to husbands' mean of just under 1.8). On balance, though, both husbands and wives reported greater rewards than stressors associated with their parenting role: Overall child-care role quality for wives was just over 1.7, and that for husbands was just under 1.8 (not a statistically significant difference).

THE PARENT-CARE, OR ADULT CHILD, ROLE

Number of Parents Helping

It is not surprising that, given their younger age, wives had more living parents and stepparents (an average of 1.6) than did husbands (1.5; see Table 5.4). Between them, husbands and wives typically had three living parents, stepparents, or parents-in-law. With respect to the number of parents, parents-in-law, and stepparents that respondents actually were helping, wives were helping an average of 1.8 parents, compared to 1.7 for husbands. Although both of these differences are statistically significant, they are not practically significant.

Total Weekly Hours of Parent Care

In terms of the amount of time spent in parent care overall, both husbands and wives were highly engaged in parent care. Respondents were asked to list the gender, age, and relationship of up to five parents, stepparents, or parents-in-law whom they were helping, along with the approximate number of hours they spent weekly in providing care to each. On the basis of totals computed of the hours spent caring for these various parents, both husbands and wives spent the equivalent of at least 1 workday each week, on average, helping parents, stepparents, or parents-in-law. Wives spent even more time than husbands, on average. Specifically, wives reported spending a total of 9.8 hours per week, on average, caring for parents, step-parents, or parents-in-law compared to husbands' reports of 7.5 hours weekly, on average.

Characteristics of the Parent Being Helped the Most

When asked about the one parent for whom they, personally, were provid-ing the most assistance,[2] both husbands and wives were more likely to re-port helping a parent than a parent-in-law. More husbands, however, were helping parents-in-law (42%) than were wives (31%). This likely was the case because husbands were older and had slightly fewer living parents of their own. Also, wives, who were providing somewhat more care overall, may have involved their husbands in the care of their parent.

Husbands were helping a parent who was, on average, 73 years of age; wives were helping a parent who was 72. Both husbands and wives were likely to be helping a female parent, although this was true for more wives (77%) than husbands (71%). In general, the parent was not married; only about one third of both husbands and wives reported that the parent they were helping the most was married (34% and 36%, respectively; this was not a statistically significant difference).

Typically, both husbands and wives perceived the parent they were helping the most as having a reasonably adequate income. On a scale that ranged from 1 (*can't make ends meet*) to 4 (*always has money left over*), both re-ported an average of about 3, or "has just enough, with a little extra some-times." In fact, compared with respondents' perceptions of the adequacy of their own incomes (see Table 5.1), the parent's income generally was perceived as being more adequate.

Only about 6% of husbands and wives reported sharing a household with the parent for whom they were providing the most help. Most were caring for a parent who lived independently in his or her own home or apartment (not retirement or group housing), although this was the case

---

[2]In the survey, after providing some basic information for up to 5 parents, stepparents, and/or parents-in-law whom they or their spouse were helping (i.e., age, gender, relationship, hours helped per week), each respondent was asked to indicate the one parent, stepparent, or parent-in-law whom he or she was helping the most. Thus, within a given couple, the parent being helped the most might be different for the husband and the wife. For example, the hus-band might be providing the most assistance to his mother, and the wife might be assisting her father the most.

somewhat more often for husbands than for wives (76% of husbands and 69% of wives). With respect to distance from the parent, wives lived an average of 28 miles away, compared to the average of 55 miles reported by husbands (this was not a statistically significant difference). In terms of average time to reach the parent's residence, again there was no difference between husbands and wives, with wives reporting an average travel time of about 31 minutes one way, compared to an average of 38 minutes for husbands, but there was considerable variability here. A total of 33 wives and 32 husbands (just under 11%) reported living 1 hour or more away from the parent they were helping the most.

In general, wives spent more time caring for the one parent whom they were helping the most than did husbands: about 6.8 hours compared to 5.1 hours per week, on average. Husbands had been helping their parent for about 8.5 years, and wives for 8 years, on average. With respect to the level of responsibility that both members of the couple, as a unit, assumed for the parent's care, husbands and wives reported at least equal responsibility with other family members or friends, if not main or sole responsibility. In particular, husbands reported an average of 2.5 and wives reported an average of 2.6 (not a significant difference) on a 4-point scale recoded such that 4 = one or both members of the couple had been the *only* ones who had provided the needed help (16% of husbands, 14% of wives); 3 = one or both were the *main* ones (41% of husbands, 49% of wives); 2 = the couple *shared care equally with others* (21% of husbands, 25% of wives); and 1 = *others* had been the main ones, with some help from the husband and/or wife (20% of husbands, 12% of wives). Thus, on average, husbands and wives fell midway between sharing the care of their parent equally with others and being the main providers of care to the parent.

The parent being cared for had fair health, on average (M = about 3.3 for both husbands and wives on a scale that ranged from 1 [*extremely poor*] to 6 [*excellent*]. In general, the parent needed some but not a great deal of assistance with activities of daily living. More specifically, we asked about the amount of help the parent needed with 14 different activities of daily living (5 personal and 9 instrumental), each assessed on a scale that ranged from 0 (*no help needed*) to 3 (*totally dependent*). Combining the scores for help needed on all 14 activities (ranging from 0 to 42) yielded an average score of about 8 for husbands' parents and 9 for wives' (not a statistically significant difference).

To learn more about the nature of husbands' and wives' parent-care responsibilities, we next asked respondents to indicate with which of those 14 tasks they, themselves, helped the parent. We found that, of the 14 tasks, on average, wives helped with a greater number than husbands: 2.4 compared to 1.7 tasks. When we examined the provision of help with each task separately, we found that husbands and wives were similarly involved in helping their parent with 7 of the 14 tasks. For the other 7, more wives provided help than husbands. It is noteworthy, but not surprising given the work status of these couples, that relatively few respondents, husbands or wives, helped with the five personal activities of daily living (i.e., bathing, dressing, transferring, toileting, eating): Husbands helped with an average of only .16 personal activities of daily living tasks, and wives helped with an average of .24 (not a significant difference). Between only 2% and 8% of respondents were providing assistance with any given personal activities of daily living task. Husbands and wives differed in their provision of only one personal activities of daily living: 6% of wives helped their parent with dressing, compared with just 2% of husbands.

The bulk of assistance provided, then, was with instrumental activities of daily living. The most commonly provided tasks were help with transportation (47% of wives, 40% of husbands; not a significant difference), shopping (37% of wives, 29% of husbands), making care decisions (33% of wives, 21% of husbands), managing money (24% of wives, 19% of husbands; not a significant difference), and housekeeping and chores (27% of wives, 15% of husbands). Of these nine instrumental activities of daily living, wives were helping with more tasks, on average: about 2.2, compared to 1.5 for husbands. More wives than husbands provided assistance with six of the nine tasks: shopping (see above), cooking (16% of wives, 6% of husbands), housekeeping (see above), medication management (18% of wives, 10% of husbands), laundry (15% of wives, 8% of husbands), and making care decisions (see above). Wives and husbands did not differ with respect to whether or not they provided transportation for their parent (see above), managed the parent's money (see above), or helped the parent with telephone use (4% of wives, 3% of husbands).

Both husbands and wives had a reasonably high-quality relationship with the parent whom they were helping the most, although wives reported relationships of slightly higher quality. Using a rating scale of 1 (*not at all*) to 4 (*very*), respondents assessed four aspects of their relationship with this parent, including the extent to which they and this parent were emotionally close, they could exchange ideas, they had similar views about life, and they got along together (Assmann, Lawrence, & Tennstedt, 1996). Wives' average score on the four items combined was 3.2, compared to 3.1 for husbands.

Parent-Care Role Quality

Finally, to discern respondents' parent-care role quality (different from the relationship quality reported above), we asked them to indicate the extent to which 10 different characteristics of the parent-care role had been stressful and 8 characteristics had been rewarding (adapted from Stephens &

Townsend, 1997). Again, items were measured on a scale that ranged from 1 (*not at all rewarding/concerned*) to 4 (*very rewarding/concerned*).[3] For example, one question asked how stressful "this parent's emotional problems or moods (e.g., depression, loss of interest, sadness)" had been in the past month. Another question asked how rewarding "seeing your relationship with this parent mature and grow" had been in the past month. Wives reported slightly higher parent-care rewards, on average, than did their husbands (3.1 compared to 2.9); at the same time, they also reported higher parent-care stressors than their husbands ($M = 1.7$ compared to 1.5). Overall parent-care role quality did not differ significantly, then, for husbands and wives (M = almost 1.5 for wives and just over 1.4 for husbands).

THE WORK ROLE

Work Role Characteristics

Regarding their work situations (see Table 5.5 in Appendix C), more wives than husbands held professional, managerial, or technical positions (46% compared to 37%). More specifically (not shown in Table 5.5), more wives than husbands held professional positions (32.5% of wives compared to 19.1% of husbands), technical positions (9.7% compared with 2.6%), and office and clerical positions (30.5% compared with 4.6%). Husbands were more likely than wives, however, to be sales workers (16.4% of husbands vs. 9.1% of wives), craft workers (21.1% vs. 1.3%), and operators (19.7% vs. 1.9%). Similar percentages of wives and husbands were officials or managers (9.9% of husbands and 9.1% of wives), laborers (2.0% of husbands and .6% of wives), and service workers (4.6% of husbands and 5.2% of wives).

With respect to the size of the organization worked for, husbands, on average, worked for larger employers than did wives (M for husbands = 23,704, compared to a mean of 7,759 for wives). At the same time, the average number of employees at the specific worksite did not differ significantly for husbands and wives: The mean number of employees at husbands' worksites was 420, compared with 266 for wives. We should note, though, that there was tremendous variability in these two variables, as reflected in the standard deviations in Table 5.5 (see Appendix C). In addition, when examining the actual percentage of respondents who worked for small companies, we found a different picture. More specifically, we found that 51% of wives and 48% of husbands worked for companies that employed fewer than 25 employees at their worksite. Furthermore, just over 50% of both men and women reported that their companies as a

---

[3]For situations that did not occur, respondents were given the opportunity to circle "0." We then recoded zeros to 1s.

whole employed 150 or fewer employees. Thus, about half of our sample worked for small to medium companies, consistent with the U.S. working population as a whole (U.S. Department of Labor, 2002).

More husbands than wives owned their own business (15% compared to 10%), and husbands had worked in their present jobs longer (12.7 vs. 9 years). Most husbands and wives worked full time (35+ hours/week), although husbands worked more hours per week, on average, than wives (49.5 compared to 38). In fact, only 2% of husbands worked less than full time, compared to 30% of wives; all, however, worked at least half time (i.e., 20 hours/week), as this was a requirement for participation in the study. Overall, both husbands and wives reported that they would prefer to work fewer hours than they were working. On a scale with 1 = fewer hours, 2 = the same hours, and 3 = more hours, the mean response for both husbands and wives was about 1.5.

More than three-fourths of both husbands and wives worked a day shift, although wives were more likely than husbands to do so (85% compared to 77%). Also, about 80% of the men in our study worked a standard full-time job schedule, compared to just 59% of the women. Among those who worked other than a standard full-time schedule (not shown in Table 5.5), about 14% of husbands and 20% of wives said they worked flexible hours, 4% each of husbands and wives worked a compressed workweek, 3% of wives (and no husbands) participated in job sharing, 1% of husbands and 14% of wives had some other type of part-time work arrangement, and 1% of husbands (and no wives) had some other full-time arrangement.

In general, both husbands and wives felt that they had at least some flexibility in their work schedules to handle family responsibilities, although wives reported higher levels of flexibility. The mean for wives was just over 3.1 compared to just under 3.0 for husbands on a scale where 1 = no flexibility, 2 = hardly any, 3 = some, and 4 = a lot. When asked about their organization's responsiveness to take time off to deal with family issues, wives rated their work organization's responsiveness more highly than did husbands, with an average score of 3.6 compared to 3.2 on a scale that ranged from 1 (*not at all*) to 5 (*extremely*). Both husbands and wives rated their work organization's responsiveness to unexpected family problems more highly. The mean for wives was 3.7, compared to 3.6 for husbands (not a significant difference). Self-employed people were instructed not to respond to these items.

Job Involvement

With respect to involvement in their job, wives reported slightly (but statistically significantly) lower job involvement than did husbands. The mean for wives was about 2.1, whereas that for husbands was 2.3 on this 4-item scale measured using a 4-point response format (1 = low, 4 = high).

It is noteworthy that both husbands' and wives' levels of job involvement were considerably lower than their levels of family involvement.

Comfort in Talking with Coworkers and Supervisors About Caregiving

Next, we asked about participants' level of comfort in talking about their dependent-care responsibilities at work, first with coworkers and then with supervisors. Wives reported significantly more comfort than husbands in talking with *coworkers* about their responsibilities related to *children* (the mean for wives was about 3.2 compared to husbands' 2.8 on a scale that ranged from 1 [*not at all comfortable*] to 4 [*very comfortable*]). Both husbands and wives were even less comfortable talking with coworkers about their responsibilities for aging *parents,* although again, wives were more comfortable ($M = 2.9$) than husbands ($M = 2.6$).

Concerning talking to *supervisors* about their responsibilities related to *children*, wives were more comfortable than husbands ($M = 2.8$, compared to 2.5). With respect to talking to supervisors about their *parent-care* responsibilities, wives' and husbands' levels of comfort did not differ significantly: The mean for wives was 2.5, whereas that for husbands was about 2.4. As was the case for talking with coworkers, however, both husbands and wives were less comfortable talking with supervisors about their responsibilities for parents than those for children.

Job Role Quality

Finally, with respect to job role quality, we asked respondents to indicate the extent to which 16 different characteristics of their work role had been rewarding and 19 characteristics had concerned them in the past month (adapted from Barnett & Brennan, 1995). Again, items were measured on a scale that ranged from 1 (*not at all rewarding/concerned*) to 4 (*very rewarding/concerned*). For example, one question asked how rewarding "challenging or stimulating work" had been in the past month. Another question asked how concerned the respondent had been about "the job's dullness, monotony, lack of variety." In our study, wives reported slightly higher job rewards than did their husbands ($M = 2.9$ compared to 2.8). Husbands' and wives' reports of job concerns did not differ significantly, however (husbands' $M = 1.9$; wives' $M = 1.8$). Wives' overall job role quality, then, was higher than that of husbands, on average (1.1 compared to 0.9).

SUMMARY

In this chapter, we examined and compared the personal characteristics, objective role demands, and subjective role characteristics (i.e., role quality) of the husbands and wives who comprised the dual-earner couples in our national sample. A profile of the typical middle-class working, sandwiched couple, based on the average responses to the survey questions is presented in Fig. 5.1. As revealed in this profile, by definition, given their multiple work and family roles, the couples in our study are busy, with responsibilities as spouses, parents, caregivers to parents, and workers. Most are in the middle of their careers and being faced with making tough choices on a daily basis as to whether work or family should or must take precedence and, within the family, whose needs to attend to first: those of their children, aging parent(s), or spouse. The "typical" working, sandwiched couple is profiled in Fig. 5.1.

In addition to the characteristics included in the profile, a few others are noteworthy. Some couples' households comprise blended families; 8% to 9% of couples have children from a prior relationship living in them. Also, in over one quarter of the couples, the husband and/or the wife have other children who do not live with them. Reasons for this include the children being older and away at college or living independently, or children who still are minors but living with another parent. Thus, these couples have additional parenting role demands that are not fully captured in this study.

There are many similarities in husbands' and wives' objective (role demands) and subjective role (quality) characteristics. In general, both husbands and wives are in the middle of their careers, and both work full time. Fortunately, both perceive that they have some flexibility in their work schedules to handle their family responsibilities when necessary. Both have considerable parent-care responsibilities, and the parent whom they are helping the most generally does not live with them but lives one half-hour away or more. The quality of their roles is reasonably high, with rewards outweighing concerns or stressors in all four roles of spouse, parent, caregiver to a parent, and worker.

Some potentially important differences between husbands and wives include wives' greater levels of negative affectivity and greater levels of family involvement, yet lower ratings of spousal role quality. Wives also take greater responsibility for the care of their children, devote even more time to parent care, and assist the parent they are helping the most with a greater number of tasks than do their husbands. At the same time, husbands' greater numbers of hours worked per week, greater levels of job involvement, and yet lower ratings of job role quality are interesting to observe.

In the next chapter, we discuss how these various characteristics of working, sandwiched husbands and wives are related to the outcomes of interest in this study, including work–family fit, well-being, and work-related outcomes.

Personal Characteristics

- The couple consists of a 44-year-old man and a 42-year-old woman, both White.
- Both the husband and the wife are fairly well educated, with 2 to 3 years of college.
- Their annual household income is about $62,500.
- The wife has higher levels both of negative affectivity and of family involvement than the husband.

Spousal Role Characteristics

- The couple has been married for almost 18 years.
- Their levels of spousal role quality are relatively high, but the husband's is higher than the wife's.

Child-Care/Parenting Role Characteristics

- The couple has two children aged 18 or younger in their household, with the youngest being 10.
- The wife takes primary responsibility for the care of the children.
- Both the husband and the wife are reasonably satisfied with the child-care arrangements for their youngest or special-needs child.
- Their levels of child-care role quality are similar and somewhat higher than those of spousal role quality.

Parent-Care/Adult Child Role Characteristics

- Together, the couple has three living parents, stepparents, or parents-in-law.
- They are each helping two parents, and each is devoting the equivalent of 1 workday or more per week to this care. The wife spends almost 10 hours per week and the husband, 7.5 hours, on parent care.
- The parent each is helping the most is their own 72-year-old widowed or divorced mother, whom they have been helping for about 8 years. The wife spends somewhat more time in caring for this parent (just under 7 hours per week) than the husband (just over 5 hours). Both are sharing care responsibilities with others.
- For both husbands and wives, their mother's income is adequate, her health is fair, and she lives independently. She also lives just over one-half hour away.
- The tasks with which each helps their mother are instrumental, not personal, activities of daily living, and involve providing transportation, shopping, making care-related decisions, housekeeping, and/or managing money.
- Their levels of parent-care role quality are similar and somewhat lower than their levels of child-care and spousal role quality.

Figure 5.1. *continues*

Work-Related Characteristics

- The husband works for a larger organization than does the wife.
- The husband spends about 49 hours per week working on the day shift on a standard full-time schedule in a sales position, a skilled craft trade, or a semiskilled trade. He has held this job for almost 13 years.
- The wife works 38 hours per week, also on the day shift on a standard full-time schedule. She has held her job for 9 years. She is as likely as not to be in a professional, managerial, or technical position.
- The wife is more comfortable than her husband in talking about her responsibilities for children and for parents at work, and both are more comfortable talking about these issues with coworkers than with their supervisor. Also, both are more comfortable talking about their child-care responsibilities than about their parent-care responsibilities.
- Both the wife and the husband would prefer to work fewer hours, although both feel they have at least some flexibility in their work schedules to handle family responsibilities.
- The wife's job role quality is higher than the husband's. For both, levels of job role quality are lower than their levels of spousal, child-care, or parent-care role quality.

Figure 5.1.   Profile of the typical middle-class working, sandwiched couple.

6

How Couples Are Doing: The Effects of Being Sandwiched on Work–Family Fit, Well-Being, and Work

---

Now it's hard just to find time to buy food and clean the house, and all those things that you just don't have the number of hours … you feel like you're shortchanging both sides … if I didn't have a family I'd probably do a better job at work … And if I didn't have a job I'd probably do a better job at home …

[I] sometimes feel torn … during spring break, I took a week off work so I could be home with my daughter and spend some time with her, but we spent a lot of time with grandparents. It's just like, "Mom, I thought we were going to do fun things!" It's kind of that torn in between trying to please too many people at the same time.

In this chapter we present our findings concerning how the working, sandwiched couples in our sample are managing, given their multiple role responsibilities. Previous research, as described in chapter 4, suggests that engaging in multiple roles affects one's work–family fit (i.e., work–family conflict and work–family positive spillover), well-being (i.e., depression, life satisfaction, overall health, and overall role performance), and work (i.e., job satisfaction, absenteeism, number of work accommodations made, and work performance). Previous work also suggests that there are differences between men and women in the ways in which their role experiences affect various outcomes and suggests that to best identify these differences in patterns, men and women should be examined separately (Aneshensel, Rutter, & Lachenbruch, 1991).

We begin by providing descriptive and comparative information for wives and husbands on these outcomes. We then describe the correlational relationships between role characteristics (personal, spousal, child care, parent care, and work) and the outcomes (work–family fit, well-being, and work). Finally, we provide results from multivariate analyses that allow us to make stronger inferences about relationships between the objective and subjective role characteristics and the outcomes, as well as examine the significant crossover effects of one spouse's role quality on the other spouse's outcomes. For all of these analyses, we use the data from the 618 individuals (309 couples) who completed the study's first mailed survey. We end with general conclusions about factors that are important for understanding ways to improve work–family fit, well-being, and work for dual-earner couples in the sandwiched generation. (Please refer to Tables 6.1–6.16 in Appendix C for complete statistical information.)

HOW ARE HUSBANDS AND WIVES IN THE SANDWICHED GENERATION DOING?

In this section, we describe and compare, for the husbands and wives in our study, the levels of work–family fit, well-being, and work outcomes experienced (see Table 6.1).

Work–Family Fit Outcomes

Measures.   As we described in chapter 4, we conceptualize work–family fit as a theoretical construct that includes both work–family conflict and work–family positive spillover. Work–family conflict and work–family positive spillover each have two dimensions: (a) work-to-family and (b) family-to-work. We measured *work–family conflict* using a scale developed by Netemeyer, Boles, and McMurrian (1996). This measure consists of 10 items, with 5 items assessing work-to-family conflict and 5 items assessing family-to-work conflict. Couples who participated in the survey indicated the extent to which they agreed or disagreed with items on a 5-point scale ranging from 1 (*strongly disagree*) to 5 (*strongly agree*). A sample work-to-family conflict item is, "The demands of my work interfere with my home and family life."

Work–family positive spillover was measured using six items adapted from the work of Stephens, Franks, and Atienza (1997) concerning positive spillover between work and caregiving for an aging parent. For the present study, the items were broadened to include care for *any* family members and consist of a work-to-family positive spillover subscale (three items) and a family-to-work positive spillover subscale (three items). Participants indicated the extent to which they agreed or disagreed with items on a 5-point scale ranging from 1 (*strongly disagree*) to 5 (*strongly agree*). A sample work-to-family positive spillover item is "Having a successful day at work puts me in a good mood to handle my family responsibilities."

Findings. The husbands and wives in our study had similar levels of work-to-family conflict (3.1 and 3.0, respectively) but differed significantly on family-to-work conflict, with husbands reporting less family-to-work conflict than wives (2.2 compared to 2.3). There were no significant differences between husbands' and wives' levels of work-to-family positive spillover (3.6 and 3.7, respectively), but husbands had significantly lower family-to-work positive spillover than did wives (3.8 vs. 4.0).

Several aspects of these findings are noteworthy. First, for both the men and the women in our study, work-to-family conflict was higher than family-to-work conflict, consistent with much of the previous work–family research (e.g., Eby, Casper, Lockwood, Bordeaux, & Brinley, 2005). Second, wives reported higher levels of family-to-work conflict, as well as family-to-work positive spillover, than did husbands, whereas no gender differences existed in levels of work-to-family conflict or work-to-family positive spillover. It appears, then, that women may be more susceptible to the influences of family on work, both positive and negative, than are men. Third, the people in our sample reported higher levels of positive spillover than conflict between work and family. This is good news! Although our findings for work–family conflict are not surprising given prior research, few studies have examined positive spillover.

Well-Being Outcomes

Measures. The indicators of well-being that we use here include self-reports of depression, life satisfaction, health, and overall role performance. *Depression* was measured using the Center for Epidemiologic Studies Depression Scale (CES–D; Radloff, 1977). This scale consists of 20 items asking respondents to describe their moods over the past week. An example item is "I was bothered by things that usually don't bother me." Scores can range from 0 to 60, with a score of 16 or higher indicative of a depressive "case" (Eaton, Smith, Ybarra, Muntaner, & Tien, 2004). *Life satisfaction* was measured using an 8-item semantic differential scale adapted from measures developed by Campbell, Converse, and Rodgers (1975); Higgins and Duxbury (1992); and Quinn and Staines (1979). Participants were asked to indicate, along a 7-point continuum, how each word pair (e.g., *hopeful–discouraging, boring–interesting* [reverse-scored]) described how they felt about their lives in general. Higher scores indicate greater life satisfaction. *Overall health* was assessed with a single item with responses ranging from *extremely poor* (1) to *excellent* (6). Using the same 6-point response format, we assessed *overall role performance*. As noted in chapter 4, this was a measure that we developed specifically for our study in an attempt to capture the essence of being sandwiched between various role responsibilities. It is a composite indicator created by taking the average of 5 items asking respondents to rate their "overall performance" in the following roles: "at your work," "as a spouse," "as a parent," "as a caregiver to the parent or parent-in-law you're helping the most," and "in taking care of your own physical and mental health needs."

Findings.   When comparing husbands and wives on their levels of *depression* (i.e., depressive symptoms), we found that the husbands in our study had an average depression score that was significantly lower than that of their wives (i.e., 10.9 compared to 13.3). To determine what percentage of participants would be considered depressed (i.e., had scores of 16 or higher), we examined the frequency distributions for all husbands (n = 287) and wives (n = 278) who responded to each of the 20 items. In Radloff's (1977) original study, he found that 21% of the general population scored at or above 16; this criterion is still commonly used today (Eaton et al., 2004). In our study, the rate for husbands was slightly higher than that of the general population (22% of husbands had scores of 16 or higher), but the rate was much higher for wives, with 35.6% of wives scoring at 16 or higher. Thus, working, sandwiched-generation couples, and wives in particular, appear to be at greater risk for depression than are members of the general population.

With respect to *life satisfaction*, husbands' and wives' reports did not differ, with both indicating moderate levels (i.e., means of 5.3 for husbands and 5.2 for wives, out of a total of 7.0). In addition, husbands and wives reported good to very good levels of *overall health* (i.e., the mean was 4.5 for both) and *overall role performance* (i.e., means of 4.4 and 4.4, respectively), with no significant differences between wives and husbands on any of these variables.

Thus, for three of the four indicators of well-being (i.e., life satisfaction, overall health, and overall role performance), we found no significant differences between wives and husbands, and the levels were moderate. On the fourth indicator, however, there was evidence of lower well-being, with husbands and wives alike appearing to be at greater risk for depressive symptoms than the general population, with the risk for wives being especially high. In addition, when we examined the individual items that composed the overall role performance measure, we found that wives reported significantly higher levels of performance as a parent and as a caregiver to a parent compared with husbands, whereas husbands reported significantly higher levels of taking care of their own physical and mental health needs compared with wives.

Work Outcomes

Measures. Job satisfaction was measured using the five-item General Job Satisfaction scale, which is a subscale of the Job Diagnostic Survey (Hackman & Oldham, 1975). We asked respondents to indicate their level of agreement with five items on a 5-point Likert-type scale, where 1 = *strongly disagree* and 5 = *strongly agree*.

Overall absence due to dependent-care responsibilities was measured via a total of eight items: Four with respect to children and four with respect to aging parents. Specifically, we asked respondents: "Because of your responsibilities for children, *in the past month,* how many times have you had to, or chosen to: (a) miss a day's work; (b) arrive late at work; (c) leave work early; and (d) spend time at work on the telephone." We asked the same questions with respect to responsibilities for parents. These items were adapted from a measure of work withdrawal behaviors developed by Neal, Chapman, Ingersoll-Dayton, and Emlen (1993) and are very similar to those used by MacEwen and Barling. Consistent with MacEwen and Barling (1994), for each type of family-care responsibility (i.e., child and parent), we combined and weighted the four work-withdrawal indicators to form one measure of absence. In particular, the number of days missed was weighted by a factor of 3, the number of times arrived late to work was weighted by a factor of 2, the number of times left work early was also weighted by a factor of 2, and the number of times spent time at work on the telephone was weighted by a factor of 1. This procedure yielded two measures, one with respect to child-care duties and another with respect to parent-care duties, each having a range of 0 to 30. We used the average of the two measures to assess overall absence due to dependent-care responsibilities.

Number of work accommodations made because of dependent-care responsibilities is a composite measure of the following seven dichotomous (*no–yes*) work accommodations made because of child- or parent-care duties: (a) "quit a job," (b) "chosen a job that gives you more flexibility to meet your family demands," (c) "refused to relocate," (d) "refused or decided not to work toward a promotion," (e) "refused or limited your travel,"(f) "working reduced hours," and (g) "working a different shift from one's spouse or partner" so that one adult is at home most of the time." Specifically, for each item we asked respondents to indicate whether they had done this in the previous year (0 = *no* and 1 = *yes*). We then calculated the total number of accommodations made.

Finally, *poor work performance due to dependent-care responsibilities* was assessed using the average of two items. Specifically, we asked respondents to indicate how often, in the past month, they had "worked less effectively because you were concerned or upset about your child(ren)" and "worked less effectively because you were concerned or upset about your parents." Responses were provided using a 5-point Likert scale, with 1 = *never* and 5 = *most or all of the time.*

Findings.   On average, both the husbands and the wives in our study reported somewhat moderate levels of job satisfaction (3.5 and 3.5, respectively, out of a total of 5.0). Wives reported significantly more absences per month due to dependent-care responsibilities than did husbands, however (5.4 vs. 2.6, respectively). When examining the specific absence items individually, we found that wives reported significantly more days missed due both to responsibilities for children and responsibilities for parents, compared with husbands. In addition, wives reported significantly higher rates of arriving to work late, leaving early, and time spent on the telephone due to responsibilities for children compared with husbands. In addition, wives reported spending significantly more time on the telephone due to parent-care responsibilities compared with husbands. Much of the research on absenteeism shows that, increasingly, absence is the result of family-care responsibilities (Martinez, 1993). Therefore, our findings may be indicative of the greater level of responsibility that the wives in our study had both for children and for aging parents, as described in chapter 5.

Wives also reported having made a greater number of work accommodations in response to work and family demands in the previous year than did husbands (1.3 vs. 0.8, respectively, on average). Specifically, compared with husbands, wives were more likely to report having worked reduced hours, chosen a job that provided more flexibility, and refused or decided not to work toward a promotion in the past year.

Finally, wives were more likely to report poor work performance due to their dependent-care demands compared to their husbands (*M*s of 2.4 and 1.9, respectively). Specifically, wives were more likely to report poor work performance due to being concerned or upset about both children and parents, compared with husbands.

These results demonstrate that although both wives and husbands were reasonably satisfied with their jobs, wives reported higher absence from work and lower work performance due to their family-related responsibilities than did their husbands, and they made more work-related accommodations because of their dependent-care duties. These results, and those with respect to work–family fit and well-being, suggest that more can and should be done to assist working, sandwiched couples, and wives especially, in their attempts to combine work and family, and that both the couples and their employers would benefit. As we describe in chapters 8 and 9, such assistance or resources can take a two-pronged approach, by focusing on work–family coping strategies and on workplace supports that help to improve work–family fit, well-being, and work outcomes.

HOW ARE ROLE CHARACTERISTICS RELATED TO WORK–FAMILY FIT, WELL-BEING, AND WORK?

In this section, we describe how the various characteristics associated with each role held (i.e., personal, spousal, child care, parent care, and work) are related to the work–family fit, well-being, and work outcomes, as depicted in our conceptual model (see Fig. 4-1, Appendix C). We begin by examining these relationships simply in terms of the correlations, or bivariate linear relationships, between the role characteristics and outcomes. We focus only on the statistically significant relationships and the relationships that are inconsistent with our expectations, based on the findings of previous research, to help in understanding the factors that affect working, sandwiched-generation couples. These correlations are presented in Tables 6.2 through 6.13 (see Appendix C). The key results are summarized in Fig. 6.1.

Personal and Spousal Characteristics and Their Associations With the Outcomes

The personal and spousal characteristics we examined within our conceptual model include years of education, ability to get along on one's income, negative affectivity, and spousal role quality, as described in chapter 5. In Tables 6.2 through 6.4 we present the correlations of these personal and spousal characteristics with the outcomes.

We found that personal and spousal characteristics were more frequently related to well-being outcomes than to either work–family fit or work outcomes. An exception was negative affectivity, which was also consistently related to the work–family fit outcomes. Because this personality characteristic tends to affect the way one sees the world, it would be expected to be related to many outcomes. It is interesting to note that perceived income adequacy was related to many of the well-being outcomes but was not consistently related to the work–family fit or work outcomes. We also found significant associations between spousal role quality and most of the work–family fit and well-being outcomes. We conclude from these findings that, at least among working, sandwiched-generation couples, the subjective perception of the quality of the spousal role is an important indicator of how these couples are doing.

Personal Characteristics

- In general, personal characteristics have stronger associations with well-being than with either work–family fit or work.

Spousal Role Characteristics

- Overall spousal role quality is related to most of the work–family fit and well-being outcomes, but not to work outcomes.

Child-Care/Parenting Role Characteristics

- Objective child-care role characteristics are most strongly related to work rather than to well-being or work–family fit outcomes.
- Overall quality of the child-care role is related more strongly to work–family fit and well-being than to work outcomes.

Parent-Care Role Characteristics

- Objective parent-care role demands, such as number of ADLs the respondent helps with, are related to work outcomes.
- Husbands' parent-care responsibilities, compared to wives', are more strongly related to work–family fit and well-being outcomes.
- Parent-care role characteristics are more often related to family-to-work conflict and family-to-work positive spillover than to work-to-family conflict or work-to-family positive spillover.

Work Role Characteristics

- Work role characteristics are related to many of the work–family fit, well-being, and work outcomes, demonstrating the importance of those characteristics not only in individuals' work lives but to their nonwork lives as well.
- Especially important is job role quality: It is associated with all of the outcomes for both husbands and wives, except for overall absence due to dependent-care responsibilities.
- These findings point to the value of high job role quality as it is associated with individuals' work–family fit, well-being, and work outcomes.

Note. ADL = activities of daily living.

Figure 6.1.   Correlations of role characteristics with work–family fit, well-being, and work.

Child-Care/Parenting Role Characteristics and Their Associations With the Outcomes

The child-care role characteristics that we examined in relation to work–family fit, well-being, and work include number of children in the household aged 18 or under, having a child with special needs, and child-care/parenting role quality. The correlations of these characteristics with the outcomes are presented in Tables 6.5 through 6.7. In general, we found that the objective child-care characteristics, or role demands, were most strongly associated with the work outcomes, rather than the well-being or work–family fit outcomes, whereas subjective child-care role quality was more strongly related to the well-being outcomes.

Parent-Care Role Characteristics and Their Associations With the Outcomes

The parent-care role characteristics in our model include a general measure of parent-care role demands (the total number of parents/in-laws being helped by the respondent) as well as the number of activities of daily living with which the respondent helps the parent whom he or she is helping the most. The relationships of these variables to the work–family fit, well-being, and work outcomes of interest in this study are presented in Tables 6.8 through 6.10.

With respect to the simple correlations between parent-care characteristics and the work–family fit, well-being, and work outcomes, we found that parent-care role quality had a strong association with the work–family fit and well-being indicators but was less strongly related to the work-related outcomes. The objective role demand variable, number of activities of daily living with which the respondent helps, was more strongly associated with the work outcomes. Although previous research has shown that women do most of the caregiving to parents, the husbands in our study were actively engaged as well, as discussed in chapter 5, and it is interesting to note that husbands' work–family fit and well-being were more highly correlated with their parent-care responsibilities than was the case for wives. With respect to work-related outcomes, however, we found more similar correlations between parent-care responsibilities and outcomes for husbands and wives, suggesting that parent-care responsibilities may have a similar effect on work for both men and women in working, sandwiched-generation couples.

Work Role Characteristics and Their Associations With the Outcomes

The work role characteristics we examined include number of hours worked per week and flexibility in work schedule to deal with family responsibilities, as well as job role quality. Their relationships to the outcomes are presented in Tables 6.11 through 6.13.

The work role characteristics had similar associations with the work family fit, well-being, and work outcomes. This demonstrates the importance of those characteristics not only in individuals' work lives but also in their family lives. Especially important is job role quality; it was related to all of the outcomes for both husbands and wives, except for overall absence due to dependent-care responsibilities. This points to the value of attempts to enhance job role quality not only for improved work outcomes but also for better work–family fit and increased well-being for individuals. Employers and employees alike stand to benefit from efforts to improve job role quality via such mechanisms as increased job control and other job design changes.

Conclusions: Simple Associations Between Role Characteristics and Work–Family Fit, Well-Being, and Work Outcomes

We have demonstrated that many associations exist between the role characteristics and work–family fit, well-being, and work outcomes that we examined. Different role characteristics, however, are differentially associated with the various outcomes. Also, the patterns of association differ somewhat for husbands and wives.

Subjective role quality in particular stands out as a critical correlate of the outcomes. For each of the roles, role quality is significantly associated with the outcomes of interest and in the expected directions. More specifically, role quality was positively related to improved work–family fit, well-being, and work outcomes. Because of these overwhelmingly consistent significant associations between role quality and the work–family fit, well-being, and work variables, we believe that these subjective indicators of one's role experience may be more important in influencing one's outcomes than are the objective role characteristics. We examine this in the next section of this chapter.

In the remainder of this chapter, then, we build on this finding of the importance of role quality by examining the relative impact of perceived role quality in the four roles (i.e., spousal, child care, parent care, and work) over and above that of the objective role characteristics, on the work–family fit, well-being, and work outcomes. We also examine the relative effects of each role, with respect to both the objective characteristics and subjective reactions (i.e., quality of the roles) and in light of all of the other roles. This is something that can be done only in a study of people who engage in all of the roles simultaneously, as we find with dual-earner couples in the sandwiched generation.

EFFECTS OF OBJECTIVE AND SUBJECTIVE ROLE CHARACTERISTICS ON WORK–FAMILY FIT, WELL-BEING, AND WORK

To be able to examine the relationships between several objective and subjective role characteristics simultaneously for the various outcomes of interest, we conducted multivariate analyses, specifically hierarchical multiple linear regression. In this way, we could determine the relative impact of objective (i.e., role demand) and subjective (i.e., role quality) characteristics for the different roles on work–family fit, well-being, and work for working, sandwiched individuals, consistent with our conceptual model. Thus, in each regression analysis we included the three personal role variables (i.e., education, income adequacy, and negative affectivity) as controls in Step 1. We then entered the six objective role characteristics variables (two each for each role: child care, parent care, and job) in Step 2. Finally, we entered the four role quality measures (spousal, child care, parent care, and job) in Step 3. Entering the sets of variables in blocks, or steps, allowed us to answer three important questions:

1. Do the effects of the objective role characteristics (i.e., number of children aged 18 or under living at home, having a child with special needs, total number of parents/in-laws helping, total number of activities of daily living with which the respondent helps, number of hours worked per week, and flexibility in work schedule) contribute significantly to the outcomes above and beyond the effects of the control variables?

2. Do the effects of the subjective role characteristics (i.e., spousal, child care, parent care, and job role quality) contribute significantly to the outcomes above and beyond the effects of the objective role characteristics?

3. What are the relative effects of spousal, child-care, parent-care, and work role characteristics (objective and subjective) on work–family fit, well-being, and work outcomes?

The findings for the first three questions are presented in Tables 6.14 through 6.16 (see Appendix C). We describe these findings below.

Work–Family Fit: Objective and Subjective Role Characteristics as Predictors

In the first set of regression analyses (see Table 6.14), we examined the effects of the objective and subjective role characteristics on the work–family fit outcomes, after controlling for the three personal characteristics of years of education, negative affectivity, and income adequacy. The findings reveal that both the objective and subjective role characteristics were significant predictors of the work–family fit outcomes for husbands and wives (see Table 6.14). The objective characteristics accounted for between 2% and 19% of the variance in the outcome measures over that of the control variables (which accounted for from 2% to 10% of the variance in the outcomes). The objective role characteristics were significant as group in predicting work-to-family conflict (for both husbands and wives), family-to-work conflict (for wives only), and work-to-family positive spillover (for wives only). After taking into consideration the objective characteristics, the role quality (subjective) measures were predictors of each of the four work–family fit outcomes for both husbands and wives, accounting for an additional 3% to 10% of the variance explained in each outcome.

Specifically, with respect to work-to-family conflict, although the objective child-care and parent-care characteristics were not significant predictors, the work role objective characteristics were, with working more hours (for both husbands and wives) and having more flexibility in one's work schedule (for husbands) being related to increased work-to-family conflict. In addition, the subjective role characteristic job role quality was a significant predictor, with increased job role quality related to decreased work-to-family conflict for both husbands and wives.

Similarly, with regard to the predictors of family-to-work conflict, working more hours (for wives) and, interestingly, having less flexible work schedules (for husbands) were both related to decreased levels of family-to-work conflict. Increased child-care role quality (for wives) and spousal role quality (for both husbands and wives) also were related to decreased family-to-work conflict. The findings for husbands regarding flexibility in work schedule demonstrate the double-edged sword of work schedule flexibility: Although that flexibility decreases work-to-family conflict, it appears to open the door for more family-to-work conflict.

With regard to work-to-family positive spillover, none of the objective role characteristics were related to this outcome. Increases in job role quality (for both husbands and wives), spousal role quality (for wives), and child-care role quality (for husbands), however, were related to higher levels of positive spillover from work to family. For family-to-work positive spillover, again the objective role characteristics were unrelated, but higher job role quality was associated with higher levels of positive spillover from family to work (for both husbands and wives), spousal role quality (for husbands), and child-care role quality (for wives).

Summary: Predictors of Work–Family Fit.   We conclude, therefore, that both objective and subjective role characteristics significantly affect work–family fit outcomes, with stronger effects stemming from the subjective compared to the objective characteristics. The one exception to this is for work-to-family conflict, in which the effects of the objective role characteristics were stronger than those of the subjective characteristics for both husbands and wives. In addition, for both types of work–family conflict, only the objective characteristics related to the work role, not those for the child- or parent-care roles, had an impact. Finally, the two subjective characteristics having the most impact on the work–family fit outcomes were job role quality and spousal role quality, although child-care role quality did affect work–family fit for wives. Parent-care role quality was not significantly related to any of these outcomes for either husbands or wives. Thus, taken together, these findings reveal that the work role has the most impact on work–family fit outcomes, followed by the spousal role, and that the quality of roles, that is, the subjective role characteristics, contribute significantly to work–family fit, above and beyond the objective characteristics for working, sandwiched couples.

Well-Being: Objective and Subjective Role Characteristics as Predictors

With respect to the predictors of the well-being outcomes (see Table 6.15), we found that the objective characteristics accounted for between 1% and 4% of the variance in these outcomes (i.e., depression, life satisfaction, overall health, and overall role performance) above and beyond that accounted for by the control variables (which accounted for from 14%–41% of the variance in the well-being outcomes). For only two outcomes, depression and life satisfaction, and mostly for husbands, were the objective role characteristics significant contributors.

After controlling for the objective role characteristics, the subjective role quality variables accounted for an additional 1% to 15% of the variance, being significantly associated with three of the four well-being outcomes for both husbands and wives. Overall health was the only outcome for which none of the role characteristics variables, subjective or objective, contributed significantly to the variance explained in the outcomes either for husbands or wives.

The results concerning the relationships between the objective role characteristics and depression and life satisfaction were unexpected. Specifically, we found that as the number of parents/in-laws being helped increased, depression decreased for both husbands and wives, and life satisfaction increased for wives. Similarly, helping an aging parent with a greater number of activities of daily living was associated, for husbands, with increased life satisfaction. It may be that the provision of more help allows these adult children to feel that they are fulfilling their filial obligations and being able to give back to their parents, thus leading to greater psychological well-being. A second possible explanation relates to the fact that when more than one aging parent is being helped, those parents may either be a couple (i.e., the respondent's mother and father, or the parents-in-law) or consist of one's own parent and an in-law. In any case, it may be especially rewarding to be able to help more than one parent or parent-in-law. A third explanation is that if the parents are a couple, caring for them may be somewhat easier, as they may be able to look after each others' needs as well as get help from their adult son or daughter. The finding that helping with more activities of daily living is associated with increased life satisfaction for husbands, however, seems to lend most support to either the first or second explanation.

In addition to the contributions by the parent-care objective role characteristics, working a greater number of hours per week also was associated with greater life satisfaction for husbands. This may be due to husbands feeling that they are contributing more to their family's well-being by earning additional income.

Turning to the impact of the subjective role characteristics on the well-being outcomes, as noted above these variables accounted for a significant amount of variance in three of the four well-being outcomes (i.e., depression, life satisfaction, and overall role performance) for both husbands and wives. In particular, higher levels of spousal role quality were related to decreased depression for both husbands and wives, and greater job role quality was related to decreased depression for husbands, whereas higher child-care role quality was related to decreased depression for wives.

With respect to life satisfaction, the subjective role characteristics that accounted for a significant amount of variance included spousal and job role quality, for husbands and wives alike, child-care role quality for wives, and parent-care role quality for husbands. In all cases, higher levels of role quality were associated with greater life satisfaction. Greater spousal role quality and child-care role quality were significant predictors of higher levels of overall role performance for both husbands and wives.

Summary: Predictors of Well-Being.

Taken together, these findings indicate that the objective role characteristics, while helping to explain some of the variance in depression and life satisfaction, had less impact as a whole on the well-being outcomes than did the subjective role characteristics. In particular, spousal role quality appeared to have the greatest impact on well-being, followed by child-care role quality and job role quality. Parent-care role quality was associated only with life satisfaction, and this relationship was significant only for husbands. It should be noted, however, that although parent-care role quality was significantly related only to husbands' life satisfaction, the parent-care objective characteristics, along with one significant relationship for number of hours worked, were the only objective characteristics that affected the well-being outcomes. These effects, however, were in the opposite direction of what we had expected, with more parent care associated with better well-being. These findings highlight some of the benefits of caregiving for husbands and wives.

Work Outcomes: Objective and Subjective Role Characteristics as Predictors

Finally, we examined the effects of the objective and subjective role characteristics on the work-related outcomes, after controlling for the three personal characteristics of years of education, negative affectivity, and income adequacy (see Table 6.16). We found that the objective role characteristics accounted for between 3% and 11% of the variance in the work outcomes (beyond the 0% to 10% of the variance accounted for by the control variables). In general, characteristics of each of the roles were related to only one of the outcomes. There were two exceptions. First, having a child with special needs was related to two outcomes, overall absence and poor work performance due to dependent-care responsibilities, for husbands only. Also, providing more help with activities of daily living to the parent was associated with more overall absence and poor work performance for both husbands and wives and with making a greater number of accommodations at work for wives. The parent-care role demands, or objective characteristics, were those that were most consistently related to the work outcomes. None of the objective role characteristics was associated with the number of work accommodations made by husbands, however.

Regarding the contribution of the subjective role characteristics, we found that the amount of variance explained in the work outcomes, over and above that contributed by the objective role characteristics, ranged from a low of 2% (wives' work accommodations made) to a high of 31% (husbands' job satisfaction). More specifically, the subjective role characteristics as a set accounted for a significant amount of variance in job satisfaction and reports of poor work performance for both husbands and wives and number of work accommodations made for husbands.

With regard specifically to job satisfaction, although the set of objective characteristics as a whole accounted for a significant amount of the variance, no one variable was a significant predictor. With respect to the subjective role characteristics, however, higher levels of job role quality were associated with job satisfaction for both husbands and wives, and for husbands, higher parent-care role quality was related to higher job satisfaction.

For overall absence due to dependent-care responsibilities, both objective child-care role characteristics (i.e., having more minor children in the household and having a child with special needs) were related to more absence for husbands. In addition, providing more help with activities of daily living for a parent was related to higher levels of absence for both husbands and wives. Having greater flexibility in one's work schedule was also related to more absence behaviors due to family responsibilities, as reported by both husbands and wives. Of the subjective role characteristics, higher job role quality was related to lower absence for both husbands and wives.

The finding that having flexibility in one's work schedule is associated with greater absence is somewhat surprising, as one might expect greater flexibility to be associated with lower levels of absence. This finding regarding flexibility may be similar to that for family-to-work conflict, with more flexibility allowing for more absence (and more intrusion of family into work). At the same time, it should not be assumed that the time missed from work when one has a flexible schedule is work time that is completely lost. In our focus groups with working, sandwiched couples, several participants noted the value of flexible work schedules that allowed them to take time off from work when they needed to in order to manage family responsibilities, but they emphasized that they made up the work by taking work home or working more hours at the workplace at a different time. Some noted that they repaid this flexibility by working even more hours than they had missed. Also, several focus group participants, generally wives, reported that they had specifically chosen their jobs because of the flexibility in work schedule that the position offered, feeling that this would help them better manage their family responsibilities while still working.

With respect to the third work outcome, number of work accommodations made in response to dependent-care responsibilities in the past year, we found that providing a parent more help with activities of daily living was associated with making a greater number of work accommodations for wives. In addition, husbands reported making more work accommodations when parent-care role quality and job role quality were low. It may be that these latter two relationships did not exist for wives because wives had made the work accommodations earlier, at first exposure to reduced role quality, as more of a preventative action, whereas husbands made such accommodations later, once role quality had deteriorated substantially.

Finally, with respect to poor work performance due to dependent-care responsibilities, the significant predictors among the objective role characteristics included having a child with special needs (for husbands) and helping more parents/in-laws (for wives). In addition, for both husbands and wives, the more activities of daily living that each reported helping their parent with, the more they reported poor work performance due to dependent-care responsibilities. Also, working more hours per week was associated with poorer work performance due to dependent-care responsibilities for husbands.

Among the subjective role characteristics, we found that higher levels of child-care role quality for both husbands and wives, and higher levels of job role quality for husbands, were related to fewer reports of poor work performance due to dependent-care responsibilities. Thus, we see that, not surprisingly, higher levels of objective role demands contribute to poorer work performance due to dependent-care responsibilities, but greater role quality contributes to positive work outcomes.

Summary: Predictors of Work Outcomes. In sum, it appears that objective parent-care role characteristics, especially helping a parent with a greater number of activities of daily living, are significant contributors to work-related outcomes, including absence, work accommodations made, and poor work performance. In addition, the objective child-care characteristics significantly affect work absence and work performance for husbands. The subjective role characteristics, and primarily job role quality, contribute to the work outcomes. Thus, it appears that the parent-care and work roles both seem to have a significant impact on work outcomes, followed by the effects of the child-care role. These findings have important implications for managers who are interested in reducing absence and improving performance in organizations (see Fig. 6.2).

Work–Family Fit

- None of the objective role characteristics are related to work–family positive spillover.
- Objective work role characteristics affect work–family conflict, while none of the objective child-care, parent-care, or spousal role characteristics relates to work–family conflict.
- Subjective role characteristics (i.e., spousal, child care, and job role quality) are related to various work–family fit outcomes in the expected directions.
  - In general, higher levels of role quality are related to lower work–family conflict and higher positive spillover, especially spousal, child-care, and job role quality.

Well-Being

- Parent-care role characteristics are the only objective role characteristics that have a significant impact on well-being; in general, objective spousal, child-care, and work role characteristics do not impact well-being.
- Our findings suggest that providing parent care (helping more parents and helping with more ADLs) can be beneficial for one's well-being, as opposed to detrimental.
- Subjective role quality is related differentially to well-being outcomes, depending on the specific role.
  - In general, higher levels of role quality are related to lower depression, higher life satisfaction, higher overall health, and higher overall role performance.

Figure 6.2 *continues*

- More relationships are found with the well-being outcomes for spousal, child-care, and job role quality as compared to parent-care role quality.

Work Outcomes

- None of the objective role characteristics are related to job satisfaction.
- All of the objective role characteristics are differentially related to work outcomes.
  - The number of ADLs a respondent helps with is the most common objective role characteristic related to work outcomes (i.e., more so even than the work characteristics).
  - Surprisingly, flexible work schedules are associated with greater absence.
- Subjective role quality is related differentially to work outcomes, depending on the specific role.
  - Spousal role quality is not related to any of the work outcomes, while job role quality is related to all of them.
  - In general, higher levels of role quality are related to higher job satisfaction, lower absence, fewer work accommodations made, and fewer reports of poor work performance.

Crossover Effects

- Spousal role quality has a significant impact on decreasing wives' work-to-family conflict and husbands' family-to-work conflict.
- Spousal role quality also has a beneficial effect on overall role performance for wives and husbands.
- There are no crossover effects of role quality (any of the roles) on the work outcomes.

Note. ADL = activities of daily living.

Figure 6.2.   Objective and subjective role characteristics in relation to work–family fit, well-being, and work: multivariate results.

Within-Couple Effects: The Crossover Effects of Subjective Role Characteristics

In this study, we were especially interested in the interactive dynamics within couples. As described in chapter 4, one way to capture such effects is to examine crossover effects, or how an employee's work–family experiences influence the work–family experiences of his or her spouse. Therefore, we were especially interested in studying the effects of one partner's role experiences on the other partner's work–family fit, well-being, and work outcomes.

Because of the importance of subjective role quality that was revealed in the preceding analyses, we decided to explore the existence of crossover effects associated with these particular variables. Therefore, we conducted a final set of regression analyses to examine the crossover effects of one spouse's role quality (spousal, child care, parent care, and job) on his or her partner's work–family fit, well-being, and work, above and beyond that partner's own control variables (partner's own personal characteristics [education, income adequacy, and negative affectivity]) and objective role characteristics (child care, parent care, and work). Note that spousal crossover effects are difficult to detect, and we are using fairly stringent criteria by examining these effects over and above one's own personal and objective role characteristics. Nonetheless, we conducted these analyses to answer the following question:

4. Do the effects of one spouse's subjective role characteristics (i.e., spousal, child care, parent care, and job role quality) contribute significantly to the outcomes for the other spouse, above and beyond the effects of the personal and objective role characteristics of that other spouse? Stated differently, does a husband's role quality affect his wife's outcomes, above and beyond the wife's personal and objective role characteristics? Similarly, does a wife's role quality affect her husband's outcomes, beyond the husband's own personal and objective role characteristics?

With respect to the work–family fit outcomes,[1] we found several significant crossover relationships. Specifically, higher levels of spousal role quality reported by husbands were related to lower levels of work-to-family conflict reported by their wives. Furthermore, higher levels of spousal role quality and parent care role quality among wives were related to higher levels of family-to-work positive spillover for their husbands.

With respect to the well-being outcomes, there were two significant crossover relationships. In particular, higher spousal role quality among wives was positively related to their husbands' overall role performance. In addition, greater spousal role quality reported by husbands was related to higher levels of overall role performance reported by their wives.

Finally, with respect to the work outcomes, there were two significant crossover relationships. Specifically, higher child-care role quality among husbands was related to more work accommodations made in the past year by wives. In addition, higher child-care role quality among wives was significantly related to lower levels of poor work performance reported by husbands.

---

[1]We describe these findings in the text but do not provide tables containing the specific data. These data can be obtained from the authors on request.

Summary: Crossover Effects.   The crossover analyses indicate that wives' subjective role characteristics (i.e., role quality) account for a significant amount of variance in husbands' positive spillover from family to work, overall role performance, and reports of poor work performance due to dependent-care responsibilities. These results suggest that when wives experience high levels of role quality, in particular spousal and parent-care role quality, their husbands benefit as well. We also found that wives benefit from higher role quality, specifically spousal role quality, on the part of their husbands, in terms of their work-to-family conflict and overall role performance. Finally, the higher the reported child-care role quality reported by husbands, the more work accommodations that had been used by wives in the previous year.

Thus, in several instances we saw significant effects of one member's role quality on their partner's outcomes. These findings are especially important given the difficulty noted earlier of detecting significant effects. Spousal role quality appears to have stronger crossover effects than do the other role quality variables, with the exception of the one significant relationship between wives' parent-care role quality and husbands' family-to-work positive spillover. Of interest is that no crossover effects were found for job role quality on work–family fit, well-being, or work.

SUMMARY

Overall, we found that objective and subjective characteristics of spousal, child-care, parent-care, and job roles have differential but important impacts on the various work–family fit, well-being, and work outcomes we examined. In addition, subjective role quality was shown, in some instances, to have significant crossover effects on spouses.

Let us now reflect back on the three questions we were attempting to answer from the first set of multivariate analyses. First, "Do the effects of the objective role characteristics (i.e., number of children aged 18 or under living at home, having a child with special needs, total number of parents/in-laws helping, total number of activities of daily living respondent helps with, number of hours worked per week, and flexibility in work schedule) contribute significantly to the outcomes above and beyond the effects of the control variables?" The answer to this question is clearly "yes." We found the objective role characteristics to be important predictors of the following outcomes for *both* husbands and wives: work-to-family conflict, job satisfaction, absence, and poor work performance due to dependent-care responsibilities. In addition, we found the objective role characteristics to be significantly related to the following outcomes for either husbands *or* wives: family-to-work conflict, work-to-family positive spillover, life satisfaction, and number of work accommodations made. Each of the objective characteristics included was significantly related to at least one of the outcomes, and some, like number of hours worked per week and number of activities of daily living with which the respondent helped his or her parent, were related to several outcomes.

The second question was: "Do the effects of the subjective role characteristics (i.e., spousal, child care, parent care, and job role quality) contribute significantly to the outcomes above and beyond the effects of the objective role characteristics?" The answer to this question also is clearly "yes." We found that the set of subjective role characteristics accounted for a significant amount of variance over and above the objective role characteristics in nearly all of the outcomes for both husbands and wives. Exceptions include the outcomes of overall health (for which neither the objective nor the subjective characteristics included predicted a significant amount of the variance for either husbands or wives), absence (for which subjective characteristics [i.e., role quality] were not a significant predictor for either husbands or wives), and number of work accommodations made (for which subjective characteristics were not a significant predictor for wives). Quality in two of the roles, spouse and job, was most frequently related to the outcomes, and the patterns of relationships varied by type of outcome. Work-related outcomes were most often associated with job role quality; well-being outcomes were most often associated with spousal role quality, child-care role quality, and job role quality; and work–family fit outcomes were most often associated with job role quality, spousal role quality, and then child-care role quality. Parent-care role quality was associated with three outcomes, but only for husbands: increased life satisfaction and job satisfaction, and decreased use of work accommodations.

A key finding from the analyses presented in this chapter concerns the importance of role quality. Although the objective role characteristics variables that are traditionally used in work–family research tended to have moderate relationships with the outcomes, more important, we found, were the subjective experiences of role quality. The role quality variables accounted for a significant amount of variance in every one of the work–family fit, well-being, and work outcomes, over and above the effects of the objective characteristics. In addition, we found significant crossover effects of role quality on work–family fit, well-being and work outcomes, suggesting the importance of examining the family system within the work–family interface. Recognizing the importance of role quality for enhancing positive outcomes is a first step, followed by identifying strategies to improve role quality. This pertains to all of the roles examined, but spousal role quality and job role quality seem to be especially crucial.

The third question asked "What are the relative effects of spousal, child-care, parent-care, and work role characteristics on work–family fit, well-being, and work outcomes?" This question addressed the issue of being sandwiched and the differential effects of each role on the outcomes.

On the basis of our findings, it appears that the work role, as measured by the objective characteristics of number of hours worked and flexibility in work schedule and the subjective characteristic of job role quality, has the most significant impact on work–family fit and the work-related outcomes. With regard to the well-being outcomes, however, spousal role quality has the most impact, followed by the child-care role (for wives), and the parent-care role (for husbands), then the job role. The importance of the job and spousal roles was somewhat surprising to us, given our sample of sandwiched generation couples: We expected the child-care and the parent-care role characteristics to predominate in importance in predicting the outcomes.

Finally, the fourth question addressed the existence of crossover effects: "Do the effects of the subjective role characteristics of one spouse (i.e., spousal, child care, parent care, and job role quality) contribute significantly to the outcomes for his or her partner, above and beyond the effects of the partner's personal and objective role characteristics?" This question addressed the couple, rather than merely the individual, offering a more systematic examination of the interactive processes occurring between a spouse's subjective role quality and his or her partner's outcomes. Several crossover effects were found from both wives to husbands and husbands to wives, suggesting that when role quality is high, work–family fit and well-being are improved for spouses. This is not surprising, and provides important evidence that dual-earner couples are operating within a complex interactive system.

Implications of the Findings for Working, Sandwiched Couples

Our findings concerning the importance of spousal role quality suggest that sandwiched couples themselves should be educated about the predominant and cross-cutting importance of spousal role quality, in particular. In addition, family-related changes, such as counseling and/or the facilitation of work–family coping strategies, may be implemented to help improve spousal role quality that would in turn, positively affect work and well-being outcomes not only for individuals but also for their spouses. We discuss some of these potential interventions in greater detail in chapters 8 and 9.

Implications for Family Care Practitioners

A general conclusion that can be drawn on the basis of our data is that people who are working and caring for children and aging parents have levels of depression that are higher than national averages, and working women, in particular, in the sandwiched generation appear to be at especially great risk for depressive symptoms. This finding indicates the need for employee assistance programs offering education and counseling for sandwiched employees related to the risks of depression and what can be done to treat it. To maximize work–family fit, well-being, and work outcomes among sandwiched couples, they should be encouraged to learn about and implement strategies for enhancing the marital relationship, despite the many demands on their time.

Implications for Employers

The findings presented in this chapter point to several potential areas for prevention and intervention. In particular, the results suggest the value of organizational changes, such as the implementation of workplace supports, which can affect both objective job role characteristics and subjective job role quality that will, in turn, positively affect work–family fit, well-being, and work outcomes for working, sandwiched couples. Managers should be educated concerning the importance of, and strategies for increasing, job role quality.

It may be similarly useful for organizations to facilitate a more family-friendly workplace culture, such as through managerial training around work and family issues. We also suggest that organizational policymakers take note of the findings related to the beneficial effects of combining work and family, as well as the drawbacks, as they engage in efforts to educate coworkers and managers about work–family issues. Finally, these finding suggest that it is useful to develop workplace interventions, in the form of family-friendly policies, benefits, and services, that assist employees not only with their child-care responsibilities but also with their parent-care responsibilities.

Implications for Research

An important conclusion that can be drawn from the findings presented in this chapter is that positive indicators, such as positive work–family spillover, job and life satisfaction, health, and overall role performance, are important to include, beyond work–family conflict and depression, in any study of how people are managing their multiple work and family care demands. Thus, we suggest that future research efforts should continue to incorporate the positive side of the equation when studying the interface between work and family, as we believe, and our data show, that combining work with child-care, parent-care, and spousal roles can have many rewarding and beneficial effects as well as challenges. This idea is consistent with the movement in positive psychology to focus on the facilitation of normal functioning through the implementation of interventions, rather than on the disease model of human functioning with a focus on treatment (Seligman & Csikszentmihalyi, 2000).

In this chapter, we have provided information on various objective and subjective role characteristics and how they are related to several work–family fit, well-being, and work outcomes. We have shown that role quality, in particular, is important for understanding the effects of being sandwiched. In chapter 10, we take a look at what happened to our sample of working, sandwiched couples over the course of 1 year and how the transitions in their role responsibilities affected their work–family fit, well-being, and work outcomes. First, however, we describe the coping strategies (chaps. 7 and 8) and workplace supports (chap. 9) used by these couples in an attempt to best manage their work and family responsibilities.

7

Development of a Model of Work–Family Coping Strategies and Advice From Couples

---

It's not easy being a working mother and a wife. Sometimes I wish God had put 32 hours in a day so I could sleep eight per night. But I look at my problems with the attitude that this, too, will come to an end. It can't last forever. Get up in the morning and first thing you say is, "It's going to be a sunshine day" and you will feel good all day no matter if it's raining or not. Live each day as if it were your last and you will have no regrets.

A key purpose of our study was to examine the work and family coping strategies used by dual-earner couples caring both for children and for aging parents, and the effects of these strategies on their work–family fit, well-being, and work. In this chapter, we describe our model of coping strategies and the types of advice suggested and used by dual-earner couples caring for children and aging parents. We conceptualize coping strategies as helping to either increase resources or decrease demands. In the next chapter, we explore the relationship between use of these coping strategies and the work–family fit, well-being, and work-related outcomes of interest in this study.

We begin by presenting a model of work and family coping strategies that we developed on the basis of existing theoretical frameworks of coping strategies, as well as data from focus groups of working, sandwiched couples that we convened locally for this purpose. We then use this model to describe the types of coping advice offered in written comments at the end of the first mailed survey and the coping strategies used, as reported by individuals comprising our national sample of 309 working, sandwiched couples.

PREVIOUS CONCEPTUALIZATIONS OF WORK–FAMILY COPING STRATEGIES

Substantial evidence demonstrates that the way we cope with stress in everyday life affects our physical and psychological well-being (Billings & Moos, 1981; Folkman & Lazarus, 1980; Skinner, Edge, Altman, & Sherwood, 2003). Moreover, type of coping strategy has been shown to be an important factor in coping effectiveness (Billings & Moos, 1981; Folkman & Lazarus, 1980; Hall, 1972; Pearlin & Schooler, 1978; Skinner et al., 2003). The literature on coping contains many models for conceptualizing or categorizing the range of possible strategies. Furthermore, work and family stressors, and the corresponding strategies that people use for coping, are just one subset within the broader area of research related to coping. Typically, work and family researchers interested in how people deal with their multiple work and family roles have relied on traditional models of coping that have been in the literature for some time (i.e., Folkman & Lazarus, 1980; Hall, 1972), or they have created work–family coping strategy taxonomies based on qualitative data specific to the particular population they are studying.

According to Lazarus (1993), *coping* refers to ongoing cognitive and behavioral efforts to master, reduce, or tolerate the internal and/or external demands created by a stressful situation between a person and his or her environment. Coping consists of the thoughts and behaviors a person uses to manage the demands of a particular person-environment transaction that has relevance to his or her well-being (Folkman, Lazarus, Gruen, & DeLongis, 1986). Coping, in this model, is viewed as having two major functions: (a) the regulation of emotions or distress, labeled *emotion-focused coping*, and (b) the management of the problem that is causing the distress, labeled *problem-focused coping* (Folkman & Lazarus, 1980). Problem-focused and emotion-focused coping can be used simultaneously, but often one predominates (Folkman, 1984; Folkman & Lazarus, 1980, 1985; Folkman et al., 1986). Problem-focused coping includes active behavioral coping, whereas emotion-focused coping includes affective/cognitive coping (Folkman & Lazarus, 1980). Both are adaptive coping mechanisms related to improved well-being.

Another model of coping with work and family role conflict was introduced by Hall in 1972. Hall (1972) argued that most previous research concerning role conflict had focused on the nature of the conflict rather than on how people cope with such conflicts, and he identified three types of coping strategies. The first type, *structural role redefinition,* involved actively working with role senders (i.e., those people who convey role expectations) to change actual role demands. An example would be negotiating a new work schedule with one's manager. The second type of coping strategy was *personal role redefinition*, which involved cognitively changing one's own perceptions of the role demands, such as prioritizing activities on the basis of one's values. The third strategy, *reactive role behavior*, involved simply trying harder to meet all existing role requirements (Hall, 1972). The first strategy is a behavioral strategy that is external to the person, whereas the second and third strategies require the person to make internal, or cognitive/emotional, accommodations. Thus, this conceptual system is similar to that proposed by Folkman and Lazarus (1980).

On the basis of Hall's (1972) typology and on a model of coping strategies developed by Billings and Moos (1981) as well as the Folkman and Lazarus (1980) model, Amatea and Fong-Beyette (1987) created a classification system for women's inter-role coping. Using data from a sample of 135 professional women, Amatea and Fong-Beyette distinguished between behavioral (i.e., problem-focused) and emotional (i.e., emotion-focused, including cognitive) strategies, both of which could use either active or passive methods. In addition, Anderson and Leslie (1991) examined how men and women cope with inter-role stress and found that people who used a problem-focused coping strategy by reframing the problem to make it more manageable reported greater marital satisfaction. Aryee et al. (1999) found that the use of emotion-focused and problem-focused coping strategies was related to both job and family satisfaction, but only emotion-focused coping was related to life satisfaction.

Some work and family researchers create their own taxonomy of coping strategies appropriate to the population under study (Menaghan, 1983; Wiersma, 1994). For example, Menaghan (1983) developed a taxonomy that included both behavioral and cognitive/emotional strategies and that addressed individual as well as family coping. The strategies identified emphasized decreasing environmental demands (e.g., negotiating role demands) and increasing individual resources (e.g., soliciting emotional support from friends) within the categories of behavioral and cognitive/emotional coping. This model focused on strategies to cope with family- (not work-) related demands; nonetheless, it introduced into the literature the idea that some coping strategies would involve increasing resources, whereas others would involve decreasing demands. In addition, Wiersma (1994) created a specialized coping taxonomy relevant to work and family role conflict among dual-earner couples from interview data using the *critical incident technique*. Focusing on behavioral strategies used by these couples for coping with work–family conflict, Wiersma (1994) identified strategies such as sharing work-related friends within the couple, setting priorities, and hiring outside help with household chores.

More recently, Baltes and Heydens-Gahir (2003) built on this coping model, or life management strategy, to identify ways to reduce work–family conflict. This model proposed the use of selection, optimization, and compensation strategies to reduce stress, and hence, to reduce work–family conflict. Also recently, Behson (2002) discussed coping strategies in terms of accommodating work for family and accommodating family for work. The existing conceptualizations of work and family coping strategies have several limitations, however. First, the models by Amatea and Fong-Beyette (1987) and Hall (1972) were developed using samples consisting primarily of women; thus, they may not be generalizable to men and to couples. Second, Wiersma's (1994) model lacked a theoretical basis, consisting instead of a list of behavioral strategies based on critical incidents. Third, Menaghan's (1983) model, although theoretically based, focused specifically on strategies for coping with family demands; it did not address coping with work-related demands. Fourth, most models of coping have offered interrelated and vague classifications (for a critique of broader coping classification systems, see Skinner et al., 2003).

There appeared to be a need, then, for the development of a new model of work and family coping strategies specific to working couples caring for children and aging parents that would integrate previous research and theory and use data from men, as well as women, in the validation process. Basing the development of the model on sandwiched-generation couples seemed optimal, as these are the very people who would be expected to experience the most stress due to their multiple family and work role responsibilities (Chapman, Ingersoll-Dayton, & Neal, 1994).

OUR MODEL OF WORK AND FAMILY COPING STRATEGIES

Our model of coping strategies is synthesized from existing theoretical frameworks developed by Amatea and Fong-Beyette (1987), Folkman and Lazarus (1980), and Menaghan (1983) but is based as well on qualitative data collected from our own national longitudinal study of working, sandwiched couples. The qualitative data were generated in the first phase of our study, when we conducted 17 focus groups with a total of 63 participants to identify the range of work and family coping strategies used and suggested by individuals who were members of dual-earner couples in the sandwiched generation. (See Appendix A for a detailed description of the study's methods.)

The transcripts of each of the focus groups were read, and relevant sections were marked. We (researchers and graduate students) then divided into two teams for the purpose of classifying the various types of coping strategies mentioned as being used or suggested. One team used existing theoretical systems (i.e., Amatea & Fong-Beyette, 1987; Folkman & Lazarus, 1980; Menaghan, 1983), sorting the statements into the theoretical categories suggested by these researchers. Another team followed an "open coding" approach (Strauss & Corbin, 1991) to identify the broadest possible range of responses based specifically on examples of coping with the demands of work and family. A categorization system then was created. We then synthesized the two classification efforts into a single conceptual system, as detailed below.

As shown in Fig. 7.1, the theoretically described and empirically identified model we developed consists of six types of work–family coping strategies that involve either (1) increasing resources or (2) decreasing demands, and doing this (a) behaviorally, (b) emotionally, or (c) cognitively. Descriptions of each of these six types of coping strategies follow. These six strategies are considered "higher order families of coping" (Skinner et al., 2003; p. 239).

	Decrease Demands	**Increase Resources**
Behavioral	Decreasing Activities (e.g., stopping or limiting activities)	Increasing Instrumental Resources (e.g., increasing flexibility in scheduling, hiring assistance)
Emotional	Decreasing Expectations of Self (e.g., reducing personal expectations)	Increasing Emotional Resources (e.g., receiving emotional support)
Cognitive	Prioritizing (e.g., prioritizing activities)	Planning (e.g., scheduling activities, future goals)

Figure 7.1.   A model of work–family coping strategies.

According to our model, work–family coping strategies are of two general types: (a) those that involve attempting to increase resources and (b) those that involve trying to decrease demands. Within each of these two general types are strategies are that involve increasing resources or decreasing demands behaviorally, emotionally, or cognitively.

Increasing Resources Behaviorally, Emotionally, and Cognitively

Increasing Resources Behaviorally

Also referred to as *problem solving* by Folkman and Lazarus (1980) and Skinner et al. (2003), this category consists of strategies that individuals actively pursue to increase their personal resources, particularly temporal resources, to manage their responsibilities. Examples of such strategies include increasing flexibility at work, alternating work shifts with one's spouse, and changing work sites to be closer to home. It should be noted, however, that using the strategy of alternating work shifts with one's spouse leads to one or both members of the couple working nonstandard shifts that are frequently associated with negative psychological and physical health outcomes (Presser, 2003). Some of our respondents' comments support the potentially negative impact of this strategy, as well. For example, as mentioned in chapter 10, some wrote that their work and family situations had improved over the course of the year between the first and second surveys because they and their spouse had abandoned this strategy.

Increasing Resources Emotionally

Strategies within this category involve seeking out additional support from friends, coworkers, supervisors, or other family members to help increase one's personal emotional resources in order to manage work and family responsibilities. Skinner et al. (2003) referred to this type of coping as *support seeking*. Spending time on the telephone with family or friends, participating in a support group, finding humor in a given situation, or incorporating religious or spiritual beliefs are all ways of trying to increase one's emotional resources.

Increasing Resources Cognitively

Also referred to as *cognitive restructuring* (Skinner et al., 2003), the strategies within this category concern the conscious, thoughtful planning of work and family schedules and activities. Examples include scheduling family time, scheduling time alone with one's spouse, planning family activities around school vacations, and having backup plans in place for child or parent care.

Decreasing Demands Behaviorally, Emotionally, and Cognitively

Decreasing Demands Behaviorally

This category of coping, which may also be referred to as either *good news* or *bad news* ways of coping, may be related to either positive or negative well-being outcomes for individuals (Skinner et al., 2003). Such strategies involve the conscious decision to stop doing certain activities in order to make time for other activities. Included are such strategies as reducing the amount of time one spends with family members, reducing the amount of personal time for oneself to make more time to care for a parent or attend a child's school activities, reducing the number of hours worked, or actually quitting a job to be able to provide more care for a parent or child. As can be seen, some examples of decreasing demands behaviorally may result in social withdrawal, leading to decreased well-being (e.g., reducing time with family members or reducing time for oneself), whereas other examples may be adaptive, leading to improved well-being (e.g., reducing number of hours worked) depending on one's appraisal of the stressors on hand.

Decreasing Demands of Emotionally

The strategies within this category concern the reduction of personal expectations and are commonly referred to as *emotional regulation* (Skinner et al., 2003). For example, several focus group participants mentioned the importance of "changing one's attitude" as a means of coping with multiple demands and responsibilities, such as changing the way one feels about a situation or telling oneself that it is all right to not do everything.

Decreasing Demands Cognitively

The strategies within this category involve prioritizing, that is, doing the most important things first, or focusing on the task at hand; they were referred to as *negotiation* by Skinner et al. (2003). For example, some participants reported making conscious decisions to put their career on hold as a way of prioritizing one's work and family demands, whereas others reported deciding to let go of certain household chores or responsibilities in lieu of more important commitments or priorities.

Summary

This six-cell coping strategies model was developed on the basis of a review of existing relevant frameworks in combination with analysis of empirical, qualitative data that we gathered through focus groups with working, sandwiched couples. Next, we use the model to describe the types of advice that the couples who participated in our national study offered to others in similar situations ($N = 309$ couples, or 618 individuals).

WHAT DO COUPLES ADVISE?

Respondents were asked to provide written comments concerning advice they would offer to other working couples in the sandwiched generation. Despite coming at the end of a lengthy survey, many respondents seemed eager to comply with this request, with some noting that sharing their strategies for coping with work and family was helpful, even cathartic in some cases. For example, one woman wrote: "P.S. This survey was good for my mental health. It gave me a chance to vent and to evaluate my feelings." Another wrote, "The process of completing this survey helped me personally to see a concrete view of what issues I'm really dealing with. It was very beneficial." A man wrote, "This questionnaire was good for me personally, because it made me think about what's going on in my life." The opposing view was stated by just one respondent, a woman. "This questionnaire made me think about how stressful and miserable a sandwich situation can be."

Using our model of work–family coping strategies, we categorized all of the advice by respondents to our mailed survey in response to the open-ended question "What advice would you offer to other working couples who have children at home and who are helping out aging or disabled parents?" Two coders independently classified the respondents' open-ended statements into the six categories. A third coder then checked and validated the codes assigned.

Of the 618 individuals who responded to the first mailed survey, 67% (235 wives and 180 husbands) volunteered written comments. A total of 891 pieces of advice were coded using the conceptual model described above. Of these, 461, or 52%, involved increasing or making use of available resources, with the remaining 48% involving decreasing demands. We address these broad categories of increasing resources and decreasing demands in the following sections.

Advice Regarding Increasing Resources

Below we describe the types of advice offered by respondents pertaining to increasing resources. We use our model as a framework, including advice involving increasing resources behaviorally, emotionally, and cognitively.

Behaviorally Increasing Resources

Behavioral ways of increasing resources, also known as *problem solving*, involve increasing resources by actively pursing formal and informal means of instrumental support (e.g., help with caregiving tasks). The advice of this nature fell into five subcategories: (a) choosing flexible jobs, (b) using family-friendly workplace policies, (c) seeking family and non-family instrumental support, and (d) using technology.

Choosing Flexible Jobs.   Choosing or obtaining a job that allows flexibility either in one's daily work schedule or in where the work is performed (e.g., work from home) in order to be able to provide family care was an important area of advice mentioned by several respondents. For example, one female respondent stated:

> I am blessed to be in a job that makes it very easy to take care of children and parents. I have not missed my children's activities, and my parent has required chemotherapy the last five months, and we've done them all. I close my office and open it up when I get back. My employer is very supportive.

Using Family-Friendly Workplace Policies.   Among the available resources that respondents encouraged others to use were family-friendly work policies. For example, a female respondent specifically endorsed the use of family leave: "Last year I was on maternity leave with my son. Being home and not working for a year was great. I was able to spend more time with my children and my mom during the day." (Of course, many families are unable to afford taking such time off as, for the most part, such leave is unpaid.)

Seeking Instrumental Support From Family Members.   Several respondents placed significant importance on pressing siblings to assist in shouldering parental care responsibilities. As we reported elsewhere, using data from the focus groups conducted as a part of the present study, we found that perceptions of conflicts over caregiving and perceived inequity in caregiving responsibilities can lead to discord among siblings (Ingersoll-Dayton, Neal, Ha, & Hammer, 2003). A male respondent who advocated the strategy of shared responsibility advised "Don't assume the entire responsibility. Let others, or demand other brothers and sisters, assume responsibilities." A female respondent suggested attending a class "for siblings to learn how to request help from each other instead of being the only one who helps [parents]."

Respondents also proposed involving children in helping to care for their grandparents as well as helping with household chores. Similarly, in the focus groups we conducted, we learned from participants that aging parents gave, as well as received, help (Ingersoll-Dayton, Neal, & Hammer, 2001). This aid from aging parents came in the form of financial help, emotional support, and help with child care and household tasks. Such help can be beneficial in terms of improving the quality of relationship between the adult child and his or her parent and in terms of improved self-ratings of performance as caregivers. At the same time, we found that it can be a mixed blessing, such as when the assistance provided by the parent is unwanted or not helpful (Ingersoll-Dayton et al., 2001).

One man suggested the strategy of enlisting children's help, in particular, not only to increase available resources but also as a method to pass along family values. Another woman similarly advised:

> Include your children in the care giving to the aging parent. Children can learn so much from being around their grandparents ... and will learn the value and see how rewarding it can be. They will always have the memory and that is very important. The children will learn to be compassionate.

Another woman recommended enlisting children to help with the household chores: "It may not be what you would do or how you would do it, but this is one way they learn on their own and the job gets done."

Several respondents suggested getting help from the aging parents, as well, such as including them in the care of their grandchildren. For example, one wrote, "Accepting help from your parents, such as for babysitting, helps them feel better about themselves." Another woman, whose mother-in-law lives in her home, stated, "I feel like we have somebody to watch over us or maybe get advice from, and [mother-in-law] really feels important."

Seeking Nonfamily Instrumental Support. Several survey respondents recommended obtaining assistance from outside the household to increase available resources. For example, one woman suggested that other working, sandwiched couples should "Hire as many people as possible to do routine jobs," as a way to free up time to manage work and family responsibilities. A male respondent encouraged the use of help from outside of the family unit to provide dependent care: "With society changing, the need for daycare for children and parents is becoming more acceptable." One man advised couples to "Look to friends or government agencies to keep on helping." Another male respondent encouraged couples to seek legal advice to help care for aging parents. He stated, "Elder care lawyers and financial planners can relieve financial burdens and anxiety over losing everything your parents have to get heavy medical coverage."

Using Technology. A few respondents wrote comments about how the use of technology had added to their ability to manage their many responsibilities. Examples included computers and microwave ovens, and one woman advised the provision of cellular phones for teenage drivers as a safety tool, "with the child responsible for the cost."[1]

Emotionally Increasing Resources

Of all of the advice given that encouraged increasing one's resources, the greatest number of suggestions advocated increasing one's *emotional* resources as a way to cope with multiple demands and responsibilities. The advice within this category touched on six themes, including those involving taking care of oneself; minding one's marital relationship; communicating and seeking emotional support from other family, friends, coworkers, and supervisors; participating in a support group; finding humor in a situation; and incorporating religious or spiritual beliefs into one's daily life.

Self-Care. Many respondents stressed the necessity of caregivers taking care of themselves. One female respondent emphasized the importance of supporting one's mental health as a way to cope with multiple demands, stating, "Our mental health is as important as our physical health." Several respondents wrote comments suggesting that individuals should take time out for themselves, including: "Take a break whenever your stress level gets too high"; "Take care of yourself physically, emotionally, socially, and spiritually so you can help others"; and [female respondent's emphases] "Take better care of yourself! Put your physical and emotional health first. You are no good to anyone if you are sick or too tired or too stressed."

Nurturing the Couple. Several respondents mentioned that it was important for couples to nurture their marital relationship as a way to

---

[1]On the basis of the focus groups we held prior to conducting the first mailed survey, we knew that use of technology was a strategy used by some couples to manage their multiple role demands. Thus, to learn more about the specific forms of technology they used, we included a question on the survey asking respondents about the most commonly available technology and its usefulness. For both husbands and wives, voice mail/answering machines, cellular phones, and Internet access were the types of technology most commonly available (see Table 7.1). All forms of technology were rated as at least somewhat helpful to respondents in managing their work and family responsibilities, with the most helpful being voicemail or answering machines, beepers or pagers, and cellular phones.

maintain or develop emotional support. This is consistent with the findings detailed in chapters 6 and 10 concerning the importance of spousal role quality as a predictor of positive work–family fit, well-being, and work outcomes. For example, a male respondent advised other working, sandwiched couples: "At the end of every day when you're alone with your spouse, take time to share and show that the two of you are still very important and loved by each other." Another man advised, "Spend time alone as a couple and make it a priority," and another, "Work to keep romance in your marriage." The difficulty of working, sandwiched-generation couples being able to find the time and energy to nourish their relationships is reflected in one man's statement that "I only wish I could have more time to spend with my wife alone." A female respondent summed up the importance of nurturing the emotional component of a marriage from a long-term perspective: "Love your spouse and hopefully your spouse returns the love. Someday you two will be the only ones in the house, so make sure you have a good relationship now."

Communication.   Several respondents reflected on the importance of communication as a way of developing emotional support. Some comments focused specifically on spousal communication as a means of maintaining a healthy relationship, overlapping with the subcategory above. This advice included such statements as, "Communication and friendship within the marriage is essential"; "Work on communication with your spouse"; and "Your spouse should be your best friend, and you should never be afraid to speak to that person about anything." Included in the advice on communication within the marriage or partnership were comments suggesting that couples discuss parenting concerns. One woman stated, "Find a way to agree on child care and discipline." Another wrote, "Discuss and agree on parenting standards for your children."

Advice on communication was not limited to that between spouses or partners, however. Also offered were suggestions for communication with other family members, including children, parents, and siblings. Recommendations included "Keep communication flowing between all involved"; "Open communication between the parties is a must"; and "Communicate, discuss, and always keep in touch with other primary family members."

Support Groups.   Support groups were suggested by several individuals as a means to increase emotional resources. A female respondent advised, "Try to find a support group regarding aging parents." Other respondents wrote, "Seek out others who have 'been there-done that' for advice and support," "Make contact with others in similar circumstances," and "Seek support groups."

Humor. Several respondents offered advice regarding the importance of humor in dealing with their multiple demands and responsibilities, writing comments such as "Don't lose your sense of humor" and "Develop a sense of humor." One woman told of the personal resources that humor added to her coping abilities in working while raising her children and dealing with aging parents, two severely handicapped brothers, and the death of another brother. She wrote, "It's an almost overwhelming circumstance. But there are also strengths, courage, and humor in this family."

Spiritual Nurturing. The importance of spiritual support and religious commitment was noted and advocated by many of the respondents. One male respondent wrote, "Pray daily, stay close to God. All good things come from heaven. Follow the commandments. Life seems to work best when we do these things." Another man said, "[Follow] the Golden Rule and the Ten Commandments." One woman stated, "Prayer is one of the biggest factors that gets me through a day that is not going well or when I am stressed out." Another woman offered, "Find your spiritual base. Whatever it is, work from within first."

Cognitively Increasing Resources

Advice related to increasing one's cognitive resources in order to cope with multiple demands and responsibilities focused on mental preparation and planning and included purposefully planning schedules, preparing for unexpected events, and planning for the couple's own future needs.

Planning Schedules. For many respondents, their advice reflected a belief in the importance of planning ahead and scheduling activities as vital for communication and for reducing conflicts. One woman suggested the use of a large calendar and a weekly family dinner for communicating family activities: "We have a large main calendar where everyone writes in schedules. We always try to have Sunday dinner together, and at that time we discuss the upcoming week and weekend and any activities, needs, transportation problems and social events." A male respondent stated, "It is extremely critical that couples organize schedules, activities, responsibilities, and roles. The workload needs to be flexible and equal as much as possible."

Preparing for the Unexpected. Noting that emergencies may arise at any time, one woman suggested that working, sandwiched couples "Be prepared for anything to happen. It's like a roller coaster, sometimes slow, sometimes fast, but always a long ride." Another woman wrote, "You need to remain flexible and realize that no matter how much planning you do that something will always happen unexpected."

Planning for the Future.   Taking a lesson from the experiences with his parents, one man advocated that couples "Plan for your future. My parents have no retirement or nest egg. Their health is also diminishing. It will be a constant struggle now, but could be easier for my children if I plan ahead." Others noted that they were planning for the future through leading by example, showing their children the importance of caring aging parents.

Advice Concerning Decreasing Demands

Forty-eight percent of the comments written by survey respondents offering advice were related to decreasing demands in the lives of working couples caring both for children and aging parents. This type of advice related to the conscious decision to stop doing certain activities, change behaviors, and/or prioritize demands. As was the case for advice concerning increasing resources, we used our conceptual model to classify the advice offered related to decreasing demands into three basic categories: (a) behavioral, (b) emotional, and (c) cognitive reduction of demands.

Behaviorally Decreasing Demands

Behavioral ways of decreasing demands included learning to say "no" to requests, working fewer hours, and simplifying one's lifestyle.

"Just Say No."   Refusing to take on additional demands was recommended as one way to decrease demands. A woman stated, "Learn how to say 'no.' It sometimes can seem impossible in the situations that come up, but you have to control your life, not let your life control you." Another woman suggested that couples "Keep a few close friends and limit other people [or] clubs trying to drain your precious time. Say 'no' to outside things if [they're] not important to you." The purpose of learning to say "no" as advised by one survey respondent was to "Find a balance that works and commit to do only what you can handle."

Reducing Work Hours.   Consciously choosing to work fewer hours in order to increase availability to family members was an area of advice offered by several survey respondents. For example, one woman advised, "If at all possible have one partner work part time in order to be able to take care of household and family matters. This will allow you to have some time to spend with each other." Another woman wrote, "Try to spend as much time with your children as possible; even if one parent must take a job earning less money and with more flexible hours."

Yet another woman described how the strategy of working part time fit into her life:

> I started working part time when my first child was born 15 years ago. My husband is a firefighter, so his hours are 24 on, 48 off. Our children were, for the most part, raised by both parents. Our situation gave us the best of both worlds. I would never have done it any other way.

Simplifying Life.   Several respondents suggested simplifying one's life as a way to decrease demands. One woman wrote:

> My advice to parents with small children would be to get used to living with less and do whatever you can, even move to a smaller house, to allow one parent to stay home with children. Too much emphasis is put on the "worldly things," such as new cars, computers, big houses, nice clothes and expensive vacations.

Another respondent stated, "People should gear down their lifestyles a bit and they would probably be happier. Spend your money where it does good, not for show." A male respondent noted that "Sometimes if you slow down, you get more done."

Emotionally Decreasing Demands

Advice concerning decreasing demands by emotional means related to reducing personal expectations and included taking one day at a time, not feeling guilty when one does not meet expectations, having patience, and changing one's attitude towards the situation.

One Day at a Time.   Taking life a day at a time was a strategy commonly advocated by respondents. One woman wrote, "Try to focus on the positive each day. Look for the strengths of each day." Another stated, "Count your blessings every day. Stay calm." Other related suggestions included such statements as "Relax and enjoy it"; "Roll with the punches"; "Take one day at a time"; and "Enjoy it all, from the smiles to frowns, to laughter to tears."

No Guilt.   Several respondents, particularly wives, advocated changing or lowering one's personal standards so as to not feel guilty when tasks were not completed to one's satisfaction or when insufficient time was available to care as much as one would like for family members. One woman stated, "Get rid of the guilt that you can't be everything to everyone." Another woman wrote, "Don't try to be Superwoman. No one cares if there's dust on the furniture, so lower your standards for house-keeping." Another respondent said, "Keep in mind that you are not a superhero. You are only human." Related comments included "There is no reason to be a perfectionist in any area of your life," "It is more important to spend time with an aging parent than have a spotless home," and "Don't try to be everything to everybody." As one woman wrote, "You have to learn not to sweat the small stuff. Spending time with your family is some-times more important than doing dishes or cleaning the house."

Patience as a Virtue. "Be patient," "Have patience," and "Patience and tolerance" were common points in many respondents' comments, indi-cating the frustrations that couples often face in coping with multiple de-mands. One woman suggested, "Be patient. There is a way to solve all problems. [Be] especially patient with aging parents. They don't always un-derstand that they are unable to do the things they did when they were younger. With patience you can solve all problems."

Attitude Adjustment. Adjusting one's attitude toward a more posi-tive focus was another area of advice offered by some of our working, sandwiched-generation couples as a way to cope with the emotional de-mands of raising children and caring for aging parents. One respondent wrote, "A person must look at what they have and not at what they do not have." Another woman said, "Consider it an honor to care for both your parents and children."

Emphasizing the importance of a positive attitude in order to cope with many conflicting responsibilities, one woman's comments embodied many other pieces of advice, as well: "'Most every day has its challenges and rewards. Try to find a bright spot in something every day, and don't lose your sense of humor. Talking to friends outside your family helps put things in perspective and often gives you new ideas for handling a situa-tion." Similarly, the difficulty that working, sandwiched-generation cou-ples face in coping with emotional stress is summed up in the woman's comments that opened this chapter.

Cognitively Decreasing Demands

Strategies involving decreasing demands cognitively are those that fo-cus on the setting of priorities. The advice of this nature that was offered by our respondents included determining life priorities, within-family prior-ities, and daily priorities.

Life Priorities. In addition to prioritizing daily activities, respon-dents also placed significant importance on prioritizing life goals. Placing family ahead of work was the most frequently cited advice of this nature. A male respondent suggested, "Always set priorities. Family members and family relationships should be the number one priority, but also do the best you can do at work." A woman wrote, "Family should be your top priority. Work is important, but family is for a lifetime." Another respondent wrote, "Remember that your children and parents are only here for a short while. Be sure to spend quality time with them." Other responses included such comments as "Family comes first. Work is a job," "Your job should not be your life," and "Never put material things ahead of family." Of all of the respondents who offered advice related to life priorities, none suggested that work should come before family.

Within-Family Priorities. A few respondents' comments centered around the difficulty that they faced in managing the conflicting responsibilities of caring for both children and parents. For example, one woman wrote, "The hardest problem I have is not the conflicting needs of work and family, but when I have to choose at any particular moment between my mother and my children." Offered as advice, another woman wrote, "If you have young children sometimes you need to make them your first priority even when you know your help is needed by your parent." A male respondent said, "Don't let parental care affect everyday obligations to raising your child." Other respondents, however, seemed to reverse these priorities, writing such comments as, "Always remember who brought you into this world," and "They sacrificed to me when I was young and I'm more than happy to sacrifice for them now. I hope my children will feel the same for me."

Daily Priorities. Respondents advised that prioritizing activities on a daily level can help allocate limited family resources more efficiently. One man wrote, "I think one thing needs [to be] addressed right up front— priorities. Find them, know them, stick with them." One woman advised that couples "Spend time each week planning and prioritizing. Work on becoming more realistic about what is possible to accomplish and let yourself let go of what's not possible. Cut corners where you can." Others' comments about daily priorities included "Set priorities and budget time accordingly" and "Insist on discussion about priorities for the family budget and family purchases."

Several respondents specifically mentioned setting aside time within one's schedule to spend with family. One woman suggested that others "Prioritize activities beyond work and school and make sure to have quality time together." A male respondent suggested to others like him that they should "Spend as much non-working time with your children [as possible]. Get involved in their school activities." Finally, another man noted:

Make sure family always comes before work because your children will grow up before you know it. And your parents won't be around forever, so spend quality time with them also, even if it is helping. You only live once and what's more important than the ones you love.

SUMMARY

In this chapter, we reviewed the coping literature and noted a lack of specific measures related to work–family coping strategies. We presented a model of coping strategies composed of a total of six categories, three each—behavioral, emotional, and cognitive—within the two dimensions of increasing resources and decreasing demands. We then used this model to describe the types of advice offered to their peers by the couples who participated in our study about how to cope and manage multiple work and family demands. We offered specific quotes from our participants to illustrate the various strategies.

As we describe in the next chapter, this model informed our development of a measure of work–family coping strategies that we then validated using our survey data. In particular, we report on the development of our measure, our effort to assess what strategies individuals and couples actually adopted themselves, and the relationships between the strategies adopted and the work–family fit, well-being, and work outcomes among our working, sandwiched-generation couples.

8

Work–Family Coping Strategies: What Are the Effects on Work–Family Fit, Well-being, and Work?

I have learned that sometimes household choices have to be left undone in order to make sure my family is provided for.

I can't seem to find time to do anything for me. If I take 5 minutes for myself I feel guilty ...

Caring for in-laws or my mother is very rewarding, as is raising our children. Work is enjoyable and I always strive to do my best. But, if given a choice, I would work part time so I could be with my family more. Heavy debt and the need for health insurance keeps me in my job, which, fortunately, is rewarding, though not in terms of money.

In this chapter, we discuss the development of our measure of coping strategies, and we analyze the simple correlational relationships between the strategies used and the outcomes. We then report the results of multivariate analyses to assess the effects of using three general types of coping strategies on individuals' own work–family fit, well-being, and work-related outcomes. Finally, we present the results of crossover analyses that examine the effects of one spouse's use of coping strategies on the other spouse.

WHAT STRATEGIES DO WORKING, SANDWICHED
COUPLES USE?

In addition to collecting advice from working couples caring for children and aging parents regarding how others like themselves could best manage their work and family lives, as reviewed in chapter 7, we were interested in learning about which coping strategies working, sandwiched couples actually were using and how using those coping strategies affected their work–family fit, well-being, and work-related outcomes. It is one thing to make suggestions to others that may be beneficial; it is another thing to make use of effective coping strategies in one's own life. Moreover, not all advice is necessarily good advice, in terms of improving outcomes.

We conceptualize coping strategies as resources that couples use to help them alleviate the demands of working and caring for children and aging parents. As such, we believed there was a need to develop a quantitative measure of work–family coping strategies used by dual-earner couples in the sandwiched generation. This would allow us to determine what couples actually did to cope with their multiple work and family responsibilities and how the strategies they used affected their lives. Our model of work–family coping strategies, described in the previous chapter, provided the structure for the measure created.

In particular, our research team developed 36 different statements describing possible individual work–family coping strategies to be included in the mailed survey (see Fig. 8.1). Items were developed on the basis of our review of previous work–family literature on coping strategies, and our model of coping strategies was created on the basis of focus groups with working, sandwiched couples (see chap. 7). Item wording was derived from the phrases used by focus group participants to describe how they managed their work and family lives. At least four items for each of the six categories of the model were developed.

In the survey, respondents were instructed as follows: "The next questions concern how YOU feel or act in response to your many work and family duties. Please indicate the degree to which each statement below describes how you feel or act." To minimize respondent burden, we elected to have respondents choose from just three possible response options: 1 = *Never*, 2 = *Sometimes*, or 3 = *Most or all of the time*.

In addition to the 36 coping items that were developed, respondents were asked to indicate whether (0 = *no*, 1 = *yes*) they had made use of any of 10 other limited or one-time use accommodations in the past year specifically because of their child- or parent-care responsibilities. A subset of these informal work and family accommodations comprised the outcome

	Decrease Demands	Increase Resources
Behavioral	Decreasing Activities (e.g., stopping or limiting activities)	Increasing Instrumental Resources (e.g., increasing flexibility in scheduling, hiring assistance)
	b. I reduce hours spent on certain tasks or demands. e. I stop doing things that are not absolutely necessary. h. I limit my volunteer work. **t. I limit my social activities.** u. I avoid taking on new tasks if others are willing to perform them. **v. I spend less time with my spouse or partner.** **w. I spent less time with other family members.** z. I limit the number of my child(ren)'s activities that I attend. dd. I limit my personal time for reading, exercise, or other leisure activities. g(r). I take on tasks if no one else is capable or available. hh. I sometimes work long hours to avoid dealing with family responsibilities	c. I involve and get help from other family members or friends to accomplish tasks or meet demands. d. I hire people who help me accomplish tasks or meet demands. r. I get help with my work from family members. x. I divide up household chores among family members bb. I use a cell phone, pager, or voice messaging so that my family can reach me. gg. When necessary, I take time off from work to care for a parent or child. p(r). I wish I could accept or ask help from others. pp. I help my spouse with his/her work
Emotional	Decreasing Expectations of Self (e.g., reducing personal expectations)	Increasing Emotional Resources (e.g., receiving emotional support)
	i. I try to realize that I can't do it all, and that it's okay. **l. I focus on the many good things I have.** m. I recognize and accept that I may not be able to do my best. aa. I lower my expectations of what should get done around the house. k(r). I feel guilty for not spending enough time with certain people or doing certain things.	**j. I get moral support and comfort from others.** **o. I try to find humor in the situation.** cc(r). I wish others would be more supportive.
Cognitive	Prioritizing (e.g., prioritizing activities)	Planning (e.g., scheduling activities, future goals)
	n. I protect or set aside time for activities that are important to me. qq. I prioritize and do the things that are most important and necessary. s(r). I lose track of what's important to me.	a. I plan how I'm going to use my time and energy. q. I have back-up systems in case things don't happen as expected. x. I attend activities separately from my spouse or partner because of conflicting schedules or responsibilities. ee. I plan my work hours around my child(ren)'s, parent'(s), or spouse's or partner's schedule. ff. I plan to work at home so that I can be close to my family.
		f(r). I don't try to plan, I just take things as they come.

Note. Items in boldface type comprise those used in the three coping scales. (r) = reverse coded.

Figure 8.1. Coping measure items by category.

145

measure "number of work accommodations" described and reported on in chapter 6.[1]

Individual-Level Coping Strategies Used

Of the 36 coping strategies (see Table 8.1 in Appendix C), the one strategy used most commonly, by both wives and husbands, was to prioritize and do the things that are most necessary: the means were 2.5 for both, on a scale from 1 to 3. (In the paragraphs that follow, the numbers in parentheses indicate means, unless otherwise noted. Similarly, differences described between husbands and wives are statistically significant at the $p \le$ .05 level unless otherwise noted.)

For wives, the next most commonly used strategies were to plan how they were going to use their time and energy (2.5); to try and find humor in the situation (2.4); to focus on the many good things they had (2.4); to limit their personal time for reading, exercise, or other leisure activities (2.4); to take on tasks if no one else were capable or available (2.3); to limit volunteer work (2.3); to limit social activities (2.3); to take time off from work to care for a parent or child (2.3); and to feel guilty for not spending enough time with certain people or doing certain things (2.3).

For husbands, after the prioritizing strategy, the next most commonly used strategies were to try and find humor in the situation (2.5); take on tasks if no one else were capable or available (2.4); limit volunteer work (2.3); focus on the many good things they had (2.3); plan how they were going to use their time and energy (2.3); try to realize that they couldn't do it all (2.2); get moral support and comfort from others (2.2); protect and set aside time for activities important to them (2.2); limit social activities (2.2); and limit personal time for reading, exercise, or other leisure activities (2.2).

The least commonly used strategy, by both husbands and wives, was to work long hours at work to avoid dealing with family responsibilities (husbands' $M = 1.2$; wives' $M = 1.2$). This finding is counter to Hochschild's (1997) basic tenet in her book, *The Time Bind*, where she describes employees who use work as a respite from stressful home lives (although the concept of work as respite did emerge among our respondents, just not in the context of actually working longer hours to avoid caregiving). The next least commonly used strategy was for respondents to hire people to assist with tasks, although husbands (1.6) were significantly more likely to do

---

[1]As described in chapter 6, 7 of these items were used to create the outcome measure "number of work accommodations made." We examine all 10 items here at the individual item level because they represent one-time use coping strategies that were implemented (or not) in the previous year as an outcome of challenging work and family situations. These items are not included in the coping strategies measure, given our wish to examine them as outcomes, consistent with the work and elder-care literature.

this than were wives (1.4), and use of this strategy was greatly influenced by household income level, as would be expected.

Sometimes strategies involve making behavioral changes in one role to make room for the demands of another role. In general, women tended to make more accommodations in their work role than did men, particularly in terms of taking time off to care for family members (2.3 compared to 2.0 for husbands) and planning work hours around family schedules (2.2 compared to 1.8 for husbands). Neither husbands nor wives reported using the strategy of planning to work at home to be close to family with much frequency (husbands' $M = 1.5$; wives' $M = 1.5$; not a significant difference).

There were fewer differences between wives and husbands with regard to accommodations made at home. Wives tended to be more likely to lower their expectations of what should be done around the house than were husbands (2.2 compared to 2.0 for husbands), whereas husbands were more likely to divide up chores among the members of the family (2.1 compared to 2.0 for wives).

In terms of the usurping of personal time by work and family roles, however, there was a marked difference between husbands and wives. Wives were more likely than husbands to limit personal time (2.4 compared to 2.2), and social activities (2.3 compared to 2.2), whereas husbands were more likely to protect and set aside time for activities that were important to them (2.2 compared to 2.0). Both wives and husbands, however, frequently reported limiting their volunteer work (the means for both were 2.3).

Limited or One-Time-Use Accommodations Used

In addition to the daily coping strategies used, we were also interested in learning about limited or one-time-use work and family accommodations that participants used in the past year in response to their child- and parent-care responsibilities. (Table 6.1, described in chap. 6, is presented in Appendix C. It lists the descriptive statistics and compares husbands and wives with respect to their use of these accommodations.)

The most commonly used accommodations of this nature were, for wives, working reduced hours (31%), refusing or limiting travel (27%), choosing a job with more flexibility to meet family demands (24%), and refusing or deciding not to work toward a promotion (21%). The limited-use accommodations made most frequently by husbands were to have refused or limited travel (23%), worked reduced hours (17%), refused to relocate (13%), or worked a different shift from their spouse so that one adult is at home most of the time (13%).

Wives and husbands differed significantly in their use of three accommodations. In particular, wives were more likely to report that they had worked reduced hours (31% vs. 17%), chosen a job that allowed them more flexibility (24% vs. 8%), and refused or decided not to work toward a promotion (21% vs. 9%). Thus, wives, in particular, have made choices or sacrifices in their jobs to allow them to participate more fully in their families.

Although they were not made as commonly, and although there were not significant gender-related differences in their use, the extent to which some other strategies were used is interesting to note as well. In the year prior to the survey, 2% of wives and 1% of husbands reported that they had quit a job because of their parent- or child-care responsibilities. Very few respondents (only 3% of wives and 1% of husbands) had participated in a support group for parents or for adult children. About 10% of wives and 8% of husbands reported that they had moved their parents or parents-in-law in with them to make it easier for them to help these parents, and 4% of wives and 3% of husbands reported having had their parents/in-laws come to live with them so these parents could help them out. Finally, about 15% of wives and 13% of husbands reported working a different shift from their spouse to enable one of them to be at home most of the time.

In sum, the working, sandwiched-generation couples in our study were using a variety of strategies and making a number of limited or one-time use accommodations in an attempt to best manage their work and family lives. However, of the 36 daily coping strategies, which were most effective in enhancing work–family fit, well-being, and work-related outcomes? In the next section, we address this question.

Development of a Composite Coping Strategies Measure

To facilitate examination of the relative effectiveness of the various coping strategies, given the relatively limited size of our sample we needed first to determine whether there were broader categories of strategies that represented groups of items and that were consistent with our model of coping strategies. To do this, we used confirmatory factor analysis, which is a data reduction technique used to group similar items and form subscales (B. Thompson, 2004). We used the data from the second wave of the survey, however, to identify these factors, because after the first survey, we realized that although having just three response options (1 = *Never*, 2 = *Sometimes*, 3 = *Most or all of the time*) for each of the coping strategies items minimized respondent burden, it also resulted in limited variability in the responses. Thus, in the second wave of the survey (1 year later), we expanded the response options to five (1 = *Never*, 3 = *Sometimes*, 5 = *Most or all of the time*) and then used those data to conduct the confirmatory factor analysis of the coping strategy items. Table 8.2 contains the final scale items for our measure of work–family coping strategies.

The confirmatory factor analysis demonstrated that our hypothesized six factors did not fit the data well. Ultimately, three factors better fit the model. The three factors covered the domains of behavioral, emotional, and cognitive coping, with two involving increasing resources and one involving decreasing demands. Thus, three of the six cells of our model were represented. On the basis of the items that comprised each factor, we named the three factors as follows: (1) Behavioral: Decreasing Social Involvement (3 items), (2) Emotional: Increasing Emotional Resources (4 items), and (3) Cognitive: Increasing Prioritization (2 items).[2]

Gender Differences in Use of the Three General Types of Coping Strategies

Looking first at similarities and differences between husbands' and wives' use of the three general types of coping strategies (see Table 8.3), using Wave 1 data, wives engaged in behavioral coping strategies involving decreasing social involvement more often than did husbands (M = 2.1 vs. 2.0). With respect to their use of emotional coping strategies that increase emotional resources, husbands and wives did not differ (the means for both were 2.3); husbands, however, engaged in cognitive coping strategies that involved increased prioritization more often than did wives (2.3 vs. 2.1).

WHAT ARE THE EFFECTS OF COPING STRATEGIES USED ON WORK–FAMILY FIT, WELL-BEING, AND WORK?

Associations Between Each of the Three General Types of Coping Strategies and the Outcomes: Simple Correlations

Our behavioral coping measure consisted of strategies that involve limiting social involvement, which in turn would be expected to lead to decreased social support; thus, we predicted that high scores on this measure would be associated with negative outcomes (i.e., poorer work–family fit,

---

[2]The internal consistency reliabilities for each factor (computed on the basis of data from the second survey) were: Behavioral: Decreasing Social Involvement (husbands = .61, wives = .65), Emotional: Increasing Emotional Resources (husbands = .47, wives = .57), and Cognitive: Increasing Prioritization (husbands = .37, wives = .47). These reliabilities are admittedly low, especially that for the cognitive coping (prioritizing) factor, but they are not unexpected given the small number of items in each factor, especially the two-item prioritizing factor. Further, these low reliabilities are similar to reliabilities of other coping measures (see, for example, Skinner, Edge, Altman, & Sherwood, 2003).

lower well-being, poorer work-related outcomes). As noted earlier, in chapter 7, this type of behavioral social withdrawal is a not an effective coping mechanism and is frequently associated with negative outcomes (e.g., Skinner et al., 2003). In contrast, because our emotional coping measure involved strategies that increase emotional resources, we expected this measure to be positively associated with work–family fit, well-being, and work outcomes (e.g., Skinner et al., 2003). Similarly, given that our cognitive coping strategies measure was composed of strategies that increase resources by prioritization, or what Skinner et al. (2003) referred to as *negotiation and cognitive restructuring*, we expected use of strategies of this nature also to be associated with positive work–family fit, well-being, and work outcomes. Our findings with respect to the simple correlational relationships are described below. (See Tables 8.4–8.6 in Appendix C.)

In brief, these correlational analyses revealed strong and consistent positive relationships between use of both emotional and cognitive coping strategies and work–family fit and well-being outcomes. In addition, use of behavioral withdrawal coping strategies was related to decreased work–family fit and well-being, as expected. We found use of coping strategies to be less consistently related to work outcomes, but the relationships that did exist were in the expected directions.

Effects of Coping Strategy Use on Work–Family Fit, Well-Being, and Work: Multivariate Analyses

To identify the unique relationships between the coping strategies used and the outcomes, we conducted hierarchical multiple regression analyses, consistent with those we presented in chapter 6. Specifically, using data from the first survey, we conducted separate analyses for husbands and wives, first entering the personal characteristics (i.e., years of education, ability to get along on one's income, negative affectivity) as control variables. In addition, we included the role quality variables as control variables, because of the significant amount of variance that these role quality measures accounted for in the outcomes, as described in chapter 6. We then entered into the regression equation the three general types of coping strategies (i.e., Behavioral: Decreasing Social Involvement; Emotional: Increasing Emotional Resources; and Cognitive: Increasing Prioritization) to determine their relationships with the work–family fit, well-being, and work outcomes over and above that of the personal characteristics and role quality. The results are described below and summarized in Fig. 8.2 (see Tables 8.5–8.7).

The Effects of Coping Strategies on Work–Family Fit. We found that, as a group, the three work–family coping strategies accounted

Work–Family Fit

- Using behavioral coping strategies that involve social withdrawal is related to higher work–family conflict for husbands and wives. There is no effect on work–family positive spillover.
- Using emotional coping strategies that increase emotional resources is related to higher levels of positive spillover for husbands and wives. There is no effect on work–family conflict.
- Using cognitive coping strategies has no effect on the work–family fit outcomes.

Well-Being

- Using behavioral coping strategies that involve social withdrawal is related to decreased well-being for husbands.
- Using emotional coping strategies that increase emotional resources is related to improved life satisfaction for both husbands and wives. There is no effect on other well-being outcomes.
- Using cognitive coping strategies that involve prioritizing is related to improved well-being outcomes for wives.

Work Outcomes

- Using behavioral coping strategies that involve social withdrawal is related only to increased number of work accommodations made by husbands.
- Using emotional coping strategies that increase emotional resources is not related to the work outcomes.
- Using cognitive coping strategies that involve prioritizing is related only to improved job satisfaction for husbands.

Crossover Effects

- Husbands' use of emotional coping strategies is related to improved work–family fit and well-being for their wives.
- Wives' use of behavioral coping strategies is related to higher life satisfaction for their husbands, contrary to expectations, and is detrimental to their own well-being.

Figure 8.2. Use of coping strategies in relation to work–family fit, well-being, and work: results of multivariate analyses.

for a small but significant amount of variance in two of the work–family fit outcomes: (a) work-to-family conflict (3% for both husbands and wives) and (b) family-to-work positive spillover (4% for husbands, and 3% for wives), over and above that of the personal characteristics and the role quality variables (which accounted for 10%–23% of the variance in each of the four outcomes).

As expected, use of behavioral coping strategies involving social withdrawal was related to higher work-to-family conflict for both husbands and wives, after taking into account personal characteristics and role quality. Use of social withdrawal strategies also was related to higher family-to-work conflict for wives. There were no significant relationships between positive work-to-family or family-to-work spillover and behavioral coping for either husbands or wives.

Use of emotional coping strategies that increase emotional resources was related to only one work–family fit outcome: family-to-work positive spillover; this was true for both husbands and wives. There were no significant relationships between use of cognitive coping strategies and any of the four work–family fit outcomes.

Thus, the findings demonstrate that using behavioral social withdrawal coping strategies has a negative effect on work-to-family conflict for both husbands and wives, and on family-to-work conflict for wives, while using emotional coping strategies has a positive impact on family-to-work positive spillover for both. Cognitive coping strategies do not affect work–family fit outcomes.

Effects of Coping Strategies on Well-Being.   As a group, the coping strategies accounted for a significant amount of variance (between 1% and 7%) in all of the well-being outcomes except overall health, for both husbands and wives, above and beyond that accounted for by the personal characteristics and role quality variables (17%–47% of the variance in each of the four well-being outcomes). Use of behavioral coping strategies involving social withdrawal was negatively related to three of the four well-being outcomes, but only for husbands. Specifically, use of this type of coping strategies was related to higher depression, lower life satisfaction, and lower overall role performance for husbands.

Use of emotional coping strategies involving increasing emotional resources was related to higher life satisfaction for both husbands and wives. There were no significant effects on the other three well-being outcomes.

Use of cognitive coping strategies involving prioritizing was related to three of the four well-being outcomes, but only for wives. These included lower depression, higher overall health, and higher overall role performance.

It is interesting to note that although use of cognitive coping strategies did not affect work–family fit, for wives, use of these strategies was related to improved well-being. Further, use of behavioral strategies had a negative effect on well-being for husbands, but not for wives. It appears that although social withdrawal is not a "healthy" coping strategy to use, it is especially unhealthy for husbands, at least when it comes to their well-being. Similarly, use of cognitive coping strategies appears to be especially important to wives' well-being.

Effects of Coping Strategies on Work.   It is interesting that the coping strategies variables, as a group, had a significant impact on only one of the work outcomes, namely, job satisfaction (accounting for 2% of the variance above and beyond the effects of the personal and role quality variables, which accounted for between 4% and 47% of the variance in the four work outcomes). Moreover, this effect was significant only for husbands. In particular, use of cognitive coping strategies involving increasing prioritizing was related to greater job satisfaction on the part of husbands.

Nonetheless, the use of behavioral coping strategies involving decreased social involvement was associated with two other work-related outcomes, one each for husbands and wives. Specifically, using these types of coping strategies was related to making a greater number of work accommodations, for husbands, and to poorer work performance, for wives. Use of emotional coping strategies involving increasing emotional resources was not related to any of work-related outcomes for either husbands or wives.

Within-Couple Effects: The Crossover Effects of Use of Coping Strategies

In addition to determining the effects of individuals' use of the three types of coping strategies on their own work–family fit, well-being, and work outcomes, we were interested in the effects of spouses' use of coping strategies on their partners' outcomes. After controlling for an individual's personal characteristics and role quality, then, we examined the effects of their spouse's use of the three types of coping strategies on the individual's outcomes.

We found that greater use by husbands of emotional and cognitive coping strategies was related to decreased family-to-work conflict for their wives. Husbands' use of emotional coping strategies was also related to higher levels of work-to-family positive spillover and of life satisfaction for wives. We conclude, then, that husbands' use of emotional coping strategies is related to improved work–family fit and well-being for their wives.

There was another significant crossover effect, as well, specifically, wives' use of behavioral coping strategies was related to higher life satisfaction for husbands. This finding is particularly interesting because it suggests that although social withdrawal is not healthy for individuals, there is some beneficial effect for their partners, at least for the husbands of wives who use this negative coping strategy. Although we do not advocate the use of such strategies, this finding demonstrates the potential spiral that may occur in families with intense work and family demands, in which one response to dealing with those demands is that one member— typically, the wife—gives up her own social contacts, to meet the family's needs. This may benefit the family (i.e., the husband) but has negative implications for the wife's own well-being.

SUMMARY

In this chapter, we examined the relationships between coping strategies used and work–family fit, well-being, and work outcomes. To do this, we first developed survey items for assessing the specific coping strategies that individuals use to manage their multiple work and family demands, using our six-factor model of coping strategies, along with data from focus groups convened for this purpose. Using the survey data, we then used a data reduction technique to develop a measure of broad types of coping strategies.

Instead of confirming the six factors in our model, however, this analysis revealed three major types of coping strategies. These included behavioral strategies that involve decreasing social involvement, emotional coping strategies that involve increasing emotional resources, and cognitive coping strategies that involve decreasing cognitive demands through prioritizing. We then investigated the effectiveness of these three general types of coping strategies, examining how they affected work–family fit, well-being, and work-related outcomes.

In general, we found that for both husbands and wives, strategies that increase emotional resources and cognitive coping strategies that increase prioritizing have beneficial effects on work–family fit and well-being, and behavioral coping strategies that involve decreasing social involvement tend to have negative effects on work–family fit and well-being. There were few effects of coping on the work outcomes, although the relationships that were significant were in the expected direction.

We also found some within-couple, or crossover, effects of the types of coping strategies used. Specifically, husbands' use of emotional coping strategies was related to improved work–family fit and well-being for their wives. Wives' use of behavioral coping strategies was related to higher life satisfaction for husbands but with negative effects on wives' well-being and work–family fit.

Implications for Working, Sandwiched Couples

These findings have a number of important implications for dual-earner couples caring for children and aging parents. First and foremost, they indicate that the natural tendency to reduce social contacts when overwhelmed with work and family is actually likely to be detrimental. At the same time, as discussed in chapter 7, use of this social withdrawal strategy was commonly advocated by respondents in their comments meant as "advice" for other working, sandwiched couples. We would urge couples not to heed this advice. Instead, we encourage them to seek out social support as a way of increasing their emotional resources, because our findings demonstrate that this coping strategy is related to a number of beneficial outcomes. In fact, a spouse can even benefit from his or her partner's use of such strategies; wives, in particular, may benefit when their husbands use strategies to increase their emotional resources.

Implications for Family-Care Practitioners

These findings also have implications for practitioners, especially family-care practitioners who counsel couples attempting to manage their work and family responsibilities. The findings suggest that the use of certain coping strategies may be beneficial not only for the individual but also for his or her partner, at least in the case of husbands' use of strategies that increase emotional resources crossing over and having beneficial effects for their wives. Informing couples of the benefits of using certain types of coping strategies (i.e., increasing emotional resources and prioritizing), as well as the detriments of using others (social withdrawal), may have positive outcomes for the family, as a whole.

Implications for Research

For researchers, we believe that the model of work–family coping strategies presented here is a useful way of conceptualizing such strategies. The three- (as opposed to six-) factor structure that we identified empirically, and the consistency of the findings with our predictions, represent a first step toward validation, but considerable additional work is needed with larger samples and possibly a larger number of coping strategy items. Problems inherent in our ability to adequately measure coping strategies used, particularly the cognitive strategies (as seen in the low reliability coefficients), may have reduced our ability to identify significant relationships, although this problem plagues most measures of coping strategies (e.g., Skinner et al., 2003).

9

Workplace Supports: Effects on Work–Family Fit, Well-Being, and Work

---

I am blessed to be in a job that makes it very easy to take care of children and parents. I have not missed my children's activities … I close my office and open it up when I get back. My employer is very supportive.

My supervisor is great. She stresses that it's important for you to have time off to be with your family. Because, you know, you're going to miss it all if you don't have a day off.

Being able to have flexible hours at work has made being a working mom more enjoyable. I am now able to participate in my children's school activities. And being able to do this brings me much joy, and does away with the guilt of not being there for them. One downfall has been that since my husband and I have chosen to work different shifts so that one of us is with the kids at all times, it has left us with a strained relationship. Working different shifts was good for the kids, but our relationship has suffered. It takes a lot of work on both parties to make the situation work.

Workplace supports, or *family-friendly practices*, defined broadly, include both formal and informal means of support within organizations. As described in chapter 3 and delineated by Neal, Chapman, Ingersoll-Dayton, and Emlen (1993), formal support comprises *policies*, such as flexible work arrangements; *services*, such as programs that provide resource and referral information about dependent-care options; and *benefits,* such as childcare subsidies. We use the term *supports* here to include all three of these types. We also believe it is important to recognize *informal support*, which refers broadly to the degree to which an organization is perceived to have a family-friendly, or positive, work–family culture. *Work–family culture* is defined as "the shared assumptions, beliefs, and values regarding the extent to which an organization supports and values the integration of employees' work and family lives" (C. A. Thompson, Beauvis, & Lyness, 1999, p. 392). Work–family culture can influence the effectiveness of more formal workplace supports (e.g., Allen, 2001).

In this chapter, we describe the findings from our study concerning both the availability and utilization of workplace supports by working couples caring for children and aging parents. In addition, we report on the types of supports that respondents wish their employers offered. We then present our findings concerning the relationship between utilization of workplace supports (specifically, alternative work schedules and dependent-care supports) and work–family fit, well-being, and work outcomes. We also report the findings from analyses conducted to determine the existence of crossover effects, or the extent to which one spouse's use of supports affects the other.

PRIOR RESEARCH ON THE AVAILABILITY AND UTILIZATION OF WORKPLACE SUPPORTS

Research regarding the effects of family-friendly workplace supports on individuals' job-related attitudes and behaviors typically has focused on the perceived availability of workplace supports (Kossek & Ozeki, 1999). In general, such research has found a positive relationship between the availability of supports and organizational attachment, such as organizational commitment and job satisfaction (e.g., Allen, 2001; Grover & Crooker, 1995; Scandura & Lankau, 1997; Sinclair, Hannigan, & Tetrick, 1995; Thomas & Ganster, 1995; C. A. Thompson et al., 1999). In addition, the presence of work–family supports has been linked to overall organizational performance. For example, Arthur (2003) found that stock market value was higher among businesses that provided family-friendly supports, and Perry-Smith and Blum (2000) found that the presence of work–family policies was related to higher perceived organizational performance.

Few studies have examined the effects of the actual utilization of workplace supports (Kossek & Ozeki, 1999). Moreover, of the existing studies, most have examined only one type of support at a time (e.g., Thomas & Ganster, 1995), as opposed to a wider variety or "bundles" of supports (Perry-Smith & Blum, 2000). In general, the types of workplace supports examined have included alternative work schedules and dependent-care supports (e.g., Bond, Thompson, Galinsky, & Prottas, 2003).

Most studies on the use of alternative work schedules have found positive effects on work–family conflict, job satisfaction, and absenteeism (for reviews, see Baltes, Briggs, Huff, Wright, & Neuman, 1999; Hammer & Barbera, 1997; Pierce, Newstrom, Dunham, & Barber, 1989). The findings regarding the use of dependent-care supports, however, have been inconsistent. For example, use of dependent-care supports has been shown by some studies to be related to decreased turnover, decreased absenteeism, and increased organizational commitment and satisfaction (e.g., Milkovich & Gomez, 1976), as well as increased organizational citizenship behaviors (Lambert, 2000). Other studies have found the utilization of on-site child care, for example, to be unrelated to work–family conflict, absenteeism (e.g., Goff, Mount, & Jamison, 1990), and performance (e.g., Kossek & Nichol, 1992; Milkovich & Gomez, 1976).

WHAT TYPES OF WORKPLACE SUPPORTS ARE AVAILABLE TO AND USED BY WORKING SANDWICHED COUPLES?

To assess the availability and utilization of workplace supports among working, sandwiched couples, we asked survey participants the following: "Please indicate whether or not each of the following workplace supports is available to you through your employer (yes/no). If YES, do you make use of this?" A list of 13 possible supports was provided. Respondents who indicated a support was not available were coded as 0 on utilization, along with those respondents who indicated that the support was available but that it was not used. Use of support was coded as 1. Respondents who did not know if a support was available were coded as 0 for availability (and, thus, 0 for use). Respondents who owned their own business (30 wives and 45 husbands) were instructed to skip the items on workplace supports. Thus, 278 wives and 257 husbands served as the sample for the analyses we present here pertaining to workplace supports.

Tables 9.1 and 9.2 (see Appendix C) present frequencies and percentages for husbands and wives, along with the results of t tests comparing husbands and wives on each of the 13 workplace supports with respect to the availability of supports to respondents (Table 9.1) and respondents' use of supports (Table 9.2). It should be noted that the percentages provided for use of supports are confounded with availability of supports (given that to use a support, it had to be available).

Availability of Supports

We found that wives were more likely than husbands to report availability of 5 of the 13 supports, including job sharing, telecommuting, unpaid leave, on-site child care, and work and family seminars. Husbands were more likely than wives to report the availability of family health insurance.

Use of Supports

With respect to use of supports, those supports used most frequently, by both husbands and wives, were family health insurance, personal time off/paid leave, flexible work hours, and unpaid leave. The least used supports, again for both husbands and wives, were on-site child care, resource and referral for child care and elder care, pretax dollars for elder care, and on-site support groups.

Wives, in general, were more likely than husbands to make use of workplace supports, consistent with previous research (e.g., Judiesch & Lyness, 1999; Rosin & Korabik, 2002). More wives than husbands used 5 of the 13 supports: flexible work hours, telecommuting, unpaid leave, personal time off/paid leave, and work–family seminars.

The finding regarding flexible work hours is likely explained by wives' explicit choice of jobs that inherently are more flexible, as indicated by the women in our focus groups. The greater use of telecommuting by wives is especially interesting given that husbands reported greater availability of the option of telecommuting; this provides an even stronger indication that these wives may have chosen their jobs at least in part because of this option. Similarly, although more husbands than wives reported having the option to take unpaid leave, more wives did so. This may be explained by women's generally lower salaries and the lessened financial impact on the family than if the husband took unpaid time off. Wives' taking more paid time off than husbands is consistent with wives' generally greater care-giving responsibilities and again, possibly their choice of jobs that offered this support.

An alternative explanation for husbands' lower utilization of supports may be their fear of being perceived as less committed to their company (Haas, Allard, & Hwang, 2002). Finally, the use by more husbands than wives of the family health insurance provided by their organization is interesting, given the greater availability of such insurance reported by wives. Wives may have been using the plan available through their husband's organization; perhaps the health insurance plans available to the husbands were better in some way (e.g., more comprehensive coverage, less expensive). At the same time, because more wives than husbands reported having health insurance available, it may be that some wives chose their jobs specifically for this coverage.

Factors That Affect the Availability and Use of Supports

A number of factors can influence both the use and availability of workplace supports, as described in chapter 2. First, utilization of a support clearly is limited to the extent that the support is actually made available by the organization. Second, as mentioned previously, the work–family culture may influence an individual's decision to use a support. Third, as in the case of unpaid family leave, it may simply be that although a support is available to employees, it may not be adequate. Fourth, some supports, such as with the case of some workplace-based federal programs, like dependent-care tax benefits, may simply be too complex for the majority of workers to understand and, hence, use. Fifth, the availability of supports may be affected by the size of companies, with larger corporations being more likely to provide more formal policies and programs. Finally, even in some organizations where supports are offered, little may be done in the way of advertising the supports' availability to workers, thus limiting the number of people who actually make use of the support.

In the present study, the low utilization rates for many of the dependent-care supports are due largely to the lack of availability of such supports. For example, only 21 wives and 10 husbands indicated that on-site child care was available, and only 3 wives and 5 husbands reported actually using this support. These low utilization rates are especially interesting among these working, sandwiched couples, who would be expected to have the highest need for such supports because of their multiple caregiving demands. These findings indicate that other factors, such as work–family culture, in addition to availability, may affect the utilization of supports (e.g., Allen, 2001; Haas et al., 2002; Sahibzada, Hammer, Neal, & Kuang, 2005). More research is needed in this area to better understand what factors contribute to an individual's decision to use, or not use, a particular workplace support.

Although use of a support is clearly related to its availability, we found that some supports tend to be available but not used, whereas others are widely used when they are available. Specifically, in the case of use of unpaid leave for family care, although about 67% of husbands and 49% of wives indicated that this support was available to them, only 12% and 23%, respectively, indicated that they actually used the support. Given our sample of employees caring both for dependent children and aging parents, this finding suggests that low utilization of such leave is due not to lack of need but rather to the unpaid nature of this leave. That most American employees are not in a position to take leave without pay raises the question of whether unpaid leave should even be considered as a form of formal workplace support.

By comparison, the percentages for use and availability are much more similar when examining the workplace support "personal time off/paid leave." Specifically, among the men in our sample, 68% had such leave available to them, and 41% reported using it; among the women, 64% had paid leave available to them, and 51% used it. Even more interesting is the comparison of utilization rates for unpaid leave compared to paid leave (i.e., 12% vs. 41% for husbands; 23% vs. 51% for wives, respectively). This clearly suggests that paid, rather than unpaid, leave is preferable to people attempting to manage multiple family and work demands.

The findings regarding company-sponsored federal programs that allow for pre-tax dollars to be spent on child- or elder-care expenses are noteworthy as well. Although 36% of husbands reported that such support for child care was available, only 8% used the program. Similarly, although about 14% reported the availability of such programs for elder care, just under 2% used them. The data are similar for wives. As discussed in chapter 2, underutilization of supports may be due to a variety of factors, but in this case a key factor may be program complexity or particularly with respect to elder care, program eligibility limitations. Finally, although between 9% (elder care) and 15% (child care) of survey participants reported the availability of information resource and referral services for child and elder care, less than 2% actually reported that they used these supports.

Similar to utilization, several factors affect the availability of supports. Key among these factors is the size of the organization. Most small organizations do not have the resources to provide a wide variety of supports compared to larger, more established companies. For example, among the companies included in *Working Mother* magazine's list of "most family-friendly companies," the majority, if not all, are large, resource-rich firms. Most of the U.S. working population, however, is employed by small companies that are less likely to provide workplace supports, as described above and in chapter 2. This was true among our study participants as well: Fifty-one percent of the wives and 48% of the husbands worked for companies with fewer than 25 employees at their worksite. In addition, when asked about the number of employees that their company as a whole employed, 53.4% of wives and 50.5% of husbands indicated that number as 150 employees or fewer. Thus, the majority of our sample, consistent with the country as a whole, worked for small organizations that are less likely to have the resources to provide some workplace supports. We believe that it is especially important for companies that do not provide formal workplace supports to develop and embrace a culture that is supportive of working families. Indeed, in our focus groups with working, sandwiched couples, many participants indicated that the small companies they worked for did this, and as a result they felt a great deal of loyalty to their employers.

Another factor that affects reports of availability, as well as utilization, of workplace supports is how well the company makes the supports known among its employees. For example, if workplace supports are available, but few employees are aware of them, people obviously will not be able to make use of the supports. Thus, the effort that the company puts forth in terms of advertising the various family-supportive programs, policies, and supports will have an impact on reports of availability and, ultimately, actual utilization of supports.

What Supports Do Respondents Wish Their Companies Offered?

To identify additional supports that working, sandwiched individuals would find beneficial, we asked survey participants to respond to an open-ended question asking about the types of workplace supports that they wished their employer offered. A total of 424 individuals (out of 618) responded. Of those who responded, 121 indicated that they were satisfied with their current benefits. Thus, a total of 303 individuals provided some information on the types of supports that they wished their employers provided. Child-care benefits, such as subsidized child care and after-school programs, were the most frequently cited (i.e., 70 respondents), followed by medical insurance (41 respondents), flexible work hours (36), and paid sick time and paid personal time off (35 and 36 respondents, respectively). Another 29 respondents indicated that they would like to have some retirement plan, 401K, or early retirement program, and 17 respondents indicated that they would like for their employer to allow them to work at home/telecommute. Still others indicated they would like for their employer to provide exercise/fitness benefits (14), mental health benefits (13), dental insurance (11), and eye care insurance (6). Additional comments were provided by 5 or fewer respondents each and ranged from the provision of financial planning to the provision of health insurance after retirement.

The findings on need, availability, and use of child care supports are particularly interesting, as such supports appear to be both desired and available, but not used, while other supports are desired but not available. Our data reflect trends at the national level and indicate that there is an unmet need for the provision of basic necessities such as subsidized child care, medical insurance, and paid/personal time off to care for a family member.

THE EFFECTS OF UTILIZATION OF WORKPLACE SUPPORTS ON WORK–FAMILY FIT, WELL-BEING, AND WORK: MULTIVARIATE ANALYSES

Creating Composite Measures of Workplace Supports

To summarize the data regarding availability and use of workplace supports and to create measures that could be used in the multivariate analyses, we grouped the 13 supports into the two categories most consistently examined in prior research: (a) alternative work arrangements, measured with 3 items, and (b) dependent-care supports, measured with 10 items. Utilization scale scores were computed as the mean number of supports available and used in each of the two categories (see Table 9.3 in Appendix C). Consistent with the more detailed findings reported above, these composite measures indicate that wives reported using alternative work schedules more than did husbands. Wives also reported greater availability of alternative work schedules and dependent-care supports at their place of work more than did husbands.

Similar to the approach we used in the previous chapter concerning the effects of coping strategies, we wished to examine the effects of workplace supports on work–family fit, well-being, and work over and above those of respondents' personal characteristics and subjective role experiences (perceived role quality) in the spousal, child-care, parent-care, and job roles. This decision was based on the significant relationships we found between role quality and work–family fit, well-being, and work outcomes among working, sandwiched couples, as presented in chapter 6. This approach allows us to identify the effects of formal workplace supports after taking into account respondents' personal characteristics and role quality. Again, as before, we conducted separate analyses for husbands and wives. In the first step of each analysis, we entered the personal role characteristics (i.e., years of education, ability to get along on one's income, negative affectivity) and the role quality measures (spousal, child care, parent care, and job) as control variables. In the second step of the analyses, the two composite workplace supports measures were entered (i.e., alternative work schedules and dependent-care supports). Given that the relationships between role quality and the outcomes were examined in detail in chapter 6, we focus here only on the amount of variance accounted for by the utilization variables and their unique contributions to the outcomes. The results are summarized in Fig. 9.1. (See Tables 9.4–9.7 in Appendix C for details.)

Effects of Utilization of Workplace Supports on Work–Family Fit

With respect to work–family fit, utilization of workplace supports accounted for significant variance in work-to-family conflict for wives (4%) and in family-to-work conflict for both husbands (3%) and wives (4%) beyond that accounted for by the personal characteristics and role quality. For husbands, there was a positive relationship between use of alternative work schedules and family-to-work conflict. For wives, there were positive relationships between use of dependent-care supports and both types of work–family conflict.

Work–Family Fit

- Using alternative work schedules is related to higher family-to-work conflict for husbands.
- Using dependent-care supports is related to higher levels of both work-to-family and family-to-work conflict for wives.
- These findings are unexpected.

Well-Being

- Using alternative work schedules is related to higher life satisfaction for husbands.
- Using dependent-care supports is related to higher life satisfaction for wives, higher overall health for husbands, and higher overall role performance for wives.

Work Outcomes

- Use of alternative work schedules is related to increased absences and more work accommodations made in response to family care responsibilities for both husbands and wives.
- Use of dependent-care supports is related to more reports of poor work performance due to dependent-care responsibilities for wives.

Crossover Effects

- In general, there is a lack of crossover effects (from one spouse to the other) in use of workplace supports.

FIG. 9.1.   Use of workplace supports in relation to work–family fit, well-being, and work: results of multivariate analyses.

These somewhat counterintuitive findings suggest that utilization of workplace supports allows sandwiched couples to reallocate or take on more family and work-related responsibilities, thus leading to increased, as opposed to decreased, work–family conflict. It is possible that use of alternative work schedules frees up time that then is filled with additional work or family responsibilities. Thus, the net effect is either no change, or even increases in role responsibilities, leading to negative effects on such outcomes as work–family conflict.

Effects of Utilization of Workplace Supports on Well-Being

The utilization of supports accounted for a significant amount of variance, above and beyond the personal characteristics and role quality variables, in two of the well-being outcomes, and only for husbands. Specifically, 3% of the variance in husbands' overall health and overall role performance was accounted for by the two types of supports as a group. Use of supports did not contribute significantly to the variance explained in any of the well-being outcomes for wives.

Unlike the findings with respect to work–family fit, the relationships for husbands were in the expected direction. Specifically, for husbands, utilization of alternative work schedules was positively related to life satisfaction, and utilization of dependent-care supports was positively related to overall health and overall role performance. For wives, use of dependent-care supports was also related to higher life satisfaction (even though the utilization measures as a whole did not explain a significant amount of unique variance in this outcome). Therefore, it appears that utilization of workplace supports, and especially use of dependent-care supports, has beneficial effects on well-being. These are important findings, as little previous research exists on the benefits of workplace supports for general well-being.

Effects of Utilization of Workplace Supports on Work

Finally, beyond the variance accounted for by the personal characteristics and role quality, utilization of supports accounted for a significant amount of variance in two of the work outcomes for husbands and three for wives. Specifically, for husbands, use of supports contributed an additional 3% to the variance explained in overall absence and 2% of the variance in number of work accommodations, whereas for wives, use of supports accounted for a an additional 10% of the variance in overall absence, 3% of that in the number of work accommodations made, and 3% of that in poor work performance due to dependent-care responsibilities.

For both husbands and wives, use of alternative work schedules was related to higher, not lower, levels of absence and higher numbers of work accommodations made in response to family responsibilities. In addition, higher levels of use of dependent-care supports for wives were related to higher levels of absence reported and more reports of poor work performance. These findings are similar to those concerning work–family fit and suggest that the sandwiched individuals who are making use of workplace supports are having a difficult time managing work and family (e.g., Boise & Neal, 1996), as manifested here in their work outcomes, and that use of supports alone is not sufficient to minimize absence from work due to dependent-care responsibilities. These findings are also consistent with those of Ingersoll-Dayton, Chapman, and Neal (1990), who studied the effects of use of workplace seminars on elder care. They determined that absenteeism increased, not decreased, after attendance at the seminars, perhaps because participants had learned about community services that could be accessed only during the day, when most participants were working.

Summary of the Effects of Use of Workplace Supports on Work–Family Fit, Well-Being, and Work

It is interesting that our findings reveal that although use of supports, both alternative work schedules and dependent-care supports, has beneficial effects on some well-being outcomes, the effects of these supports on work–family fit and work outcomes are not as expected. Specifically, we found that the utilization of supports was related to higher levels of work–family conflict and higher levels of absenteeism. As explained earlier, we believe that for these sandwiched couples, the ability to make use of workplace supports enables them to redistribute and possibly take on more work and family demands, sometimes leading to more conflict and absenteeism, but also improving well-being, at least in the form of overall life satisfaction. Thus, the ultimate effectiveness of utilization of supports depends on the type of outcome examined.

USE OF FORMAL VERSUS INFORMAL SUPPORTS AND THE EFFECTS ON WORK–FAMILY FIT, WELL-BEING, AND WORK

To explore the contributions of informal support (work–family culture) beyond those of use of formal supports in explaining the outcomes, we conducted additional follow-up analyses. Specifically, we examined the effects of individuals' reports of the organization's responsiveness to employees' need to take time off for planned family responsibilities, over and above the effects of utilization of workplace supports, on work–family fit, well-being, and work. We selected this organizational responsiveness variable as a proxy for organizational work–family culture.

The findings of these analyses revealed that, for husbands, greater perceived organizational responsiveness to planned family responsibilities was associated with less experience of work-to-family conflict. In addition, there was a positive relationship between an organization's responsiveness to planned family responsibilities and overall role performance for wives; however, there also was a positive relationship with absence behaviors. Thus, we found some, but limited, support for the idea that work–family culture is more important in influencing work and family outcomes than the actual utilization of formal supports. This issue clearly merits examination in future research, especially in light of our findings concerning the potential negative effects of utilization of workplace supports on work–family fit and work.

WITHIN-COUPLE EFFECTS: THE CROSSOVER EFFECTS OF UTILIZATION OF WORKPLACE SUPPORTS

We also were interested in the effects of one partner's use of workplace supports on the other partner's work–family fit, well-being, and work outcomes, given the family systems perspective that guided our research. Thus, we examined the impact of a spouse's use of workplace supports on his or her partner's outcomes, over and above the effects of the partner's personal characteristics and role quality.

We found only one significant relationship, and that was between one spouse's use of supports and the other's well-being—in particular, the other's overall role performance. Specifically, wives' use of dependent-care supports was related to lower overall role performance reported by husbands. The two composite workplace support variables as a group, however, did not account for a significant amount of variance in husbands' overall role performance.

The relative lack of crossover effects is surprising, given the perspective offered by systems theory, in which the couple is seen a unit, with each member's behaviors and attitudes affecting the other's. It is possible that given the magnitude and complexity of their work and family responsibilities, working, sandwiched couples may not see themselves as being able to interconnect with one another to the same degree to which other couples are able and thus may not benefit from each other's use of workplace supports.

Another explanation is based on information from both our focus group and survey participants, who reported that one strategy they use for managing their work and family responsibilities is to work opposite shifts (see chap. 7). It is possible that use of such a strategy lessens the ability of individuals' own use of workplace supports to have a beneficial impact on their spouses' work–family fit, well-being, and work outcomes. Hence, individuals within our sandwiched couples may be more likely to operate and manage independently of one another, given their multiple work and family demands.

SUMMARY

In this chapter, we provided national-level data on the utilization and availability of workplace supports. To our knowledge, the only other national data available to this extent are those provided by the Families and Work Institute, based on its 1998 Business Work-Life survey and its 2005 National Study of Employers, as well as its National Study of the Changing Workforce (Bond et al., 2003). This information is useful from a policy standpoint, as it not only demonstrates levels of workplace support availability, as reported by our respondents, but also provides information about utilization rates. Further, we outlined a number of possible reasons why supports are not more available or utilized more by employees. These findings have implications for both organizational and government policymakers.

Implications for Employers and Government Policymakers

First, the results of our study and its focus on utilization and availability of workplace supports suggest that there are things employers can do to help improve employee awareness of and utilization of workplace supports. Specifically, we know that the work–family culture may influence an individual's decision to use a support. Enhancing an organization's work–family culture may create an atmosphere that is more conducive to employees making use of workplace supports, which may ultimately have beneficial affects on employee health and well-being. Clearly, if employee health is improved, this could lead to a reduction in employer health care costs, which will in turn have beneficial effects on organizations' bottom lines. In addition, ways of improving the family-friendliness of organizations may prove useful, such as through developing and implementing supervisory training programs focused around being sensitive to employees' work and family responsibilities.

Second, we also suggest that employers clearly publicize their existing supports to enable the maximum number of employees to use the necessary supports. Our findings, as well as those of others (Rosin & Korabik, 2002), show that women are more likely than men to use workplace supports. One solution is to better market these supports to male employees. In addition, it is important to address the organizational barriers to the use of workplace supports by employees, and by men in particular, such as those outlined in chapter 2.

Third, we argue that although the provision of family leave is important, it tends to be *unpaid* and thus not frequently used. We suggest that this issue be considered at the federal level, as many employees in the United States are unable to afford to take advantage of family leave that is not associated with pay. We also encourage employers to consider ways of making paid leave available to employees.

Our findings concerning the effects of use of workplace supports on work–family conflict were unexpected, as they demonstrated positive, not negative, relationships with work–family conflict. In particular, we found that as utilization of supports increases, so does work–family conflict. We argue that this is not a reason for employers to forego providing workplace supports, however; instead, it points to the complexity of the work and family system. Because wives are still considered the traditional care-givers, despite their participation in the workforce, it is possible that when given the opportunity to relieve work–family stress through the use of family-friendly workplaces supports, wives in particular are more likely to take on even more family-care responsibilities. Thus, the net result is an increase, as opposed to a decrease, in work–family conflict.

In results presented elsewhere (Hammer, Neal, Newsom, Brockwood, & Colton, 2005b), these data were examined longitudinally, and similar re-sults were found: Utilization of supports at Wave 1 predicted higher levels of work–family conflict at Wave 2 (specifically, family-to-work conflict). Of interest, however, is that wives and husbands alike reported higher lev-els of job satisfaction associated with utilization of supports over time. Thus, although the use of supports may not be beneficial to wives in terms of work–family conflict, it is beneficial to both wives and husbands in terms of job satisfaction, which in turn is related to a number of other im-portant outcomes, such as organizational commitment and thus, potentially, job performance.

In sum, these findings indicate that the provision of formal workplace supports alone is not sufficient to minimize negative outcomes that may be associated with attempting to integrate work and multiple family care-giving roles. Thus, we suggest that employers consider other ways of re-ducing work–family conflict. One such way is to develop a more family-friendly workplace culture within their companies, where work–family is-sues are valued and where everyone, from top management to the first-line supervisors, is socialized to be sensitive and supportive of employees' work and family responsibilities.

The relationships found between utilization of workplace supports and the well-being outcomes were more consistent with our expectations. We found use of supports to be positively related to overall health and overall role performance for husbands. Use of workplace supports, as a whole, however, did not account for significant incremental variance in any of the well-being outcomes for wives.

Similar to the effects for work–family fit, we found unexpected relation-ships between utilization of workplace supports and a number of the neg-ative work outcomes (i.e., absence, number of workplace accommodations used, and poor work performance (the last for wives only). A possible ex-planation for these nonintuitive findings is that use of supports is not as important in influencing these work–family conflict and work outcomes as are perceptions of the extent to which one's organization's culture is family friendly (e.g., Allen, 2001; Sahibzada et al., 2005; C. A. Thompson et al, 1999). The follow-up analyses that we conducted provided some support for this idea and suggest that ways of improving the family-friendliness of organizations may prove useful and thus should be considered by organizations.

Implications for Research

As we found in our follow-up analyses, there was support for the idea that work–family culture is more important than formal workplace supports in influencing work–family fit, well-being, and work outcomes. This issue needs to be addressed in future research, especially in light of our findings concerning the potential negative effects of utilization of workplace supports on work–family fit and work outcomes.

We encourage organizations to focus on ways to improve their informal work–family culture, as our findings reveal the importance of both formal and informal supports for assisting workers in their efforts to integrate their work and family lives.

10

Changes in Work and Family Roles and Outcomes Over Time

I am now separated which has hurt my kids, in return it hurts me to see them sad. I also spend more time with my mother, she's in the final stages of emphysema that has also taken it's toll on me. This is why I am so late getting this back to you. I work, take care of my mother, and my youngest is 4 years old.

I have taken on 2 part-time jobs because I am more comfortable having my bills paid off and providing my children with the opportunity to get a 4-year college degree. I am very grateful we both have parents who are still living. I don't feel we are missing out on anything by helping both our parents and children. Instead, we stay connected and gain valuable insights, into each others' lives.

Improvements in one area are compensated by setbacks in others—zero sum game ... I now know the meaning of "lives of quiet desperation."

To this point in the book, the findings we have presented have been derived primarily from the data gathered through the first survey that was completed by both members of the 309 dual-earner, sandwiched couples who comprised our national sample. Thus, the results have been cross-sectional in nature, as has been the bulk of work–family research to date. These cross-sectional data allowed us to highlight the characteristics of this population and describe the relationships between these characteristics and the outcomes in a straightforward way. However, the cross-sectional analyses have not allowed us to consider the changes, objective and subjective, that occur over time in work and family roles and the effects of those changes on work–family fit, well-being, and work (Eby, Casper, Lockwood, Bordeaux, & Brinley, 2005).

In this chapter, we use our longitudinal data, gathered through two surveys administered 1 year apart, to examine the shifts in objective and subjective role characteristics that occur over the course of a year among working couples caring for children and aging parents. We also analyze the effects of those shifts on changes in work–family fit, well-being, and work outcomes over the 1-year time period. Because data from two time points are required in order to assess change, we use only the data from the 234 couples (468 individuals; 76% of the original 309 couples) who returned both the first (Wave 1) and second (Wave 2) surveys.

In this chapter, then, we ask two key questions. First, what changes in role demands and role quality occurred in the year between the two surveys? Second, how did those changes affect the outcomes of interest in this study, including work–family fit, well-being, and work-related outcomes?

To address the first question, we examine the changes that occurred in key characteristics of the roles of spouse, parent to dependent children (the child-care role); caregiver to aging parent or parents (the parent-care role), and worker. We examine the same variables as were included in chapter 6 in describing the cross-sectional relationships between the role characteristics (objective role demands and subjective role quality) and the outcomes.

In particular, we examine change in role characteristics in three different ways. First, we investigate the extent to which the couples in our study continued even to occupy each of the four roles of interest—that is, spouse or partner, caregiver to a child aged 18 or younger, caregiver to an aging parent, and worker—1 year after administration of the first survey. Second, we compare the means, or average values, for the objective and subjective role characteristics, and also the outcomes, at Waves 1 and Wave 2. These descriptive analyses allow us to determine the average level of change that occurred. Third, because examining only the average changes that occur in roles tends to obscure the nature of individual variability, we also consider the distribution of the objective role changes, in particular, by depicting the percentages of husbands and wives who experienced an increase in the selected role demands, those who experienced a decrease, and those who experienced no change in these demands. This presents a more dynamic picture of the changes in work and family roles held by the men and women in our sample.

To address the second question—that is, what the effects of these role changes were—we use hierarchical multiple regression to investigate the overall effects of changes in role demands and role quality on the outcomes and to learn specifically *which* role changes, objective and/or subjective, are the strongest predictors of changes in the outcomes over time. As in previous chapters, the outcomes we examine include changes in work–family fit (i.e., work-to-family and family-to-work conflict and work-to-family and family-to-work positive spillover), well-being (i.e., depression, life satisfaction, overall health, and overall role performance), and work (i.e., job satisfaction, overall absence, number of accommodations made at work, and poor work performance).

Finally, to better understand the changes that occurred in roles, and the effects of these changes on the outcomes experienced by dual-earner couples caring for children and aging parents, we examined respondents' responses to two open-ended questions at the end of the survey. These questions asked respondents (a) whether they felt their work–family situations had stayed the same, improved, or worsened, and why, and (b) how they felt they were handling their work and family situation as compared to the previous year and why they felt this way.

CHANGES THAT OCCURRED IN THE OBJECTIVE AND SUBJECTIVE ROLE CHARACTERISTICS

Couples Who No Longer Were Dual-Earner Couples in the Sandwiched Generation: Findings Regarding Role Occupation

An important consideration in thinking about the changes in role demands that occurred in the year between the two surveys is the extent to which couples in the study remained "dual-earner couples in the sandwiched generation," as defined by our study criteria. At the time of the first survey (Wave 1), all couples in the sample had been married or partnered for at least 1 year and had children aged 18 or younger in their household. One or both members also were caring for an aging parent for a minimum of 3 hours per week, and both members were employed, with one member of the couple working 35 hours per week or more and the other working at least 20 hours per week. One year later, when the survey was again administered by mail (Wave 2), however, some couples no longer occupied these roles of spouse, parent, caregiver to an aging parent, and/or worker.

Specifically, with respect to occupation of the *child-care* or *parenting role*, in 9 of the 234 couples (about 4%), there were no longer any children aged 18 or younger living in the household.

Concerning occupation of the *parent-care or caregiver to an aging parent role*, 35 wives out of 234 (15%) and 37 husbands out of 234 (16%) were no longer helping any parents. In 22 of the 234 couples (9%), neither the husband nor the wife was providing parent care any longer. Reasons for loss of the parent-care role included that the parent had died, someone else was now providing care, the parent no longer needed help, or the respondent stopped providing care for some other reason.[1] It is also interesting to note that, on the basis of the age and gender of the parent listed as the one parent whom the respondent was helping the most, just under one quarter of husbands and wives appeared to be providing care for a different parent at Wave 2 than at Wave 1.

Occupation of the *work role*, and, specifically, being a dual-earner couple, was determined by the number of hours worked. At Wave 2, 22 of the 234 couples (9%) no longer met the study's criterion of one member working full time (35+ hours/week) and the other working at least half time (20+ hours/week). In 17 of these couples (7%), either the wife (9 couples) or the husband (8 couples) was no longer working at all, because of their dependent-care responsibilities (wives only) or for some other reason.[2,3]

Finally, to determine whether any couples no longer occupied the *spouse/partner role*, we jointly analyzed the responses to three questions asking whether the couple: (a) was still living together, (b) had experienced a separation or divorce in the previous year, and (c) had experienced a reconciliation or marriage in the previous year. The findings revealed indications of marital instability among 6 of the 234 couples (almost 3%) from whom we received Wave 2 surveys from both members of the couple.[4] In addition, among the additional nine Wave 2 surveys that were received from only one member of the couple (and thus were not included in any subsequent analyses, given our interest in couples), three respondents (the wife, in all cases) reported that the couple had separated or divorced. Thus, of the 243 couples from whom we received a completed Wave 2 survey from one or both members of the couple, at least 9 couples, or almost 4%, were reported by one or both members of the couple to be separated at

---

[1]Twenty-nine of the 35 wives provided reasons they were no longer caring for their parent, including the parent passed away ($n = 13$); someone else was providing care ($n = 4$); the parent no longer needed help ($n = 11$); or, in the case of one woman, "My father is alcoholic and has refused to associate with me." Similarly, 29 of the 37 husbands indicated reasons, including the parent passed away ($n = 13$), someone else was providing care ($n = 4$), or the parent no longer needed help ($n = 12$).

[2]The wives reported that they had quit their jobs specifically to care for children ($n = 4$); to care for children and parents ($n = 2$); or were not working for other, nonspecified reasons ($n = 3$). The husbands indicated that they had been laid off ($n = 3$); had retired ($n = 2$); or were not working for other, nonspecified reasons ($n = 3$). None of the husbands reported that they were no longer working because of dependent-care reasons. In only 1 of the 17 couples did the remaining member with a job work less than full time; in this couple, the wife worked 25 hours per week, and the husband had been laid off. In an additional 5 couples (2%), although the husband still worked full time, the wife now worked fewer than 20 hours per week.

[3]Although not a role per se, all couples continued, at Wave 2, to meet the income criterion of $40,000 or greater (according to at least one member of the couple), as set by the study's funder, the Alfred P. Sloan Foundation.

[4]Some respondents had missing data on one or more of the three questions, so their status could not be determined with certainty. Also, interestingly, some husbands' and wives' reports did not agree as to whether they had separated, reconciled, or even were currently living together.

the time of the Wave 2 survey or to have lived separately from one another at some point(s) over the course of the year. Moreover, as we describe later, several respondents, both husbands and wives, wrote comments at the end of their Wave 2 surveys indicating that they were experiencing problems in their relationship with their spouse.

Average Change and Proportional Increases and Decreases in Role Demands and Role Quality

In this section, we examine the average (mean) changes in roles, as well as in the outcomes, that occurred in the year between the two administrations of the mailed survey. For these and subsequent analyses, individuals no longer occupying a role received a score of 0 (e.g., for number of children or aging parents being cared for) or had missing data on certain characteristics (e.g., parent-care role quality if they were no longer caring for a parent).[5]

Specifically, we compared the means at Waves 1 and 2 for selected personal characteristics, role characteristics (objective and subjective), and the outcomes for husbands and wives, respectively (see Tables 10.1 and 10.2). Below, we describe the results of those analyses, indicating whether the amount of change between the two time points was significant from a statistical standpoint. We should note that such changes over time are susceptible to the phenomenon of regression toward the mean, with individuals at the extremes at the first time of measurement more likely to move toward moderate scores at the next measurement point (Allison, 1990; Lehman, 1991).

In addition, because the mean is not a good measure of central tendency when variables are not normally distributed (Downie & Heath, 1970; Schutt, 1996), we look at the distribution of the changes specifically with respect to the role demand and role quality measures. We do this by examining the proportions of individuals who experienced increases and decreases in role demands and role quality in the year between the two surveys (see Table 10.3). This enables us to gain a better understanding of the degree of variation between individuals with respect to change in work and family roles. The key findings from our analyses concerning the changes that occurred in role characteristics and outcomes are summarized in Fig. 10.1.

---

[5]Participants were instructed to respond to complete the child-care role quality measures at Wave 2 on the basis of either their youngest child (even if he or she was now over the age of 18) or their child with special needs. Respondents who were no longer providing parent care were instructed to skip the parent-care quality questions, but some respondents chose to answer anyway; their responses were retained, given the importance these respondents seemed to place on these items. In retrospect, we would ask all respondents except those whose parent had died to complete the parent-care role quality measures, as the relationship with the parent would continue to exist, despite the change in care arrangements.

Changes in Role Occupancy From Wave 1 to Wave 2

- In about 9% of the couples, one member had stopped working or had reduced his or her hours below half-time.
- About 4% of couples no longer had children ≤ 18.
- About 9% of couples were no longer providing parent care.
- About 4% became temporarily or permanently separated from his or her spouse or partner.

Changes in Role Demands From Wave 1 to Wave 2

- There were no increases, on average, in role demands over the course of the year.
- There were decreases, on average, in three of the six role demand measures: fewer numbers of children, fewer aging parents, fewer wives who reported having children with special needs in their household.

Changes in Role Quality From Wave 1 to Wave 2

- There was no difference in spousal, child-care, or job role quality for either husbands or wives.
- Parent-care role quality decreased significantly for wives but not for husbands.
- Scores for child-care role quality were the highest and those for job role quality the lowest for both husbands and wives.
- For all four roles, role quality remained positive (i.e., rewards continued to outweigh concerns) for both husbands and wives.

Changes in the Outcomes

- The patterns of changes in the outcomes between Waves 1 and 2 of the survey were similar for husbands and wives.
- Work-to-family and family-to-work conflict declined, on average, for wives and husbands, along with depression (for wives) and use of work accommodations (wives and husbands).
- Positive family-to-work spillover and life satisfaction also declined, on average, for both husbands and wives.
- Husbands' average level of overall health declined (wives' remained the same).
- There was no change in positive work-to-family spillover, overall role performance, job satisfaction, overall absence due to dependent-care responsibilities, or poor work performance for either husbands or wives.

Figure 10.1.   Average changes in role characteristics and outcomes among dual-earner couples caring for children and aging parents over the course of 1 year.

Changes in Personal Characteristics

With respect to the three personal characteristics variables, level of education was assessed only at Wave 1, so change in this variable could not be assessed. With regard to ability to get along on the household's income, husbands' ratings increased, on average, while wives' perceptions of their household's income adequacy did not change significantly. For both husbands and wives, the average levels of negative affectivity decreased significantly over the year.

Changes in Spousal Role Demands

Aside from reporting the number of couples who indicated separations or reconciliations over the year between the two surveys (see section titled "Average Change and Proportional Increases ..."), no other data existed pertaining to changes in objective role characteristics for the spousal role that could be hypothesized to positively or negatively affect the outcomes.[6] Also, because of the relatively small number of couples who experienced separations from their spouse or partner, and especially given the fluid nature of these separations over the 1-year period, we are able to report this aspect of spousal/partner role change only descriptively; we cannot examine the effects on work–family fit, well-being, and work. We will, however, examine change in spousal role quality, both descriptively and as a predictor of the outcomes.

Changes in Child-Care Role Demands

As shown in Tables 10.1 (husbands) and 10.2 (wives), in terms of child-care role demands, for both husbands and wives the average number of children aged 18 or under in the household decreased significantly in the year between the two surveys. This was due to such factors as children leaving home to go to college, live independently, or live with another parent. Also, significantly fewer wives (but not husbands) reported having a child with special needs than reported this in the first survey. With respect to the distributions of responses (see Table 10.3), only a few wives (about 3%) and husbands (about 1%) reported a greater number of children aged 18 or under living in the home at Wave 2 than at Wave 1. More common were decreased numbers of minor children (16% of husbands

---

[6]For example, there would not have been enough variability in change in the number of years together, given the small number of couples who appeared to have permanently separated over the course of the year, to detect a change in the outcomes, and all other couples would simply have been together 1 year longer. Similarly, there would have been no variability in change in whether each member of the couple had been married previously.

and 15% of wives). About 5% of husbands and 6% of wives reported having fewer children with special needs, compared with less than 3% of husbands and just over 1% of wives who reported an increased number of children with special needs.[7]

Changes in Parent-Care Role Demands

With respect to parent care, the average number of parents being helped decreased significantly over the year both for husbands (from about 1.7 to 1.3) and wives (from about 1.8 to 1.3; see Tables 10.1 and 10.2, respectively). The number of personal and instrumental activities of daily living with which respondents assisted the parent they were helping the most, however, increased somewhat, on average, for husbands (from 1.6 to 2.0) and wives (from 2.5 from 2.6), although neither increase was statistically significant.

With respect to the distributions of responses (see Table 10.3), for both wives and husbands, decreased role demands were reported more frequently than were increased demands. Specifically, number of parents being helped dropped for about 36% of husbands and 39% of wives, while increasing for about 10% of husbands and 6% of wives. At the same time, the number of activities of daily living with which the respondent helped the parent for whom he or she was providing the most care increased for about 30% of husbands and wives, while falling for about 32% of wives and 28% of husbands.[8]

Changes in Work Role Demands

In terms of the work role, the average number of hours worked per week did not change significantly for either husbands or wives, remaining at about 49 hours for husbands and 38 for wives (see Tables 10.1 and 10.2). Similarly, no significant changes in flexibility in work schedule to handle family responsibilities occurred, on average, for either husbands or wives.

With respect to the distribution of responses (see Table 10.3), the number of hours worked per week decreased for about 33% of husbands and

---

[7]Although not shown in Table 10.3, and not included in the multivariate analyses for the sake of consistency with earlier analyses, it is interesting to note the change in level of responsibility reported for children among husbands and wives. Specifically, more wives reported a lower level of child-care responsibility (15%), rather than a higher level of responsibility (8%) in Wave 2 than they had in Wave 1, but this was not the case for husbands. Instead, about 20% of husbands reported a higher level of responsibility for the care of their children in Wave 2 than in Wave 1, compared with the 12% who reported a lower level of responsibility in Wave 2 than in Wave 1.

[8]Similarly, although not shown in Table 10.3, the total number of weekly hours of parent care fell for about 61% of wives and 52% of husbands and increased for 31% of wives and for 33% of husbands.

increased for about 27%. Among wives, about 30% worked fewer hours per week than they had in the previous year, with 29% working more. Flexibility in the work schedule to handle family responsibilities increased for 19% of husbands and decreased for 22%, whereas about 21% of wives reported an increased level of work schedule flexibility, and almost 20% reported decreased flexibility.

Changes in Role Quality

With respect to *spousal role quality,* the findings reveal that there was no statistically significant change between Wave 1 and Wave 2 for either husbands or wives (see Tables 10.1 and 10.2). Spousal role quality remained positive (i.e., rewards continued to outweigh concerns). In terms of the proportions of husbands and wives who experienced increases and decreases in spousal role quality (see Table 10.3), about 49% of both husbands and wives experienced a decrease in spousal role quality, while 42% of husbands and 44% of wives experienced an increase.

Child-care role quality also remained stable, and positive, for both husbands and wives, with no significant change in mean role quality between the two waves of the survey (see Tables 10.1 and 10.2). Approximately equal percentages of husbands had increases (48%) and decreases (49%) in child-care role quality (see Table 10.3). Among wives, child-care role quality decreased for 53% and increased for 44% (nonetheless, the difference in mean levels at Waves 1 and 2, as noted earlier, was not statistically significant).

For wives, there was a small but statistically significant decline in *parent-care role quality,* although it remained positive (with rewards outweighing concerns). There was no change for husbands (see Tables 10.1 and 10.2). Proportionately, parent-care role quality declined for more wives (about 50%) and husbands (44%) than it increased (for about 36% of wives and 39% of husbands), although the mean difference was statistically significant only for wives, as reported earlier.

Job role quality was stable for both husbands and wives (see Tables 10.1 and 10.2). About 49% of husbands and 47% of wives experienced increased job role quality, while 46% of husbands and 48% of wives experienced decreased job role quality (see Table 10.3 in Appendix C).

Changes in the Outcomes

We turn now to the average changes that occurred in the outcomes between the two surveys. With respect to the four measures of *work–family fit,* for both husbands and wives there were significant decreases in the mean levels of both work-to-family and family-to-work conflict. Positive family-to-work spillover, however, also decreased significantly, on average, over the year between the surveys, for both husbands and wives. Positive work-to-family spillover did not change over time for either husbands or wives.

On the four measures of *well-being*, both husbands and wives experienced significant drops in life satisfaction, on average, over the course of the year. Husbands also experienced a decrease in overall health. On a positive note, wives experienced significantly lower average levels of depression at Wave 2 compared with Wave 1, and husbands' scores declined slightly as well, but the difference was not statistically significant. Neither husbands' nor wives' reports of poor work performance due to concerns about children or aging parents differed significantly between the two surveys.

For the four *work-related outcomes* we examined, there were significant changes between the two waves of the survey in only one of the outcomes. Overall levels of job satisfaction did not change significantly for either husbands or wives, nor did those of overall absence due to dependent-care responsibilities or poor work performance due to child- and/or parent-care concerns. Both husbands and wives did report making fewer work accommodations due to child- and/or parent-care duties at Wave 2 than at Wave 1 in the month preceding the survey. This latter finding is consistent with the couples' reduced dependent-care responsibilities, because, on average, they were caring for fewer children and parents. A summary of the changes that occurred in role occupation and the average changes in objective and subjective role characteristics and outcomes are provided in Fig. 10.1.

THE EFFECTS OF CHANGES IN ROLE CHARACTERISTICS ON WORK–FAMILY FIT, WELL-BEING, AND WORK: RESULTS FROM THE MULTIVARIATE ANALYSES

To determine the effects of changes in role demands and quality on changes in work–family fit, well-being, and work, we conducted analyses separately for husbands and wives for each outcome, as in the previous multivariate analyses in this book. This allowed us to look at the patterns across the sets of outcomes and to compare those patterns for husbands and wives.

Consistent with our conceptual model, we examined the same objective and subjective role characteristics that were included in earlier chapters, such as chapter 6. For the multivariate analyses here, however, we needed to create the measures of change. To do this, for each of the objective role characteristics, subjective role quality measures, and outcome measures, we created "difference scores" (Rogosa & Willett, 1983) by subtracting the Wave 1 value from the Wave 2 value (i.e., Wave 2 – Wave 1; e.g., Shields, 2002). As a result, a positive score indicates that the Wave 2 survey value was higher than the Wave 1 survey value and thus that there was an increase in the objective role characteristic, subjective role quality, or outcome over the year between the two surveys. A negative score indicates that there was a decrease. Using these difference or *change* scores, after controlling for the outcome at Wave 1, allows us to examine the extent to which changes in work–family fit, well-being, or work are predicted by changes in role demands and/or role quality (Allison, 1990).

We then conducted hierarchical linear regression analyses, in which we entered sets of variables in blocks, or steps. In the first step of the analyses, as in analyses presented in previous chapters, we included the three personal characteristics, including years of education, perceived income adequacy, and negative affectivity (specifically, the baseline [Wave 1] values). In addition, we entered the Wave 1 value of the dependent variable for that particular analysis. Including the Wave 1 dependent variable provided the starting point for the absolute amount of change that occurred between the surveys (e.g., Shields, 2002). In this way, we could take into account whether a respondent began the study with a high level of depression, for example, or a low level.

In the second step of the analyses, we entered the changes in objective role characteristics (the difference scores), to determine what amount of variance in the outcomes they accounted for, beyond the control variables and Wave 1 value of the outcome variable. Finally, in the third step of the analyses, we entered the subjective role quality difference scores to determine the extent to which the subjective role characteristics explained any additional variance in the change in outcome measures.

We selected $p \leq .10$ as the criterion for statistical significance in the multivariate analyses because of the comparatively small sample size, the somewhat low internal consistency of some of our measures, and because of the difficulty of detecting significant effects in longitudinal analyses (Murphy & Myors, 2004). The findings and significance levels of all relationships are depicted in Tables 10.4 through 10.6 (see Appendix C).

Effects on Work–family Fit

Effects of Changes in Objective Role Characteristics on Work–family Fit

After controlling for years of education, ability to get along on one's household income, and negative affectivity at Wave 1, as well as the Wave

1 measure of the dependent variable (e.g., Wave 1 work-to-family conflict for the outcome "change in work-to-family conflict"), the objective role characteristics variables, as a group, significantly increased the amount of variance explained in only one of the four work–family fit outcomes (see Table 10.4). Specifically, we found that the objective role characteristics accounted for a significant additional amount of variance only in change in work-to-family conflict and only for wives, contributing an additional 8% over the variance explained by the control variables. This variance was contributed primarily by the objective role characteristic "change in number of hours worked." As might be expected, for both wives and husbands, working more hours at Wave 2 than at Wave 1 increased the amount of work-to-family conflict they experienced.

In addition, increased flexibility in work schedule was a significant predictor, for husbands, of increased positive spillover from family to work, although as a group the objective role characteristics variables did not add significantly to the variance explained in this outcome. Similarly, the two parent-care objective role characteristics variables predicted two different work–family fit outcomes, even though the objective role characteristics variables as a group did not add significantly to the variance explained in these outcomes. In particular, for wives, helping fewer parents was associated with greater family-to-work positive spillover over time. It is interesting that helping with more activities of daily living predicted a decrease in family-to-work conflict over time for husbands. One possible explanation for this counterintuitive finding is that perhaps doing more for one's parent than one was doing previously helps to ease one's mind, leading to less guilt and a reduction in the amount of family-to-work conflict that is felt.

Effects of Changes in Subjective Role Quality on Work–family Fit

The change in subjective role quality variables predicted three of the four work–family fit outcomes for either husbands or wives, accounting for an additional 1% (not significant) to 11% of the variance explained. Change in family-to-work conflict was the only work–family fit outcome that was not predicted by the role quality variables as a group for either husbands or wives.

Among the specific predictors, spousal role quality was a significant predictor for wives, but not for husbands. For wives, an increase in spousal role quality was associated with a decrease in work-to-family conflict, an increase in family-to-work positive spillover, and an increase in work-to-family positive spillover over time.

An increase in parent-care role quality predicted an increase in both types of positive spillover for wives. It also was associated with reduced family-to-work conflict for husbands over time.

An important predictor of the work–family fit outcomes was change in job role quality; specifically, an increase in job role quality was associated with a decrease in work-to-family conflict for both husbands and wives over time and with an increase in both types of positive spillover for wives. It also was a predictor of decreased family-to-work conflict for husbands over time.

Effects on Well-Being

Effects of Changes in Objective Role Characteristics on Well-Being

After inclusion of the Wave 1, or baseline, personal characteristics and the Wave 1 value of the well-being outcome of interest, the addition of the objective role characteristics variables as a block did not significantly increase the amount of variance explained in any of the well-being outcomes for either husbands or wives. Moreover, only one role demand variable predicted a change in any of the well-being outcomes, and this predictor was significant only at the $p \leq .10$ level. Specifically, helping an aging parent with more activities of daily living over time contributed to an increase in life satisfaction for wives.

Effects of Changes in Subjective Role Quality on Well-Being

As a group, it was the subjective role quality variables that contributed the most to change in well-being, beyond the personal characteristics and the respective Wave 1 dependent variables. This was true for three of the four well-being outcomes for wives and for one well-being outcome for husbands. Only change in overall health was not predicted by changes in role quality for either husbands or wives. In particular, an increase in spousal role quality predicted decreased depression and increased life satisfaction for wives and increased overall role performance for both husbands and wives. An increase in parent-care role quality, however, was the most important predictor of increased life satisfaction for wives and of increased overall role performance for husbands. In addition, an increase in child-care role quality predicted increased overall role performance for wives. Change in job role quality did not significantly affect the well-being outcomes

Effects on Work-Related Outcomes

Effects of Changes in Objective Role Characteristics on Work

The changes in role demand variables, as a group, contributed significantly to the variance in three of the four work-related outcomes over and above that explained by the baseline personal characteristics and the Wave 1 dependent variable. Specifically, for wives, helping a parent with an increased number of activities of daily living and working fewer hours predicted an increase in reports of poor work performance due to concern about children and/or aging parents.

The relationship between providing help with more activities of daily living and poor work performance is expected, given the likely time conflict between the two roles. The link between working fewer hours and increased reports of poor work performance is not quite as straightforward, but it may not be as strange as it might first appear. A possible explanation is that the increase in help provided to the parent required the adult child to decrease the number of hours worked, resulting in a perception of poorer performance at work than previously.

The amount of variance explained by the objective role characteristics variables was significant for two additional outcome variables: (a) overall absence from work due to dependent-care responsibilities, for wives, and (b) job satisfaction, for husbands. As a group, though, none of the individual role quality measures contributed significantly to the variance in job satisfaction. The predictors of increased overall absence from work were working more hours (for both wives and husbands) and an increase in work schedule flexibility (for wives).

It may be that working more hours required respondents to take time off from work to deal with their dependent-care responsibilities, and the additional flexibility in their work schedule actually enabled them to take this greater amount of time off. Alternatively, perhaps respondents needed to work more hours to compensate for the additional time that they had to take off from work to fulfill their responsibilities for children and aging parents.

In sum, the change in objective role characteristics variables, as a group, contributed a significant amount of additional variance in three of the four work-related outcomes for either husbands or wives. Three of the six objective role demand change variables—that is, working more hours, having greater work schedule flexibility, and helping an aging parent with more activities of daily living—significantly predicted decreased work performance and/or increased absence due to dependent-care responsibilities for wives. For husbands, working more hours was a significant predictor of increased absence from work due to dependent-care responsibilities.

Effects of Changes in Subjective Role Quality on Work

We turn now to the change in role quality variables. These contributed significantly to the amount of variance accounted for in two of the four work-related outcomes, above that explained by the baseline personal characteristics, Wave 1 dependent variables, and change in objective role characteristic variables: (a) change in job satisfaction and (b) poor work performance. Specifically, and not surprisingly, increased job satisfaction was predicted by an increase in job role quality for husbands and wives alike. In addition, for wives only, a decrease in child-care role quality also contributed to an increase in job satisfaction. One possible explanation for this latter finding is afforded by the notion of work as a respite from family, that is, that work can serve as a respite from dependent-care responsibilities, particularly when these responsibilities are especially stressful (e.g., Fredriksen-Goldsen & Scharlach, 2001; Hochschild, 1997).

The second outcome predicted by the subjective role quality variables was an increase in poor work performance due to concern about children or aging parents. As might be expected, an increase in poor work performance was predicted by a decrease in child-care role quality for both husbands and wives. Similarly, a decrease in parent-care role quality was a significant predictor of poorer work performance, but for husbands only. Poorer perceived work performance also was predicted, however, by an increase in spousal role quality for husbands and for wives. Perhaps husbands and wives were giving priority to their spousal relationship, over their job, during especially trying times with their children and/or their aging parents.

As a group, the change in role quality variables did not contribute significantly to any additional variance explained in use of work accommodations over time. Nonetheless, two of the variables, a change in spousal role quality and in parent-care role quality for husbands, and a change in child-care role quality for wives, were significant predictors of change in use of work accommodations. For husbands, it seems that when there was less support at home from their spouse, and/or when things got worse with their parent, they needed to make more accommodations at work. For wives, it seems that having a better relationship with their children led them to make more accommodations at work, possibly because of the greater salience of the child-care role for them than the work role.

A summary of the findings with respect to the predictors of changes in the three sets of outcomes is presented in Fig. 10.2.

Changes in Work–Family Fit

- Increased role quality is related to increased work–family fit.
- In general, change in subjective role quality, rather than change in objective role demands, results in improvement or decline in work–family fit.
- Job role quality is an important predictor of work–family fit for both husbands and wives, followed by parent-care role quality (for both) and spousal role quality (for wives only).

Changes in Well-Being

- Change in role quality, rather than in role demands, is most responsible for change in well-being.
- Changes in the quality of family roles, especially spouse and parent care, rather than the work role, are the most important predictors of change in well-being.

Changes in Work-Related Outcomes

- Changes in role quality, especially in the child-care and spousal roles, but also in the job and parent-care roles, are more consistent predictors of changes in the work-related outcomes than changes in role demands.
- The exceptions are:
    - Working more hours per week (for both husbands and wives) and greater flexibility in work schedule (for wives) predict increased overall absence due to dependent-care responsibilities; changes in role quality are not significant predictors of this outcome.
    - For wives, poorer work performance over time is predicted by providing increased help with activities of daily living to a parent and working fewer hours, along with lowered child-care role quality and an increase in spousal role quality.

Note. ADL = activities of daily living.

Figure 10.2.   Predictors of changes in work–family fit, well-being, and work over time.

IN THEIR OWN WORDS: RESPONDENTS' ASSESSMENTS OF CHANGE IN THEIR WORK AND FAMILY SITUATIONS

In a attempt to better understand the nature and effects of role transitions undergone by dual-earner couples in the sandwiched generation from their own perspective, at the end of the Wave 2 survey we asked respondents to think back to the previous year, at the time of the first survey, and indicate whether they felt their work–family situations had stayed the same, improved, or worsened. We then asked the reasons for their response. We also asked respondents how they felt they were handling their work and family situation compared with the previous year and why they felt this way.

Our results revealed that approximately equal proportions of husbands and wives felt their situations had changed for the better, for the worse, or stayed the same.[9] Among the 230 husbands who responded, 12% said their work–family situation had worsened, 50% said it had stayed the same, and 38% said it had improved. With respect to how they felt they were handling their situation, 5% felt they were handling it worse than previously, 66% felt they were handling it about the same as before, and 29% felt they were handling it better than in the previous year. Among the 231 wives who responded, 20% said their work–family situation had worsened, 41% said it had stayed the same, and 39% said it had improved. About 7% felt that they were handling their work and family situation worse than previously, 59% felt they were handling it about the same as before, and 34% felt they were handling it better than in the previous year.

The general categories of reasons offered for both improvements and decrements in the work and family situation, and also in how the respondent was handling the situation, were similar. They pertained to respondents' jobs or businesses, their children, aging parents, spouse, their own physical or mental health, and physical amenities. Typically, more than one reason was given, and reasons were interrelated. The findings are described below.

Improvements in the Work and Family Situation

Work-Related Reasons

A commonly cited work-related cause for improvement in the work and family situation included better pay or income. This was especially true for husbands but was mentioned by some wives as well. For example, one man stated "Our income has increased, easing the burden of financial responsibilities along with making some of our goals materialize." This man went on to note that "The job has given me better choices along with better pay." A woman wrote, "I have a better paying job," and another wrote that "I am not working full time, but the pay is better so we can do more." Other respondents, too, cited a job change as one of the reasons their work and family situation had improved, with a job being "better" because it was

---

[9]Paired-sample t tests between husbands' and wives' means revealed no statistically significant differences between the two groups' assessments of change in their work and family situation ($n = 227$; husbands' mean = 2.26, wives' mean = 2.19), $t(226) = 121$, $p = .23$, or in how they were handling their work and family situation compared to the previous year ($n = 226$; husbands' mean = 2.23, wives' mean = 2.27), $t(225) = 0.70$, $p = .48$, compared to the previous year (1 = worse, 2 = same, 3 = better).

more interesting or challenging or simply different (e.g., "I'm working in a new industry with a new company," "New job responsibilities providing more challenge," "I took a teaching job this year … [I'm doing] 'better' because it's fulfilling and because I have the most supportive husband ever").

Other respondents commented that their job situation was better because they now had more flexibility in work schedule or work place (e.g., "[I now] work from home so I can oversee [our] child at home," "I work full time flextime gratefully …"). Some noted that their new job was located closer to home (e.g., "new job, smaller commute, home more"), had less stress, was less physically demanding, or was with a "more stable company." Changing the shift one worked, generally to a day shift, led to improvements for some respondents (e.g., "I had been working the night shift and things at home were tense"; "Better job situation, now working 1st shift not 3rd"; "My spouse is home more now that she has a day job"). And some respondents noted that their situations had improved because they or their spouse had reduced their hours (e.g., "[I] reduced hours at work to allow more time at home") or had even quit a job. Exemplifying this latter reason and also demonstrating how multiple, interrelated reasons for improvement often were offered is the comment by a man who wrote: "My wife quit her stressful job and it has given us more quality time together. Plus I have an easier and less physically demanding job."

Additional work-related reasons for improvement included that business had improved (for small business owners), respondents had better support from their supervisor or coworkers, they had experienced better performance or advancement at work (e.g., "more accomplishments on my job," "work advancement"), or they had undergone a change in attitude regarding work (e.g., "Relating to work, [I] realize that I can't do everything and that the 'grass isn't always greener on the other side'").

Child-Related Reasons

Several respondents cited reasons for improvement that pertained to their children. These included a child's improved academic performance or attainment of academic goals (e.g., "My son is happier in school and doing great …," "Daughter graduated from college. Son graduated from high school"). The advantages of children who are a year older also were often cited as reasons for improved situations. These included children's maturity (e.g., "The kids are a bit more mature than last year—not always, but sometimes a parent gets that sustaining glimpse of maturity within a child that wasn't there before") and greater independence (e.g., "Children are more self-supporting, allowing us more time to spend on ourselves"). Also, respondents noted that older children were able to contribute more (e.g., "The kids are growing up and are helping us more," "[My] daughter got her license so she can help out") or even able to leave home (e.g., "Two children moved out, so the house is not so hectic)." One woman said she was handling her work and family situation better because "I am getting used to my son being away at college." Another said things were better for her even with having children who were still young, "Because I did not change jobs but I found a better daycare for my children."

Parent-Care-Related Reasons

Reasons for improvement in respondents' work and family situation often related to aging parents. Not surprisingly, these included improvement in the parent's health (e.g., "My dad's health has gotten a little better so I don't feel as needed [that's good]") and the respondent's having learned how to be a better caregiver. For example, one man noted "[I'm] learning to make decisions for my mother … that keep things on an even keel; how to care for her with good people who care; things [are] in control for now." A woman noted, "my mom has more help from other agencies; that takes the burden off me."

Other reasons were more bittersweet, however, and included the parent's move to a care facility or, for many, the parent's death. For example, one woman wrote:

> My spouse's mom has been placed in a nursing home—more difficult in some ways emotionally, plus physically he has been the main sibling cleaning out, sorting, emptying out his parent's home. It has been easier because he (and I) don't worry about her all the time and know that her quality of life has improved.

And a man wrote: "My mother became more seriously ill and [I] had to bring her into my home for almost a year. We finally, after Christmas, moved her to a rest home." Several others responded similarly (e.g., "Because my mother is now in a nursing home [less stress]"). A man whose parent had died wrote, "My father passed away after a long illness. [I'm] still very sad, but [I'm] not watching him suffer … I am able to begin spending time with my family (wife and children) that was spent with my dad." Others felt similarly: "Mother died; she was my primary parent that needed support," and "[My] father-in-law passed away. He took a lot more of my wife's time." A woman explained, "Last year at this time I was helping frequently with my father who was very ill and dying. I miss him very much … But the pressure is off, and my mom only needs some help even though we do help each other in so many ways." And another woman described her situation, which also had improved because of the death of her father, the end of his suffering, and her ability to get on with the rest of her life:

[Last year] my father, who lived 2 hours away ... was in and out of nursing homes, hospitals and living briefly at home with assistance. I drove up to visit or care for him at least one day of most weekends during that time ... Most of his last year he was extremely depressed which made visits and caregiving very stressful ... [Then] he was once again admitted to a nursing home where the depression was lifted with the proper dosage of medication. I am truly grateful for the care and concern for him at this facility because for the last 3 months of his life I was once again able to have the father I had loved for so many years ... After [his] death ... my brothers and I spent at least one day of most weekends [for months] cleaning out his house to prepare it for sale. For the first time in a year and a half I have been able to focus on my family and job and plan some activities that we all enjoy.

Finally, some respondents noted that their situations had improved because they had been able to overcome the grief they felt over the loss of their parent, who had died earlier in the year.

Spouse-Related Reasons

Several respondents cited reasons for improvement pertaining to their relationship with their spouse (e.g., "because of our bond"), or sometimes simply their "family." Husbands wrote, for example: "[My] spouse and myself are happier with each other. More caring, more giving. Not easily upset with each other. Better family situation"; "The family has gotten closer"; "[We] work as a team (family). Working towards [the] same goal"; and "[I] spend more time with family ... The family situation is perfect. No arguing with my wife and we work together on everything concerning family and finances." Sample comments from wives regarding why their situation had improved include "Relationship with spouse improved"; "[My] spouse is very supportive and this helps to cope with the load increase [parent more dependent]"; "Both of us went to marital counseling"; "We have been working with a counselor on marital problems"; and, starkly, the reverse, "Because my divorce is final."

Reasons Related to Personal Characteristics

Changes in personal characteristics played a key role in improvements in work and family situations, according to several respondents. Reasons included better physical and/or mental health on the part of the respondent and/or the spouse. For example, one man wrote, "[My] spouse and I have lost weight to a good condition but not too much") and another explained "[I am] on Prozac, high blood pressure pills—help to stabilize mood swings, stress, temper, etc." A woman wrote, "Grandmother is now in [a] nursing home. [My] diabetic father seems to be a little better. My diabetes [is] under control although [I'm] pregnant." Another woman wrote, "Last year, at this time, I was very depressed. Since [then], I've been hospitalized and on daily medication for depression which helps my overall outlook and availability to my family and spouse ... I was not functioning well at home or at work. This has changed drastically since last year." And a man wrote, "I became very ill this past year and while being down I had time to think about work and family."

Others, too, talked about changes in attitudes and in improved coping strategies and personal growth. This was especially true for women, but some men also cited these as reasons. For example, men wrote "Improved emotions"; "I've learned to become more tolerant and more appreciative of family and work situations and events ... I try and leave problems at work so they don't affect my family"; "[I] plan ahead better, wiser decisions, etc." Women wrote, for example, "I continue working towards 'balance'"; "[I've] been working on my spiritual life—can calm self down"; "[I] have been reading books on self-awareness and becoming more effective. Goal setting and reaching for dreams"; and "[I'm] working on my own stress level mostly through prayer. [I] talked to [my] husband about us working harder on our relationship and *both* of us being more considerate of each other ... [I'm] getting better at time management and prioritizing." Other respondents described their situations as being about the same as last year, rather than improved, but felt they were handling them better, such as one man, who said, "My wife's mother passed away and I have been traveling 40% of the time, but we have managed well in handling these events."

Financial and Other Reasons

Several respondents, especially men but also some women, cited an improvement in the family's financial situation. Although they sometimes related this to an increase in pay or salary, as noted above in the work-related reasons offered, this was not always the case. Sample comments include: "Have reduced debts by several thousand dollars"; "Bills are all paid off"; "Handling major college expenses; better off financially, i.e., less stress"). And some respondents indicated that their work and family situations had improved because of various physical amenities, such as acquisition of a new (generally bigger) home or a boat, "better lifestyle," and so on.

Worsened Work and Family Situations

With respect to the reasons offered for work and family situations that had worsened, these mirrored, in reverse, the reasons for improvement. Again, many respondents cited multiple reasons, such as "Job situation unstable, marital relationship growing more distant"; "Spending more time with parent. Financial difficulties"; and "Job more demanding—parent less competent and more miserable." Exemplifying the multiple demands and a situation that is worsening on many fronts are the following two women's comments:

> I've now taken on the responsibility of caring for a terminal (cancer) aunt … This leaves less time for the family and also my parents … I can't seem to find time to do anything for me. If I take 5 minutes for myself I feel guilty … My husband is last on the list for my time; next comes the kids, who are wanting more time. My parents get their time each week but first is the Aunt. When the job is factored in, "my" time is not practical. Everyone is to the point of hoping the Aunt dies very soon and at the same time realizing how much she was a very important part of our life. Guilt is felt by all but sometimes most by me who has lost control of deciding how to ration my own time.

> As my children grow older, their school projects and homework increases [sic]. Also, my children participate in many activities. I feel like I am overloaded with responsibilities. When my father broke off his relationship with me—it was a relief in one aspect because he was one less burden [I] had to bear. I feel like I don't always do a good job at home or at work. I also have two adult daughters—one who is married with two small children. My married daughter's life is in upheaval due to marital problems. I often have to watch her [young] children along with my usual responsibilities. My husband works constantly and is just not available to help very often.

Work-Related Reasons

In addition to the work-related comments above, problems with the U.S. economy were noted by some respondents. For example, one man wrote, "As a small business owner, times are slow." Also, some respondents cited problems with having been laid off and still out of work and looking for a job. Others described management and leadership problems. For example, one man said, "[We] had management problems at work that caused bad feelings all around." Another said his situation was worsened "due to being overworked and understaffed at work," and another wrote, "I have the boss who is a poor leader and doesn't like most [things] I do. I now have to work long hours to pay for our son's college." A woman noted, "Work demands have taken time away from family—added stress … having to work adds to stress and prevents important times from being what you want them to be."

Spouse-Related Reasons

Some respondents commented on their relationship with their spouse as a reason for their deteriorated work and family situation. Male respondents wrote, for example, "We almost separated a couple of months ago—things should be getting better!! ... Stressful days—wife works 8 hours—school 4 hours daily. Lonely," and "Events have happened at home to create a poor living condition (marital problems)."

The woman quoted at the beginning of this chapter wrote that she and her husband actually had separated. Another woman linked problems with her spouse to her parent-care situation, among other things, explaining:

> My relationship with my husband is changing due to my mother's illness and the fact that she has been living with us. I have also changed churches which displeases my spouse ... I try to make the best of every situation, but I feel that I do not get support, wholeheartedly, from my husband. I have always tried to do things with and for him and the children. I enjoy my spouse less and less.

Reasons Related to Parent Care

Other reasons for a deteriorated work and family situation dealt primarily with parent care, such as this man's description of his situation:

> My father's health has worsened. He is very hard to talk with. He doesn't want to take his medicine correctly. He is very hard headed. He doesn't let me do things that ought to be done. My father won't show me where his life insurance papers are or anything like that. I am his power of attorney, but he thinks when the time comes, I can find the thing and take care of it. I have no idea what his monthly bills are and where important financial items are (CD's, etc.). He causes a lot of grief because of his desires to keep his life so private.

Another noted that his situation had worsened because he had a "sick in-law living in [the] home." A woman wrote, "Mother's Alzheimer's is progressing and we're trying to plan future care (not living with us in [the] future)," and another said, "One parent has had a physical setback with his health, leaving me to totally take care of it all." Yet another woman cited both parent-care and child-related reasons: "[My] parent's health has dramatically changed—senile dementia, and it's hard to deal with. [My] daughter had an assault on her and this too [was] very stressful. Many ups and downs in one year."

One man asserted that his situation had stayed the same but his handling of it had worsened, explaining, "My father's physical and emotional state is continuing to decline. As an only child much falls upon me/my wife." And others said their situations had worsened because the parent had died and they were grieving the loss.

A final reason related to a worsened work and family situation concerned parent care as well but had specifically to do with the lack of involvement in siblings in the care of the parent(s). For example, one woman wrote, "[My mother] is [slowly] wasting away and at times I wish God would just take her and save me the pain of watching her in her helplessness. Also [I] have lots of anger toward my siblings who do little to nothing to help." Another woman volunteered:

> The major stressor I have experienced is the lack of support in the care of my mother by my brother. I have spent a lot of time keeping him informed over the last year and have been frustrated and ultimately embittered by his lack of response(s). In addition, this has been the major issue encountered by 3 close girlfriends in the case of their parents(s). This stress gets compounded by the "prodigal son" phenomenon of my mother. [I] spend a lot of time with supportive friends in similar situation talking about "how did you get your brother(s) involved." One friend actually wrote a 5 page script to talk to her brother. [I'm] not sure if it's gender-based—or generational—low expectations of sons, high of daughters. Finally, the insistence of my mother that "we are all such a close knit family" is frustrating. Difference in parent care levels/expectations. Although my husband never says anything, I feel guilty.

Child-Related Reasons

Several respondents cited child-related issues. Women noted difficulties with "babysitting availability" and the cost of preschool. A man wrote: "We had twin boys two months ago. Many of the answers on this survey reflect a snapshot in time of a very rapidly changing atmosphere of joy, stress and love. Things are presently tough, but getting better rapidly." Although children's getting older often was cited as a reason for improvement, some respondents noted difficulties with this too, both due to the increase in homework and number of activities, as noted earlier, but also due to adolescence:

> Both stepsons are adolescents. They have been around less and don't want/need us involved as much. The youngest tends to be moody and uncommunicative at times. The oldest stepson is driving. He has already had 2 accidents and a speeding ticket. These are areas that cause stress between my husband and I.

> My daughter takes up a lot of my time and emotional energy. She puts tremendous pressure on herself and therefore on us. I hear this is normal for teenage girls these days. I do understand it. I tend to be overprotective so I'm pretty much in her face all the time. In a year she'll be off to college and then the answer to your question will probably change. But I'm not sure better or worse will apply, maybe just different.

> My 18-year-old son has rebelled against my spouse [wife] and I and moved out. In his high school senior year he went from being in honor society to barely getting passing grades. He has admitted to smoking marijuana and cigarettes ... Most of the frustrations and disappointments that

occurred in my family life this past year pertain to my older son. I have often felt helpless to affect his behavior.

Both child-care and parent-care concerns contributed to a deteriorated situation for some respondents. For example, a husband wrote that his situation had worsened because "The problems with my older children from my first marriage have become much worse. My mother-in-law now lives with us." He went on to say that he also was handling the situation worse because "I am much more upset with my older children and I am having trouble focusing on work."

Personal Characteristics and Other Reasons

Personal physical and mental health issues contributed to worsening situations for some (e.g., "[I] had a fall off a building and was seriously injured and [am] still recovering at work"; "I have grown older and tired of [the] same routine"). Another comment included a combination of reasons addressing financial, personal and child mental health issues: "Financial strain has increased. My depression hasn't improved as much as I would like. My oldest daughter (away at college) is having problems with depression … Overall, things seem worse. Counseling and anti-depression meds don't seem to be helping as much as I had hoped."

Work and Family Situations That Stayed About the Same

Reasons offered for the work and family situation staying the same were simple, for example, "No major changes in my life"; "Things haven't improved"; or "Same job and same family, different day and year." This last respondent noted that he was handling the situation about the same, as well, because "It's something you have to do, so I do it. I don't like to be a quitter or called a quitter."

Several respondents, however, felt that some things had become more difficult while others improved, making the situation, on balance, the same. Consistent with this phenomenon, except for the simple types of response noted above, in nearly all cases when the work and family situation was classified as "about the same," multiple reasons were cited.

For example, one husband stated that his spouse was working more, which was hard on the home life, but she also was earning more, which made things easier financially. Another wrote, "New problems and new opportunities ($) to deal with the problems." Another said, "Did not make a job change to keep somewhat more time for childcare vs. new job with 0 flexibility in schedule." Another wrote, "Work stayed the same. My wife lost her sister and father last year. We are adjusting to the loss." Another man said his situation was the same and explained, "My father died so it's a little better. I don't have to take care of him. [But] My wife and I think opposite about 90 [%] of time. I keep in shape, she doesn't."

One man stated that his work and family situation was "about the same" even though there had been an addition to the family: "Had a child one year ago but everything else stayed the same." Another man indicated that his ability to handle his work and family situation was "about the same" but expressed considerable conflict when explaining his response (i.e., "I'm handling [my] boss as best I can and my wife wishes I were home more"), and in additional comments he volunteered at the end of the survey that touched on several aspects of work and family life, including his parent-in-law's feelings of worthlessness, a poor supervisor at work, guilt over his mother's loneliness, and distress over his children's lack of appreciation of "how good we have made it for them." In contrast, a woman quoted at the beginning of this chapter indicated that she felt things had "stayed the same" but went on to write that she had "taken on 2 part-time jobs" to help pay her bills and save for her children to be able to attend college.

It is clear that for some respondents, "about the same" meant that their situations remained quite difficult. For example, one respondent who said his work–family situation had stayed the same stated that "[My] mother-in-law died last year at this time. My mother died last week. [My] oldest child moved away." Some respondents who said their situations had stayed the same attributed this to financial reasons, explaining, for example, "I don't feel I make enough money to make me happy (i.e., working car, money for travel)," "Financially no growth. Everything is routine," or "Stayed the same because I still work two jobs to make ends meet." Finally, and poignantly, another said his work and family situation and how he was handling it were "about the same" as the previous year because, as included among the quotes beginning this chapter, noting "Improvements in one area are compensated by setbacks in others—zero sum game … I now know the meaning of 'lives of quiet desperation.'"

SUMMARY

To examine the nature and effects of changes in role responsibilities and role quality that occurred over the course of 1 year in the lives of dual-earner, sandwiched-generation couples, we performed three sets of analyses. The findings with respect to the first two sets of analyses—that is, of change in role occupancy (i.e., whether couples continued to be dual-earner couples sandwiched between their work and care for children and aging parents 1 year after the first survey), and change in the degree of role demands and quality (i.e., the proportions of husbands and wives who experienced increases and decreases)—reveal the dynamic nature of work and family roles. Our findings demonstrate that, at the individual level, employees' family and work lives change, sometimes quite dramatically, over the course of just 1 year. Some individuals begin working more hours; others quit their jobs or cut back on their hours, voluntarily or because they are forced to. Some couples have children who leave home to go to college, to live on their own, or to live with their other parent; for some couples, this means that they become empty-nesters and no longer have any children living at home. A few couples acquire additional children, such as through birth, adoption, marriage and/or a change in a child's or stepchild's living arrangements with another parent. Some individuals' aging parents die; others' parents' health improves or someone else assumes responsibility for the parents' care, resulting in loss or reduction of the parent-care role. Still others take on additional parent-care responsibilities, for the same parent or parents as before, or for another parent for whom they had not been providing care a year earlier, or had not been providing as much care as they now are. A few couples divorce or separate, and some experience reconciliation, or even marry.

Our findings concerning the separation or even divorce among 4% of the couples in our study in the year between the two surveys are sobering, and they may well be an underestimate, given that we have no Wave 2 data for 66 of the original couples. The extent to which marital instability occurs more frequently for working, sandwiched couples than for couples without this configuration of work and family roles cannot be answered here, unfortunately, given our lack of a comparison group. Future research should explore this issue, taking care to obtain data from both members of each couple whenever possible, given the variations in husbands' and wives' reports, and gathering data at more than one additional time point and possibly at more frequent intervals than 1 year to best capture fluctuations.

On average, among our study participants, role responsibilities, or demands, tended to decrease or remain stable over the year, rather than increase. This is most likely due to the fact that only individuals who already had these multiple family and work responsibilities were included in the sample; thus, reductions in role demands over time would be expected overall, especially because some members of the sample would be expected to no longer occupy particular roles at all (e.g., due to children leaving home and/or parents dying). It would be interesting to compare those who no longer held the parent-care role with those who continued in the role; similarly, longitudinal research comparing couples who became empty-nesters with those who continued to have minor children living in their household would be useful, although the role of parent persists even after the child comes of age and/or is no longer living at home. To do such comparisons would require a larger sample than was afforded by the present study.

It is interesting that the findings from this study reveal that role quality remains fairly stable, on average, after 1 year. The exception may be parent-care role quality. In our study, for both husbands and wives, spousal role quality, child-care role quality, and job role quality did not change significantly in the year between the two surveys; parent-care role quality, however, decreased significantly for wives who continued to have parent-care responsibilities. This decrease may be due to fatigue resulting from having carried parent-care responsibilities for another year, or to strain placed on the relationship due to increased needs or expectations for help by the parent. Also, data on role quality generally were not available for respondents who no longer had parent-care duties, such as those whose parent had died.

Similarly, in a 1-year interval, work–family fit, well-being, and work-related outcomes appear to remain fairly stable or even to improve, on average, with a few exceptions. In our study, the working men and women caring for children and aging parents experienced no significant changes in many of the outcomes and, on the plus side, both husbands and wives had lower levels of work-to-family and family-to-work conflict, wives had lower levels of depression, and husbands were using fewer work accommodations at the time of the second survey compared to the first. These findings are consistent with the reduced role demands experienced, as described above.

The exceptions were that, on the downside, both husbands and wives reported less family-to-work positive spillover and lower levels of life satisfaction, and husbands reported poorer overall health at the time of the second survey. Over 1 year, then, for dual-earner, sandwiched couples, except for husbands' health, it appears that on average, negative outcomes become less bad, and positive outcomes become less good. Once again, this is probably due in part to the fact that we initially surveyed couples who already were actively engaged in each of these work and family roles. For those who continued to occupy all roles, after another year of bearing these multiple responsibilities, perhaps weariness set in, resulting in less positive outcomes. At the same time, these individuals became accustomed to and more skilled with managing their multiple role demands, thus reducing negative impacts. Regarding the loss of caregiving roles, our data show that this can be experienced as simultaneously positive and negative. For example, as noted by many of our respondents whose parent died, they felt both grief due to the death of the parent and relief because the parent was no longer suffering and/or because their caregiving role was now over. Similarly, respondents whose children went away to college, for example, had mixed feelings about their loss of daily parenting duties.

With respect to predicting changes over time in work–family fit, well-being, and work-related outcomes, the results from the multivariate analyses indicate that changes in subjective role quality exert additional influence over and above changes in objective role demands. Greater spousal role quality, in particular, has positive effects for wives, especially, in terms of improved work–family fit and greater well-being

Furthermore, increased job role quality is an important predictor of the work–family fit and the work-related outcomes, but not the well-being outcomes, and improved child-care role quality appears to have effects only on work-related outcomes. Improved parent-care role quality has effects on the work–family fit and the well-being outcomes, but less so on the work-related outcomes.

With respect to the changes in objective role characteristics (i.e., role demands) as significant predictors of the outcomes, only changes in work role demands predict the work–family fit outcomes, and only changes in work role demands and parent-care role demands predict the work-related outcomes. As a group, changes in role demands have little effect on well-being. One explanation for this relative failure of the objective role characteristics to predict change in the outcomes may be the relatively small amounts of change, on average, that occurred between Wave 1 and Wave 2 in some of the characteristics and the outcomes. The optimal time frame for assessing change in these variables is not known. A longer time frame in between data collection points might yield more significant results of this nature. Alternatively, a shorter time frame might be more sensitive to the effects of role demand changes, in particular.

A second explanation concerns three interrelated issues: (a) the very complicated nature of family caregiving roles, (b) the difficulties associated with measuring "increases" and "decreases" in these roles, and (c) the potential interactions among roles (e.g., spouse, parent, caregiver to aging parent, job). For example, an employed adult daughter who is also a wife and a mother may be caring for her aging mother and father. Over the course of the year, the father dies. On the one hand, this may represent a decrease in role responsibility, as she now has one less parent to care for. On the other hand, her remaining parent may need more attention, which may or may not involve additional hours spent in caregiving but which may very well weigh heavily on the daughter's mind as she anticipates the future. At the same time, she is grieving the loss of her father. She may also have had a child leave home to attend college (and be feeling loss and/or glee). The quality of her relationship with her spouse may have changed for the better or the worse; similarly, her work situation and/or job role quality may have changed. On the basis of our findings, we would expect that this woman's perceptions of the quality of her roles would be the most important predictors of increased or decreased work–family fit, well-being, and work outcomes, outweighing the objective role demand characteristics of a reduced number of parents and children under her care.

Implications for Working, Sandwiched Couples

Several implications of the findings emerge from these analyses that have specific relevance for working couples caring for children and aging parents. Most important, from the standpoint of what working, sandwiched couples can do themselves to enhance their work and well-being, our findings clearly point to the importance of paying careful attention to one's role as spouse and striving to preserve and enhance one's marital relationship. As described in chapter 8, one strategy that is commonly used to cope with the multiple demands of work and family involves cutting back on time for oneself, one's spouse, and one's friends. In fact, our findings reveal that working, sandwiched couples may be at risk for marital instability. The cross-sectional findings presented in chapter 6 and the longitudinal findings described here point to the importance of preserving—and, indeed, working to enhance—one's relationship with one's spouse.

Implications for Employers

Managers, human resource professionals, business owners, and other organizational policymakers also should take note of the importance of spousal role quality to employees, as it has implications not only for increased personal well-being of employees but also for decreased levels of work–family conflict and positive work–family spillover. A possible way in which these employers can help employees improve their spousal role quality is to provide educational seminars and counseling emphasizing the value of a solid marital relationship, strategies for improving communication between spouses, and helping spouses to find ways to spend more time together.

Even more directly relevant to employers are the findings pertaining to the importance of enhanced job role quality. Our findings demonstrate that identifying ways in which job role quality can be improved, such as through enhancing the amount of decision-making ability employees have in their jobs, will yield benefits in terms of greater job satisfaction on the part of employees and thus less costly turnover.

The findings concerning the effects of changes in the number of hours worked and flexibility in work schedule are interrelated with those concerning job role quality and also have implications for managers. Working an increased number of hours results in increased work-to-family conflict for both men and women, and there are indications that it reduces job satisfaction as well, especially for men. It also appears to result in increased absence from work for men. In light of these findings, managers may wish to consider minimizing long work hours and attempting to find ways to increase work schedule flexibility.

In addition, managers should pay special attention to the finding that, especially for women, working an increased number of hours per week results in a greater amount of work-to-family conflict. Managers and human resource professionals should be aware of this and seek to make available, and advertise the availability of, informal and formal workplace supports that can minimize this conflict, such as offering more flexibility in the hours and place of work.

Finally, greater awareness on the part of employers concerning the fluid and ever-changing nature of employees' family care responsibilities is important. For employment-based work–family programs to be maximally useful to as many employees as possible, they will need to be flexible and wide ranging in the nature of assistance provided, and employees and managers alike will need to be reminded regularly of the availability of these supports so that when an employee's situation changes and a given support becomes salient, there is awareness of its existence. Finally, programs that are designed to enhance not only spousal but also job, childcare, and parent-care role quality, as well as to improve employees' parenting and parent-care skills, will be especially helpful.

Implications for Future Research

In this chapter, we have examined the impact of role transitions over a 1-year period at two points in time, both in terms of objective role characteristics and subjective role quality, on changes in work–family fit, well-being, and work-related outcomes. As noted above, future research should include additional points of data, at least three waves and ideally more, so that trends can be established and stronger causal inferences made. Also, given the relatively small amount of change that occurred, on average, in the outcome measures and the role demand and role quality measures, different data collection intervals, both longer and shorter than 1 year, should be considered. Finally, larger sample sizes would increase the statistical power of the analyses, enable inclusion of additional variables (i.e., role demands and interaction effects) that might better predict the outcomes, and enable comparisons of respondents who continued in roles with those in did not.

It is important to note, as well, that the multivariate analyses presented here, because they used listwise deletion of missing data, meant that the analyses included only people who had responses on each variable. Consistently excluded, then, were respondents who no longer had parent-care duties and thus did not have a score on parent-care role quality. We conducted the same analyses using pairwise deletion, however, and the patterns of results remained the same, with the same conclusions. Still, future research with larger samples should be conducted to compare respondents who no longer held the parent-care role with those who continued in the role to identify improvements and decrements in the outcomes associated with the loss of this particular role.

EFFECTING CHANGE: WHERE DO WE GO FROM HERE?

11

Summary of Major Findings and Recommendations for Next Steps

Caring for in-laws or my mother is very rewarding, as is raising our children. Work is enjoyable and I always strive to do my best. But, if given a choice, I would work part time so I could be with my family more. Heavy debt and the need for health insurance keeps me in my job, which fortunately is rewarding, though not in terms of money.

To date, most work–family research has studied the effects of managing paid work on the nuclear family (children and spouse) and vice versa, or, to a much lesser degree, managing care for elders while working. Only a few studies have focused on individuals who are employed and who have multiple dependent care responsibilities, such as for children *and* elders or adults with disabilities, and even fewer that have examined multiple caregiving and work roles within the context of the dual-earner couple, that is, from the perspective of both members of the couple. Thus, the study we have described here offers information not provided in previous research, to our knowledge, making a significant contribution to the understanding of the intersection between work and family.

Guided by family systems theory and by role theory, and taking into account subjective role quality, not just number of roles occupied, we studied dual-earner couples from across the United States who were caring simultaneously for dependent children and aging parents, or the "sandwiched generation." The study covered issues of critical importance to work–family researchers, employers, and sandwiched couples themselves.

Our main goal in conducting the study was to discover which personal, child-care, parent-care, and work factors best predicted positive work–family fit, well-being, and work outcomes. The findings would then form the basis for suggestions for policy, research, and practice, including recommendations for the design of workplace and community-based programs to best meet the needs of working, sandwiched couples. In conducting the study, we used mixed methods, involving holding focus groups locally, surveying a national sample of couples by mail and then surveying them again 1 year later, and interviewing by telephone a subgroup of individuals who had changed the most for the better or for the worse in the year between the surveys.

We focused our analyses on how various factors affect work–family fit, well-being, and work outcomes. In particular, the factors we examined included personal, family, and work characteristics; role quality in the four roles of spouse, parent, caregiver to an aging parent, and job; coping strategies devised; and workplace supports used. The work–family fit outcomes that we studied included both work–family conflict and work–family positive spillover. The measures of well-being included depression, life satisfaction, overall physical health, and combined role performance. The work outcomes that we examined included job satisfaction, absence from work, number of work accommodations made, and work performance. Thus, in contrast to much of the existing work–family research, we focused on positive as well as negative outcomes of having multiple work and family responsibilities.

Here we highlight what we see as the major findings of our study of working couples caring both for children and aging parents. We then discuss the implications of the findings for sandwiched-generation couples themselves, for family care practitioners, for policymakers, and for employers and managers. Finally, we discuss the methodological limitations associated with the study and make suggestions for future research.

MAJOR FINDINGS

Prevalence of Working, Sandwiched Couples

Although a few prior studies have estimated the prevalence of individuals caring for both children and elders, regardless of employment status (e.g., Nichols & Junk, 1997), or of employees caring for children and elders (Durity, 1991), we know of none that have provided an estimate of the number of U.S. households containing working, sandwiched couples. On the basis of telephone recruitment for our national survey, we found prevalence rates indicating that **dual-earner, sandwiched-generation couples comprise between 9% and 13% of American households having telephones** and one or more persons aged 30 through 60. This was based on use of a targeted list of telephone numbers of households containing adults in this age range. In 2000, there were 72,261,780 households with householders between the ages of 30 and 60; thus, the low prevalence estimate of 9% would suggest a total of over 6.5 million (i.e., 6,503,560) households of working, sandwiched couples, and the high prevalence estimate of 13% would yield almost 9.4 million (i.e., 9,394,013) households comprised of working, sandwiched couples (U.S. Department of Commerce, 2000).

A Profile of the Working, Sandwiched Couple

As we detailed in chapter 5, our findings reveal that **the typical working, sandwiched couple** consists of a 44-year-old man and a 42-year-old woman who have been married for about 18 years. The husband works about 49 hours per week, and the wife works about 38 hours per week. They have two children aged 18 or younger in the household, and they each help two aging parents, stepparents, or parents-in-law. The help they provide these aging parents is primarily with instrumental, not personal, activities of daily living and includes help with transportation, shopping, making care-related decisions, housekeeping, and managing money. Both the husband and the wife spend the equivalent of at least 1 workday each week caring for these parents, although the wife spends about 2 hours more per week, or a total of 9.8 hours per week, compared with the husband's total of about 7.5 hours. The couple has a median household income of around $62,500 (among couples with a minimum household income of $40,000—a criterion for participation in the study).

Our study involved only working couples caring both for children and aging parents, and not workers caring only for children or only for aging parents or workers without family care responsibilities. As a result, for the most part we are not able to compare directly the characteristics or outcomes of working, sandwiched couples with those of working couples with fewer or no family responsibilities.

We can, however, compare men and women, or the husbands and wives who participated in the survey, to determine differences and similarities in their personal characteristics, role responsibilities, and role quality, and their outcomes. Our findings reveal that wives report higher levels of both negative affectivity and family involvement, and lower levels of spousal role quality, than do husbands. Furthermore, although wives take on more of the responsibility for child care compared with husbands, there were no differences in overall child-care role quality between the two. Although wives are spending more hours each week caring for aging parents than are husbands (9.8 vs. 7.5, respectively), we were impressed that husbands were taking on a significant amount of responsibility with parent care. In addition, wives and husbands report similar levels of overall parent-care role quality. Wives work fewer hours per week than do husbands (38 vs. 49.5, respectively); however, both report that they would prefer to work fewer hours per week overall. Wives also report greater flexibility in their work schedules to handle family responsibilities compared with husbands, as well as greater comfort in talking about both their child-care and parent-care responsibilities with coworkers than do husbands. Finally, although husbands report higher levels of overall job involvement than do wives, wives report higher overall job role quality compared with husbands.

With respect to the outcomes we examined in this study (as per the summary that follows), wives report higher levels of both family-to-work conflict, and family-to-work positive spillover, than do husbands. In addition, wives report higher levels of depressive symptoms, higher overall absence, more work accommodations made in response to family responsibilities, and poorer work performance due to concerns about children and parents, compared with husbands. Thus, the findings from this study concerning mean comparisons between husbands and wives reveal not only many similarities but also several important gender differences in husbands' and wives' role characteristics as well as the outcomes they experience in integrating work and family.

What Are the Effects, or Outcomes, of Being "Sandwiched "?

Important Mean Differences in Outcomes

Our findings concerning the outcomes experienced by working couples caring for children and aging parents indicate that for both working, sandwiched men and women, **work-to-family conflict is higher than family-to-work conflict;** that is, work interferes with family to a greater extent than family interferes with work. This finding, although consistent with much of the previous work–family research (see Eby, Casper, Lockwood, Bordeaux, & Brinley, 2005, for a review), remains noteworthy.

Another important finding concerning the outcomes experienced by working, sandwiched couples is that, compared with the results of other national studies of depression using the Center for Epidemiologic Studies Depression Scale (Radloff, 1977) in the general population, greater percentages of both the wives and the husbands in our study experienced depressive symptoms. Thus, we conclude that **working, sandwiched men and women are at greater risk for depression than the general population.**

Effects of Objective Role Characteristics

We also can compare the relative effects of the different roles with respect to their objective and subjective characteristics. With respect to the impact of objective *child-care role characteristics*, we find that these **do not affect work–family fit or well-being outcomes and only minimally affect work outcomes.** More specifically, greater child care demands negatively impact husbands', but not wives', work outcomes.

We do find, however, that objective **parent-care role characteristics are important in predicting how working, sandwiched-generation couples do in terms of their well-being and work outcomes.** In particular, our findings suggest that **providing parent care (helping more parents and helping with more activities of daily living) can be beneficial for one's well-being but detrimental for one's work.** Specifically, husbands and wives who were helping a greater number of parents reported lower depression and, for wives, this was also related to greater life satisfaction. Furthermore, the more activities of daily living husbands and wives reported helping with, the higher their reports of absence and the greater their reports of poor work performance. Wives helping with more activities of daily living also reported making a greater number of accommodations at work. These findings concerning the effects on work are especially salient in light of the increasing number of older workers and the growing percentage with parent-care responsibilities.

With respect to the work role, we find that **objective work role characteristics significantly affect work–family fit and work outcomes.** Specifically, working a greater number of hours per week is associated with higher levels of work-to-family conflict for both husbands and wives and with more family-to-work conflict for wives, and with more reports of poor work performance for husbands (but also with greater life satisfaction for husbands). Flexibility in work schedules is related to lower work-to-family conflict but higher levels of family-to-work conflict for husbands, and to higher levels of absence for both husbands and wives. It is clear, then, that these objective work characteristics have mixed effects.

Effects of Subjective Role Characteristics Over and Above Those of Objective Role Characteristics

A unique finding of our study is that subjective role quality is a significant predictor of work–family fit, well-being, and work outcomes over and above objective role characteristics or demands. Spousal role quality, in general, is related to improved work–family fit and well-being but is not related to work outcomes. When it comes to child-care role quality, there are minimal effects on work–family fit, well-being, and work outcomes. Parent-care role quality is not related to work–family fit and only minimally related to well-being and work outcomes. Finally, job role quality is positively related to improved work–family fit, well-being, and work outcomes, with the most significant effects on improved job satisfaction and decreased absenteeism.

What this means is that for working, sandwiched couples, the effects of being sandwiched are dependent to some extent not only on such objective factors as number of hours spent in a role or number of dependents for whom one is caring, but also, and importantly, on how one experiences the roles. That is, the perceived quality of the role experience is a key factor that affects one's work–family fit, well-being, and work outcomes. In particular, we found that **role quality in the work and spousal roles is especially important in predicting these outcomes.** This was somewhat surprising to us; we expected that the role demands and rewards associated with the caregiving roles (child care and parent care) would take precedence. Instead, child-care and parent-care role quality did not, for the most part, have as significant an impact on the outcomes we examined. Thus, our findings indicate that one role does not dominate in affecting the outcomes, but rather the roles have differing effects, overall, on work–family fit, well-being, and work outcomes.

An additional key finding concerns the benefits of combining work and family, in addition to the difficulties. We found that **combining work and family can have an up side as well as be stressful.** It is interesting that the couples in our sample actually reported higher levels of *positive* spillover than *conflict* between work and family. In addition, there is another benefit of combining work and care to aging parents: **Couples receive help from, as well as give help to, their aging parents.** Among the couples in our study, this aid from aging parents came in the form of financial help, emotional support, and help with child care and household tasks. This help received is beneficial in terms of improving the quality of relationship between the adult child and his or her parent and in terms of improved self-ratings of performance as caregivers (see Ingersoll-Dayton, Neal, & Hammer, 2001, for details).

Use and Effects of Coping Strategies

Our review of the literature; our focus group data; and respondents' advice to other working, sandwiched couples revealed six basic types of strategies for coping with work–family demands (see chaps. 4, 7, and 8). **These coping strategies center around increasing resources and decreasing demands, and doing so behaviorally, emotionally, and cognitively,** yielding a total of six types of strategies. To best summarize these six strategies here, we draw specifically on the advice offered by respondents for other working, sandwiched couples.

Increasing resources behaviorally, as suggested by working, sandwiched-generation couples themselves, involved actively pursing formal and informal means of instrumental support to help them with their caregiving tasks. In particular, the couples in this study advised their peers to increase job flexibility, make use of workplace policies, enlist family support and nonfamily support (hiring outside help), and make use of technology (e.g., voicemail, cell phones). *Emotional ways of increasing resources* also were suggested and included taking care of oneself and one's marital relationship; seeking emotional support from family, friends, coworkers, and supervisors; participating in a support group; finding humor in a situation; and incorporating religious or spiritual beliefs into one's daily life. Advice was also offered related to *cognitively increasing resources* in order to cope with multiple demands and responsibilities and included such things as purposefully planning schedules, preparing for unexpected events, and planning for the couple's own future needs.

The other major type of strategy advised involved decreasing demands. *Behavioral ways of decreasing demands* that the working, sandwiched couples in our study advocated included learning to say no to requests, working fewer hours, and simplifying one's lifestyle. Advice concerning *decreasing demands by emotional means* included reducing personal expectations, taking one day at a time, not feeling guilty when one does not meet expectations, having patience, and changing one's attitude toward the situation. *Ways of decreasing demands cognitively* included determining overall life priorities, within-family priorities, and daily priorities and using these to guide behavior.

Of course, not all advice is actually adhered to by those offering it, nor is all advice necessarily good advice. As a result, we developed a measure of work–family coping strategies to enable us to examine which coping strategies were in fact used and, of these, which were associated with the most positive, and the most negative, outcomes.

Our measure included emotional, behavioral, and cognitive dimensions yielding the following three coping strategies: (a) **emotional/increasing emotional resources,** (b) **behavioral/decreasing social involvement,** and (c) **cognitive/increasing prioritizing.** We found some gender differences in the types of strategies used: **Wives engage in coping strategies involving decreasing social involvement more often than do husbands, and husbands engage in coping strategies that involve increased prioritizing more often than do wives.** We found no significant gender differences, however, in the frequency of use of coping strategies that increase emotional resources.

With respect to the effectiveness of the three types of coping strategies, we found that **coping strategies that involve social withdrawal are related to negative work and family outcomes.** Alternatively, **coping strategies that are centered on seeking emotional support are beneficial, as are those focused on conscious attempts to prioritize tasks,** although to a lesser extent. In general, our findings reveal that **the type(s) of coping strategies used have more effects on work–family fit and well-being than on work outcomes.**

In addition to asking respondents about the coping strategies they regularly used, we asked respondents whether or not they had made certain limited- or one-time use work and family accommodations in the past year in response to their child- and parent-care responsibilities. We found that the most commonly used **accommodations by wives** were working reduced hours (31%), refusing or limiting travel (27%), choosing a job with more flexibility to meet family demands (24%), refusing or deciding not to work toward a promotion (21%), and working a different shift from their spouse so that one adult is at home most of the time (15%). The most frequently used **accommodations by husbands** were to have refused or limited travel (23%), worked reduced hours (17%), refused to relocate (13%), or to have worked a different shift from their spouse so that one adult is at home most of the time (13%). These findings indicate that **wives, in particular, are more likely to make work accommodations for family than are husbands.**

Use and Effects of Workplace Supports

When examining the use of workplace supports, we found that **the workplace supports used most frequently are family health insurance, personal time off/paid leave, flexible work hours, and unpaid leave. Paid leave is clearly preferred over unpaid leave, when it is available;** 40.9% of husbands and 51% of wives used paid leave when available, compared with 11.7% of husbands and 23% of wives who used unpaid leave. **Least-used supports are those related specifically to family-care needs,** including on-site child care, resource and referral for child care and elder care, pre-tax dollars for elder care, and on-site support groups for parents of dependent children or for caregivers to elders. It is important to note, however, that because policies, benefits, and services cannot be used if they are not available, or if employees do not know about them, these findings reflect, in part, availability and knowledge of supports.

We also found that, in general, **wives are more likely to make use of workplace supports than are husbands,** consistent with previous research (e.g., Judiesch & Lyness, 1999; Rosin & Korabik, 2002). In our study, wives were more likely than husbands to use flexible work hours, telecommuting, unpaid leave, personal time off/paid leave, and work–family seminars. One exception was that husbands were more likely to use the family health insurance offered by their employer than were wives. Possible reasons for the differential health insurance utilization rate may be that husbands' plans were better than those available to their wives, or because wives, who were more likely to work part time than husbands, were not eligible to receive benefits at their own place of work, although such health insurance benefits were available to most employees.

Our results indicate that using workplace supports positively affects well-being (i.e., life satisfaction, overall health, and overall role performance) for husbands and/or wives. Some of the findings were inconsistent with our expectations, however. Specifically, we found that, **at the same time, use of workplace supports is related to decreased work–family fit and more negative work outcomes** (i.e., increased work–family conflict, higher absenteeism, more work accommodations, and poorer work performance for husbands and/or wives). Some of these findings appear to hold over time, as well: When we examined the findings related to work–family conflict further using our longitudinal data (see Hammer, Neal, Newsom, Brockwood, & Colton, 2005), we found that, for women, use of workplace supports was related to higher family-to-work conflict over time. One explanation is that when people who have extensive family demands make use of workplace supports, they then use the extra time or flexibility or assistance to enable them to take on additional work and family responsibilities. This then results in more work–family conflict, but perhaps better feelings about the workplace for providing the supports in the first place. Similarly, use of supports may lead to employees taking time off from work or making other accommodations at work in order to access previously unknown but needed resources (e.g., Ingersoll-Dayton, Chapman, & Neal, 1990). Another explanation is that the most stressed employees are those who are most likely to need and use supports (e.g., Fredriksen-Goldsen & Scharlach, 2001); thus, it would not be surprising that these employees would report poorer work performance.

"Crossover Effects" of One Spouse on the Other

A key advantage to collecting data from both members of working, sandwiched couples is the ability to examine the effects of one spouse's behaviors and perceptions on the other's outcomes. We found significant crossover effects of role quality and, in particular, *spousal* role quality, on both husbands' and wives' work–family fit, well-being, and work outcomes. That is, we found that **one's spousal role quality affects his or her partner's work and family outcomes in positive ways.**

Similarly, **the types of coping strategies used by one member of the couple also have beneficial effects on the other member's outcomes.** More specifically, husbands' use of emotional coping strategies had beneficial effects on wives' work–family fit and well-being.

With respect to the use of workplace supports, however, we did not find crossover effects on one's spouse. This may be due to greater reliance on the part of sandwiched individuals on emotional support from their spouse (i.e., spousal role quality) or on limited- or one-time use accommodations, particularly by wives, thus mitigating the effects of use of workplace supports by one spouse on the other's outcomes.

Changes Over Time in Work–Family Roles and Outcomes

The findings from our longitudinal analyses indicate that working, sandwiched couples have extremely dynamic lives. The characteristics associated with working and caring for children and aging parents affect these couples in profound ways, as reflected in the analysis of two waves of survey data and in the comments shared by participants who were part of our focus groups and interviews.

We found that over the course of a year, **some couples' work and family lives change dramatically.** For example, after 1 year, a few couples actually no longer held one or more roles and thus no longer met the study criteria. Specifically, some couples no longer had children aged 18 or under, no longer were providing parent care, no longer were together as a couple, and/or had a member who was no longer working. Others had less drastic reductions in demands, including having fewer children aged 18 or younger living in their household, having fewer children with special needs, caring for fewer aging parents, helping parents with fewer activities of daily living, working fewer hours, and having more flexibility in their work schedules to deal with family-related demands.

When examined in the aggregate (by comparing the means at Wave 1 and Wave 2), however, the only significant changes in role demands were reductions in demands, including decreases in the number of dependent children in the household and the number of aging parents/in-laws being helped (as reported by both husbands and wives), and a decreased number of children with special needs (as reported by wives only). Still, some couples experienced increases in role demands, including having a greater number of children living in their household, having more children with special needs, caring for a greater number of parents, helping parents with more activities of daily living, working more hours, and having less flexibility in their work schedules to deal with family-related demands.

With respect to role quality, few participants maintained the same exact levels of role quality over the year. Instead, approximately equal percentages experienced declines and increases. It is interesting that when we looked at the *average* amount of change that occurred in role outcomes, we found no change overall for husbands and wives in several of the outcomes, including one of the four work–family fit outcomes (positive work-to-family spillover), one of the four well-being outcomes (overall role performance), and three of the four work outcomes (job satisfaction, absence due to dependent-care responsibilities, and poor work performance due to dependent-care responsibilities).

At the same time, **when there** *were* **changes in the outcomes, some were positive and some were negative.** We found that, on the one hand, for either husbands or wives, or both, as a whole, the amount of work–family conflict, depression, and use of work accommodations declined, *on average*, over the course of the year between surveys. On the other hand, positive spillover from family-to work and life satisfaction declined for both husbands and wives, and overall health declined for husbands. In other words, at the aggregate level, over the year, some bad things became less bad, but some good things also became less good.

In addition, again at the aggregate level, **role demands either stayed the same or in some cases decreased over time.** Simple examination of overall mean changes, however, provided little information concerning what was happening with the couples in our sample and what factors contributed to improvements or decrements in work and family outcomes. Thus, we examined the impact of changes in objective and subjective role characteristics on changes in the outcomes.

We found that **changes in objective role demands do affect the outcomes; however, changes in role quality are even more important.** In general, as would be expected, we found that **increases in role demands are related to increased negative outcomes, and increases in role quality result in increases in positive outcomes.** For example, an increase in job role quality was related to improved work–family fit, as was an increase in parent-care role quality, for both husbands and wives; an increase in spousal role quality was associated with better work–family fit for wives. Changes in job demands and parent-care demands also predicted some of the work–family fit outcomes, with working more hours resulting in more work-to-family conflict for both husbands and wives and having increased flexibility at work predicting an increase in positive family-to-work spillover for wives.

Changes in the quality of family roles, especially spousal and parent-care role quality, rather than changes in the work role, were the most important predictors of changes in well-being. Similarly, changes in role quality, especially in the child-care and spousal roles, but also the job and parent-care roles, were more consistent predictors of changes in the work-related outcomes than changes in role demands, although there were exceptions. For example, more overall absence due to dependent-care responsibilities was predicted by working more hours per week (presumably to make up for time lost from work) and gaining greater flexibility in work schedule (which allowed participants to take more time off during regular work hours). Also, wives who reported poorer work performance tended to be providing more help with activities of daily living to a parent and working fewer hours. Lowered child-care role quality and increased spousal role quality, however, also predicted poorer work performance for wives. **In sum, these longitudinal findings indicate the salience of role quality in predicting work and family outcomes and thus have important implications for practice, policy, and research.**

IMPLICATIONS OF THE FINDINGS

Implications for Working, Sandwiched-Generation Couples Themselves

We draw our implications for actions to be taken by working couples caring for children and aging parents themselves from several of our findings. These include the advice offered to couples by study participants (as summarized earlier in the section on use and effects of coping strategies); our quantitative findings concerning which coping strategies are most effective in terms of being associated with greater levels of work–family fit, well-being, and positive work outcomes; and our findings concerning other predictors of positive outcomes.

In general, working, sandwiched couples are advised to strive to increase their resources and to decrease the demands they face. **On the basis of the findings from this study, however, we caution sandwiched-generation couples against using coping strategies that involve social withdrawal.** We found that use of social withdrawal strategies is related to negative work and well-being outcomes. What this means is that the natural tendency to reduce social contacts when overwhelmed with work and family can actually be detrimental to one's well-being. In fact, the strategy of reducing social contacts as a means of coping with multiple work and family demands was commonly mentioned by our respondents in their comments meant as "advice" for other sandwiched couples. Our findings clearly indicate, though, that this strategy can lead to reduced, not improved, well-being.

Alternatively, use of emotional coping strategies that involve seeking emotional support is beneficial for individuals themselves, and the benefits extend to one's spouse, at least when wives make use of such strategies. Thus, we would encourage working, sandwiched individuals to seek out social support as a way of increasing their own, and their spouse's, emotional resources.

A key finding of this study is the centrality of spousal support and spousal role quality for achieving work–family fit, well-being, and positive work outcomes. The value of a supportive relationship with one's spouse is a consistent theme that emerged in this study. These findings suggest the importance of nurturing and enhancing the marital relationship for working, sandwiched couples, despite the difficulty of doing so in the face of limited time and competing demands from work, children, and aging parents.

In addition to the crossover effects of use of coping strategies that involve seeking emotional support, we found that one spouse's role quality sometimes "crosses over" and affect his or her spouse's outcomes. Working, sandwiched couples are urged to keep this in mind and seek emotional and tangible support to improve not only their own work–family fit and well-being, but also their spouse's.

Finally, a secondary analysis of our data revealed that there can be significant financial costs associated with the provision of parent care, in particular, of which working, sandwiched couples should be aware. On the basis of the responses to a survey item asking respondents how much they spent each month on caregiving expenses for the parent they were helping the most (e.g., for hiring outside help, transportation expenses, giving the parent money, telephone charges, etc.), Lottes (2005) estimated the annual out-of-pocket expenses for couples at $976.92. The same study also sought to value the time sandwiched couples spend providing elder care, using replacement and opportunity cost approaches, and found the value of care provided by working, sandwiched couples to range between $4,576.70 and $13,894.76. These findings point to the potential financial impact, in addition to the other outcomes addressed here, of combining work and family, specifically, parent care.

Implications for Family Care Practitioners

Our findings have several implications for counselors, social workers, family therapists, employee assistance professionals, psychiatrists, and other family care practitioners. First, our results suggest that family care practitioners can assist working, sandwiched individuals by encouraging them to make use of coping strategies that increase their emotional resources, such as through seeking social support, as these types of coping strategies lead to improved well-being. In addition, because our findings indicate that the use of social withdrawal coping strategies has negative effects on work–family fit and well-being, individuals should be encouraged to maintain their significant social relationships, even when they are feeling overwhelmed and stressed and feel they do not have time for these relationships.

Another implication for family care practitioners is the importance of recognizing that working, sandwiched individuals are at greater risk for depression, especially women. Being more aware of this risk may assist practitioners with earlier diagnosis, as well as with identifying strategies for preventing depression, including the provision of adequate information about the possible risks of depression and making available resources to help support these families.

Our findings suggest as well that family care practitioners can help working, sandwiched couples by emphasizing to them the importance of spousal role quality and working with them to identify ways to enhance the quality of their marital relationship. Helping couples to improve their communication techniques and counseling them with respect to ways of managing multiple role demands together may help to enhance spousal role quality. Moreover, on the basis of the findings concerning the cross-over effects of one spouse on the other, counselors and other family care practitioners are urged to help couples understand how one member's behaviors and attitudes affects the other's experiences.

Finally, although detailed elsewhere (i.e., Ingersoll-Dayton et al., 2001), and mentioned only briefly in this book (see chap. 5), findings from our data demonstrate the importance of conceptualizing caregiving to aging parents, in particular, as a *mutual* help-giving process between adult children and their aging parents for whom they are caring, rather than a uni-lateral, one-way process involving only care by the adult children to their aging parents. Family care practitioners can help caregivers by assisting them to identify psychological and/or tangible ways in which their older parents can serve as a source of help and by encouraging caregivers to seek such support from their parents.

Implications for Public Policymakers

In chapters 2 and 3 of this book, we offered evidence that the United States has not kept pace with other industrialized (and some nonindustrialized) countries when it comes to providing national programs and policies needed to support working caregivers (Heymann, 2000). In most industri-alized nations other than the United States, responsibility for addressing workers' and their families' needs is seen as being in the public domain. In those countries, the government has assumed leadership, with family care provisions legislated, as opposed to being voluntarily initiated and imple-mented by employers; there, employers generally are not expected to as-sist employees in managing their family care responsibilities (Andersson, 1999; Reichert & Naegele, 1999). In contrast, in the United States, responsi-bility for addressing workers' and their families' needs is shared among individuals, employers, nongovernmental organizations, and last, gov-ernment agencies. As Hammer, Cullen, and Shafiro (2006) noted, the heavier reliance on workplace-based family-friendly human resource pol-icies in the United States than in other countries is due to the lack of sup-port at the national level. Unfortunately, such reliance on employers to provide support for working families is inadequate because of the preponderance of small and family-owned businesses in this country. For example, in our national sample of working, sandwiched couples, over 50% of respondents worked in companies with fewer than 25 people. Smaller companies often do not have the resources to provide formal supports.

Universal child care and paid family leave are the key governmental supports that typically are provided for working families in other industrialized nations (M. F. Davis & Powell, 2003). In the United States, there are no universal child-care programs. Indeed, of 193 United Nations member countries, the United States and Somalia are the only ones that failed to ratify the International Convention on the Rights of the Child, a document that asserts the obligation of the state to assist parents, especially working parents, with the upbringing and the development of children (M. F. Davis & Powell, 2003). Moreover, although federally mandated family leave in the United States protects the employee's job (or guarantees a job of equivalent status and pay), the employer is not required to pay the employee while she or he is on leave (except where state law has mandated paid family leave, such as in California; M. F. Davis & Powell, 2003). Many other countries also pay family caregivers to children and/or elders, whereas in the United States, such payments are the exception rather than the rule (M. F. Davis & Powell, 2003; Lechner & Neal, 1999).

We believe that in the United States, paid leave should be provided to support working families. This is supported by our findings related to couples' utilization rates of paid versus unpaid family leave: When paid leave was available, it was, of course, used much more often than was unpaid leave. Many working families in today's society are unable to take advantage of such "supports" as unpaid family leave; they simply cannot afford to do so. Paid leave should be legislated by the federal government, perhaps with tax incentives to lessen the short-term costs to employers.

With respect to elder care, in other countries as well in as the United States, there is limited awareness of issues surrounding employees' responsibilities for aging parents and other relatives, and fewer supports specifically related to elder care, as opposed to child care, are provided by either the government or by employers. As described in chapters 2 and 3, those supports that are available tend to be recent and not to be targeted specifically to employed caregivers of elders but to all employees or, in some cases, to elders themselves.

With the growing number of workers caring both for aging parents and children, it becomes even more important to implement public policies that support the needs of working, sandwiched couples. In the United States, we must, as do other industrialized nations, recognize the critical importance of high-quality and affordable child care, for the benefit of working parents, our children, the economy, and society as a whole. We must identify funding mechanisms and make provisions so that such child care is available. Similarly, we can learn from other countries about the need for paid parental and family care leave (for sick and disabled children as well as aging parents and other adult relatives); policymakers should examine the specific details of other countries' provisions for such leave and implement new and/or more extensive provisions here to support working families.

In addition, policymakers should consider ways to support employers' provision of flexible work arrangements, including flexible work hours, alternative work schedules and places of work (e.g., telecommuting), and part-time work, and efforts to train managers to be more supportive of employees' family (child-, adult-, and elder-care) responsibilities, perhaps through tax breaks or incentives. The implementation of additional tax breaks and payments to family caregivers should be supported as well. Finally, the provision of universal health care, along with long-term care insurance, would go a long way toward easing the burdens faced by working families caring for children and aging parents.

Implications for Employers

Many of the findings from our study have important implications for managers, human resource professionals, business owners, and other organizational policymakers. These include the findings related to objective role demands, subjective role demands (i.e., spousal, child care, parent care, and job role quality) and formal and informal workplace supports.

Effects of Objective Role Demands

To begin, we found that extensive caregiving responsibilities have a negative impact on a number of work-related outcomes, further making the case that employers should be concerned with addressing the issues faced by working families. For example, we found that objective parent-care role demands, especially helping a parent with a greater number of activities of daily living, are significant contributors to various forms of workplace absence; are related to the number of work accommodations made, such as reducing work hours; and are related to increased reports of poor work performance. In addition, objective child-care demands significantly affect absence and work performance for husbands, in particular.

These findings suggest that it would be helpful for employers to develop a basic understanding of the demographics of their workforce in terms of caregiving demands. This knowledge would assist organizational policymakers in determining the types of programs and support systems to provide that would be most useful. The necessary information can be identified by conducting a needs analysis, as mentioned earlier, using an instrument similar to that which we provide in the Work–family Sourcebook for Employers, which we developed as a part of this research project and which can be found at http://www.sandwich.pdx.edu.

The objective work characteristics that we examined in detail in this study were the extent to which study participants had flexibility in their work schedules to handle their family responsibilities and the number of hours participants worked per week. We know from our research reported elsewhere that providing employees flexibility at work to make certain accommodations (e.g., reducing hours when needed, changing work schedules) has beneficial effects on employees' work lives and on their family lives (Brockwood, Hammer, Neal, & Colton, 2001).

In this study, our findings with respect to the importance of flexibility were consistent across our focus group and survey participants. For example, several focus group participants, generally wives, noted that they had specifically chosen their jobs *because of* the flexibility in work schedule that the position offered, realizing that this would help them better manage their family responsibilities while still working. Thus, there are potential recruitment benefits that may accrue from the implementation of flexible work schedule options. Moreover, the significant relationships between flexibility in the workplace and the work–family fit variables indicate that designing jobs to increase employee autonomy and control over when and where work gets done may be of particular importance in promoting work and family integration. In addition, increased job control and reduced job demands are related to important long-term health outcomes such as decreased risk for cardiovascular disease (Schnall, Belkic, Landsbergis, & Baker, 2000), which could reduce employers' health care costs and workers' compensation claims.

Our findings concerning the effects of changes in the number of hours worked also have important implications for employers. Working more hours results in increased work-to-family conflict for both men and women, and there are indications that it reduces job satisfaction as well, especially for men. Our findings revealed that working more hours also results in increased absence from work for men. In light of these findings, employers may wish to consider minimizing long work hours for employees.

Effects of Subjective Role Quality

Although our research suggests a number of important implications for employers with respect to objective role characteristics, such as the number of children and aging parents for whom one cares, and the structure of jobs in terms of work hours and schedule flexibility, we also found that subjective perceptions about the quality of various roles were important to participants and thus have significant implications for employers. These perceptions, which we refer to as *spousal, child-care, parent-care,* and *job role quality,* have a profound impact on individuals' work–family fit, well-being, and work outcomes.

Of particular importance to employers is the importance of spousal role quality to employees, as higher levels of quality in this role are related to increased personal well-being, decreased levels of work–family conflict, and positive work–family spillover. Employers can help by providing educational seminars for employees that emphasize the value of a solid relationship with their spouse, help employees to identify strategies for improving communication with their spouse, and help them to find ways to spend more time together with their spouse.

In addition, programs that are designed to enhance child-care and parent-care role quality, as well as programs to enhance employees' practical skills with respect to helping their parents with activities of daily living, will be helpful. Given our findings on the prevalence of working, sandwiched-generation couples in the United States (between 9% and 13% of households with an adult aged 30–60), as well as the national data projecting the aging of the population and the workforce in the years to come, along with the increased numbers of workers who are reporting that they provided elder care in the past year (i.e., 35%; Bond, Thompson, Galinsky, & Prottas, 2003), heightened attention to the provision of elder-care programs, in particular, is crucial for employers. Such programs may ultimately affect employers' ability to be successful in recruiting workers in the future, many of whom will be older and likely to have parent-care responsibilities.

Finally, our findings suggest that employers can directly affect and improve work–family fit, well-being, and work outcomes for employees by implementing changes that have the potential of influencing worker perceptions of job role quality that will ultimately affect such outcomes as job satisfaction and absenteeism in positive ways. We have mentioned a number of these strategies throughout the book; they include providing supervisory support to employees, giving employees greater degrees of autonomy and control over what they are doing and where they are doing it, and providing employees with meaningful work that they find rewarding. Much effort in the organizational sciences has been devoted to such job redesign efforts aimed at changing the characteristics of a job. We suggest that interested employers seek out additional readings on this topic, such as the seminal work by Hackman and Oldham (1975) on the job characteristics model. These efforts on the part of managers and supervisors aimed at directly changing the nature of the job itself to make it a more positive experience for workers will lead to higher levels of overall job role quality and improved outcomes for workers and employers alike.

Effects of Formal and Informal Workplace Supports

Our study provides evidence of the positive effects of using formal workplace supports on employee well-being, in particular. At the same time, we also found that utilization of formal workplace supports was related to higher levels of work–family conflict, possibly because those who are making use of the supports are the very people in most need of the supports. It is important that employers be aware of this fact. Thus, we urge the development of a two-pronged approach consisting not only of formal supports but also, as elaborated below, of informal support in the form of a developing a family-friendly organizational culture.

The low utilization rates of workplace supports intended specifically for employees with dependent-care responsibilities that we found in this study are due largely to the lack of availability of such supports. Thus, the findings do not indicate lack of employee interest in such supports. Similarly, although use of unpaid leave in order to fulfill family care responsibilities was fairly common, this clearly was not the leave option preferred by employees; instead, this finding, too, is in large part a reflection of the lack of availability of paid leave.

Our finding that women are more likely than men to use workplace supports may be an indicator that men feel less comfortable than women using such supports. It is consistent with our finding that women generally are more comfortable than men in talking about their dependent-care responsibilities with coworkers and supervisors. Employers may wish to make special formal and visible attempts, such as through advertising of supports and through training supervisors, to encourage male employees to make use of available support options.

In recognition of our finding that individual employees' family care responsibilities can change considerably over the course of just 1 year, we suggest that for employment-based work–family programs to be maximally useful to as many employees as possible, they should be flexible and wide ranging in the nature of assistance provided. Also, and importantly, because employees often do not pay attention to the types of supports that are offered until those supports become salient to them, employees will need to be reminded regularly of those formal supports that are available to them.

At the same time, other factors may also affect the utilization of supports, such as an unsupportive work–family culture (e.g., Allen, 2001; Sahibzada, Hammer, Neal, & Kuang, 2005). In fact, previous research has shown that a supportive work–family culture can have positive outcomes over and above those simply of utilization of formal supports (Allen, 2001; C. A. Thompson, Beauvais, & Lyness, 1999). The findings from this study demonstrate that even when formal supports are available, employees do not always use them. Reasons for this may include fear that such action would jeopardize their jobs, the need to negotiate with an unsympathetic supervisor for the benefits, lack of awareness of the benefits and how to use them, failure to identify oneself as a caregiver and thus as someone eligible for the supports, and/or because the employee simply does not expect assistance from others with his or her caregiving responsibilities (Lechner, 1999; Martin-Matthews, 1999; Phillips, 1999; Reichert & Naegele, 1999; Wagner & Hunt, 1994). Thus, in addition to providing more formal workplace supports, it is important to identify ways to decrease or eliminate barriers to using available supports. In particular, we encourage employers to strive to improve their organization's work–family culture, such as through developing and implementing supervisory training programs focused around being sensitive to employees' work and family responsibilities. These informal strategies may actually prove to be more effective and a better use of resources than the implementation of formal policies pertaining to work and family.

Thus, it is important to periodically train management and supervisors to be more sensitive to employees' work–family issues and to communicate with employees about their work and family needs. This will enhance the organization's work–family culture so that men and women alike feel no stigma associated with having family responsibilities, using the available formal supports, and working informally with their supervisor to find ways of accommodating their work and family needs. Ultimately, the only way to significantly influence the work–family culture of an organization is to demonstrate support for families at all levels within the company.

If organizations provide both formal and informal supports, their employees will have more positive attitudes at work and be more committed to the organization, thereby improving job satisfaction and employee retention. Furthermore, providing such supports is likely as well to help organizations in terms of recruiting employees by improving the attractiveness of the organization.

STRENGTHS AND LIMITATIONS OF THE STUDY AND SUGGESTIONS FOR FUTURE RESEARCH

Strengths

In this book, we have presented a description of working, sandwiched-generation couples from across the United States with respect to their personal characteristics, the nature of their caregiving responsibilities, the strategies that they have adopted to help them manage their multiple roles, and the outcomes they are experiencing. We have analyzed which characteristics and strategies are linked to positive outcomes, including those that occur over time. We also have examined the effects of one spouse's behavior and attitudes on the other's outcomes. The study that yielded these data addresses many of the problems associated with previous work–family research: We focused not just on women but also men; we included both members of couples rather than only one; we examined the nature and effects of family care responsibilities for elders (i.e., aging parents) as well as for children; and we looked at how situations, behaviors, and attitudes change over time and the effects of these changes. Also, the study was national, not local, in scope. At the same time, the study has limitations of its own.

Limitations

An important limitation concerns the potential generalizability of the findings from the study. This limitation stems from the composition of the sample. Although the telephone screening sampling procedure used for identifying study participants was national in scope, non-White couples were underrepresented in the final sample, as were same-sex couples. Also, by using a targeted list of telephone numbers, some members of the population were not represented (e.g., persons without telephones or with unlisted numbers). Also because of the funder's special interest in middle- and upper income couples, low-income couples were not included in the study; neither were single parents caring for children and aging parents. Similarly, our focus was on couples in which both members were employed, one full time and the other at least half time, and both members of the couple were required to participate. As a result, the findings may not accurately represent couples who are members of racial, ethnic, or sexual minority groups; those who do not have telephones or have unlisted numbers; those with low annual household incomes; those in which both members would not participate; those in which both members were not working at least half time; and single workers caring for children and parents.

Additional limitations concern the nature of the sample. With respect to the number of hours of parent care, we should note that the criteria for participation in this study were more stringent than those of most other studies and required that, together, couples spent at least 3 hours per week helping out an aging parent. Similarly, couples were required to have minor children living in their household at least 3 days per week. Thus, our findings concerning the amount of time that working, sandwiched individuals spend helping parents (either all parents combined or the one parent being helped the most) would be an overestimate if generalized to working, sandwiched couples who spend fewer hours in parent care than the minimum criterion we stipulated for participation in this study. Also, the responsibilities of couples whose children or stepchildren do not live with them, or do so for less than an average of 3 days per week, are not reflected here; neither are those of single parents. In addition, as noted above, the responsibilities of blended families may not be fully captured. Also as mentioned above, because couples in which both members worked less than full time were not included in the study, the findings regarding the number of hours worked by working, sandwiched-generation couples would be overestimated for those couples.

Also of concern is the overall response rate, whether calculated on the basis of all households that met the study criteria, regardless of their willingness to participate in the mailed survey, or, less conservatively, on the basis of the number of surveys originally mailed out (see Appendix A for details). Follow-up calls to encourage participation lead us to believe that those couples who received surveys but did not complete them may have been even busier and/or more stressed than the couples who did participate. At the same time, however, we found no significant differences on key characteristics between those respondents who were screened via telephone and found to meet the study's criteria but who did not return surveys compared to those who did return surveys. Of course, couples who were most busy or in crisis may have been less likely to agree to participate in the 3-minute screening call, or even to have answered the telephone. Thus, the findings from this study may well actually underestimate the level of stress experienced by working, sandwiched couples.

Another limitation is that there is no comparison group, making it difficult to judge how well these couples were doing in comparison with working couples with fewer or no caregiving responsibilities. The longitudinal data, however, did allow determination of changes that occurred in respondents' outcomes and the predictors of these changes. One explanation for the relative lack of significant contribution by the objective role demand variables in predicting change in the outcomes may be the limited amount of change overall, in the aggregate, that occurred in the year between the two surveys with respect to those variables, and especially in the outcome variables themselves. A longer time frame in between data collection points might yield more significant results of this nature. Alternatively, a shorter time interval might be more sensitive to the effects of changes in role demands, in particular. Furthermore, as discussed earlier, more than two time points of data are necessary to establish trends.

Finally, the relatively small sample size (i.e., 309 couples) limited the number of variables that could be included in analyses based on the power to detect significant effects. To overcome these various limitations, future research with larger, more diverse samples is needed to further explore the complex interrelationships among role demands, role quality, and outcomes for working families.

Recommendations for Future Research

This study represents an important first step in understanding the situations and needs of sandwiched-generation, dual-earner couples. Considerable work remains to be done, however. In particular, we have seven recommendations concerning future research in this arena.

First, the findings from our longitudinal analyses, as presented in chapter 10, reveal the dynamic nature of work and family roles at the individual level, demonstrating that employees' family and work lives change, sometimes quite dramatically, over the course of just 1 year. As such, they point to the importance of studying role changes over time and the need for future longitudinal research.

Thus, we recommend, first, that data should be gathered at multiple time points. In this study, we gathered data from couples at two time points, 1 year apart. Whether a longer or a shorter time interval between data collection points would be best is uncertain; however, multiple observation points (more than two) clearly would be very beneficial. Our analyses of the changes that occurred between the two mailed surveys administered 1 year apart indicate considerable change and fluidity in work and family situations over the year (e.g., divorce, birth or adoption of children, children leaving the home, the death of parents, increased parent-care responsibilities). Examined in the aggregate, the findings from the study revealed that, over the course of the year between the two mailed surveys, among study participants as a whole, role responsibility, or demands, tended to decrease rather than increase. This may be the result of regression toward the mean. To qualify for the study, couples had to have fairly high levels of parent-care responsibilities and to have children who were anywhere from 0 to 18 years of age at the outset. Thus, it is logical that some couples would, in essence, "age out" of being in the sandwiched generation as parents died or children reached maturity and moved out. At the same time, however, subjective role quality also decreased overall across all four roles. This finding is an indicator that the subjective experience of multiple family and work responsibilities may deteriorate over time. To fully understand these findings and to make stronger causal inferences, additional points of data are required.

One approach would be to collect survey data annually, or even semiannually, for 3 or more years. Another option would be to collect more detailed, fine-grained data over a shorter period of time using, for example, daily diary methodology (e.g., Crouter, Bumpus, Maguire, & McHale, 1999). Such data could help to further elucidate the specific caregiving demands, role rewards, and coping strategies that are linked to positive and negative outcomes. Regardless, future studies should include gathering data at a minimum of three time points, and ideally more.

A second, related suggestion for future research is that careful consideration should be given to the time frame *between* data collection points, consistent with the research questions and outcomes of interest. In our study, the limited amount of change in the aggregate measures over the course of 1 year suggests either that there is considerable stability in these outcomes or that a year-long time frame is either too short or too long to detect change at the aggregate level. Future research should explore the appropriate time interval between data collection points.

A third suggestion is that future research should endeavor to include, at a minimum, the gathering and analysis of data from both members of working, sandwiched-generation couples. Our findings demonstrated that what one member of the couple does and experiences at work and at home does indeed affect the other member both at work and at home. The use of a systems framework will contribute to greater understanding of individuals', and families', well-being and work-related outcomes.

Expanding on this idea, consideration should be given to the inclusion of more members of the family system as well as members of the work system. Very few studies have examined the effects of work on other family members' well-being, such as children (for an exception, see Crouter et al., 1999), and especially aging parents. To better reflect the larger family system, gathering data from children, aging parents, and siblings of the adult child caregivers to parents would be very beneficial. Collection of data from work supervisors and/or coworkers would be similarly useful to better represent the work system. Such a design would afford a much more complete view of both the family and the work contexts of dual-earner, sandwiched-generation couples. The need to rely solely on self-report data would be eliminated, and the multiple perspectives obtained would add to the validity of results.

A fourth suggested area for future research concerns how information from this study can be used for further theory development. Here we have presented results that clearly indicate the critical impact of subjective role quality on work–family fit, well-being, and work outcomes. Although research on the work–family interface frequently examines objective role characteristics as indicators of well-being, rarely are the subjective role experiences of individuals included in models. Incorporating the role quality construct in future models of the work–family interface will expand researchers' understanding of the complex factors that affect work–family outcomes.

A fifth area suggested for future research also will contribute to theory development and concerns the importance of examining positive as well as negative outcomes of combining work and family. In our study, work–family positive spillover was clearly related to a number of role characteristics and demands. As positive spillover and the related construct of work–family enrichment (Greenhaus & Powell, 2006) begin to be more completely examined in the literature, models of the work–family interface will expand to regularly include the positive aspects of combining work and family, as opposed to the more narrow traditional stress perspective. With a focus on how to facilitate normal, positive functioning, the work–family field will join with other similar movements in positive psychology (Seligman & Csikszentmihalyi, 2000).

A sixth suggestion relates to the importance of distinguishing between the effects of formal and informal workplace supports. Our findings indicate the value of informal work–family culture/workplace supports, over and above that of formal workplace supports, similar to the findings of Allen (2001) and others. On the basis of the follow-up analyses we reported in chapter 9, it appears that an organization's work–family culture is important, over and above the employee's actual utilization of supports, for better work–family fit, well-being, and work outcomes. Thus, we recommend that future research should focus on identifying ways to improve the work–family culture of an organization. We believe that this is important because many smaller companies may not have the resources or systems in place to implement formal work–family policies. If they, or their managers, were provided with specific information that would help improve the work–family culture, they might see more significant impact on their employees than even larger organizations that have formal supports in place. Such information would be beneficial to larger companies, as well, because improving the work–family culture may be more cost-effective than implementing formal supports.

A seventh area for future research stems from our use of some outcome measures in this study, which are fairly new to the work–family field. The role of these various concepts in future work–family models needs to be assessed. For example, the extent to which work accommodations are made, although common as an outcome in the work and elder-care literature, traditionally has been seen in the organizational literature as a "resource" contributing to decreased work–family stress (e.g., Behson, 2002). It is interesting that our findings suggest that higher levels of role demands and low levels of role quality are related to using a greater number of work accommodations. Thus, making accommodations at work may be a way that sandwiched couples attempt to manage their work and family responsibilities, and thus this should be examined in future organizational research as a outcome resulting from combining work and multiple family care responsibilities similar to how the measure is used in the work and elder-care literature.

Finally, we recommend that future work–family research used mixed methods, gathering and analyzing both qualitative and quantitative data, as has been elaborated elsewhere (Neal, Hammer, & Morgan, 2006). The focus groups we conducted helped greatly in the development of the survey tool, and the comments volunteered by respondents on the back of their mailed surveys, as well as in the telephone interviews we conducted, were invaluable in providing context and helping us to interpret the quantitative findings.

CONCLUSION

To our knowledge, this is the most comprehensive study to date on families that work and have caregiving responsibilities both for children and for elders. The study has made a number of contributions toward advancing knowledge in the areas of work and family issues, multiple roles, and mid-life caregiving to dependent children and aging parents. This national study on work and multiple caregiving roles has made use of both quantitative and qualitative data, using both members of the couple and involving multiple waves of data. The use of a mixed-methods approach, a family systems framework, and a longitudinal design has allowed for a rich understanding of the complexities of the lives of these working, sandwiched couples.

A primary purpose of this research was to provide a description of the work and family lives of dual-earner couples caring both for children and aging parents. We sought to determine the prevalence of these couples in the United States and to understand the effects of being sandwiched on work–family fit, well-being, and work outcomes. In addition, we sought to understand the work and family coping strategies and workplace supports that were most effective in helping couples best integrate work and family. On the basis of our findings, we have provided suggestions for practice and policy for human resources personnel; employee assistance programs; work-life professionals; and working, sandwiched couples themselves.

We have based our work on a role quality perspective, which contends that roles such as spouse, parent, caregiver to a parent, and worker have both positive and negative aspects and that these rewards and stressors are reflected in both positive and negative consequences of role experiences for individuals. Thus, we have investigated not only the detrimental but also the beneficial aspects of combining work and family, taking into account not only the nature of role responsibilities but also how individuals experienced those roles. In fact, we found that role quality was generally more often a predictor of work and family outcomes than were objective role demands.

We also investigated the effects of occupying various social roles in the context of the other roles held. This has yielded a more complete view of work–family issues than is possible when only one family role is examined in conjunction with the work role. Thus, we have been able to examine the relative contribution of the spousal, child-care, parent-care, and work roles on work–family fit, well-being, and work.

Moreover, the study included both members of each couple, providing a more complete view of families and work. Much previous work–family research has focused exclusively on women, thus ignoring work and family issues among men. Indeed, the findings of the present study reveal men's involvement in both child and parent care and greater effects on men than women of certain child-care and parent-care duties. They call into question the notions of family caregiving as "women's work" and work–family issues as "women's issues." Our study demonstrates that considering the broader family context is not only useful but also necessary for understanding how sandwiched individuals are managing work and family.

Even those studies that have included both men and women have used the views of just one adult to represent the household. By having data from both members of each couple, we have been able to compare husbands' and wives' attitudes and experiences and identify similarities and differences. Also, we have been able to examine crossover effects of one spouse's attitudes or behaviors on the other, and we found some clear effects. Additional analyses of crossover effects, as well as dyadic analyses that use the couple as the unit of analysis, although not presented here, are possible, as are numerous other analyses, given the wealth of these data.

Finally, the longitudinal design of the study represents a major contribution. Most research on the work–family interface has been cross-sectional. By using a longitudinal design—that is, collecting data at two or more points in time—stronger inferences about causal relationships could be made. It also allowed us to see the ever-changing nature of roles.

The findings of this study have revealed the importance of role quality, particularly spouse and job role quality, for work–family fit, individual well-being, and positive work-related outcomes. Examination of role quality, as opposed to examining only role occupation, has been neglected in much of the previous research. The particular importance of spousal role quality that emerged in this study provides a clear indication that couples cannot afford to neglect their relationships with their spouse, despite their many competing caregiving and work role demands. The findings suggest the potential value of interventions that would identify ways to enhance the marital relationships of working, sandwiched couples and ways to encourage individuals to take care of themselves personally. Furthermore, the findings concerning the centrality of job role quality for positive work outcomes signal the merit of examining the structure of work and jobs to enhance not only individual well-being but also employers' bottom line.

It is our sincere hope that the findings presented here will be used to inform the development of public and workplace policies and programs to assist working families. We hope, too, that they will offer some helpful strategies to couples who find themselves simultaneously in the roles of workers, spouses or partners, parents, and caregivers to aging parents. Finally, we hope that the findings from this study will guide future research on the intersection between work and family, with the ultimate goal of enhancing the quality of lives of working couples caring for children and aging parents.

References

AARP. (2001). *In the middle: A report on multicultural boomers coping with family and aging issues.* Washington, DC: Author.

Adams, G. A., King, L. A., & King, D. W. (1996). Relationships of job and family involvement, family social support, and work–family conflict with job and life satisfaction. *Journal of Applied Psychology, 81,* 411–420.

Administration on Aging. (1999, May). Family caregiver fact sheet. Retrieved December 2, 2004, from http://www.aoa.dhhs.gov/May99/caregiver.html

Aldous, J. (1990). Specification and speculation concerning the politics of workplace family policies. *Journal of Family Issues, 11,* 355–367.

Allen, T. D. (2001). Family-supportive work environments: The role of organizational perspectives. *Journal of Vocational Behavior, 58,* 414–435.

Allison, P. D. (1990). Change scores as dependent variables in regression analysis. *Sociological Methodology, 20,* 93–114.

Amaro, H., Russo, N. F., & Johnson, J. (1987). Family and work predictors of psychological well-being among Hispanic women professionals. *Psychology of Women Quarterly, 11,* 505–521.

Amatea, E. S., & Fong-Beyette, M. L. (1987). Through a different lens: Examining professional women's interrole coping by focus and mode. *Sex Roles, 17,* 237–252.

American Business Collaborative for Dependent Care. (2004). Retrieved August 23, 2004, from www.abcdependentcare.com

Anderson, E. A., & Leslie, L. A. (1991). Coping with employment and family stress: Employment arrangement and gender differences. *Sex Roles, 24,* 223–237.

Andersson, L. (1999). Sweden and the futile struggle to avoid institutions. In V. M. Lechner & M. B. Neal (Eds.), *Work and caring for the elderly: International perspectives* (pp. 101–119). Philadelphia: Brunner/Mazel.

Aneshensel, C. S., Rutter, C. M., & Lachenbruch, P. A. (1991). Social structure, stress, and mental health: Competing conceptual and analytic models. *American Sociological Review, 56,* 166–178.

Arthur, M. M. (2003). Share price reactions to work–family human resource decisions: An institutional perspective. *Academy of Management Journal, 46,* 497–505.

Aryee, S. (1992). Antecedents and outcomes of work–family conflict among married professional women: Evidence from Singapore. *Human Relations, 45,* 816–837.

Aryee, S., Luk, V., Leung, A., & Lo, S. (1999). Role stressors, inter-role conflict, and well-being: The moderating influence of spousal support and coping behaviors among employed parents in Hong Kong. *Journal of Vocational Behavior, 54,* 259–278.

Assmann, S. F., Lawrence, R. H., & Tennstedt, S. L. (1996, November). *Quality of the caregiver–care recipient relationship: Does it offset negative consequences of caregiving?* Paper presented at the 49th Annual Scientific Meeting of the Gerontological Society of America, Washington, DC.

Axel, H. (1985). *Corporations and families: Changing practices and perspectives* (Report No. 868). New York: Conference Board.

Baltes, B. B., Briggs, T. E., Huff, J. W., Wright, J. A., & Neuman, G. A. (1999). Flexible and compressed workweek schedules: A meta-analysis of their effects on work-related criteria. *Journal of Applied Psychology, 84,* 496–513.

Baltes, B. B., & Heydens-Gahir, H. A. (2003). Reduction of work–family conflict through the use of selection, optimization, and compensation behaviors. *Journal of Applied Psychology, 88,* 1005–1018.

Barling, J., MacEwen, K. E., Kelloway, E. K., & Higginbottom, S. F. (1994). Predictors and outcomes of elder-care-based interrole conflict. *Psychology and Aging, 9,* 391–397.

Barnett, R. (1998). Toward a review and reconceptualization of the work/family literature. *Genetic, Social, and General Psychology Monographs, 124*(2), 125–183.

Barnett, R. C., & Baruch, G. K. (1985). Women's involvement in multiple roles and psychological distress. *Journal of Personality and Social Psychology, 45,* 135–145.

Barnett, R. C., & Brennan, R. T. (1995). The relationship between job experiences and psychological distress: A structural equation approach. *Journal of Organizational Behavior, 16,* 259–276.

Barnett, R. C., & Hyde, J. S. (2001). Women, men, work, and family: An expansionist theory. *American Psychologist, 56,* 781–796.

Barnett, R. C., & Marshall, N. L. (1992). Worker and mother roles, spillover effects and psychological distress. *Women and Health, 18,* 9–40.

Barnett, R. C., Marshall, N. L., Raudenbush, S. W., & Brennan, R. T. (1993). Gender and the relationship between job experiences and psychological distress: A study of dual-earner couples. *Journal of Personality and Social Psychology, 64,* 794–806.

Barnett, R. C., Raudenbush, S. W., Brennan, R. T., Pleck, J. H., & Marshall, N. L. (1995). Change in job and marital experiences and change in psychological distress: A longitudinal study of dual-earner couples. *Journal of Personality and Social Psychology, 69,* 839–850.

Barnett, R. C., & Rivers, C. (1996). *She works/he works: How two-income families are happier, healthier, and better-off.* New York: HarperCollins.

Barr, J. K., Johnson, K. W., & Warshaw, L. J. (1992). Supporting the elderly: Workplace programs for employed caregivers. *The Milbank Quarterly, 70,* 509–533.

Baruch, G. K., & Barnett, R. C. (1986a). Consequences of fathers' participation in family work: Parents' role strain and well-being. *Journal of Personality and Social Psychology, 51,* 983–992.

Baruch, G. K., & Barnett, R. C. (1986b). Role quality, multiple role involvement, and psychological well-being of mid-life women. *Journal of Personality and Social Psychology, 51*, 578–585.

Bedian, A. G., Burke, B. G., & Moffett, R. G. (1988). Outcomes of work–family conflict among married male and female professionals. *Journal of Management, 14*, 475–491.

Behson, S. J. (2002). Coping with family-to-work conflict: The role of informal work accommodations to family. *Journal of Occupational Health Psychology, 7*, 324–341.

Bengtson, V. L., & Lowenstein, A., Putney, N. M., & Gans, D. (2003). In V. L. Bengtson & A. Lowenstein (Eds.), *Global aging and challenges to families* (pp. 1–24). Hawthorne, NY: Aldine de Gruyter.

Beutell, N. J., & Greenhaus, J. H. (1982). Interrole conflict among married women: The influence of husband and wife characteristics on conflict and coping behavior. *Journal of Vocational Behavior, 21*, 99–110.

Bialik, R. (1999). Urbanization in Mexico affects traditional family caregiving of the elderly. In V. M. Lechner & M. B. Neal (Eds.), *Work and caring for the elderly: International perspectives* (pp. 160–173). Philadelphia: Brunner/Mazel.

Billings, A. G., & Moos, R. H. (1981). The role of coping responses and social resources in attenuating the stress of life events. *Journal of Behavioral Medicine, 4*, 139–157.

Bird, C. E., & Fremont, A. M. (1991). Gender, time use, and health. *Journal of Health & Social Behavior, 32*, 114–129.

Birg, H. (2001). *Die demographische Zeitenwende* [The changing demographic tide]. Munich, Germany: C. H. Beck.

Boaz, R., & Muller, C. (1992). Paid work and unpaid help by caregivers of the disabled and frail elders. *Medical Care, 30*, 149–158.

Boise, L., & Neal, M. B. (1996). Family responsibilities and absenteeism: Employees caring for parents versus employees caring for children. *Journal of Managerial Issues, 8*, 218–238.

Boles, J. S., Johnston, M. W., & Hair, J. F. (1997). Role stress, work–family conflict and emotional exhaustion: Inter-relationships and effects on some work-related consequences. *Journal of Personal Selling & Sales Management, 1*, 17–28.

Bolger, N., DeLongis, A., Kessler, R. C., & Wethington, E. (1989). The contagion of stress across multiple roles. *Journal of Marriage and the Family, 51*, 175–183.

Bond, J. T., Galinsky, E., Kim, S. S., & Brownfield, E. (2005). *The 2005 National Study of Employers*. New York: Families and Work Institute.

Bond, J. T., Galinsky, E., & Swanberg, J. (1998). *The 1997 National Study of the Changing Workforce*. New York: Families and Work Institute.

Bond, J. T., Thompson, C. A., Galinsky, E., & Prottas, D. (2003). *Highlights of the 2002 National Study of the Changing Workforce*. New York: Families and Work Institute.

Brennan, Rosenzweig, Ogilvie, Wuest, & Shindo (in press). Employed parents of children with mental health disorders: Achieving work–family fit, flexibility, and role quality. *Families in Society*.

Brockwood, K. J., Hammer, L. B., Neal, M. B., & Colton, C. L. (2001). Effects of accommodations made at home and at work on wives' and husbands' family and job satisfaction. *Journal of Feminist Family Therapy, 13*, 41–64.

Brody, E. M. (1981). "Women in the middle" and family help to older people. *The Gerontologist, 21,* 471–480.

Bronfenbrenner, U. (1977). Toward an experimental ecology of human development. *American Psychologist, 32,* 513–531.

Bronfenbrenner, U., McClelland, D., Wethington, E., Moen, P., & Ceci, S. J. (1996). *The state of Americans.* New York: Free Press.

Buffardi, L. C., Smith, J. L., O'Brien, A. S., & Erdwins, C. J. (1999). The impact of dependent-care responsibility and gender on work attitudes. *Journal of Occupational Health Psychology, 4,* 356–367.

Bureau of National Affairs. (1988). 33 ways to ease work/family tensions—An employer's checklist (Special Report No. 2). Rockville, MD: Buraff.

Burke, R. J. (1988). Some antecedents and consequences of work–family conflict. *Journal of Social Behavior and Personality, 3,* 287–302.

Burke, R. J. (1994). Stressful events, work–family conflict, coping, psychological burnout, and well-being among police officers. *Psychological Reports, 75,* 787–800.

Byars, L. L., & Rue, L. W. (2004). *Human resource management.* New York: McGraw-Hill/Irwin.

Caldwell, B. (1992, August). Long-term care: Demographics drive insurance industry, employer response to long-term care. *Employee Benefit Plan Review, 47*(2), 28–47.

Campbell, A., Converse, P. E., & Rodgers, W. L. (1975). *The quality of American life.* Ann Arbor, MI: Social Science Archive.

Canan, M. J., & Mitchell, W. D. (1991). *Employee fringe and welfare benefits plans: 1991 Edition, including coverage of the Omnibus Budget Reconciliation Act of 1990.* St. Paul, MN: West.

Casper, L. M., & Bianchi, S. M. (2002). *Continuity and change in the American family.* Thousand Oaks, CA: Sage.

Chan, D. (2001). Modeling method effects of positive affectivity, negative affectivity, and impression management in self reports of work attitudes. *Human Performance, 14,* 77–96.

Chapman, N. J., Ingersoll-Dayton, B., & Neal, M. B. (1994). Balancing the multiple roles of work and caregiving for children, adults, and elders. In C. P. Keita & J. J. Hurrel, Jr. (Eds.), *Job stress in a changing workforce* (pp. 283–300). Washington DC: American Psychological Association.

Chi, I. (1999). China and the family unit: Implications for employed caregivers. In V. M. Lechner & M. B. Neal (Eds.), *Work and caring for the elderly: International perspectives* (pp. 177–193). Philadelphia: Brunner/Mazel.

Childs, T. (1993, November). *IBM survey findings and program responses to eldercare.* Presentation given to the National Association of Women Legislators, New York.

Christensen, K. A., Stephens, M. A., & Townsend, A. L. (1998). Mastery in women's multiple roles and well-being: Adult daughters providing care to impaired parents. *Health Psychology, 17,* 163–171.

Christensen, K. E., & Staines, G. L. (1990). Flextime: A viable solution to work/family conflict? *Journal of Family Issues, 11,* 455–476.

Cleveland, J. N. (2005). What is success? Who defines it? Perspectives on the criterion problem as it relates to work and family. In E. E. Kossek & S. J. Lambert

(Eds.), *Work and life integration: Organizational, cultural, and individual perspectives* (pp. 319–346). Mahwah, NJ: Lawrence Erlbaum Associates.

Coberly, S., & Hunt, G. G. (1995). *The MetLife study of employer costs for working caregivers.* Washington, DC: Washington Business Group on Health.

Committee for Economic Development. (1987). *Work and change: Labor market adjustment policies in a competitive world.* New York: Author.

Committee for Economic Development. (1999). *New opportunities for older workers.* New York: Research and Policy Committee of the Committee for Economic Development.

Cook, W. L. (1994). A structural equation model of dyadic relationships within the family system. *Journal of Consulting and Clinical Psychology, 62,* 500–509.

Creedon, M. A. (1987). Introduction: Employment and eldercare. In M. Creedon (Ed.), *Issues for an aging America: Employees & eldercare: A briefing book* (pp. 2–4). Bridgeport, CT: University of Bridgeport, Center for the Study of Aging.

Creedon, M. (1995). Eldercare and work research in the United States. In J. Phillips (Ed.), *Working carers* (pp. 93–115). London: Avebury.

Creedon, M. A., & Tiven, M. (1989). *Eldercare in the workplace.* Washington, DC: National Council on the Aging.

Crouter, A. C., Bumpus, M. F., Maguire, M. C., & McHale, S. M. (1999). Linking parents' work pressure and adolescents' well-being: Insights into dynamics in dual-earner families. *Developmental Psychology, 35,* 1453–1461.

Dautzenberg, M., Diederiks, J., Philipsen, H., & Stevens, F. (1998). Women of a middle generation and parent care. *International Journal of Aging & Human Development, 47,* 241–262.

Dautzenberg, M. G. H., Diederiks, J. P. M., Philipsen, H., Stevens, F. C. J., Tan, F. E. S., & Vernooij-Dassen, M. J. F. (2000). The competing demands for paid work and parent care: Middle-aged daughters providing assistance to elderly parents. *Research on Aging, 22,* 165–187.

Davis, E., & Krouze, M. K. (1994). A maturing benefit: Eldercare after a decade. *Employee Benefits Journal, 19*(3), 16–20.

Davis, M. F., & Powell, R. (2003). The International Convention on the Rights of the Child: A catalyst for innovative childcare policies. *Human Rights Quarterly, 25,* 689–719.

Day, R. D. (1995). Family-systems theory. In R. D. Day, K. R. Gilbert, B. H. Settles, & W. R. Burr (Eds.), *Research and theory in family science* (pp. 91–101). Pacific Grove, CA: Brooks/Cole.

den Dulk, L. (2005). Workplace work–family arrangements: A study and explanatory framework of differences between organizational provisions in different welfare states. In S. Poelmans (Ed.), *Work and family: An international research perspective* (pp. 211–238). Mahwah, NJ: Lawrence Erlbaum Associates.

Downie, N. M., & Heath, R. W. (1970). *Basic statistical methods* (3rd ed.). New York: Harper & Row.

Dube, A., & Kaplan, E. (2002). *Paid family leave in California: An analysis of costs and benefits* (Working Paper No. 2). Berkeley: University of California, Labor Project for Working Families.

Durity, A. (1991). The sandwich generation feels the squeeze. *Management Review, 80*(12), 38–41.

Duxbury, L. E., & Higgins, C. A. (1991). Gender differences in work–family conflict. *Journal of Applied Psychology, 76,* 60–74.

Eaton, W. W., Smith, C., Ybarra, M., Muntaner, C., & Tien, A. (2004). Center for Epidemiological Studies Depression scale: Review and revision (CESD and CESD–R). In M. E. Maruish (Ed.), *The use of psychological testing for treatment planning and outcomes assessment* (pp. 363–377). Mahwah, NJ: Lawrence Erlbaum Associates.

Ebert, P., & Neal, M. (1988, November). *Gaining corporate participation in an employee survey and demonstration project.* Paper presented at the 41st annual scientific meeting of the Gerontological Society of America, San Francisco.

Eby, L. T., Casper, W. J., Lockwood, A., Bordeaux, C., & Brinley, A. (2005). Work and family research in IO/OB: Content analysis and review of the literature (1980–2002). *Journal of Vocational Behavior, 66,* 124–197.

Edwards, J. R., & Rothbard, N. P. (1999). Work and family stress and well-being: An examination of person–environment fit in the work and family domains. *Organizational Behavior and Human Decision Processes, 77,* 85–129.

Edwards, J. R., & Rothbard, N. P. (2000). Mechanisms linking work and family: Clarifying the relationships between work and family constructs. *Academy of Management Review, 25,* 178–199.

Eldercare referrals for employees. (1994). *Small Business Reports, 19*(2), 19–20.

Emlen, A. C. (1996). *Oregon Child Care Research Partnership, Re: Scale Development.* Unpublished technical report, Portland State University.

Employee Benefit Research Institute. (1990). *Fundamentals of employee benefit programs* (4th ed.). Washington, DC: Author.

Esping-Andersen, G. (1990). *The three worlds of welfare capitalism.* Princeton, NJ: Princeton University Press.

Esping-Andersen, G. (1999). *Social foundations of postindustrial economies.* New York: Oxford University Press.

Family Caregiver Alliance (2003). Paid Family Leave Act—SB 1661: Ten quick facts. San Francisco: Author.

Federal Interagency Forum on Aging-Related Statistics. (2000). *Older Americans 2000: Key indicators of well-being.* Washington, DC: U.S. Government Printing Office.

Federal Interagency Forum on Aging-Related Statistics. (2004). *Older Americans 2004: Key indicators of well-being.* Washington, DC: U.S. Government Printing Office.

Feinberg, L. F., & Newman, S. L. (2004). A study of 10 states since passage of the National Family Caregiver Support Program: Policies, perceptions, and program development. *The Gerontologist, 44,* 760–769.

Feinberg, L. F., Newman, S. L., & Steenberg, C. V. (2002). *Family caregiver support: Policies, perceptions and practices in 10 states since passage of the national caregiver support program.* San Francisco: Family Caregiver Alliance.

Fernandez, J. P. (1990). *The politics and reality of family care in corporate America.* Lexington, MA: Heath.

Fierman, J. (1994, March 21). Are companies less family-friendly? *Fortune, 129*(6), 64–67.

Flynn, G. (1994). Elder relocation may become a factor in employee moves. *Personnel Journal, 73*(7), 18.

Folkman, S. (1984). Personal control and stress and coping processes: A theoretical analysis. *Journal of Personality and Social Psychology, 46,* 839–852.

Folkman, S., & Lazarus, R. S. (1980). An analysis of coping in a middle-aged community sample. *Journal of Health and Social Behavior, 21,* 219–239.

Folkman, S., & Lazarus, R. S. (1985). If it changes it must be a process: Study of emotion and coping during three stages of a college examination. *Journal of Personality and Social Psychology, 48,* 150–170.

Folkman, S., Lazarus, R. S., Gruen, R. J., & DeLongis, A. (1986). Appraisal, coping, health status, and psychological symptoms. *Journal of Personality and Social Psychology, 50,* 571–579.

Fredriksen-Goldsen, K. I., & Scharlach, A. E. (2001). *Families and work: New directions in the twenty-first century.* New York: Oxford University Press.

Freudenheim, M. (2003). Employees paying ever-bigger share for health care. *New York Times.* Retrieved September 10, 2003, from http://www.nytimes.com/2003/09/10/business/10CARE.html

Friedman, D. E. (1986, June). Eldercare: The employee benefit of the 1990s? *Across the Board, 23*(6), 45–51.

Friedman, D. E., & Johnson, A. A. (1997). Moving from programs to culture change: The next stage for the corporate work–family agenda. In S. Parasuraman & J. H. Greenhaus (Eds.), *Integrating work and family: Challenges and choices for a changing world* (pp. 192–208). Westport, CT: Quorum Books.

Froberg, D., Gjerdingen, D., & Preston, M. (1986). Multiple roles and women's mental health: What have we learned? *Women and Health Review, 11,* 79–96.

Frone, M. R. (2000). Work–family conflict and employee psychiatric disorders: The National Comorbidity Survey. *Journal of Applied Psychology, 85,* 888–895.

Frone, M. R., & Rice, R. W. (1987). Work–family conflict: The effect of job and family involvement. *Journal of Occupational Behavior, 8,* 45–55.

Frone, M. R., Russell, M., & Cooper, M. L. (1992). Antecedents and outcomes of work–family conflict: Testing a model of the work–family interface. *Journal of Applied Psychology, 77,* 65–78.

Frone, M. R., Russell, M., & Cooper, M. L. (1997). Relation of work–family conflict to health outcomes: A four-year longitudinal study of employed parents. *Journal of Occupational & Organizational Psychology, 70,* 325–335.

Frone, M. R., Yardley, J. K., & Markel, K. S. (1997). Developing and testing an integrative model of the work–family interface. *Journal of Vocational Behavior, 50,* 145–167.

Fukuda, N. (1993). Comparing family-friendly policies in Japan and Europe: Are we in the same or a different league? *Journal of Population and Social Security (Population)1* (Suppl.), 31–45.

Gabel, J., Levitt, L., Pickreign, J., Whitmore, H., Holve, E., Rowland, D., et al. (2001). Job-based health insurance in 2001: Inflation hits double digits, managed care retreats. *Health Affairs, 20,* 180–186.

Galinsky, E., & Bond, J. T. (1998). *The 1998 business work–life study: A sourcebook.* New York: Families and Work Institute.

Galinsky, E., Friedman, D. E., Hernandez, C. A. (with Axel, H.). (1991). *Corporate reference guide to work–family programs.* New York: Families and Work Institute.

Galinsky, E., & Stein, P. J. (1990). The impact of human resource policies on employees: Balancing work/family life. *Journal of Family Issues, 11,* 368–383.

Garrison, A., & Jelin, M. A. (1990, October). *The Partnership for Eldercare Research Study.* New York: New York City Department for the Aging.

Gignac, M. A. M., Kelloway, E. K., & Gottlieb, B. H. (1996). The impact of caregiving on employment: A mediational model of work–family conflict. *Canadian Journal on Aging, 15,* 525–542.

Goff, S. J., Mount, M. K., & Jamison, R. L. (1990). Employer supported child care, work/family conflict, and absenteeism: A field study. *Personnel Psychology, 43,* 793–809.

Gonyea, J. G. (1997). The *real* meaning of balancing work and family. *Public Policy and Aging Report 8*(3), 6–8.

Goode, W. J. (1960). A theory of role strain. *American Sociological Review, 25,* 483–496.

Gorey, K. M., Brice, G. C., & Rice, R. W. (1990). An elder care training needs assessment among employee assistance program staff. *Employee Assistance Quarterly, 5*(3), 71–93.

Gorey, K. M., Rice, R. W., & Brice, G. C. (1992). The prevalence of elder care responsibilities among the work force population: Response bias among a group of cross-sectional surveys. *Research on Aging, 14,* 399–418.

Gottlieb, B. H., Kelloway, E. K., & Fraboni, M. (1994) Aspects of eldercare that place employees at risk. *The Gerontologist, 34,* 815–821.

Grandey, A. A. (2001). Family friendly policies: Organizational justice perceptions of need-based allocations. In R. Cropanzano (Ed.), *Justice in the workplace: From theory to practice* (pp. 145–173). Mahwah, NJ: Lawrence Erlbaum Associates.

Grant, D. B. (1992). "Total compensation" plan design—Beyond dependent care benefits: The life cycle allowance. *Compensation & Benefits Management, 8*(4), 73–75.

Greenhaus, J. H., & Beutell, N. J. (1985). Sources of conflict between work and family roles. *Academy of Management Review, 10,* 76–88.

Greenhaus, J. H., & Parasuraman, S. (2002). The allocation of time to work and family roles. In D. L. Nelson & R. J. Burke (Eds.), *Gender, work stress, and health* (pp. 115–128). Washington, DC: American Psychological Association.

Greenhaus, J. H., & Powell, G. N. (2006). When work and family are allies: A theory of work–family enrichment. *Academy of Management Review, 31,* 1–21.

Grover, S. L., & Crooker, K. J. (1995). Who appreciates family-responsive human resource policies: The impact of family-friendly policies on the organizational attachment of parents and non-parents. *Personnel Psychology, 48,* 271–288.

Gryzwacz, J. G. (2000). Work–family spillover and health during midlife: Is managing conflict everything? *American Journal of Health Promotion, 14,* 236–243.

Grzywacz, J. G., Almeida, D. M., & McDonald, D. A. (2002). Work–family spillover and daily reports of work and family stress in the adult labor force. *Family Relations: Interdisciplinary Journal of Applied Family Studies, 51,* 28–36.

Grzywacz, J. G., & Marks, N. F. (2000a). Family, work, work–family spillover and problem drinking during midlife. *Journal of Marriage and the Family, 62,* 336–348.

Grzywacz, J. G., & Marks, N. F. (2000b). Reconceptualizing the work–family interface: An ecological perspective on the correlates of positive and negative spillover between work and family. *Journal of Occupational Health Psychology, 5,* 111–126.

Gutek, B. A., Searle, S., & Klepa, L. (1991). Rational versus gender role explanations for work–family conflict. *Journal of Applied Psychology, 76,* 560–568.

Haas, L., Allard, K., & Hwang, P. (2002). The impact of organizational culture on men's use of parental leave in Sweden. *Community, Work, and Family, 5,* 319–342.

Hackman, J. R., & Oldham, G. R. (1975). Development of the Job Diagnostic Survey. *Journal of Applied Psychology, 60,* 159–170.

Hall, D. T. (1972). A model of coping with role conflict: The role behavior of college educated women. *Administrative Science Quarterly, 17,* 471–486.

Hammer, L. B., Allen, E., & Grigsby, T. (1997). Work–family conflict in dual-earner couples: Within-individual and crossover effects of work and family. *Journal of Vocational Behavior, 50,* 185–203.

Hammer, L. B., & Barbera, K. M. (1997). Toward an integration of alternative work schedules and human resource systems. *Human Resource Planning, 20*(2), 28–36.

Hammer, L. B., Bauer, T. N., & Grandey, A. A. (2003). Work–family conflict and work-related withdrawal behaviors. *Journal of Business and Psychology, 17,* 419–436.

Hammer, L. B., Colton, C. L., Caubet, S., & Brockwood, K. B. (2002). The unbalanced life: Work and family conflict. In J. C. Thomas & M. Hersen (Eds.), *Handbook of mental health in the workplace* (pp. 83–101). Newbury Park, CA: Sage.

Hammer, L. B., Cullen, J. C., Neal, M. B., Sinclair, R. R., & Shafiro, M. (2005). The longitudinal effects of work–family conflict and positive spillover on experiences of depressive symptoms among dual-earner couples. *Journal of Occupational Health Psychology, 10,* 138–154.

Hammer, L. B., Cullen, J. C., & Shafiro, M. (2006). Work–family best practices. In F. Jones, R. Burke, & M. Westman (Eds.), *Work-life balance: A psychological perspective* (pp. 261–275). East Sussex, England: Psychology Press.

Hammer, L. B., Neal, M. B., Newsom, J., Brockwood, K. J., & Colton, C. (2005). A longitudinal study of the effects of dual-earner couples' utilization of family-friendly workplace supports on work and family outcomes. *Journal of Applied Psychology, 90,* 799–810.

Hanson, B. G. (1995). *General systems theory beginning with wholes.* Washington, DC: Taylor and Francis.

Hanson, G., Hammer, L. B., & Colton, C. (in press). Development and validation of a multidimensional scale of work–family positive spillover. *Journal of Occupational Health Psychology.*

Haupt, J. (1992). Eldercare: The next frontier in family benefits. *Pension World, 28*(7), 10–13.

Hayden, L. C., Schiller, M., Dickstein, S., Seifer, R., Sameroff, A. J., Miller, I., et al. (1998). Levels of family assessment: I. Family, marital, and parent–child interaction. *Journal of Family Psychology, 12,* 7–22.

Hayghe, H. V. (1988, September). Employers and child care: What roles do they play? *Monthly Labor Review, 111,* 38–44.

Hayward, L., Davies, S., Robb, R., Denton, M. & Auton, G. (2004). Publicly funded and family-friend care in the case of long-term illness: The role of the spouse. *Canadian Journal on Aging, 23* (Suppl. 1), S39–S48.

He, W., Sengupta, M., Velkoff, V. A., & DeBarros, K. A. (2005). *65+ in the United States: 2005.* U.S. Census Bureau, Current Population Reports, P23–209. Washington, DC: U.S. Government Printing Office. Retrieved April 8, 2006, from http://www.census.gov/population/www/socdemo/age.html#elderly

Health Action Forum of Greater Boston. (1989). *Eldercare: The state of the art.* Boston: Author.

Hepburn, C. G., & Barling, J. (1996). Eldercare responsibilities, interrole conflict, and employee absence: A daily study. *Journal of Occupational Health Psychology, 1,* 311–318.

Heymann, J. (2000). *The widening gap: Why America's working families are in jeopardy and what can be done about it.* New York: Basic Books.

Higgins, C. A., & Duxbury, L. E. (1992). Work–family conflict: A comparison of dual-career and traditional-career men. *Journal of Organizational Behavior, 13,* 389–411.

Higgins, C. A., Duxbury, L. E., & Irving, R. H. (1992). Work–family conflict in the dual-career family. *Organizational Behavior and Human Decision Processes, 51,* 51–75.

Hill, E. J., Miller, B. C., Weiner, S. P., & Colihan, J. (1998). Influences of the virtual office on aspects of work and work/life balance. *Personnel Psychology, 51,* 667–683.

Hochschild, A. R. (1997). *The time bind: When work becomes home and home becomes work.* New York: Metropolitan Books.

Hoffman, C. (2000). Dependent care in the 21st century: Broadening the definition for employee assistance practice. *Employee Assistance Quarterly, 16,* 15–32.

Honeycutt, T. L., & Rosen, B. (1997). Family friendly human resource policies, salary levels, and salient identity as predictors of organizational attraction. *Journal of Vocational Behavior, 50,* 271–290.

Hooyman, N. R., & Kiyak, H. A. (2005). *Social gerontology: A multidisciplinary perspective* (7th ed.). Boston: Allyn & Bacon.

Huang, Y. E., Hammer, L. B., Neal, M. B., & Perrin, N. (2004). The relationship between work-to-family and family-to-work conflict: a longitudinal study. *Journal of Family and Economic Issues, 25,* 79–100.

Hughes, D., & Galinsky, E. (1988). Balancing work and family lives: Research and corporate applications. In A. E. Gottfried & A. W. Gottfried (Eds.), *Maternal employment and children's development: Longitudinal research* (pp. 233–268). New York: Plenum.

Ingersoll-Dayton, B., Chapman, N., & Neal, M. (1990). A program for caregivers in the workplace. *The Gerontologist, 30,* 126–130.

Ingersoll-Dayton, B., Neal, M. B., Ha, J., & Hammer, L. B. (2003). Collaboration among siblings providing care for older parents. *Journal of Gerontological Social Work, 40,* 51–66.

Ingersoll-Dayton, B., Neal, M. B., & Hammer, L. B. (2001). Aging parents helping adult children: The experience of the sandwiched generation. *Family Relations: Interdisciplinary Journal of Applied Family Studies, 50,* 263–271.

Ishii-Kuntz, M. (1999). Japan and its planning toward family caregiving. In V. M. Lechner & M. B. Neal (Eds.), *Work and caring for the elderly: International perspectives* (pp. 84–100). Philadelphia: Brunner/Mazel.

Jacobs, J. A., & Gerson, K. (2004). *The time divide: Work, family, and gender inequality.* Cambridge, MA: Harvard University Press.

John, O. P. (1989). Towards a taxonomy of personality descriptors. In D. H. Buss & N. Cantor (Eds.), *Personality psychology: Recent trends and emerging directions* (pp. 261–271). New York: Springer-Verlag.

Johnston, W. B., & Packer, A. H. (1987). *Workforce 2000: Work and workers for the twenty-first century.* Indianapolis, IN: Hudson Institute.

Jones, F., & Fletcher, B. C. (1993). An empirical study of occupational stress transmission in working couples, *Human Relations, 46,* 881–903.

Judge, T. A., Boudreau, J. W., & Bretz, R. D., Jr. (1994). Job and life attitudes of male executives. *Journal of Applied Psychology, 79,* 767–782.

Judiesch, M. K., & Lyness, K. S. (1999). Left behind? The impact of leaves of absence on managers' career success. *Academy of Management Journal, 42,* 641–651.

Judy, R. W., & D'Amico, C. (1997). *Workforce 2020.* Indianapolis, IN: Hudson Institute.

Kahn, R., & Antonucci, T. (1980). *Social networks in adult life: Principal questionnaire.* Unpublished manuscript, University of Michigan, Survey Research Center.

Kahn, R. L., Wolfe, D. M., Quinn, R., Snoek, J. D., & Rosenthal, R. A. (1964). *Organizational stress.* New York: Wiley.

Kahn, S., Long, B. C., & Petersen, C. (1989). Marital and parental status and quality of life of female clerical workers. *Canadian Journal of Counseling, 37,* 185–194.

Kaiser Family Foundation & Health Research and Educational Trust. (2003). *Employer health benefits: 2003 annual survey.* Retrieved November 14, 2004, from http://www.kff.org

Kamerman, S. B. (1983). *Meeting family needs: The corporate response* (Work in America Institute Studies in Productivity, Vol. 33). New York: Pergamon.

Kamerman, S. B. (1991). Child care policies and programs: An international overview. *Journal of Social Issues, 47,* 179–196.

Kamerman, S. B., & Kingston, P. W. (1982). Employer responses to the family responsibilities of employees. In S. B. Kamerman & C. D. Hayes (Eds.), *Families that work: Children in a changing world* (pp. 144–208). Washington, DC: National Academy Press.

Katz, D., & Kahn, R. (1978). *The social psychology of organizations* (2nd ed.). New York: Wiley.

Katz, S., Ford, A. B., & Moskowitz, R. W. (1963). Studies of illness in the aged. The Index of ADL: A standardized measure of biological and psychosocial function. *Journal of the American Medical Association, 185,* 914–919.

Kingston, P. W. (1990). Illusions and ignorance about the family-responsive workplace. *Journal of Family Issues, 11,* 438–454.

Kinnunen, U., & Mauno, S. (1998). Antecedents and outcomes of work–family conflict among employed women and men in Finland. *Human Relations, 51,* 157–177.

Kirchmeyer, C. (1992). Nonwork participation and work attitudes: A test of scarcity vs. expansion models of personal resources. *Human Relations, 45,* 775–795.

Kirchmeyer, C. (1993). Nonwork-to-work spillover: A more balanced view of the experiences and coping of professional men and women. *Sex Roles, 28,* 531–552.

Kirchmeyer, C., & Cohen, A. (1999). Different strategies for managing the work/non-work interface: A test for unique pathways to work outcomes. *Work & Stress, 13,* 59–73.

Koludrubetz, W. W. (1974, April). Two decades of employee benefits plans, 1981. *Social Security Bulletin, 37*, 17–35.

Kossek, E. E. (1990). Diversity in child care assistance needs: Employee problems, preferences, and work-related outcomes. *Personnel Psychology, 43*, 769–791.

Kossek, E. E., DeMarr, B. J., Backman, K., & Kollar, M. (1993). Assessing employees' emerging elder care needs and reactions to dependent care benefits. *Public Personnel Management, 22*, 617–638.

Kossek, E. E., & Lambert, S. J. (1995). *Work and life integration: Organizational, Cultural, and individual perspectives.* Mahwah, NJ: Lawrence Erlbaum Associates.

Kossek, E. E., & Lambert, S. (Eds.). (2005). *Work and life integration: Organizational, cultural and psychological perspectives.* Mahwah, NJ: Lawrence Erlbaum Associates.

Kossek, E. E., & Nichol, V. (1992). The effects of on-site child care on employee attitudes and performance. *Personnel Psychology, 45*, 485–509.

Kossek, E. E., & Ozeki, C. (1998). Work–family conflict, policies, and the job–life satisfaction relationship: A review and directions for organizational behavior–human resources research. *Journal of Applied Psychology, 83*, 139–149.

Kossek, E. E., & Ozeki, C. (1999). Bridging the work–family policy and productivity gap: A literature review. *Community, Work and Family, 2*, 7–32.

Koyano, W. (2003). Intergenerational relationships of Japanese seniors: Changing patterns. In V. L. Bengtson & A. Lowenstein (Eds.), *Global aging and challenges to families* (pp. 272–283). Hawthorne, NY: Aldine de Gruyter.

Kramer, B. J. (1993). Expanding the conceptualization of caregiver coping: The importance of relationship-focused coping strategies. *Family Relations, 42*, 383–391.

Kramer, B. J., & Kipnis, S. (1995). Eldercare and work-role conflict: Toward an understanding of gender differences in caregiver burden. *The Gerontologist, 35*, 340–348.

Kuzmits, F. E. (1998). Communicating benefits: A double-click away. *Compensation & Benefits Review 14*(9), 60–64.

Lambert, S. J. (2000). Added benefits: The link between work-life benefits and organizational citizenship behavior. *Academy of Management Journal, 43*, 801–815.

Lawton, M., & Brody, E. (1969). Assessment of older people: Self-maintaining and instrumental activities of daily living. *The Gerontologist, 9*, 179–186.

Lazarus, R. S. (1993). Coping theory and research: Past, present, and future. *Psychosomatic Medicine, 55*, 234–247.

Lechner, V. (1999). Final thoughts. In V. M. Lechner & M. B. Neal (Eds.), *Work and caring for the elderly: International perspectives* (pp. 211–232). Philadelphia: Brunner/Mazel.

Lechner, V. M., & Creedon, M. A. (1994). *Managing work and family life.* New York: Springer.

Lechner, V. M., & Neal, M. B. (1999). The mix of public and private programs in the United States: Implications for employed caregivers. In V. M. Lechner & M. B. Neal (Eds.), *Work and caring for the elderly: International perspectives* (pp. 120–139). Philadelphia: Brunner/Mazel.

Lehman, R. S. (1991). *Statistics and research design in the behavioral sciences.* Belmont, CA: Wadsworth.

Leiter, V., Krauss, M. W., Anderson, B., & Wells, N. (2004). The consequences of caring: Effects of mothering a child with special needs. *Journal of Family Issues, 25*, 379–403.

Lewis, S., Rapoport, R., & Gambles, R. (2003). Reflections on the integration of paid work and the rest of life. *Journal of Managerial Psychology, 18*, 824–841.

Liebig, P. S. (1993). Factors affecting the development of employer-sponsored elder-care programs: Implications for employed caregivers. *Journal of Women & Aging, 5*, 59–78.

Litwak, E., Silverstein, M., Bengtson, V., & Hirst, Y. W. (2003). Theories about families, organizations, and social supports. In V. L. Bengtson & A. Lowenstein (Eds.), *Global aging and challenges to families* (pp. 27–53). Hawthorne, NY: Aldine de Gruyter.

Loerch, K. J., Russell, J. E., & Rush, M. C. (1989). The relationships among family domain variables and work–family conflict for men and women. *Journal of Vocational Behavior, 35*, 288–308.

Loomis, L. S., & Booth, A. (1995). Multigenerational caregiving and well-being: The myth of the beleaguered sandwich generation. *Journal of Family Issues, 16*, 131–148.

Lottes, J. (2005). *An investigation of the value of informal care to aging parents.* Unpublished doctoral dissertation, Portland State University.

MacEwen, K. E., & Barling, J. (1994). Daily consequences of work interference with family and family interference with work. *Work and Stress, 8*, 244–254.

Major, V. S., Klein, J., & Ehrhart, M. G. (2002). Work time, work interference with family, and psychological distress. *Journal of Applied Psychology, 87*(3), 427–436.

Marks, N. F. (1998). Does it hurt to care? Caregiving work–family conflict, and mid-life well-being. *Journal of Marriage and the Family, 60*, 951–966.

Marks, N. F. (2001). Caregiving across the lifespan: National prevalence and predictors. *Family Relations, 45*, 27–36.

Marks, S. R. (1977). Multiple roles and role strain: Some notes on human energy, time and commitment. *American Sociological Review, 42*, 921–936.

Marshall, N. L., & Barnett, R. C. (1993). Work–family strains and gains among two-earner couples. *Journal of Community Psychology, 21*, 64–78.

Marshall V. W., Clarke P., & Ballantyne, P. (2001). Instability in the retirement transition: Effects on health and well being in a Canadian study. *Research on Aging, 23*, 379–409.

Martin-Matthews, A. (1996). Why I dislike the term "eldercare." *Transition, 26*(3), 16.

Martin-Matthews, A. (1999). Canada and the changing profile of health and social services: Implications for employment and caregiving. In V. M. Lechner & M. B. Neal (Eds.), *Work and caring for the elderly: International perspectives* (pp. 11–28). Philadelphia: Brunner/Mazel.

Martin-Matthews, A., & Campbell, L. D. (1995). Gender roles, employment and informal care. In S. Arber & J. Ginn (Eds.), *Connecting gender and ageing: Sociological reflections* (pp. 129–143). Buckingham, England: Open University Press.

Martinez, M. N. (1993). Family support makes business sense. *HRMagazine, 38*(1), 38–43.

Martire, L. M., & Stephens, M. A. P. (2003). Juggling parent care and employment responsibilities: The dilemmas of adult daughter caregivers in the workforce. *Sex Roles, 48*, 167–173.

Martire, L. M., Stephens, M. A. P., & Atienza, A. A. (1997). The interplay of work and caregiving: Relationships between role satisfaction, role involvement, and caregiver's well-being. *Journal of Gerontology: Social Sciences, 52B*, S279–289.

Martocchio, J. J. (2003). *Employee benefits: A primer for human resource professionals.* New York: McGraw-Hill/Irwin.

Matsui, T., Ohsawa, T., & Onglatco, M. (1995). Work–family conflict and the stress-buffering effects of husband support and coping behavior among Japanese married working women. *Journal of Vocational Behavior, 47,* 178–192.

McDowell, I., & Newell, C. (1996). *Measuring health: A guide to rating scales and questionnaires.* New York: Oxford University Press.

Meeker, S. E., & Campbell, N. D. (1986). Providing for dependent care. *Business and Health, 3*(7), 18–22.

Menaghan, E. G. (1983). Marital stress and family transitions: A panel analysis. *Journal of Marriage and the Family, 45,* 371–386.

MetLife & National Alliance for Caregiving. (1997). *The MetLife study of employer costs for working caregivers.* Westport, CT: Author.

MetLife Mature Market Institute & National Alliance for Caregiving. (2006, June). The MetLife caregiving cost study: Productivity losses to U.S. business. Westport, CT: Authors.

Miech, R. A., & Shanahan, M. J. (2000). Socioeconomic status and depression over the life course. *Journal of Health and Social Behavior, 41,* 162–176.

Milkovich, G. T., & Gomez, L. R. (1976). Day care and selected employee work behaviors. *Academy of Management Journal, 19,* 111–115.

Miller, D. A. (1981). The "sandwich" generation: Adult children of the aging. *Social Work, 26,* 419–423.

Moen, P. (2003). *It's about time: Couples and careers.* Ithaca, NY: Cornell University Press.

Morgan, H., & Tucker, K. (1991). *Companies that care: The most family-friendly companies in America—What they offer and how they got that way.* New York: Simon & Schuster/Fireside.

Murphy, K. R., & Myors, B. (2004). *Statistical power analysis: A simple and general model for traditional and modern hypothesis tests.* Mahwah, NJ: Lawrence Erlbaum Associates.

National Alliance for Caregiving. (2005). *International caregiving legislation.* Retrieved October, 28, 2005, from http://www.caregiving.org/intcaregiving/intlindex.htm

National Alliance for Caregiving & AARP. (2004). *Caregiving in the U.S.* Washington, DC: Authors.

National Alliance for Caregiving (NAC) & American Association of Retired Persons. (1997). *Family caregiving in the U.S.: Findings from a national survey.* Washington, DC: Authors.

National Research Council & Institute of Medicine. (2004). *Health and safety needs of older workers.* Washington, DC: National Academies Press.

Neal, M. (1990, November). *Employer-sponsored long-term care insurance: Factors in decisions to offer.* Paper presented at the 43rd Annual Scientific Meeting of the Gerontological Society of America, Boston.

Neal, M. (1999). Historische Entwicklung und Perspektiven betrieblicher Maßnahmen zur Unterstützung erwerbstätiger Pflegender in den USA [Employers' elder care activities in the United States of America: History and evolution]. In G. Naegele & M. Reichert (Eds.), *Vereinbarkeit von Erwerbstätigkeit und Pflege: Nationale und Internationale Perspektiven II* [Combining work and caregiving: National and international perspectives] (pp. 191–237). Hannover, Germany: Vincentz Verlag (English translation available from the author).

Neal, M. B., Chapman, N. J., Ingersoll-Dayton, B., & Emlen, A. C. (1993). *Balancing work and caregiving for children, adults, and elders*. Newbury Park, CA: Sage.

Neal, M. B., Chapman, N. J., Ingersoll-Dayton, B., Emlen, A. C., & Boise, L. (1990). Absenteeism and stress among employed caregivers of the elderly, disabled adults, and children. In D. E. Biegel & A. Blum (Eds.), *Aging and caregiving: Theory, research, and policy* (pp. 160–183). Newbury Park, CA: Sage.

Neal, M. B., & Hammer, L. B. (with Brockwood, K. J., Caubet, S., Colton, C., Hammond, T., Huang, E., Isgrigg, J., & Rickard, A.). (2001). *Supporting employees with child and elder care needs: A work–family sourcebook for employers*. Portland, OR: Portland State University.

Neal, M. B., Hammer, L. B., & Morgan, D. (2006). Using mixed methods in research related to work and family. In M. Pitt-Catsouphes, E. E. Kossek, & S. Sweet (Eds.), *The work and family handbook: Multi-disciplinary perspectives, methods and perspectives* (pp. 587–606). Mahwah, NJ: Lawrence Erlbaum Associates.

Neal, M. B., Ingersoll-Dayton, B., & Starrels, M. E. (1997). Gender and relationship differences in caregiving patterns and consequences among employed caregivers. *The Gerontologist, 37*, 804–816.

Neal, M. B., & Wagner, D. L. (2002). *Working caregivers: Issues, challenges and opportunities for the aging network*. Retrieved March 3, 2004, from http://www.aoa.gov/prof/aoaprog/caregiver/careprof/progguidance/background/program_issues/special_caregiver_pop.asp.

Netemeyer, R. G., Boles, J. S., & McMurrian, R. (1996). Development and validation of work–family conflict and family–work conflict scales. *Journal of Applied Psychology, 81*, 400–410.

New York Business Group on Health. (1986). *Employer support for employee caregivers*. New York: Author.

Nichols, L. S., & Junk, V. W. (1997). The sandwich generation: Dependency, proximity, and task assistance needs of parents. *Journal of Family and Economic Issues, 18*, 299–326.

Norton, T. R., Stephens, M. P., Martire, L. M., Townsend, A. L., & Gupta, A. (2002). Change in the centrality of women's multiple roles: Effects of role stress and rewards. *Journals of Gerontology: Series B: Psychological Sciences & Social Sciences. 57B*(1), S52–S62.

Offerman, L. R., & Gowing, M. K. (1990). Organizations of the future: Changes and challenges. *American Psychologist, 45*, 95–108.

Olmsted, B., & Smith, S. (1989). *Creating a flexible workplace: How to select and manage alternative work options*. New York: American Management Association.

Ontario Women's Directorate. (1990). *Work and family: The crucial balance*. Toronto, Ontario, Canada: Author.

Parasuraman, S., Greenhaus, J. H., & Granrose, C. S. (1992). Role stressors, social support, and well-being among two-career couples. *Journal of Organizational Behavior, 13*, 339–356.

Pavalko, E. K., & Artis, J. E. (1997). Women's caregiving and paid work: Causal relationships in late midlife. *Journals of Gerontology: Psychological Sciences and Social Sciences, 52B*, S170–S179.

Pavalko, E. K., & Woodbury, S. (2000). Social roles as process: Caregiving careers and women's health. *Journal of Health and Social Behavior, 41*, 91–105.

Pearlin, L. I., & Schooler, C. (1978). The structure of coping. *Journal of Health and Social Behavior, 19*, 2–21.

Penning, M. J. (1998). In the middle: Parental caregiving in the context of other roles. *Journal of Gerontology: Social Sciences, 4*, S188–S197.

Perry-Smith, J. E., & Blum, T. C. (2000). Work–family human resource bundles and perceived organizational performance. *Academy of Management Journal, 43*, 1107–1117.

Phillips, J. (1999). Developing a caregivers' strategy in Britain. In V. M. Lechner & M. B. Neal (Eds.), *Work and caring for the elderly: International perspectives* (pp. 47–67). Philadelphia: Brunner/Mazel.

Phillips, J., Bernard, M., & Chittenden, M. (2002). *Juggling work and care: The experiences of working carers of older adults.* Bristol, England: The Polity Press.

Piacentini, J. S., & Cerino, T. J. (1990). *EBRI databook on employee benefits.* Washington, DC: Employee Benefit Research Institute.

Pierce, J. L., & Newstrom, J. W. (1983). The design of flexible work schedules and employee responses: Relationships and process. *Journal of Occupational Behavior, 4*, 247–262.

Pierce, J. L., Newstrom, J. W., Dunham, R. B., & Barber, A. E. (1989). *Alternative work schedules.* Newton, MA: Allyn & Bacon.

Piotrkowski, C. S. (1979). *Work and the family system: A naturalistic study of working class and lower-middle-class families.* New York: Free Press.

Pleck, J. H., Staines, G., & Lang, L. (1980). Conflicts between work and family life. *Monthly Labor Review, 103*, 29–32.

Poelmans, S. A. (2005). *Work and family: An international research perspective.* Mahwah, NJ: Lawrence Erlbaum Associates.

Presser, H. B. (2003). *Working in a 24/7 economy: Challenges for American families.* New York: Russell Sage Foundation.

Probst, T. (2005). Economic stressors. In J. Barling, E. K. Kelloway, & M. R. Frone (Eds.), *Handbook of work stress* (pp. 267–298). Thousand Oaks, CA: Sage.

Pruchno, R. A., Burant, C. J., & Peters, N. D. (1997). Coping strategies of people living in multigenerational households: Effects on well-being. *Psychology and Aging, 12*, 115–124.

Queensland Government (2003). *Queensland government carer recognition policy.* Queensland, Australia: Queensland Government Press.

Quinn, R. P., & Staines, G. L. (1979). *The 1977 Quality of Employment Survey.* Ann Arbor: University of Michigan, Institute for Social Research.

Raabe, P. H. (1990). The organizational effects of workplace family policies: Past weaknesses and recent progress toward improved research. *Journal of Family Issues, 11*, 477–491.

Raabe, P. H., & Gessner, J. C. (1988). Employer family-supportive policies: Diverse variations on the theme. *Family Relations, 37*, 196–202.

Radloff, L. S. (1977). The CES–D scale: A self-report depression scale for research in the general population. *Applied Psychological Measurement, 1,* 385–401.

Raphael, D., & Schlesinger, B. (1993). Caring for elderly parents and adult children living at home: Interactions of the Sandwich Generation family. *Social Work Research and Abstracts, 29*(1), 3–8.

Reichert, M., & Naegele, G. (1999). Elder care and the workplace in Germany: An issue for the future? In In V. M. Lechner & M. B. Neal (Eds.), *Work and caring for the elderly: International perspectives* (pp. 29–46). Philadelphia: Brunner/Mazel.

Research Institute of America. (1995). *Internal Revenue Code of 1995.* Deerfield, IL: Callaghan.

Resource for Enhancing Alzheimer' Caregiver Health. (1998). *Data collection forms and instructions* (Version 1.2) (CD-ROM). Pittsburgh, PA: University of Pittsburgh.

Rickard, A. (2002). *The effects of parent care and child care role quality on work outcomes among dual-earner couples in the sandwiched generation.* Unpublished doctoral dissertation, Portland State University.

Rogosa, D. R., & Willett, J. B. (1983). Demonstrating the reliability of the difference score in the measurement of change. *Journal of Educational Measurement, 20,* 335–343.

RoperASW, & Zapolsky, S. (2004). *Baby boomers envision retirement II: Survey of baby boomers' expectations for retirement.* Retrieved November 13, 2005, from http://www.aarp.org/research/work/retirement/aresearch-import-865.html

Roper Starch Worldwide. (1999). *Baby boomers envision their retirement: An AARP segmentation analysis.* Retrieved November 13, 2005, from http:// www.aarp.org/research/reference/publicopinions/aresearch-import-299.html

Rosenthal, C. J., Martin-Matthews, A., & Matthews, S. H. (1996). Caught in the middle? Occupancy in the middle roles and help to parents in a national probability sample of Canadian adults. *Journal of Gerontology: Social Sciences, 51B,* S274–S283.

Rosin, H. M., & Korabik, K. (2002). Do family-friendly policies fulfill their promise? An investigation of their impact on work–family conflict and work and personal outcomes. In D. L. Nelson & R. J. Burke (Eds.), *Gender, work stress, and health* (pp. 211–226). Washington, DC: American Psychological Association.

Rothausen, T. J., Gonzalez, J. A., Clarke, N. E., & O'Dell, L. L. (1998). Family-friendly backlash—Fact or fiction? The case of organizations' on-site child care centers. *Personnel Psychology, 51,* 685–706.

Sahibzada, K., Hammer, L. B., Neal, M. B., & Kuang, D. C. (2005). The moderating effects of work–family role combinations and work–family organizational culture on the relationship between family-friendly workplace supports and job satisfaction. *Journal of Family Issues, 26,* 1–20.

Scandura, T. A., & Lankau, M. J. (1997). Relationships of gender, family responsibility and flexible work hours to organizational commitment and job satisfaction. *Journal of Organizational Behavior, 18,* 377–391.

Scharlach, A. (1994). Caregiving and employment: Competing or complementary roles? *The Gerontologist, 34,* 378–385.

Scharlach, A. E., Lowe, B. F., & Schneider, E. L. (1991). *Elder care and the work force: Blueprint for action.* Lexington, MA: Lexington.

Scharlach, A., Midanik, L., Runkle, C., & Soghikian, K. (1997). Health practices in adults with elder care responsibilities. *Preventative Medicine, 26,* 155–161.

Scharlach, A. E., Sansom, S. L., & Stanger, J. (1995). The Family and Medical Leave Act of 1993: How fully is business complying? *California Management Review, 37*(2), 66–79.

Schnall, P. L., Belkic, K., Landsbergis, P., & Baker, D. (2000). The workplace and cardiovascular disease: Occupational medicine—State of the art reviews. Philadelphia: Hanley & Belfus.

Schutt, R. K. (1996). *Investigating the social world: The process and practice of research.* Thousand Oaks, CA: Pine Forge.

Schwartz, F. (1989). Management women and the new facts of life. *Harvard Business Review, 67,* 65–76.

Sekaran, U. (1983). Factors influencing the quality of life in dual-career families. *Journal of Occupational Psychology, 56,* 161–174.

Sekaran, U. (1986). *Dual-career families.* San Francisco: Jossey-Bass.

Seligman, M., & Csikszentmihalyi, M. (2000). Positive psychology: An Introduction. *American Psychologist, 55,* 5–14.

Shamir, B. (1983). Some antecedents of work–nonwork conflict. *Journal of Vocational Behavior, 23,* 98–111.

Shellenberger, S., & Hoffman, S. S. (1995). The changing family–work system. In R. H. Mikesell & D. D. Lusterman (Eds.), *Integrating family therapy: Handbook of family psychology and systems theory* (pp. 461–479). Washington, DC: American Psychological Association.

Shields, M. (2002). Shift work and health. *Health Reports, 13*(4), 11–33.

Shore, R. (1998). *Ahead of the curve: Why America's leading employers are addressing the needs of new and expectant parents.* New York: Families and Work Institute.

Sieber, S. D. (1974). Toward a theory of role accumulation. *American Sociological Review, 39,* 467–478.

Sinclair, R. R., Hannigan, M. A., & Tetrick, L. E. (1995). Benefit coverage and employee attitudes: A social exchange perspective. In L. E. Tetrick & J. Barling (Eds.), *Changing employment relations: Behavioral and social perspectives* (pp. 163–185). Washington, DC: American Psychological Association.

Skinner, E., Edge, K., Altman, J., & Sherwood, H. (2003). Searching for the structure of coping: A review and critique of category systems for classifying ways of coping. *Psychological Bulletin, 129,* 216–269.

Smith, J. L. , Buffardi, L. C., & Holt, R. W. (1999, April). Antecedents and consequences of elder care responsibilities and the role of organizational and supervisory support. In L. C. Buffardi (Chair), *Work–family conflict and the influence of perceived organizational support.* Symposium conducted at the 14th Annual Convention of the Society for Industrial and Organizational Psychology, Atlanta, GA.

Snyder, R., Rice, T., & Kitchman, M. (2003). *Paying for choice: The cost implications of health plan options for people on Medicare.* Menlo Park, CA: Kaiser Family Foundation.

Society for Human Resource Management. (2003). *2003 Benefits Survey.* Alexandria, VA: Author.

Solomon, C. M. (1994). Work/family's failing grade: Why today's initiatives aren't enough. *Personnel Journal, 73,* 72–87.

Spillman, B. C., & Pezzin, L. E. (2000). Potential and active family caregivers: Changing networks and the "sandwich generation." *Milbank Quarterly, 78,* 347–374.

Spitze, G., & Logan, J. (1990). Sons, daughters, and intergenerational social support. *Journal of Marriage and the Family, 52,* 420–430.

Stephens, M. A. P., & Franks, M. M. (1995). Spillover between daughters' roles as caregiver and wife: Interference or enhancement? *Journal of Gerontology: Psychological Sciences, 50B,* 9–17.

Stephens, M. A. P., Franks, M. M., & Atienza, A. A. (1997). Where two roles intersect: Spillover between parent care and employment. *Psychology and Aging, 12,* 30–37.

Stephens, M. A. P., Franks, M. M., & Townsend, A. L. (1994). Stress and rewards in women's multiple roles: The case of the women in the middle. *Psychology and Aging, 9,* 45–52.

Stephens, M. A. P., & Townsend, A. L. (1997). Stress of parent care: Positive and negative effects of women's other roles. *Psychology and Aging, 12,* 376–386.

Stephens, M. A. P., Townsend, A. L., Martire, L. M., & Druley, J. A. (2001). Balancing parent care with other roles: Interrole conflict of adult daughter caregivers. *Journal of Gerontology: Psychological Sciences, 56B,* P24–P34.

Stewart, B., & Archbold, P. (1996). *Oregon family caregiving survey.* Unpublished manuscript, Oregon Health Sciences University, School of Nursing.

Stoller, E. P., & Pugliesi, K. L. (1989). Other roles of caregivers: Competing responsibilities or supportive resources. *Journal of Gerontology: Social Sciences, 44,* S231–S238.

Stone, R., Cafferata, G. L., & Sangl, J. (1987). Caregivers of the frail elderly: A national profile. *The Gerontologist, 27,* 616–626.

Stone, R. I., & Short, P. F. (1990). The competing demands of employment and informal caregiving to disabled elders. *Medical Care, 28,* 513–526.

Stone-Romero, E. F. (2005). Personality-based sigmas and unfair discrimination in work organizations. In R. L. Dipboye & A. Colella (Eds.), *Discrimination at work: The psychological and organizational bases* (pp. 255–280). Mahwah, NJ: Lawrence Erlbaum Associates.

Strauss, A., & Corbin, J. M. (1991). *Basics of qualitative research: Grounded theory procedures and techniques.* Thousand Oaks, CA: Sage.

Tennstedt, S. L., & Gonyea, J. G. (1994). An agenda for work and eldercare research: Methodological challenges and future directions. *Research on Aging, 16,* 85–108.

The Travelers Insurance Companies. (1985). The Travelers employee caregiver survey: A survey of caregiving responsibilities of Travelers employees for older Americans. Hartford, CT: Author.

Thomas, L. T., & Ganster, D. C. (1995). Impact of family-supportive work variables on work–family conflict and strain: A control perspective. *Journal of Applied Psychology, 80,* 6–15.

Thompson, B. (2004). *Exploratory and confirmatory factor analysis: Understanding concepts and applications.* Washington, DC: American Psychological Association.

Thompson, C. A., Beauvais, L. L., & Lyness, K. S. (1999). When work–family benefits are not enough: The influence of work–family culture on benefit utilization, organizational attachment, and work–family conflict. *Journal of Vocational Behavior, 54,* 392–415.

U.S. Bureau of Labor Statistics. (2000). *USDL 00-127*. Retrieved May 21, 2004, from http://stats.bls.gov/news.release/famee.nr0.htm

U.S. Bureau of Labor Statistics. (2001a). *Employment characteristics of families*. Retrieved June 18, 2004, from http://www.bls.gov/news.release/famee.t02.htm

U.S. Bureau of the Census. (1996). *Current population reports, special studies, P23-190, 65+ in the United States*. Washington, DC: U.S. Government Printing Office.

U.S. Census Bureau. (2001b, October). *The 65 years and over population: 2000—Census 2000 brief*. Retrieved September, 30, 2004, from www.census.gov/prod/2001pubs/c2kbr01-10.pdf

U.S. Census Bureau. (2001a, October). *Age: 2000—Census 2000 brief*. Retrieved October 25, 2004, from www.census.gov/prod/2001pubs/c2kbr01-12.pdf

U.S. Census Bureau. (2003, October). *Grandparents living with grandchildren: 2000*. Retrieved May 30, 2006, from http://wwwcensus.gov/prod/2003pubs/c2kbr-31.pdf

U.S. Census Bureau. (2004, August 26). Table 2b: Projected population change in the United States, by age and sex: 2000 to 2050. Retrieved November 12, 2005, from http://www.census.gov/ipc/www/usinterimproj/

U.S. Census Bureau. (2006, May 10). Statistics about business size (including small business) from the U.S. Census Bureau. Retrieved May 30, 2006, from http://www.census.gov/epcd/www/smallbus.html

U.S. Department of Commerce. (2000). *Profiles of general demographic characteristics: 2000 census of population and housing*. Washington, DC: U.S. Census Bureau.

U.S. Department of Labor. (2002). *Working in the 21st century*. Washington, DC: U.S. Bureau of Labor Statistics. (Available at http://www.bls.gov/opub/working/home.htm)

U.S. Department of Labor, Bureau of Labor Statistics. (1993). *Work experience of the population in 1992*. Retrieved September 21, 2003, from ftp://ftp.bls.gov/pub/news.release/History/work.102093.news

U.S. Department of Labor, Office of the Secretary, Women's Bureau. (n.d.). *Work and family resource kit*. Washington, DC: Author.

U.S. Department of Labor, Bureau of Labor Statistics. (2005, May). *Women in the labor force: A databook*. Retrieved February 16, 2006, from http://www.bls.gov/cps/wlf-databook2005lhtm

U.S. Department of Labor, Bureau of Labor Statistics. (2005, December 22). *Work experience of the population in 2004*. Retrieved August 14, 2006, from http://www.bls.gov/news.release/work.nr0.htm

U.S. Department of the Treasury, Internal Revenue Service. (2005). *Publication 503 (2005) child and dependent care expenses*. Retrieved May 30, 2006, from http://www.irs.gov/publications/p503/index.html

U.S. Equal Employment Opportunity Commission. (1996). *EEO-1 job classification guide: A guide which maps 1990 census job codes and titles into the nine (9) EEO-1 survey job categories*. Washington, DC: U.S. Equal Employment Opportunity Commission

Vanderkolk, B. S., & Young, A. A. (1991). *The work and family revolution: how companies can keep employees happy and business profitable*. New York: Facts on File.

Vinokur, A. D., Pierce, P. F., & Buck, C. L. (1999). Work–family conflicts of women in the Air Force: Their influence on mental health and functioning. *Journal of Organizational Behavior, 20,* 865–878.

Voydanoff, P., & Donnelly, B. W. (1999). Multiple roles and psychological distress: The intersection of the paid worker, spouse, and parent roles with the adult child role. *Journal of Marriage and the Family, 61,* 725–738.

Wagner, D. L. (2000). The development and future of workplace eldercare. In *Dimensions of family caregiving: A look into the future.* Westport, CT: MetLife Mature Market Institute.

Wagner, D. L. (2003). *Workplace programs for family caregivers: Good business and good practice.* Retrieved November 13, 2004, from http://www.caregiver.org/caregiver/jsp/content_node.jsp?nodeid=953

Wagner, D. L., Creedon, M. A., Sasala, J. M., & Neal, M. B. (1989). *Employees and eldercare: Designing effective responses for the workplace.* Bridgeport, CT: University of Bridgeport, Center for the Study of Aging.

Wagner, D. L., & Hunt, G. G. (1994). The use of workplace eldercare programs by employed caregivers. *Research on Aging, 16,* 69–84.

Wagner, D. L., & Neal, M. B. (1994). Caregiving and work: Consequences, correlates, and workplace responses. *Educational Gerontology, 20,* 645–663.

Ward, R. A., & Spitze, G. (1998). Sandwiched marriages: The implications of child and parent relations for marital quality in midlife. *Social Forces, 77,* 647–666.

Watkins, C. E., & Subich, L. M. (1995). Annual review, 1992–1994: Career development, reciprocal work/non-work interaction, and women's workforce participation. *Journal of Vocational Behavior, 47,* 109–163.

Watson, D., Clark, L. A., & Carey, G. (1988). Positive and negative affect and their relation to anxiety and depressive disorders. *Journal of Abnormal Psychology, 97,* 346–353.

Wayne, J. H., Musisca, N., & Fleeson, W. (2004). Considering the role of personality in the work–family experience: Relationships of the Big Five to work–family conflict and facilitation. *Journal of Vocational Behavior, 64,* 108–140.

Westman, M. (2001). Stress and strain crossover. *Human Relations, 54,* 557–591.

Westman, M., & Etzion, D. (1995). Crossover of stress, strain and resources from one spouse to another. *Journal of Organizational Behavior, 16,* 169–181.

Westman, M., & Piotrkowski, C. S. (1999). Introduction to the special issue: Work–family research in occupational health psychology. *Journal of Occupational Health Psychology, 4,* 310–306.

Westman, M., & Vinokur, A. D. (1998). Unraveling the relationship of distress levels within couples: Common stressors, empathic reactions, or crossover via social interaction? *Human Relations, 51,* 137–156.

Westman, M., Vinokur, A. D., Hamilton, V. L., & Roziner, I. (2004). Crossover of marital dissatisfaction during military downsizing among Russian army officers and their spouses. *Journal of Applied Psychology, 89,* 769–779.

Wiatrowski, W. J. (1990, March). Family-related benefits in the workplace. *Monthly Labor Review, 113*(3), 28–33.

Wiersma, U. J. (1994). A taxonomy of behavioral strategies for coping with work–home role conflict. *Human Relations, 47,* 211–221.

Wiley, D. L. (1987). The relationship between work/nonwork role conflict and job-related outcomes: Some unanticipated findings. *Journal of Management, 13,* 467–472.

Wilensky, H. L. (1960). Work, careers, and social integration. *International Social Science Journal, 12,* 543–560.

Williams, K. J., & Alliger, G. M. (1994). Role stressors, mood spillover, and perceptions of work–family conflict in employed parents. *Academy of Management Journal, 37,* 837–868.

Yeandle, S., Wigfield, A., Crompton, R., & Dennet, J. (2002). *Employed carers and family-friendly employment policies.* Bristol, England: The Polity Press.

Youngblood, S. A., & Chambers-Cook, K. (1984). Child care assistance can improve employee attitudes and behavior. *Personnel Administrator, 29,* 45–46, 93–95.

Zedeck, S. (1992). Introduction: Exploring the domain of work and family concerns. In S. Zedeck (Ed.), *Work, families, and organizations* (pp. 1–32). San Francisco: Jossey-Bass.

Zedeck, S., & Mosier, K. L. (1990). Work in the family and employing organization. *American Psychologist, 45,* 240–251.

A

Methods and Procedures
of the Study

The findings presented in this book are based on data from the "Dual-Earner Couples in the Sandwiched Generation Study" that we conducted at Portland State University with funding from the Alfred P. Sloan Foundation. The 3-year project began in 1997 and involved the collection of dyadic, longitudinal qualitative and quantitative data.

Specific criteria for participation in the study were: (a) the couple had been married or living together for at least 1 year; (b) one person in the couple worked at least 35 hours per week, and the other worked at least 20 hours per week; (c) there were one or more children aged 18 or younger living in the household at least 3 days a week; and (d) altogether, one or both members of the couple spent a minimum of 3 hours per week caring for one or more aging parents or parents-in-law. The fifth and final study criterion was that the couple have a combined household income of $40,000 or greater. This stipulation was made because of the specific interest of the Alfred P. Sloan Foundation in middle- and upper income couples.

DATA COLLECTION

We collected a variety of types of data, using both qualitative and quantitative modes of data collection. Specifically, we conducted focus groups, two mailed surveys 1 year apart, follow-up focus groups, and telephone interviews. The data for the study were collected over a 3-year period. The bulk of the findings presented in this book were derived from the survey data.

Focus Groups

Purpose

The project began with focus groups held in Portland, Oregon, with a sample of working, sandwiched couples. These focus groups were convened for three purposes. The primary purpose was to learn about the work and family accommodations made, and coping strategies used, by these couples in an effort to balance their work and family roles. We then used these items to formulate items for a survey instrument to be sent by U.S. mail to a national sample of dual-earner sandwiched generation couples. The third purpose was to test a variety of methods for recruiting eligible study participants. A second purpose of the focus groups was to develop a prototype sampling strategy to be used in recruiting participants for the national mailed survey to follow.

Sampling Procedure

To realize the secondary purpose of these focus groups, three different sampling strategies were used to gauge their effectiveness and efficiency in recruiting the sample. Twenty-five percent of the sample was identified and recruited via computer-assisted telephone interviews (CATI) conducted with a sample generated from random-digit dialing techniques. Another 25% was obtained through advertising in local newspapers. The remaining 50% of the sample was recruited via CATI using a targeted list of telephone numbers of households believed to have at least one adult between the ages of 30 and 60.

Recruitment for both the random-digit dialed and targeted list samples (75% of the sample) consisted of identifying potential participants via telephone screening interviews conducted by trained interviewers. These screening interviews (see screening criteria above) were completed using the university's CATI laboratory during evening hours on weekdays and daytime hours on weekends. Each completed interview took approximately 3 minutes. Interviewees who met the criteria and who were willing to participate in the focus groups either signed up for a group at a specific date and time during the telephone screening call, or a subsequent call was placed to schedule their participation in a group. The remaining 25% of the sample was recruited through advertisements in three local newspapers. All individuals and couples who agreed to attend the focus groups were given a reminder call before the actual date of the focus group.

Of the three recruitment strategies tested, the one that proved most effective, from both a cost and a yield perspective, was the telephone screening using a targeted list of households.

We used four strategies to help increase success in participant recruitment and actual participation. First, on-site child care was provided during the focus groups. To facilitate the provision of this child care, the groups were convened at the university's child development center. Several participants took advantage of this free service. Second, although the original design called for both members of each couple to participate (albeit in separate focus groups), some individuals ultimately were permitted to participate without their spouse. We allowed this because it proved difficult to coordinate the participation of both members of all couples due to a variety of factors typically related to their multiple role demands (e.g., sick children or parents, couple working different shifts). Third, a $20 incentive, per individual, was provided at the conclusion of the focus group session. Fourth, all individuals and couples who agreed to attend the focus groups were given a reminder call before the actual date of the focus group.

Description of the Focus Group Sample. A total of 17 focus groups were held. The majority of the groups had at least 4 members. The sample consisted of representatives of 38 couples, with a total of 63 individuals. For 25 couples, both members attended, and 13 couples were represented by 1 member.

The average age of the wives was 41.4 years, and the husbands' average age was 44.1 years. Couples had been together an average of 16.2 years and reported a median income of approximately $57,500 per year. They had an average of two children aged 18 or under living in the household. On average, wives reported spending 9.7 hours per week in caring for a parent, and husbands reported spending 6.2 hours of parent care per week. Some wives and husbands were caring for up to four different parents, stepparents, and/or parents-in-law. Wives worked an average of 32.7 hours per week, and husbands worked an average of 44.6 hours per week.

Data Analysis

Data from the focus groups were analyzed as follows. The transcripts of each of the focus groups were read, and relevant sections (i.e., coping strategies) were marked. Researchers and graduate students then divided into two teams for the purpose of classifying the various types of coping strategies mentioned as being used or suggested. One team used existing theoretical systems (e.g., Amatea & Fong-Beyette, 1987; Folkman & Lazarus, 1980; Menaghan, 1983), sorting the statements into the theoretical categories suggested by these researchers. Another team followed an "open coding" approach (Strauss & Corbin, 1991) to identify the broadest possible range of responses related to examples of coping with the demands of work and family. A categorization system was created from the key themes mentioned by the focus group participants. The two classification efforts then were synthesized into a single conceptual system. This framework was later used to code all open-ended statements describing the advice that survey participants reported using to manage their multiple demands of work and family. In particular, two coders independently classified the respondents' open-ended statements into the six categories. A third coder checked and validated the codes assigned.

The National Longitudinal Mailed Survey

After completing the focus groups, we began (a) developing the mail survey instrument for use in the national study and (b) recruiting couples nationally for participation.

Sampling Procedure

Recruitment for the national mailed survey consisted of identifying potential participants from across the continental United States via telephone screening interviews conducted by trained interviewers during the winter and spring of 1998. Specifically, the sample was recruited using the university's CATI laboratory during evening hours on weekdays and daytime hours on weekends.

Rather than using random-digit dialing, which proved too costly for identifying couples who met the study criteria (see section titled "Focus Groups"), we purchased a targeted list of telephone numbers of households in the continental United States composed of one or more adults aged 30 through 60. Telephone numbers on the list were called until someone answered or until they had been tried a minimum of 10 times and a maximum of 20 times each at various times during weekday evenings and weekends.

The telephone screening interview took approximately 3 minutes to complete. If a respondent's answers to the screening questions indicated that the household met the study criteria, the respondent was asked if he or she and his or her spouse or partner each might be willing to complete a survey to be sent by mail. Respondents were informed that, as a token of appreciation, couples who returned each member's surveys would receive a check for $40. If the respondent expressed willingness, on the part of the couple, to consider participating, the names and address of both members of the couple were obtained, and separate survey packets containing a cover letter, survey instrument, and return envelope were mailed.

Study participants in the national mailed survey consisted of both members of dual-earner couples in the sandwiched generation from across the continental United States. A total of 309 couples (618 individuals) meeting the study's criteria returned the first survey (Wave 1), which was mailed in the spring and summer of 1998; 234 of these couples returned the second survey (Wave 2), which was virtually identical to the first instrument and was mailed 1 year later. (See Appendix B for the Wave 1and Wave 2 survey instruments.)

During the sample recruitment process, a total of 33,037 calls were placed to 8,787 telephone numbers. Interviews were completed with 5,565 households (63.3%). Another 1,997 households were reached but refused to complete the screening interview (22.7%). Interviews could not be completed with 104 households (1.2%) because of a language barrier or hearing or speech impairment. The remaining telephone numbers were persistently unavailable (e.g., always busy, always answered by an answering machine; $n = 602$, or 6.9%), belonged to business or group quarters ($n = 156$, or 1.8%), or were nonworking numbers ($n = 363$, or 4.1%). Excluding this last set of numbers from the initial sample yielded a completion rate of 73.6% (5,565 divided by 7,562).

A total of 741 households contacted met the criteria for participation. These households represent 8.97% of the 8,268 apparently working, nonbusiness numbers, or 13.3% of the 5,565 households with whom interviews were completed. These findings would indicate that between 9% and 13% of American households with telephones and having one or more persons aged 30 through 60 are comprised of dual-earner, sandwiched-generation couples. These results are comparable, although somewhat lower, than those of Nichols and Junk (1997).

Of the 741 couples, 96 (12.3%) respondents reported household incomes below $40,000, and 35 (4.7%) refused to say whether their income was below or at or above $40,000. Of the 741 couples, 624 agreed to participate in the study or to consider participating, and so they were mailed surveys. Both members of the couple were sent separate cover letters and instructed to independently complete and return the survey using the postage-paid, addressed envelopes provided for each of them. Once surveys from both members of the couple had been received, a check for $40 was mailed to the couple.

Surveys from both members of 360 couples (57.7% of 624, or 48.6% of 741) were returned. A review of responses, however, revealed that 22 of the 360 couples (6.1%) no longer met the study criteria. Of the remaining 338 couples, 309 ($N = 618$ individuals) met the income criterion and serve as the basis for the sample in the study described herein. (Couples not meeting the income requirement for the larger study were reimbursed with funds from a secondary source.)

It should be noted that the sampling procedure resulted in a sample that was national in scope, although by using a targeted list of telephone numbers in the continental United States, some members of the population were not represented (e.g., persons without telephones or potentially, those with unlisted numbers, U.S. households in Alaska or Hawaii, and non-English speaking participants). Also, caution must also be exercised in generalizing from the results because of the relatively high percentage of refusals to complete the screening interview. To determine the representativeness of the 309 couples, at least as compared with those originally screened by telephone and found to meet the study's criteria (including income) but who did not complete mailed surveys ($n = 265$), t tests were conducted. These analyses revealed that the two groups of couples did not differ significantly on any of several key characteristics, including average age, number of children living in the household all or some of the time, age of youngest child, number of living parents, number of hours spent helping parents, or number of hours worked or screened respondent's gender.

Participating couples were resurveyed by mail 1 year later to assess changes in work and family characteristics, outcomes, and work and family accommodations. Responses to the second survey were received from both members of 234 (75.7%) of the 309 couples. Again, once surveys from both members of the couple had been received, a check for $40 was mailed to the couple. The characteristics of the 309 couples who participated in the first wave of the survey are detailed in chapter 5.

Follow-Up Focus Groups

After the administration of both waves of the national mailed survey, the study's design called for reconvening the focus groups to aid in interpretation of the study's findings and to learn more about the changes in the lives of couples who are combining work and family and how they are deal with those changes.

All participants in the first set of focus groups were invited to return 3 years later to participate in another focus group. A total of 13 participants (7 wives and 6 husbands) returned, and participants were split into two groups. The average age of the wives who participated was 42.7 years; the husbands' average age was 45.8 years. Couples had been together an average of 16.2 years and reported a median income of approximately $56,500 per year. All participants indicated that they still had children aged 18 or under living at home, and they had an average of 2.1 children per household. Two wives and 3 husbands no longer provided parent care. Wives reported spending an average of 6.2 hours per week caregiving for a parent, and husbands reported spending an average of 7.0 hours per week providing parent care. One husband and 1 wife were no longer employed. The remaining wives worked an average of 32.7 hours per week, and the husbands worked an average of 39 hours per week.

Telephone Interviews

To gain a better understanding of what had happened to study couples since the last contact with them 1 year earlier, when they had completed the Wave 2 mailed survey, follow-up telephone interviews were conducted with a subsample of participants. A set of standard questions for these interviews was developed. Included were a series of questions to ascertain the extent of the caregiving and work responsibilities that each person had. Next, questions were asked about changes that had occurred at work and at home over the past year, how these changes had affected their ability to manage their work and family demands, and what changes they anticipated in the coming year. Participants then were asked about the advantages and drawbacks of combining work and family and specific things that made it easier or harder to manage their various responsibilities. Finally, participants were asked to indicate how easy or difficult it was for them to manage their work and family demands.

Our study design called for interviewing approximately 50 individuals, half of whom had had experienced the most change for the better between the two waves of the mailed survey, and the other half of whom had experienced the most change for the worse. Further, we wished to interview approximately equal numbers of men and women.

To choose the individuals whom we would interview, we calculated individual change scores for several outcome variables, including depression, work–family conflict, life satisfaction, and job satisfaction, by subtracting the value on the Time 1 variable from the value on the Time 2 variable. Thus, positive scores indicated an increase in the variable from Time 1 to Time 2, and negative scores indicated a decrease in the variable between the two time points. The change scores for work–family conflict and depression were both multiplied by –1 so that they would be in the same direction as the satisfaction measures. Each individual's values on the four change variables were then summed and divided by the number of change variables (i.e., 4) to yield an overall mean change score on the outcomes for each individual in the sample. This procedure was implemented first for husbands ($n = 234$) and then for wives ($n = 234$).

After the overall change score was created, two rank-ordered lists, one for husbands and one for wives, were created. The 13 men at the top of the list of husbands (i.e., those who experienced the most change for the better) and the 13 men at the bottom of the list (i.e., those who had experienced the most change for the worse) were selected for the sample of husbands. Similarly, the 13 women who had experienced the most improvement, and the 13 whose situations had worsened the most, were identified. Thus, the total initial sample was 52. In the data set containing both waves of survey data for husbands and wives, a new variable, "change," was created by assigning a 1 to those who had been selected in the "changed for the better" category, assigning a –1 to those who had been selected in the "changed for the worse" category, and assigning a 0 to the remainder, indicating no or minor change overall.

After identification of the individuals to be interviewed, a list of their names, addresses, and telephone numbers was compiled. A personalized letter was sent to each potential participant telling him or her that an interviewer from the study would be calling and asking him or her to participate in a telephone interview. The types of questions that would be asked were described, and individuals were informed that they would receive $40 in appreciation of their participation, if they chose to do so.

Potential participants were called by one of five trained interviewers on weekends or evenings (in the participant's time zone). If the time when a respondent was reached was inconvenient for him or her, an appointment for a return call was made. All interviews were tape-recorded to capture all of the data (permission of the respondent was requested), and interviewers took notes as well. At the end of the interview, respondents were given the opportunity to add anything else they felt was relevant or to ask questions about the study. Respondents then were thanked for their time and told that they should receive their $40 check within the next 2 weeks. After the interview, tapes were labeled with the respondents' respective identification numbers and then were transcribed. After transcription of the telephone interviews, the questions were divided up among teams of project staff members, who then identified the themes that captured the responses to the questions assigned to them.

Description of Participants in the Telephone Interview. A total of 48 individuals completed the telephone interview. From the initial sample, 7 people were unreachable by phone, did not want to participate, or had passed away. Replacements for 4 of these individuals then were identified by selecting those next on the list whose situations had improved or declined, as appropriate. Responses were gathered from 26 wives and 22 husbands, and 24 each from the "worse" or "better" categories (i.e., 11 husbands from each category and 13 wives from each category). Three (6.3%) of the respondents indicated that they were no longer with their spouse or partner, and 5 (10.4%) no longer had a child 18 or under living at home. Two respondents were no longer employed outside the home (4.2%) either because of care responsibilities for both parents and children or some other reason, and another 2 (4.2%) indicated that their spouse was no longer employed outside the home because of child-care responsibilities. A total of 14 (29.8%) respondents indicated that neither they nor their spouse/partner had parent-care responsibilities any longer, and 4 (8.5%) other indicated that they were not involved in parent care but that their spouse/

partner was. An additional 3 (6.7%) couples had fallen below the original household income criterion of $40,000 per year.

MEASURES

Independent Variables

Below is a description of the various measures that we used to describe study participants and their work–family fit, well-being, and work-related outcomes. Means and standard deviations are presented in the tables associated with chapters 5 through 10 (see Appendix C). Internal consistency reliability coefficients (α) for multi-item indices are presented here where appropriate, based on the Wave 1 data.

Demographic, Socioeconomic, and Personal Information

Data of this nature included: *age, race* (0 = non-White, 1 = White), *years of education, annual gross household income, marital status* (0 = unmarried but living together, 1 = married), *number of years married/living together*, whether the respondent had been *previously married* (0 = *no*, 1 = *yes*), the *ages and relationships of all persons living in the household*, whether any of the *children were from a previous relationship*, and whether they had *children who are not living with them* (0 = *no*, 1 = *yes*). *Perceived adequacy of income* was measured using an item developed by Stewart and Archbold (1996): "Which of the following four statements describes your ability to get along on your income? 1 = *We can't make ends meet;* 2 = *We have just enough, no more;* 3 = *We have enough, with a little extra sometimes;* and 4 = *We always have money left over.*" Finally, a measure of *major life events* was adapted from R. Kahn and Antonucci's (1980) work. Respondents were asked to indicate whether they had experienced each of 15 events in the previous year (e.g., changed or left a job, changed place of residence, married, had a decline in financial status; 0 = no, 1 = yes).

Negative affectivity is a measure of personality that has been demonstrated previously to be associated with many of the work and well-being outcomes of interest here (see chap. 2). The instrument we used was a 7-item measure developed by John (1989), with responses ranging from 1 (*disagree strongly*) to 5 (*agree strongly*). Examples of items are "I see myself as someone who": "gets nervous easily," "worries a lot," "is relaxed" (reverse coded; John, 1989). The internal consistency reliability of this measure in the present study was .77 both for husbands and for wives.

Family involvement is a measure of the extent to which participants are involved in their families. A sample item from the 4-item scale by Frone and Rice (1987), which we used, is "Most of my interests are centered around my family." Response options ranged from 1 (*strongly disagree*) to 4 (*strongly agree*), such that a high score indicated high family involvement. The internal consistency reliability of this measure in the present study was .85 for husbands and .84 for wives.

Child-Care Related Characteristics, Arrangements, and Responsibility

The *number of children aged 18 and younger* and the *age of the youngest child* in the household were derived from the household composition information provided. Respondents also were asked if any of these children had *special needs* (e.g., due to physical disabilities, poor physical health, substance abuse, emotional or behavioral problems or learning disabilities; 0 = no, 1 = yes). *Satisfaction with the care arrangement* used most frequently for their youngest or special-needs child then was determined using a measure consisting of a seven-item, 5-point Likert scale (1 = *strongly disagree*, 5 = *strongly agree*) adapted from Emlen (1996). Higher scores indicated greater satisfaction with the child-care arrangement. The internal consistency reliability of this measure in the present study was .82 for husbands and .85 for wives.

Responsibility for child care was gauged by a single item asking respondents to indicate the extent to which they or their spouse/partner takes most responsibility to seeing to the care of the children in their household (recoded such that 1 = low [mostly spouse], 2 = medium [self and spouse share equally], and 3 = high [mostly self]).

Parent-Care Related Characteristics and Responsibilities

Respondents were asked to indicate the *number of living parents and step-parents* they had; the *relationship*, *age*, and *gender* of those *parents, including parents-in-law, whom they were helping*; and approximately how many *hours per week they were helping each*.

Next, respondents were asked to identify which *one* of these parents or parents-in-law they were *helping out the most*, and a number of questions then were asked specifically regarding that parent. These questions included the *number of years* the respondent had been providing assistance, the *marital status* of the parent (0 = not married, 1 = married), how many *miles away* the parent lives, how much *time it takes to get to this parent's residence*, the *parent's ability to get along on his/her income* (modified from Stewart & Archbold, 1996; see earlier description of demographic characteristics), and the parent's *overall health* (1 = *extremely poor*, 6 = *excellent*).

This parent's *need for assistance with 14 activities of daily living* was assessed on a 4-point scale (recoded such that 0 = *no help needed*, 3 = *totally de-*

pendent). Five of the 14 items measured the need for assistance with personal activities of daily living and were adapted from S. Katz, Ford, and Moskowitz (1963). Nine of the 14 items measured the amount of assistance needed with instrumental activities of daily living; these items were adapted from Lawton and Brody (1969). Information from Stephens and Townsend (1997) and McDowell and Newell (1996) was used in adapting these measures. Respondents then were asked to indicate *with which tasks they helped the parent*, along with the degree to which they *found each task stressful*. This latter variable was not used in the present study. Summary scores were computed for the need-help and the provide-help sets of variables by summing the scores. The ratings of help needed by the parent in accomplishing each of the 14 activities of daily living ranged from 0 to 42. The internal consistency reliability of the 14-item scale was .95 for husbands and .94 for wives. The internal consistency reliability for the five-item personal activities of daily living scale was .92 for husbands and .93 for wives, and that for the nine-item instrumental activities of daily living scale was .93 for husbands and .92 for wives.

The *quality of the relationship with the parent* was assessed using a measure adapted from Assmann, Lawrence, and Tennstedt (1996). This measure consisted of four items rated on a 4-point scale: "Please indicate the extent to which you and this parent: (1) are emotionally close; (2) can exchange ideas; (3) have similar views about life; and (4) get along together" (1 = *not at all*, 4 = *very*). Thus, higher scores indicate a higher perceived quality of the relationship between the respondent and the parent. The internal consistency reliability of this measure in the present study was .83 for husbands and .87 for wives.

The next set of questions concerned the various *coping strategies* respondents' used to deal with their multiple work and family responsibilities. These items were developed on the basis of the results of the focus groups held. Respondents were asked to indicate the degree to which 36 different statements described how they felt or acted in response to their many work and family duties (1 = *never*, 2 = *sometimes*, 3 = *most or all of the time*). Examples include "I plan how I'm going to use my time and energy" and "I lower my expectations about what should get done around the house." In the Wave 2 survey, the response format was changed to a 5-point response scale (1 = *never*, 3 = *sometimes*, 5 = *most or all of the time*).

In addition, respondents were asked about each of 10 other accommodations in the past year that they may have made specifically because of their child- or parent-care responsibilities. These accommodations included strategies that were likely to have been made only once or rarely in that time frame, such as quitting a job, refusing to relocate, or having parents move in. As a result, these were dichotomous variables, in which respondents simply indicated whether they had made each accommodation because of their child- or parent-care responsibilities (0 = no, 1 = yes). The statements used to describe the above strategies or accommodations were developed as a result of data gathered through the focus groups. The number of work-related accommodations made were summed and treated as a dependent variable, as described below.

Respondents also were asked about 7 types of *technology*, specifically, whether they had this technology and, if so, how helpful each type was to respondents in managing their work and family responsibilities (1 = *not at all*, 2 = *somewhat*, 3 = *very helpful*). The types of technology included voice-mail/answering machine; fax; cellular phone; beeper/pager; portable computer; remote access to computer used for work; and Internet/World Wide Web access (for information and support; see chap. 7 and Table 7.1). In addition, a single item asked "To what extent does technology (like portable computers and voice mail) make it harder or easier for you to manager both your work and family responsibilities?" The response options ranged from 1 (*much harder*) to 7 (*much easier*).

Work Characteristics

Questions regarding respondents' work-related characteristics included *occupation*,[1] whether the respondent was *self employed*, number of *years in current job*, number of *hours worked per week*, *number of hours preferred to work* (1 = *fewer*, 2 = *same*, 3 = *more*), *shift worked* (1 = *day*, 0 = *other*), *type of work schedule* (1 = *standard full time*, 0 = *other*), *perceived work schedule flexibility to deal with family matters* (1 = *no flexibility at all*, 4 = *a lot of flexibility*), and level of *comfort with talking about dependent-care responsibilities at work*. This last measure included four items that asked respondents how comfortable they felt talking with (a) *coworkers* and (b) *supervisors* about their responsibilities first *for children* and then *for parents* (1 = *not at all*, 4 = *very*; respondents without coworkers or supervisors circled 0, *not applicable*). *Job involvement* also was measured using a 4-item scale by Frone and Rice (1987) that parallels the family involvement measure. A sample item is "The most important things that happen to me involve my present job." Response options ranged from 1 (*strongly disagree*) to 4 (*strongly agree*) and were recoded as necessary, such that a high score indicated high job involvement.

---

[1]Respondents were asked (a) their job title and (b) to describe their work. These open-ended data were coded using the EEO-1 Survey Job Classification Guide (U.S. Equal Employment Opportunity Commission, 1996). A dichotomous variable then was created, such that professional, managerial, and technical positions were coded 1, and all others were coded 0.

Role Quality Measures

As Barnett and Hyde (2001) noted, it is important to assess role quality, or what we call *subjective role quality*, as well as quantity, or what we call the *objective role characteristics* or *role demands*. To assess *spousal role quality*, we asked respondents to indicate how rewarding nine different characteristics of the spousal role had been in the previous month and how concerned they had been about 8 different role characteristics, on a scale that ranged from 1 (*not at all*) to 4 (*very;* adapted from Barnett, Marshall, Raudenbush, & Brennan, 1993). For example, one question asked "How rewarding has it been having a spouse or partner who is easy to get along with?" Another asked, "How concerned have you been about poor communication with your spouse or partner?" The internal consistency reliability of the spousal role rewards subscale was .92 both for husbands and wives. The internal consistency reliability of the spousal role concerns subscale was .91 for husbands and .90 for wives.

To compute a composite spousal role quality score, (a) an average was computed of the concerns/stressors items, (b) an average was computed of the rewards items, and then (c) the stressors were subtracted from the rewards. Thus, a positive score indicated that, overall, rewards outweighed stressors, whereas a negative score indicated that, overall, stressors outweighed rewards. This same procedure was used to compute overall role quality in the child-care, parent-care, and job roles as well. Although we would have preferred to analyze the two dimensions (i.e., rewards and stressors) separately, this was not possible given the already large number of variables included in the analyses relative to the size of the sample.

Child-care role quality was assessed by asking respondents to indicate how rewarding each of 8 parental role characteristics had been in the past month and how much of a concern 13 different role characteristics had been, on a scale that ranged from 1 (*not at all*) to 4 (*very;* adapted from Barnett et al., 1993). For potentially stressful situations that might not have occurred for some respondents, these respondents were given the opportunity to circle "0." We then recoded these 0s to 1s. For example, one question asked respondents how stressful it had been for them in the past month due to "your child(ren) having problems at school," and another asked about stress due to "your child(ren)'s possible alcohol or other substance use." The internal consistency reliability of the child-care role rewards subscale was .91 for husbands and .87 for wives. The internal consistency reliability of the child-care role concerns subscale was .86 for husbands and .88 for wives.

Parent-care role quality was measured by asking respondents to indicate the extent to which 10 different characteristics of the parent-care role had been stressful and 8 characteristics had been rewarding (adapted from Stephens & Townsend, 1997). Again, items were measured on a scale that ranged from 1 (*not at all rewarding/concerned*) to 4 (*very rewarding/concerned*), and again, for situations (both positive and negative, in this case) that did not occur, respondents were given the opportunity to circle "0." We then recoded 0s to 1s. For example, one question asked how stressful "this parent's emotional problems or moods (e.g., depression, loss of interest, sadness)" had been in the past month. Another question asked how rewarding "seeing your relationship with this parent mature and grow" had been in the past month. Indicating 0 in such cases indicated an absence of reward or stress due to this situation, or the equivalent of 1, "not rewarding/stressful" at all. The internal consistency reliability of the parent-care role rewards subscale was .91 for husbands and .92 for wives. The internal consistency reliability of the parent-care role concerns subscale was .88 for husbands and .78 for wives.

Finally, with respect to *job role quality*, we asked respondents to indicate the extent to which 16 different characteristics of their work role had been rewarding and 19 characteristics had concerned them in the past month (adapted from Barnett & Brennan, 1995). Again, items were measured on a scale that ranged from 1 (*not at all rewarding/concerned*) to 4 (*very rewarding/concerned*). For example, one question asked how rewarding "challenging or stimulating work" had been in the past month. Another question asked how concerned the respondent had been about "the job's dullness, monotony, lack of variety." For respondents who were self-employed, some items did not apply (e.g., questions about supervisors or coworkers or benefits). For these items, respondents circled "0," and these items were omitted from the calculation of the subscale scores. The internal consistency reliability of the job role rewards subscale was .92 for husbands and .86 for wives. The internal consistency reliability of the job role concerns subscale was .91 for husbands and .87 for wives.

Coping Strategies

The development of measures of coping strategies is described in detail in chapter 8 and thus is not repeated here. The descriptive statistics for these measures are presented in Table 8.3.

Workplace Supports

Respondents were asked about the availability of several workplace supports and, if available, whether they used the support. For this study, items concerning the use of 13 supports were examined. To assess availability and utilization of workplace supports, participants were asked the following at Wave 1: "Please indicate whether or not each of the following workplace supports is available to you through your employer. If YES, do you make use of this?" Respondents who indicated that a support was available to them received a score of 1, and those who indicated that this support was not available to them received a score of "0." With respect to utilization of supports, respondents for whom a support was not available received a score of 0 on that item, because if a support were not available, they could not use it, as did those respondents who indicated that the support was available but that it was not used. Respondents who used a support received a score of 1 for that item.

We also created composite variables by grouping the 13 supports into two categories: (a) alternative work arrangements, measured with 3 items, and (b) dependent-care supports, measured with 10 items. Specifically, four composite variables were created separately for husbands and wives: composite *availability* of alternative work arrangements and of dependent-care supports, and composite *use* of alternative work arrangements and of dependent-care supports (see Table 9.3). The score for each composite variable was computed as the mean number of supports available/used. For example, if an individual had available to him or her 2 of the 10 dependent-care supports, then the score on the composite use of dependent care supports variable was .2.

Dependent Variables

Twelve different outcome measures were included in the present study: 4 work–family fit, 4 well-being, and 4 work-related outcome measures.

Work–Family Fit

We measured work–family conflict using a scale with two subscales developed by Netemeyer, Boles, and McMurrian (1996). This measure consists of 10 items, with 5 items assessing *work-to-family conflict* (internal consistency reliability was .90 for husbands and .91 for wives) and 5 assessing *family-to-work conflict* (internal consistency reliability was .88 for both husbands and wives). Participants indicated the extent to which they agreed or disagreed with items on a 5-point scale ranging from 1 (*strongly disagree*) to 5 (*strongly agree*).

Work–family positive spillover was measured using six items adapted from the work of Stephens, Franks, and Atienza (1997) concerning positive spillover between work and caregiving for an aging parent. For the present study, the items were broadened to include care for any family members and consist of a *work-to-family positive spillover* subscale (three items; internal consistency reliability was .83 for husbands and .82 for wives) and a *family-to-work positive spillover* subscale (three items; internal consistency reliability was .79 for husbands and .72 for wives). Participants indicated the extent to which they agreed or disagreed with items on a 5-point scale ranging from 1 (*strongly disagree*) to 5 (*strongly agree*).

Well-Being Measures

Depression was measured using Radloff's (1977) Center for Epidemiologic Studies Depression Scale. This measure consists of 20 items (e.g., "During the past week": "I was bothered by things that usually don't bother me; I felt depressed; I was happy") scored from 0 (*rarely or none of the time*) to 3 (*most of the time*), with positively worded items reverse coded. The maximum score is 60; a score of 16 or above is considered to be indicative of clinical depression (Radloff, 1977). The internal consistency reliability of this measure in the present study was .87 for husbands and .90 for wives.

Life satisfaction was measured using an eight-item semantic differential scale adapted from Campbell, Converse, and Rodgers (1975) and Quinn and Staines (1979). Specifically, the measure was worded: "Consider each of the word pairs and circle the number that best indicates how you feel about your life in general: boring–interesting; miserable–enjoyable; useless–worthwhile; lonely–friendly; empty–full; discouraging–hopeful; disappointing–rewarding; doesn't give me much of a chance–brings out the best in me." Responses were made on a 7-point scale and scored such that 1 = *low* and 7 = *high life satisfaction*. The internal consistency reliability of this measure in the present study was .95 for both husbands and wives.

Overall health was assessed using a single item that asked respondents to rate their overall health on a 6-point response scale (1 = *extremely poor*, 6 = *excellent*).

Overall role performance was ascertained by taking the average of five single items that asked respondents to rate their overall performance in each of their roles: (a) at work, (b) as a spouse, (c) as a parent, (d) as a caregiver to the parent whom they help the most, and (e) in taking care of their own mental and physical health. A 6-point response scale (1 = *extremely poor*, 6 = *excellent*) was used. Husbands and wives did not differ significantly with respect to their assessments of their performance at work or as a spouse, but wives rated their performance as parents (*M* = 4.84 compared to 4.57 for husbands) and as caregivers to their parents (*M* = 4.36 compared to 4.11 for husbands) significantly higher than did husbands. Husbands gave themselves higher ratings with respect to taking care of themselves than did wives (husbands = 3.85, wives = 3.49). The internal consistency reliability of this measure in the present study was .77 for husbands and .69 for wives.

Work-Related Outcomes

Job satisfaction was measured using the five-item General Job Satisfaction scale, which is a subscale of the Job Diagnostic Survey (Hackman & Oldham, 1975). Respondents were presented with each of five statements and asked to indicate their level of agreement on a 5-point Likert-type scale (1 = *strongly disagree*, 5 = *strongly agree*). Higher scores indicate higher levels of perceived job satisfaction. The internal consistency reliability of this measure in the present study was .72 for husbands and .69 for wives.

Overall absence from work as a result of dependent-care responsibilities was measured with a total of 8 items. Specifically, respondents were asked how many times in the past month they had (a) missed a day's work; (b) arrived late at work; (c) left work early; and (d) spent time at work on the telephone due, first, to responsibilities for any of their children, and second, due to responsibilities for any of their parents, stepparents, or parents-in-law. These items were adapted from a study by Neal, Chapman, Ingersoll-Dayton, and Emlen (1993) and are very similar to those used by MacEwen and Barling. Consistent with MacEwen and Barling, for each type of family care responsibility (i.e., child and parent) we combined and weighted the four work withdrawal indicators to form one measure of absence. The number of days missed was weighted by a factor of 3, the number of times arrived late to work was weighted by a factor of 2, the number of times left work early was also weighted by a factor of 2, and the number of times spent time at work on the telephone was weighted by a factor of 1. This procedure yielded two measures, one with respect to child-care duties and another with respect to parent-care duties, each having a range of 0 to 30. We then computed the average of the two measures to assess overall absence due to dependent-care responsibilities. (Internal consistency reliability is not computed given the nature of this measure.)

Number of work accommodations made due to dependent-care responsibilities is a composite measure of seven dichotomous (no–yes) work accommodations made because of child- or parent-care duties. These accommodations consisted of strategies that were likely to have been made only once or rarely in the previous year. The statements used to describe these strategies or accommodations were developed as a result of data gathered through the focus groups. Items include: "quit a job," "chosen a job that gives you more flexibility to meet your family demands," "refused to relocate," "refused or decided not to work toward a promotion," "refused or limited your travel" "worked reduced hours," and "worked a different shift from one's spouse or partner" so that one adult is at home most of the time." For each item, we asked respondents to indicate whether they had done this in the previous year (0 = no and 1 = yes). We then calculated the total number of accommodations made.

Poor performance at work due to dependent-care responsibilities was measured using the average of two items. Respondents were asked to indicate the extent to which their work performance was negatively affected by, first, their child-care responsibilities and second, their parent-care responsibilities. Specifically, we asked "In the past month, how often have you worked less effectively because you were concerned or upset: (a) about your child(ren); (b) about your parent(s)?" Responses were provided using a 5-point Likert scale, with 1 = *never* and 5 = *most or all of the time*. These items were adapted from Neal et al. (1993). The internal consistency reliability of this measure was .64 for husbands and .73 for wives.

ANALYSES

All quantitative data were entered and analyzed using SPSS (Statistical Package for the Social Sciences), version 11.5. Qualitative data (i.e., textual data from focus group transcripts, responses to open-ended questions on both waves of the mailed survey, and telephone interview transcripts) were entered using word-processing software (Word), then imported into The Ethnograph software. This software enables the coding and retrieval of sections of textual data. The quantitative data form the basis of the majority of the analyses presented here, except for the development of the coping measures. In addition to helping in the development of the coping strategies measure, the qualitative data are used here primarily to provide quotations for illustrative purposes and to help in the interpretation of the quantitative findings.

Descriptive statistics (e.g., means, standard deviations, *t* tests) were used to describe the sample (chap. 5), the outcomes experienced (chap. 6), the coping strategies used (chap. 8), the workplace supports used (chap. 9), and the types of role changes that occurred in the year between the two waves of the survey (chap. 10). Correlational analyses (bivariate) were used to assess the degree to which selected objective and subjective role characteristics were associated with each of the eight outcomes of interest. Confirmatory factor analysis was used to test the factor structure of the coping strategies (chap. 8). Hierarchical multiple regression was conducted to enable us to identify whether the subjective role quality variables were predictive of the well-being and work-related outcomes (chap. 6), after taking into account personal characteristics and objective role characteristics. Finally, to analyze crossover effects, in which one spouse's subjective role characteristics, coping strategies, and use of workplace supports affect the other's, we again used hierarchical multiple linear regression.

B

Survey Instruments
(Waves 1 and 2)

Portland State University

National Survey
of
Dual-Earner Couples in the Sandwiched Generation

A study of working couples
caring for children and aging parents
conducted by
Dr. Margaret B. Neal and Dr. Leslie B. Hammer
at
Portland State University, Portland, Oregon
with funding by the Alfred P. Sloan Foundation

Winter 1998

ID#_____

Thank you for participating in our study of couples who are both working, have children living with them, and are providing help to one or more aging parents or parents in-law. Please answer the following questions by circling your response or by writing your answer in the blank provided.

1. Are you:

    1 Married
    2 Not married, but living together
      (referred to as "partner" in this survey)

2. How long have you and your spouse or partner been living together?

    _____ years

3. Have you ever been married before?
    0 No
    1 Yes

4. Please list the ages and relationships to you of all persons, **besides yourself,** who live with you 3 or more days per week.

	Age	Relationship
1	_____	_____
2	_____	_____
3	_____	_____
4	_____	_____
5	_____	_____
6	_____	_____
7	_____	_____

5. Are any of these your or your spouse's or partner's children from a previous relationship?

    0 No
    1 Yes -- Please write their ages below

    ____ ____ ____ ____ ____

6. Do you or your spouse or partner have other children who are <u>not</u> living with you at least 3 days a week?

    0 No
    1 Yes

7. Would you say that:

    1 **You** are the person who takes most responsibility for seeing to the care of the children in your household.

    2 **You and your spouse or partner share** this responsibility equally.

    3 **Your spouse or partner** takes on the most responsibility.

8. How much travel time does taking your child(ren) to and/or from school or child care add to your trip to and/or from work? If none, write "0".

    _____ minutes

9. **Think about your relationship with your SPOUSE OR PARTNER in the past month.** How REWARDING have the following been?

	Not at all rewarding	Just a little rewarding	Somewhat rewarding	Very rewarding
a. Having a spouse or partner who is easy to get along with	1	2	3	4
b. Your spouse or partner appreciating you	1	2	3	4
c. Good communication	1	2	3	4
d. Your spouse or partner backing you up in what you want to do	1	2	3	4
e. Having a spouse or partner who is a good friend	1	2	3	4
f. Your spouse or partner liking you as a person	1	2	3	4
g. Being able to disagree without threatening the relationship	1	2	3	4
h. Having a spouse or partner who is a good listener	1	2	3	4
i. Having a spouse or partner who shares in household responsibilities	1	2	3	4

10. **Still thinking about your relationship with your SPOUSE OR PARTNER, in the past month** how CONCERNED have you been about the following?

	Not at all concerned	Just a little concerned	Somewhat concerned	Very concerned
a. Poor communication with your spouse or partner	1	2	3	4
b. Your spouse or partner not understanding who you really are	1	2	3	4
c. Arguing or fighting	1	2	3	4
d. Your spouse or partner not backing you up in what you want to do	1	2	3	4
e. Lack of companionship	1	2	3	4
f. Your spouse or partner being critical of you	1	2	3	4
g. Not getting along	1	2	3	4
h. Your spouse or partner not helping around the house	1	2	3	4

1

276

11. What is the age of this child? _____ years (_____ months if child is under 1 year)

12. Does this child have special needs, such as due to physical disabilities, poor physical health, substance abuse, emotional or behavioral problems or learning disabilities?

      0 No   1 Yes

13. Please circle the number of the statement that best describes the care arrangement currently used most for this child:

    1 Child looks after him or herself (SKIP TO QUESTION 15)
    2 Care is in your home by an older brother or sister
    3 Care is in your home by you or your spouse or partner
    4 Care is in your home by another relative or non-relative
    5 Care is in someone else's home, a child-care center, or a before or after school program or activity

14. How many hours per week is this child in this arrangement? _____ hours/week

15. **Please indicate the extent to which you agree or disagree with each statement by circling the appropriate number. Please answer even if this child looks after him or herself. Circle "0" if a statement is not applicable to your situation.**

	Strongly disagree	Disagree	Neutral	Agree	Strongly agree	NA
a. This arrangement is just what this child needs	1	2	3	4	5	0
b. I feel good about this arrangement for this child	1	2	3	4	5	0
c. This has been a good experience for this child	1	2	3	4	5	0
d. If I had to do it over, I would choose this arrangement again	1	2	3	4	5	0
e. I have good back-up arrangements in case of emergency	1	2	3	4	5	0
f. In choosing child care I have had to take what I could get	1	2	3	4	5	0
g. I have difficulty paying for child care	1	2	3	4	4	0

16. **Now think about being a PARENT to any or all of your children. Please indicate how STRESSFUL each of the following has been in the past month.**

	Not at all stressful	Just a little stressful	Somewhat stressful	Very stressful	NA
a. Your child(ren) having problems at school	1	2	3	4	0
b. Your child(ren) not living up to their potential or to your expectations	1	2	3	4	0
c. Your child(ren) not doing what they're supposed to do without being asked	1	2	3	4	0
d. Problems in communicating with your child(ren)	1	2	3	4	0
e. Your child(ren)'s possible alcohol or other substance use	1	2	3	4	0
f. Your child(ren)'s conflicts with others (including their siblings)	1	2	3	4	0

How STRESSFUL has it been to:	Not at all stressful	Just a little stressful	Somewhat stressful	Very stressful	NA
g. Discipline or correct your child(ren)	1	2	3	4	0
h. Supervise or check on your child(ren)	1	2	3	4	0
i. Offer guidance or advice to your child(ren)	1	2	3	4	0
j. See that your child is (children are) cared for when they are sick	1	2	3	4	0
k. Help with your child(ren)'s school work or school activities	1	2	3	4	0
l. Help with your child(ren)'s personal care (e.g., grooming, dressing)	1	2	3	4	0
m. Arrange or provide transportation for your child(ren)	1	2	3	4	0

17. **Now let's focus on the more positive aspects of being a PARENT to any or all of your children. Please indicate how REWARDING each of the following has been in the past month.**

	Not at all rewarding	Just a little rewarding	Somewhat rewarding	Very rewarding
a. Doing things to help your child(ren)	1	2	3	4
b. Feeling needed by your child(ren)	1	2	3	4
c. Sharing in your child(ren)'s accomplishments	1	2	3	4
d. Doing things with your child(ren)	1	2	3	4
e. Seeing your relationship with your child(ren) mature and grow	1	2	3	4
f. Watching your child(ren) develop as (an) individual(s)	1	2	3	4
g. Fulfilling family obligations or expectations	1	2	3	4
h. Passing on to your child(ren) some of the care that your parents gave you	1	2	3	4

Now we're going to ask you about your and your spouse/partner's parents and step-parents.

18. How many living parents, including step-parents, do you have? _____

19. How many living parents, including step-parents, does your spouse or partner have? _____

20. **Please think now about those parents (including step-parents) and/or parents-in-law whom you and/or your spouse or partner are HELPING OUT in some way. By helping out we mean everything that you each do to assist a parent, such as shopping, home maintenance, transportation to appointments, providing emotional support, financial manage-ment, checking on them by phone, making arrangements for care, making meals, bathing, time spent traveling to and from their residence, etc. Please complete the chart below for EACH parent for whom you or your spouse or partner are helping out.**

	Relationship: Your Parent (P) or Parent-in-law (PIN)		Male or Female		Parent's Age (Approx.)	Average hours per week helped by:	
						You	Your Spouse or Partner
1.	P	PIN	M	F	_____	_____	_____
2.	P	PIN	M	F	_____	_____	_____
3.	P	PIN	M	F	_____	_____	_____
4.	P	PIN	M	F	_____	_____	_____
5.	P	PIN	M	F	_____	_____	_____

21. WHICH ONE of these parents or parents-in-law (1-5 from the above question) are you helping out the MOST: _____ (If you help all equally, please just choose one.)

22. What is the marital status of this parent?
1 Married/partnered
2 Divorced or separated
3 Widowed
4 Never married

23. About how long have you been helping this parent?

_____ years OR _____ months

24. Did you begin helping because of:
1 A crisis
2 A gradual worsening
3 Other _____

25. **In the past year,** when this parent has needed help, who has usually been the one who has given it or seen that it was given? ("Others" include family members, neighbors, friends, or paid care providers)
1 You/your spouse or partner have been the only ones
2 You/your spouse or partner have been the main ones, with some help from others
3 You/your spouse have shared equally with others
4 Others have been the main ones, with some help from you/your spouse or partner

26. How would you rate the overall health of this parent? Would you say it is:
1 Extremely poor   4 Good
2 Poor   5 Very good
3 Fair   6 Excellent

27. Which of the following best describes this parent's living arrangements?
1 Lives in the same household as you
2 Lives with another adult child or non-spouse relative
3 Lives in a nursing facility
4 Lives in group housing for less independent elderly
5 Lives in housing for active/independent retirees
6 Lives in own home/apartment in the community (with or without spouse)

28. How many miles away from you does this parent live?

_____ miles

29. How long (one way) does it usually take you to get to this parent's place of residence?

_____minutes OR _____hours OR_____days

30. How satisfied are you with the help this parent receives from his or her other adult children? (Please circle "0" if there are no other adult children.)

Not at all satisfied						Extremely satisfied	NA
1	2	3	4	5	6	7	0

31. Which of the following four statements describes this parent's ability to get along on his or her income?
1 Can't make ends meet
2 Has just enough, no more
3 Has just enough, with a little extra sometimes
4 Always has money left over

32. Overall, on average, how much do you spend each month on caregiving expenses for this parent (such as for hiring outside help, transportation expenses, giving the parent money, telephone charges, etc.)?

$_____ per month

33. **Please indicate the extent to which you and this parent:**

	Not at all	Just a little	Somewhat	Very
a. Are emotionally close	1	2	3	4
b. Can exchange ideas	1	2	3	4
c. Have similar views about life	1	2	3	4
d. Get along together	1	2	3	4

34. **Even though parents may need help, they sometimes provide help as well. How often does this parent provide the following types of help to you?**

	Never	Not often	Sometimes	Frequently
a. Financial assistance (money)	1	2	3	4
b. Emotional support (someone to talk with)	1	2	3	4
c. Help with watching/caring for your children	1	2	3	4
d. Help with household tasks	1	2	3	4
e. Other help _____	1	2	3	4

3

35. These next questions ask you: (A) how much help this parent requires with various activities, (B) whether you provide or arrange for this help, and if so, (C) how stressful you find it to do this.

A. How much help does this parent require with:	Needs no help (SKIP TO NEXT ITEM)	Can do, but needs to be reminded or supervised	Needs some help from others	Totally dependent upon others	B. Do you help with this activity or arrange for it to be done? (IF NO, SKIP TO NEXT ITEM)		C. IF YES: How stressful is it for you to do this? Not at all	Just a little	Somewhat	Very much
a. Bathing or showering	1	2	3	4	No	Yes	1	2	3	4
b. Dressing or undressing	1	2	3	4	No	Yes	1	2	3	4
c. Getting in or out of a chair or bed	1	2	3	4	No	Yes	1	2	3	4
d. Using the toilet or getting to the bathroom on time	1	2	3	4	No	Yes	1	2	3	4
e. Eating or feeding him/herself	1	2	3	4	No	Yes	1	2	3	4
f. Shopping for necessities	1	2	3	4	No	Yes	1	2	3	4
g. Cooking	1	2	3	4	No	Yes	1	2	3	4
h. Housekeeping	1	2	3	4	No	Yes	1	2	3	4
i. Transportation	1	2	3	4	No	Yes	1	2	3	4
j. Taking or managing medications	1	2	3	4	No	Yes	1	2	3	4
k. Managing money	1	2	3	4	No	Yes	1	2	3	4
l. Using the telephone	1	2	3	4	No	Yes	1	2	3	4
m. Doing laundry	1	2	3	4	No	Yes	1	2	3	4
n. Making decisions about his/her care	1	2	3	4	No	Yes	1	2	3	4

36. Still thinking about this parent, please indicate how STRESSFUL each of the following has been for you in the past month. If a particular problem did not occur with this parent in the past month, please circle "0."

	Not at all stressful	Just a little stressful	Somewhat stressful	Very stressful	Did not occur
a. This parent's emotional problems or moods (e.g., depression, loss of interest, sadness)	1	2	3	4	0
b. This parent's memory or cognitive problems (e.g., living in the past, forgetfulness, confusion, repetitive questions)	1	2	3	4	0
c. This parent endangering him/herself (e.g., wandering off, driving when they shouldn't)	1	2	3	4	0
d. This parent's aggressive or inappropriate behaviors (e.g., not respecting others' privacy, accusing others)	1	2	3	4	0
e. This parent's communication problems (e.g., inability to express him/herself)	1	2	3	4	0
f. This parent's agitation (e.g., being constantly restless, pacing)	1	2	3	4	0
g. This parent's possible alcohol or other substance use	1	2	3	4	0
h. This parent's difficulty sleeping	1	2	3	4	0
i. This parent's complex medical care needs	1	2	3	4	0
j. This parent's criticisms and complaints	1	2	3	4	0

37. Next, we focus on the more positive aspects of being a caregiver. Please indicate how REWARDING each of the following has been in the past month. If something did not occur in the past month, please circle "0."

	Not at all rewarding	Just a little rewarding	Somewhat rewarding	Very rewarding	Did not occur
a. Doing things to help this parent	1	2	3	4	0
b. Feeling needed by this parent	1	2	3	4	0
c. Seeing this parent do things for him or herself	1	2	3	4	0
d. Doing things with this parent	1	2	3	4	0
e. Seeing your relationship with this parent mature and grow	1	2	3	4	0
f. Fulfilling family obligations or expectations	1	2	3	4	0
g. This parent showing appreciation for what you do for him/her	1	2	3	4	0
h. Giving back to this parent some of the care s/he gave to you	1	2	3	4	0

4

279

38. Now, we'd like you to think about **YOUR FAMILY IN GENERAL**, including your spouse or partner, each of your children, and your parents and your spouse's or partner's parents. For each statement below please circle the response indicating the extent to which you agree or disagree.

	Strongly disagree	Disagree	Agree	Strongly agree
a. The most important things that happen to me involve my family	1	2	3	4
b. I am very much personally involved with my family	1	2	3	4
c. Most of my interests are centered around my family	1	2	3	4
d. To me, my family is a very large part of who I am	1	2	3	4
e. The most important things that happen to me involve my present job	1	2	3	4
f. Most of my interests are centered around my job	1	2	3	4
g. I am very much involved in my job	1	2	3	4
h. To me, my job is only a small part of who I am	1	2	3	4

39. Again, for each statement below, please circle the response indicating the extent to which you agree or disagree. When thinking about your family, please continue to include your spouse or partner, your child(ren) and your parents or parents-in-law.

	Strongly disagree	Disagree	Neither agree nor disagree	Agree	Strongly agree
a. The demands of my work interfere with my home and family life	1	2	3	4	5
b. The amount of time my job takes up makes it difficult to fulfill family responsibilities	1	2	3	4	5
c. Things I want to do at home do not get done because of the demands my job puts on me	1	2	3	4	5
d. My job produces strain that makes it difficult to fulfill family duties	1	2	3	4	5
e. Due to my work-related duties, I have to make changes to my plans for family activities	1	2	3	4	5
f. The demands of my family or spouse/partner interfere with work-related activities	1	2	3	4	5
g. I have to put off doing things at work because of demands on my time at home	1	2	3	4	5
h. Things I want to do at work don't get done because of the demands of my family or spouse/partner	1	2	3	4	5
i. My home life interferes with my responsibilities at work, such as getting to work on time, accomplishing daily tasks, and working overtime	1	2	3	4	5
j. Family-related strain interferes with my ability to perform job-related duties	1	2	3	4	5
k. Having my family well cared for puts me in a good mood at work	1	2	3	4	5
l. I have had more positive feelings about myself at work because I have felt good about myself and my handling of family responsibilities	1	2	3	4	5
m. I have had greater confidence in myself at work because I have been able to handle family responsibilities well	1	2	3	4	5
n. Having a successful day at work puts me in a good mood to handle my family responsibilities	1	2	3	4	5
o. I have had greater confidence in my ability to handle family responsibilities because I have been able to handle my job responsibilities well	1	2	3	4	5
p. I have had more positive feelings about myself and my ability to handle my family responsibilities because I have felt good about myself at work	1	2	3	4	5
q. My family responsibilities provide me a needed break from work	1	2	3	4	5
r. My work provides me a needed break from my family responsibilities	1	2	3	4	5
s. Generally speaking, I am very satisfied with my family	1	2	3	4	5
t. I frequently think I would like to change my family situation	1	2	3	4	5
u. I am generally satisfied with the role I play in my family	1	2	3	4	5
v. I am generally satisfied with the degree to which I am managing my work and family responsibilities	1	2	3	4	5
w. Generally speaking, I am very satisfied with my job	1	2	3	4	5
x. I frequently think of quitting my job	1	2	3	4	5
y. I am generally satisfied with the kind of work I do in my job	1	2	3	4	5
z. Most people in this job are very satisfied with the job	1	2	3	4	5
aa. People in this job often think of quitting	1	2	3	4	5
bb. I will probably look for a new job in the next year	1	2	3	4	5

5

280

Now we're going to ask you some questions about your and your spouse/partner's jobs.

40. What is your occupation?

_____

41. Please describe briefly the kind of work that you do:

_____

_____

42. About how many hours per week do you work?

_____ hours/week

43. Would you prefer to work more, fewer, or the same number of hours?
    1 More
    2 Fewer
    3 The same

44. Usually, do the number of hours you work:
    1 Stay nearly the same every week
    2 Vary from week to week

45. Do you mostly:
    1 Work for someone else
    2 Own your own business

46. How many people do you supervise or manage?

_____

47. Are you sometimes able to do your regularly scheduled work at home?
    1 No
    2 Yes -- If yes: On average, how any hours per week do you work at home? _____ hours/week

48. What is your best estimate of the number of employees who work at the site where you work most often?

_____

49. What is your best estimate of the number of employees who work for your organization/employer overall?

_____

50. Are you:
    1 Salaried
    2 Paid by the hour
    3 Paid by commission
    4 Paid by the hour and by commission
    5 Other_____

51. What shift do you work?
    1 Days
    2 Nights
    3 Swing
    4 Rotating
    5 Other _____

52. About how many hours per week does your spouse or partner work?

_____ hours/week

53. What shift does your spouse or partner work?
    1 Days
    2 Nights
    3 Swing
    4 Rotating
    5 Other _____

54. Which type of work schedule best describes your work situation?
    1 Standard full time
    2 Flexible work hours
    3 Compressed work week (such as four 10-hour days or three 12-hour days)
    4 Job sharing (part time)
    5 Other part time

55. Are you a temporary or a contract worker?
    0 No
    1 Yes

56. How long have you been employed in this job?
    _____ years

57. What is your approximate commuting time (one way) to work?
    _____ minutes

58. How much flexibility do you have in your work schedule to handle family responsibilities?
    1 No flexibility at all
    2 Hardly any flexibility
    3 Some flexibility
    4 A lot of flexibility

59. How much flexibility does your spouse or partner have in his/her work schedule to handle family responsibilities?
    1 No flexibility at all
    2 Hardly any flexibility
    3 Some flexibility
    4 A lot of flexibility

60. How responsive is your organization to your need to take time to deal with planned family responsibilities?
    1 Not at all
    2 A little
    3 Somewhat
    4 Quite a bit
    5 Extremely
    0 Not applicable -- self-employed

61. How responsive is your organization to your need to take time to deal with unexpected family problems?
    1 Not at all
    2 A little
    3 Somewhat
    4 Quite a bit
    5 Extremely
    0 Not applicable -- self-employed

6

281

62. In your current JOB, in the past month how REWARDING to you have the following been:

		Not at all rewarding	Just a little rewarding	Somewhat rewarding	Very rewarding
a.	Challenging or stimulating work	1	2	3	4
b.	The income	1	2	3	4
c.	Being able to set your own work schedule	1	2	3	4
d.	Having a variety of tasks	1	2	3	4
e.	Having hours that fit your needs	1	2	3	4
f.	Your job being flexible enough that you can respond to non-work situations	1	2	3	4
g.	Having the authority you need to get your job done	1	2	3	4
h.	The job fitting your skills	1	2	3	4
i.	The opportunity for learning new things	1	2	3	4
j.	Making good money compared to other people in your field	1	2	3	4

In the past month, how REWARDING have the following been: (Please circle "0" NA if something has not applied to your situation in the past month.)

		Not at all rewarding	Just a little rewarding	Somewhat rewarding	Very rewarding	NA
k.	Your supervisor's respect for your abilities	1	2	3	4	0
l.	Your supervisor's concern about the welfare of those under him/her	1	2	3	4	0
m.	Your supervisor paying attention to what you have to say	1	2	3	4	0
n.	Job security	1	2	3	4	0
o.	The amount of support from co-workers	1	2	3	4	0
p.	Your job offering good benefits, for example, paid sick leave	1	2	3	4	0

63. In your current JOB, in the past month how CONCERNED have you been about the following:

		Not at all concerned	Just a little concerned	Somewhat concerned	Very concerned
a.	The job's dullness, monotony, lack of variety	1	2	3	4
b.	The job's not using your skills	1	2	3	4
c.	Having to do tasks you don't feel should be part of your job	1	2	3	4
d.	Having to juggle conflicting tasks or duties	1	2	3	4
e.	The income	1	2	3	4
f.	Having too much to do	1	2	3	4
g.	The job's taking too much out of you	1	2	3	4
h.	Having to do things against your better judgment	1	2	3	4
i.	People in jobs like yours being laid off or unemployed	1	2	3	4
j.	Making less money than other people in your line of work	1	2	3	4
k.	Making less money than you feel you deserve	1	2	3	4

In the past month, how CONCERNED have you been about: (Please circle "0" if something has not applied to your situation in the past month.)

		Not at all concerned	Just a little concerned	Somewhat concerned	Very concerned	NA
l.	Lack of job security on this job	1	2	3	4	0
m.	Your supervisor's lack of appreciation for your work	1	2	3	4	0
n.	The possibility of unemployment	1	2	3	4	0
o.	Your supervisor's having unrealistic expectations for your work	1	2	3	4	0
p.	Not being able to get your own job done because of other people or red tape	1	2	3	4	0
q.	Lack of support from your supervisor	1	2	3	4	0
r.	Lack of support from co-workers	1	2	3	4	0
s.	Lack of good benefits, for example, paid sick leave	1	2	3	4	0

7

282

64. **Please indicate the degree to which each statement below describes how you and your spouse or partner, AS A COUPLE, feel and act in response to your many work and family duties.**

		Never	Sometimes	Most or all of the time
a.	We work out who will have responsibility for particular family tasks	1	2	3
b.	Together we decide changes in each other's work, such as work hours and job changes	1	2	3
c.	We set aside time to talk about major issues and make decisions	1	2	3
d.	We pick up the slack if the other is having a demanding time at work	1	2	3
e.	We take time away just for us, without the kids or parent care responsibilities	1	2	3
f.	We lean on and look to each other for moral support	1	2	3
g.	We try to be understanding when the other is stressed	1	2	3
h.	We wish one of us didn't have to work	1	2	3

65. **The next questions concern how YOU feel or act in response to your many work and family duties. Please indicate the degree to which each statement below describes how you feel or act.**

		Never	Sometimes	Most or all of the time
a.	I plan how I'm going to use my time and energy	1	2	3
b.	I reduce hours spent on certain tasks or demands	1	2	3
c.	I involve and get help from other family members or friends to accomplish tasks or meet demands	1	2	3
d.	I hire people who help me accomplish tasks or meet demands	1	2	3
e.	I stop doing things that are not absolutely necessary	1	2	3
f.	I don't try to plan, I just take things as they come	1	2	3
g.	I take on tasks if no one else is capable or available	1	2	3
h.	I limit my volunteer work	1	2	3
i.	I try to realize I can't do it all, and that it's okay	1	2	3
j.	I get moral support and comfort from others	1	2	3
k.	I feel guilty for not spending enough time with certain people or doing certain things	1	2	3
l.	I focus on the many good things I have	1	2	3
m.	I recognize and accept that I may not be able to do my best	1	2	3
n.	I protect or set aside time for activities that are important to me	1	2	3
o.	I try to find humor in the situation	1	2	3
p.	I wish I could accept or ask for help from others	1	2	3
q.	I have back-up systems in case things don't happen as expected	1	2	3
r.	I get help with my work from family members	1	2	3
s.	I lose track of what's important to me	1	2	3
t.	I limit my social activities	1	2	3
u.	I avoid taking on new tasks if others are willing to do them	1	2	3
v.	I spend less time with my spouse or partner	1	2	3
w.	I spend less time with other family members	1	2	3
x.	I attend activities separately from my spouse or partner because of conflicting schedules or responsibilities	1	2	3
y.	I divide up household chores among family members	1	2	3
z.	I limit the number of my child(ren)'s activities that I attend	1	2	3
aa.	I lower my expectations of what should get done around the house	1	2	3
bb.	I use a cell phone, pager, or voice messaging so that my family can reach me	1	2	3
cc.	I wish others would be more supportive	1	2	3
dd.	I limit my personal time for reading, exercise, or other leisure activities	1	2	3
ee.	I plan my work hours around my child(ren)'s, parent'(s), or spouse's or partner's schedule	1	2	3
ff.	I plan to work at home so that I can be close to my family	1	2	3
gg.	When necessary, I take time off from work to care for a parent or child	1	2	3
hh.	I sometimes work long hours to avoid dealing with family responsibilities	1	2	3
pp.	I help my spouse or partner with his/her work	1	2	3
qq.	I prioritize and do the things that are most important and necessary	1	2	3

283

66. Because of your responsibilities for children or parents, in the past month, how many times have you had to, or chosen to:

	Due to responsibilities for any of your **children**	Due to responsibilities for any of your **parents or parents-in-law**
a. Miss a day's work	_____ times	_____ times
b. Arrive late at work	_____ times	_____ times
c. Leave work early	_____ times	_____ times
d. Spend time at work on the telephone	_____ times	_____ times

67. **In the past month**, how often have you worked less effectively because you were concerned or upset:

	Never	Seldom	Sometimes	Frequently	Most or all of the time
a. About your child(ren)	1	2	3	4	5
b. About your parent(s)	1	2	3	4	5

68. How comfortable are you talking with co-workers and with your supervisor at work about your responsibilities for children and parents? (Circle 0 if you do not have co-workers or a supervisor.)

	Comfortable talking about child(ren)					Comfortable talking about parent(s)				
	Not at all	Just a little	Somewhat	Very	NA	Not at all	Just a little	Somewhat	Very	NA
a. Co-workers	1	2	3	4	0	1	2	3	4	0
b. Supervisor	1	2	3	4	0	1	2	3	4	0

69. When a child or parent you are caring for needs assistance and you take time off from work, which ONE of the following is most likely to make this possible? (Please circle only one response.)

0 I am not able to take time off work
1 I use sick leave
2 I have flexible hours
3 I use emergency leave
4 I take a day off without pay
5 I use vacation or personal leave
6 I do my work at home
7 I never need to take time off for this reason
8 Other: _____

70. Please indicate whether or not each of the following workplace supports is available to you through your employer. If YES, do you make use of this? Please skip to the next question if you are self-employed.

	Don't know	No	Yes ------->	IF YES: Do you use? No	IF YES: Do you use? Yes
a. Flexible work hours	8	0	1	0	1
b. Job-sharing	8	0	1	0	1
c. Option to work at home/telecommute	8	0	1	0	1
d. Unpaid leave to care for a family member	8	0	1	0	1
e. Personal Time Off or other paid leave which can be used to care for a family member	8	0	1	0	1
f. Family health care insurance	8	0	1	0	1
g. Pension/retirement plan	8	0	1	0	1
h. Program that allows workers to set aside pre-tax dollars to pay for child care	8	0	1	0	1
i. Program that allows workers to set aside pre-tax dollars to pay for care of a parent	8	0	1	0	1
j. Subsidy for child care	8	0	1	0	1
k. Subsidy for parent care	8	0	1	0	1
l. On-site child care center	8	0	1	0	1
m. On-site adult day care center	8	0	1	0	1
n. Resources and referral services for child care	8	0	1	0	1
o. Resources and referral services for elder care	8	0	1	0	1
p. On-site support groups on family-related issues	8	0	1	0	1
q. Seminars on work and family issuess	8	0	1	0	1
r. Employee assistance program (EAP)	8	0	1	0	1
s. Other family-friendly benefits/programs (Specify:_____)	8	0	1	0	1

9

71. What workplace supports or services do you <u>wish</u> your employer offered?

---

72. Because of your child or parent care responsibilities, <u>in the past year</u>, have you:

	No	Yes
a. Quit a job	0	1
b. Chosen a job that gives you more flexibility to meet your family demands	0	1
c. Refused to relocate	0	1
d. Refused or decided not to work toward a promotion	0	1
e. Refused or limited your travel	0	1
f. Had your parent(s) or parent(s)-in-law live with you so they can help you out	0	1
g. Had your parent(s) or parent(s)-in-law live with you to make it easier for you to help them	0	1
h. Participated in a support group for parents or for adult children	0	1
i. Worked reduced hours	0	1
j. Worked a different shift from your spouse or partner so that one adult is at home most of the time	0	1
k. Other (related to your work or family) _____	0	1

---

73. For each of the following types of technology, please indicate whether or not you currently have this technology. If you do have it, please note how helpful it is to you in managing your work and family responsibilities.

	Do you have?		If YES: How helpful is it?		
	No	Yes ---------->	Not at all	Somewhat	Very
a. Voice mail/answering machine	0	1	1	2	3
b. Fax	0	1	1	2	3
c. Cellular phone	0	1	1	2	3
d. Beeper/Pager	0	1	1	2	3
e. Portable computer	0	1	1	2	3
f. Remote access to computer used for work	0	1	1	2	3
g. Internet/WWW access (for information, support)	0	1	1	2	3

---

74. To what extent does technology (like portable computers and voice mail) make it harder or easier for you to manage both your work and family responsibilities?

	Much Harder					Much Easier	
Technology makes it:	1	2	3	4	5	6	7

---

75. Please indicate which of the following have happened to you in the past year. During the past year, have you. .

	No	Yes
a. Changed or left a job?	0	1
b. Changed your place of residence?	0	1
c. Been robbed or burglarized?	0	1
d. Become divorced or separated?	0	1
e. Had someone close to you either move in with you or leave your home?	0	1
f. Gotten married or had a marital reconciliation?	0	1
g. Had a family member or close friend who was seriously ill or injured?	0	1
h. Lost a parent through death?	0	1
i. Lost a child through death?	0	1
j. Lost a beloved family pet?	0	1
k. Experienced the death of some other family member or close friend?	0	1
l. Been seriously ill or injured yourself?	0	1
m. Been arrested or involved in a court case?	0	1
n. Had a decline in financial status?	0	1
o. Other (Specify:_____)	0	1

10

285

76. **Shown below are opposite pairs of words that may indicate how people feel overall about their life. Consider each of the word pairs and circle the number that best indicates how YOU feel about your life in general.**

a.	Interesting	1	2	3	4	5	6	7	Boring
b.	Enjoyable	1	2	3	4	5	6	7	Miserable
c.	Worthwhile	1	2	3	4	5	6	7	Useless
d.	Friendly	1	2	3	4	5	6	7	Lonely
e.	Full	1	2	3	4	5	6	7	Empty
f.	Hopeful	1	2	3	4	5	6	7	Discouraging
g.	Rewarding	1	2	3	4	5	6	7	Disappointing
h.	Brings out the best in me	1	2	3	4	5	6	7	Doesn't give me much of a chance

77. **Taking all things together, how would you say things are these days? Would you say that you are:**

    1 very happy   2 pretty happy   3 not too happy

78. **In general, how satisfying do you find the ways you're spending your life these days?**

    1 completely satisfying   2 pretty satisfying   3 not very satisfying

79. **Below is a list of ways you might have felt or behaved. Please indicate how often you have felt this way during the past week by circling the appropriate number.**

During the past week:	Rarely or none of the time (less than 1 day)	Some or a little of the time (1-2 days)	Occasionally or a moderate amount of time (3-4 days)	Most of the time (5-7 days)
a. I was bothered by things that usually don't bother me	1	2	3	4
b. I did not feel like eating; my appetite was poor	1	2	3	4
c. I felt that I could not shake off the blues even with help from my family or friends	1	2	3	4
d. I felt that I was just as good as other people	1	2	3	4
e. I had trouble keeping my mind on what I was doing	1	2	3	4
f. I felt depressed	1	2	3	4
g. I felt that everything I did was an effort	1	2	3	4
h. I felt hopeful about the future	1	2	3	4
i. I thought my life had been a failure	1	2	3	4
j. I felt fearful	1	2	3	4
k. My sleep was restless	1	2	3	4
l. I was happy	1	2	3	4
m. I talked less than usual	1	2	3	4
n. I felt lonely	1	2	3	4
o. People were unfriendly	1	2	3	4
p. I enjoyed life	1	2	3	4
q. I had crying spells	1	2	3	4
r. I felt sad	1	2	3	4
s. I felt that people disliked me	1	2	3	4
t. I could not get "going"	1	2	3	4

80. Below are a number of characteristics that may or may not apply to you. Please circle the number next to each statement to indicate the extent to which you agree or disagree with each statement.

I see myself as someone who:	Disagree strongly	Disagree a little	Neither agree nor disagree	Agree a little	Agree strongly
a. Is depressed, blue	1	2	3	4	5
b. Is relaxed	1	2	3	4	5
c. Can be tense	1	2	3	4	5
d. Is emotionally stable, not easily upset	1	2	3	4	5
e. Worries a lot	1	2	3	4	5
f. Remains calm in tense situations	1	2	3	4	5
g. Gets nervous easily	1	2	3	4	5

81. Please indicate the extent to which you agree or disagree with the following statements reflecting beliefs about appropriate behaviors for men and women in families.

	Strongly disagree	Disagree	Agree	Strongly agree
a. A working mother can establish just as warm and secure a relationship with her children as a mother who does not work	1	2	3	4
b. It is more important for a wife to help her husband's career than to have a career herself	1	2	3	4
c. It is much better for everyone involved if the man is the achiever outside the home and the woman takes care of the home and family	1	2	3	4
d. Men should share the work around the house, such as doing dishes, cleaning, and so forth	1	2	3	4
e. A preschool child is likely to suffer if his/her mother works	1	2	3	4
f. A woman's job should be kept for her when she is having a baby	1	2	3	4
g. Men make better supervisors on the job than women do	1	2	3	4
h. Fathers should be as involved in caring for the children as mothers, such as taking them to doctors, changing diapers, etc.	1	2	3	4
i. If there is a limited number of jobs, it is all right for a married woman to hold a job when her husband is able to support her	1	2	3	4

These last questions cover the basics about you.

82. What is your age?_____ years

83. Your gender?
0 Male   1 Female

84. Were you born in the United States?
0 No   1 Yes

85. Do you consider yourself Hispanic or Latino?
0 No   1 Yes

86. Do you consider yourself primarily:
1 White/Caucasian
2 Black/African American
3 American Indian or Alaska Native
4 Asian
5 Hawaiian or Pacific Islander
6 Other _____

87. What is the highest grade/degree in school that you completed?
1 Grade school or less
2 Some high school
3 Graduated high school
4 Some college
5 Graduated college
6 Some graduate study
7 Graduate degree

88. What would you say is your and your spouse's or partner's approximate combined household income before taxes?

$_____ per year

89. Which of the following four statements describes your ability to get along on your income?
1 We can't make ends meet
2 We have just enough, no more
3 We have enough, with a little extra sometimes
4 We always have money left over

90. Which one response best describes you and your day-to-day priorities:
1 I am primarily a family person
2 I am a family and career person, but I lean a bit more towards family
3 I am a career person and a family person
4 I am a career and family person but lean a bit more towards career
5 I am primarily a career person

91. Circumstances differ and some people find it easier than others to combine working with family responsibilities. In general, how easy or difficult is it for you?
1 Very easy   4 Somewhat difficult
2 Easy   5 Difficult
3 Somewhat easy   6 Very difficult

92. How would you rate your overall health; would you say it is:	Extremely poor	Poor	Fair	Good	Very good	Excellent
	1	2	3	4	5	6

93. How would you rate your spouse's or partner's overall health?	Extremely poor	Poor	Fair	Good	Very good	Excellent
	1	2	3	4	5	6

94. How would you rate your overall performance:	Extremely poor	Poor	Fair	Good	Very good	Excellent
a. at your work	1	2	3	4	5	6
b. as a spouse	1	2	3	4	5	6
c. as a parent	1	2	3	4	5	6
d. as a caregiver to the parent or parent-in-law you're helping the most	1	2	3	4	5	6
e. in taking care of your own physical and mental health needs	1	2	3	4	5	6

95. What advice would you offer to other working couples who have children at home and who are helping out aging or disabled parents?

96. Any other comments you'd like to add? (Please continue on next page if necessary.)

13

THANK YOU FOR YOUR HELP!

Please return in the postage-paid envelope to:

Institute on Aging
Portland State University
P.O. Box 751
Portland, OR 97207-0751

Portland State University

National Survey
of
Dual-Earner Couples in the Sandwiched Generation

Wave 2 of a study of working couples
caring for children and aging parents

conducted by
Dr. Margaret B. Neal and Dr. Leslie B. Hammer
at
Portland State University, Portland, Oregon
with funding by the
Alfred P. Sloan Foundation

Spring, 1999

ID#_____

1. Besides you and your spouse/partner, please list the ages and relationships to you of all persons who <u>live with you 3 or more days per week.</u>

	Age	Relationship		Age	Relationship
1	_____	_____	5	_____	_____
2	_____	_____	6	_____	_____
3	_____	_____	7	_____	_____
4	_____	_____	8	_____	_____

2. Do you still have one or more children age 18 or under living with you at least 3 days per week?

      1 Yes   0 No   - IF NO, which of the following best describes your situation?

                        1 Youngest child is now 19 and still lives with us —> **SKIP TO QUESTION 5**
                        2 Youngest child is now 19 and no longer lives with us
                        3 Youngest child is 18 or under but is living elsewhere —> **SKIP TO QUESTION 9**
                        4 Other – Please explain; _____

3. Would you say that:

    1 You are the person who takes most responsibility for seeing to the care of the children in your household.
    2 You and your spouse or partner share this responsibility equally.
    3 Your spouse or partner takes on the most responsibility.

4. What is the age of this child? _____ years (Write "0" if the child is under 1 year of age.)

5. Does this child have special needs, such as due to physical disabilities, poor physical health, substance abuse, emotional or behavioral problems or learning disabilities?   0 No   1 Yes

6. Please circle the number of the statement that best describes the care arrangement currently <u>used most</u> for this child:

    1 Child looks after him or herself —> **SKIP TO QUESTION 8**   5 Care is in someone else's home
    2 Care is in your home by an older brother or sister   6 Care is in a child-care center
    3 Care is in your home by you or your spouse or partner   7 Care is in a before or after school program or activity
    4 Care is in your home by another relative or non-relative

7. How many hours per week is this child in this arrangement? _____ hours/week

8. **Please indicate the extent to which you agree or disagree with each statement by circling the appropriate number. Please answer even if this child looks after him or herself. Circle "0" if a statement does not apply to you.**

	Strongly disagree	Disagree	Neutral	Agree	Strongly agree	NA
a. This arrangement is just what this child needs	1	2	3	4	5	0
b. I feel good about this arrangement for this child	1	2	3	4	5	0
c. This has been a good experience for this child	1	2	3	4	5	0
d. If I had to do it over, I would choose this arrangement again	1	2	3	4	5	0
e. I have good back-up arrangements in case of emergency	1	2	3	4	5	0
f. In choosing child care I have had to take what I could get	1	2	3	4	5	0
g. I have difficulty paying for child care	1	2	3	4	5	0

9. **Now think about being a PARENT to any or all of your children. Please indicate how STRESSFUL each of the following has been <u>in the past month</u>. Circle "0" if a statement does not apply to you.**

	Not at all stressful	Just a little stressful	Somewhat stressful	Very stressful	NA
a. Your child(ren) having problems at school	1	2	3	4	0
b. Your child(ren) <u>not</u> living up to their potential or to your expectations	1	2	3	4	0
c. Your child(ren) <u>not</u> doing what they're supposed to do without being asked	1	2	3	4	0
d. Problems in communicating with your child(ren)	1	2	3	4	0
e. Your child(ren)'s possible alcohol or other substance use	1	2	3	4	0
f. Your child(ren)'s conflicts with others (including their siblings)	1	2	3	4	0

1

292

9A. How STRESSFUL has it been to:

	Not at all stressful	Just a little stressful	Somewhat stressful	Very stressful	NA
g. Discipline or correct your child(ren)	1	2	3	4	0
h. Supervise or check on your child(ren)	1	2	3	4	0
i. Offer guidance or advice to your child(ren)	1	2	3	4	0
j. See that your child is (children are) cared for when they are sick	1	2	3	4	0
k. Help with your child(ren)'s school work or school activities	1	2	3	4	0
l. Help with your child(ren)'s personal care (e.g., grooming, dressing)	1	2	3	4	0
m. Arrange or provide transportation for your child(ren)	1	2	3	4	0

10. Now let's focus on the more _positive_ aspects of being a PARENT to any or all of your children. Please indicate how REWARDING each of the following has been _in the past month._

	Not at all rewarding	Just a little rewarding	Somewhat rewarding	Very rewarding
a. Doing things to help your child(ren)	1	2	3	4
b. Feeling needed by your child(ren)	1	2	3	4
c. Sharing in your child(ren)'s accomplishments	1	2	3	4
d. Doing things with your child(ren)	1	2	3	4
e. Seeing your relationship with your child(ren) mature and grow	1	2	3	4
f. Watching your child(ren) develop as (an) individual(s)	1	2	3	4
g. Fulfilling family obligations or expectations	1	2	3	4
h. Passing on to your child(ren) some of the care that your parents gave you	1	2	3	4

Now we're going to ask you about your spouse or partner.

11. Are you and your spouse or partner of last year still living together?

    1   Yes

    2   No - we're separated or divorced ⎯⎯⎯⎯

    3   No - s/he passed away ⎯⎯⎯⎯ **---> SKIP TO QUESTION 14**

12. Think about your relationship with your SPOUSE OR PARTNER _in the past month_. How REWARDING have the following been?

	Not at all rewarding	Just a little rewarding	Somewhat rewarding	Very rewarding
a. Having a spouse or partner who is easy to get along with	1	2	3	4
b. Your spouse or partner appreciating you	1	2	3	4
c. Good communication	1	2	3	4
d. Your spouse or partner backing you up in what you want to do	1	2	3	4
e. Having a spouse or partner who is a good friend	1	2	3	4
f. Your spouse or partner liking you as a person	1	2	3	4
g. Being able to disagree without threatening the relationship	1	2	3	4
h. Having a spouse or partner who is a good listener	1	2	3	4
i. Having a spouse or partner who shares in household responsibilities	1	2	3	4

13. Still thinking about your relationship with your SPOUSE OR PARTNER, _in the past month_ how CONCERNED have you been about the following?

	Not at all concerned	Just a little concerned	Somewhat concerned	Very concerned
a. Poor communication with your spouse or partner	1	2	3	4
b. Your spouse or partner not understanding who you really are	1	2	3	4
c. Arguing or fighting	1	2	3	4
d. Your spouse or partner not backing you up in what you want to do	1	2	3	4
e. Lack of companionship	1	2	3	4
f. Your spouse or partner being critical of you	1	2	3	4
g. Not getting along	1	2	3	4
h. Your spouse or partner not helping around the house	1	2	3	4

Now we're going to ask you about your and your spouse/partner's parents and step-parents.

14. How many living parents, including step-parents, do **you** have? _____

If you and your spouse/partner are no longer together, answer the following questions regarding help to parents just in terms of the help **you** are providing.

15. How many living parents, including step-parents, does **your spouse or partner** have? _____

2

293

16. Are you or your spouse or partner still **HELPING OUT** one or more parents, step-parents, or parents-in-law for **a combined total of 3 or more hours per week?** By **"helping out"** we mean **everything that you each do** to assist a parent, such as shopping, home maintenance, transportation, providing emotional support, financial management, checking on them by phone, making arrangements for care, making meals, time spent traveling to and from their residence, etc.

   1 Yes   0 No -- IF NO, which of the following best describes your situation?

            1 We still help the parent(s), but less than a combined total of 3 hours per week. ---> **GO TO QUESTION 17**
            2 The parent(s) we were helping passed away.
            3 Someone else is now caring for the parent(s).   ---> **SKIP TO**
            4 The parent(s) no longer need(s) help.   **QUESTION 36,**
            5 Other - Please explain: _____   **p. 5**

17. Please complete the chart below for **each parent** whom you or your spouse or partner are **helping out.**

	Relationship: Your Parent or Parent-in-Law	Male or Female	Parent's Age (Approx.)	Average hours per week helped by **you**	Average hours per week helped by your **spouse or partner**
A.	Parent Parent-in-law	M F	_____	_____	_____
B.	Parent Parent-in-law	M F	_____	_____	_____
C.	Parent Parent-in-law	M F	_____	_____	_____
D.	Parent Parent-in-law	M F	_____	_____	_____
E.	Parent Parent-in-law	M F	_____	_____	_____

18. Identify by letter (**A - E above**) which one of these parents or parents-in-law you are currently helping the **MOST**:

_____ (If you help all equally, please just choose one.)

19. What is the marital status of this parent?
  1 Married/partnered   3 Widowed
  2 Divorced or separated   4 Never married

20. About how long have you been helping this parent?

_____ years (enter "0" if less than one year)

21. **In the past year**, when this parent has needed help, who has usually been the one who has given it or seen that it was given? ("Others" include family members, neighbors, friends, or paid care providers)

  1 You/your spouse or partner have been the **only** ones

  2 You/your spouse or partner have been the **main** ones, with some help from others

  3 You/your spouse have **shared equally** with others

  4 **Others** have been the main ones, with some help from you/ your spouse or partner

22. Which of the following best describes this parent's living arrangements?

  1 Lives with you -- **SKIP TO QUESTION 25**
  2 Lives with another adult child or non-spouse relative
  3 Lives in a nursing facility
  4 Lives in group housing for less independent elderly
  5 Lives in housing for active/independent retirees
  6 Lives in own home/apartment in the community (with or without spouse)

23. How many miles away from you does this parent live?

_____miles

24. How long (one way) does it usually take you to get to this parent's place of residence?

_____minutes OR _____hours OR_____days

25. How satisfied are you with the help this parent receives from his or her other adult children? (Please circle "0" if there are no other adult children.)

Not at all satisfied						Extremely satisfied	NA
1	2	3	4	5	6	7	0

26. How would you rate the overall health of this parent?
  1 Extremely poor   4 Good
  2 Poor   5 Very good
  3 Fair   6 Excellent

27. Which of the following four statements describes this parent's ability to get along on his or her income?

  1 Can't make ends meet
  2 Has just enough, no more
  3 Has just enough, with a little extra sometimes
  4 Always has money left over

28. Please indicate the extent to which you and this parent:

	Not at all	Just a little	Somewhat	Very
a. Are emotionally close	1	2	3	4
b. Can exchange ideas	1	2	3	4
c. Have similar views about life	1	2	3	4
d. Get along together	1	2	3	4

29. Even though parents may need help, they sometimes provide help as well. How often does this parent provide the following types of help to you?

	Never	Not often	Sometimes	Frequently
a. Financial assistance(money)	1	2	3	4
b. Emotional support (someone to talk with)	1	2	3	4
c. Help with watching/caring for your children	1	2	3	4
d. Help with household tasks	1	2	3	4
e. Other help (specify below)	1	2	3	4

(_____)

3

294

30. **Still thinking about this parent, please indicate how STRESSFUL each of the following has been for you in the past month.** If a particular problem did not occur with this parent in the past month, please circle "0."

		Not at all stressful	Just a little stressful	Somewhat stressful	Very stressful	Did not occur
a	This parent's emotional problems or moods (e.g., depression, loss of interest, sadness)	1	2	3	4	0
b.	This parent's memory or cognitive problems (e.g., living in the past, forgetfulness, confusion, repetitive questions)	1	2	3	4	0
c.	This parent endangering him/herself (e.g., wandering off, driving when they shouldn't)	1	2	3	4	0
d.	This parent's aggressive or inappropriate behaviors (e.g., not respecting others' privacy, accusing others)	1	2	3	4	0
e.	This parent's communication problems (e.g., inability to express him/herself)	1	2	3	4	0
f.	This parent's agitation (e.g., being constantly restless, pacing)	1	2	3	4	0
g.	This parent's possible alcohol or other substance use	1	2	3	4	0
h.	This parent's difficulty sleeping	1	2	3	4	0
i.	This parent's complex medical care needs	1	2	3	4	0
j.	This parent's criticisms and complaints	1	2	3	4	0

31. Next, we focus on the more positive aspects of being a caregiver. Please indicate how REWARDING each of the following has been in the past month. If something did not occur in the past month, please circle "0."

		Not at all rewarding	Just a little rewarding	Somewhat rewarding	Very rewarding	Did not occur
a.	Doing things to help this parent	1	2	3	4	0
b.	Feeling needed by this parent	1	2	3	4	0
c.	Seeing this parent do things for him or herself	1	2	3	4	0
d.	Doing things with this parent	1	2	3	4	0
e.	Seeing your relationship with this parent mature and grow	1	2	3	4	0
f.	Fulfilling family obligations or expectations	1	2	3	4	0
g.	This parent showing appreciation for what you do for him/her	1	2	3	4	0
h.	Giving back to this parent some of the care s/he gave to you	1	2	3	4	0

32. **Please indicate (A) how much help this parent requires with each of the tasks (a-o) below. If no help is needed with a task, circle 1 and skip down to the next one. If some help is needed, please circle the appropriate response (2-4), then indicate (B) whether or not you provide or arrange for this help, and if yes, (C) how stressful you find it to do this.**

A. How much help does this parent require with:	Needs no help (SKIP TO NEXT TASK)	Can do, but needs to be reminded or supervised	Needs some help from others	Totally dependent upon others	B. Do you either help with this activity or arrange for it to be done? (SKIP DOWN TO NEXT TASK IF NO)	C. IF YES: How stressful is it for you to do this? Not at all / Just a little / Somewhat / Very much
a. Bathing or showering	1	2	3	4	No ... Yes	1 ... 2 ... 3 4
b. Dressing or undressing	1	2	3	4	No ... Yes	1 ... 2 ... 3 4
c. Getting in or out of a chair or bed	1	2	3	4	No ... Yes	1 ... 2 ... 3 4
d. Using the toilet or getting to the bathroom on time	1	2	3	4	No ... Yes	1 ... 2 ... 3 4
e. Eating or feeding him/herself	1	2	3	4	No ... Yes	1 ... 2 ... 3 4
f. Shopping for necessities	1	2	3	4	No ... Yes	1 ... 2 ... 3 4
g. Cooking	1	2	3	4	No ... Yes	1 ... 2 ... 3 4
h. Housekeeping	1	2	3	4	No ... Yes	1 ... 2 ... 3 4
i. Transportation	1	2	3	4	No ... Yes	1 ... 2 ... 3 4
j. Taking or managing medications	1	2	3	4	No ... Yes	1 ... 2 ... 3 4
k. Managing money	1	2	3	4	No ... Yes	1 ... 2 ... 3 4
l. Using the telephone	1	2	3	4	No ... Yes	1 ... 2 ... 3 4
m. Doing laundry	1	2	3	4	No ... Yes	1 ... 2 ... 3 4
n. Making decisions about his/her care	1	2	3	4	No ... Yes	1 ... 2 ... 3 4
o. Car maintenance, home repair or yard work	1	2	3	4	No ... Yes	1 ... 2 ... 3 4

4

33. What, if any, other things do you do to help out this parent (e.g, checking on them by phone, visiting with them, providing emotional support)?

34. What is the **main** thing that you do to help out this parent?

35. Overall, on average, how much do you spend **each month** on caregiving expenses for this parent (such as for hiring outside help, transportation expenses, giving the parent money, telephone charges, etc.)? $_____ per month

Now we're going to ask you some questions about your and your spouse/partner's jobs.

36. Is your spouse or partner currently working?
   1 Yes
   0 No ————————
   9 No spouse or partner ——— --->**SKIP TO QUESTION 40**

37. About how many hours per week does your spouse or partner work?
   _____ hours/week

38. What shift does your spouse or partner work?
   1 Days
   2 Nights
   3 Swing
   4 Rotating
   5 Other _____

39. How much flexibility does your spouse or partner have in his/her work schedule to handle family responsibilities?
   1 No flexibility at all   3 Some flexibility
   2 Hardly any flexibility   4 A lot of flexibility

40. Are you currently working?
   1 Yes   0 No IF NO, which of the following best describes your situation?
       1 Retired
       2 Laid off
       3 Quit work to care for children   **SKIP TO**
       4 Quit work to care for parents   **QUESTION**
       5 Quit work to care for children   **81. p. 12**
         and parents
       6 Not working for other reasons

41. Do you hold more than one paid position?
   0 No   1 Yes

42. What is your primary occupation?
   _____

43. Please describe briefly the kind of work that you do:
   _____
   _____

44. How long have you been employed in this job?
   _____years

45. Are you a temporary or a contract worker?
   0 No   1 Yes

46. About how many hours per week do you work?
   _____ hours/week

47. Would you prefer to work more, fewer, or the same number of hours?
   More   Fewer   The same
   1   2   3

48. Usually, do the number of hours you work:
   1 Stay nearly the same every week
   2 Vary from week to week

49. Do you mostly:
   1 Work for someone else
   2 Own your own business

50. How many people do you supervise or manage?
   _____ (Write "0" if none)

51. Are you sometimes able to do your regularly scheduled work at home?
   1 No
   2 Yes -- IF YES - On average, how many hours per week do you work at home?
       _____hours/week

52. What is your best estimate of the number of employees who work at the site where you work most often?
   _____

53. What is your best estimate of the number of employees who work for your organization/employer overall?
   _____ (Write "same" if your worksite is the entire organization)

54. Are you:
   1 Salaried
   2 Paid by the hour
   3 Paid by commission
   4 Paid by the hour and by commission
   5 Other_____

55. What shift do you work?
   1 Days
   2 Nights
   3 Swing
   4 Rotating
   5 Other _____

5

296

56. Which type of work schedule best describes your work situation?
   1 Standard full time
   2 Flexible work hours
   3 Compressed work week (such as four 10-hour days or three 12-hour days)
   4 Job sharing (part time)
   5 Other part time

57. What is your approximate commuting time (one way) to work? _____ minutes

58. How much travel time does taking your child(ren) to or from school or child care add to your trip to or from work? If none or not applicable, write "0". _____ minutes

59. **How much flexibility do you have in your work schedule to handle family responsibilities?**

No flexibility at all	Hardly any flexibility	Some flexibility	A lot of flexibility
1	2	3	4

60. **How responsive is your organization to your need to take time to deal with PLANNED family responsibilities?**

Not at all	A little	Somewhat	Quite a bit	Extremely	Not applicable -- self-employed
1	2	3	4	5	0

61. **How responsive is your organization to your need to take time to deal with UNEXPECTED family problems?**

Not at all	A little	Somewhat	Quite a bit	Extremely	Not applicable -- self-employed
1	2	3	4	5	0

62. **How likely is it that you will actively look for a new job in the next year?**

Not at all likely		Somewhat likely		Quite likely		Extremely likely
1	2	3	4	5	6	7

63. **For each statement below please circle the response indicating the extent to which you agree or disagree.**

	Strongly disagree	Disagree	Neither agree nor disagree	Agree	Strongly agree
a. I often think about quitting	1	2	3	4	5
b. I will probably look for a new job in the next year	1	2	3	4	5

64. **Please read each statement with your place of employment in mind and then circle the response indicating the extent to which you agree or disagree. (If you are self-employed and have no employees, circle O.)**

	Strongly Disgree	Somewhat Disgree	Somewhat Agree	Strongly Agree	NA
a. There is an unwritten rule at my place of employment that you can't take care of family needs on company time	1	2	3	4	0
b. At my place of employment, employees who put their family or personal needs ahead of their jobs are not looked on favorably	1	2	3	4	0
c. If you have a problem managing your work and family responsibilities, the attitude at my place of employment is: "You made your bed, now lie in it."	1	2	3	4	0
d. At my place of employment, employees have to choose between advancing in their jobs or devoting attention to their family or personal lives	1	2	3	4	0

65. **In your current JOB, in the past month how REWARDING to you have the following been:**

	Not at all rewarding	Just a little rewarding	Somewhat rewarding	Very rewarding
a. Challenging or stimulating work	1	2	3	4
b. The income	1	2	3	4
c. Being able to set your own work schedule	1	2	3	4
d. Having a variety of tasks	1	2	3	4
e. Having hours that fit your needs	1	2	3	4
f. Your job being flexible enough that you can respond to non-work situations	1	2	3	4
g. Having the authority you need to get your job done	1	2	3	4
h. The job fitting your skills	1	2	3	4
i. The opportunity for learning new things	1	2	3	4
j. Making good money compared to other people in your field	1	2	3	4

6

65A. **In the past month,** how REWARDING have the following been: **(Please circle "0" NA if something has not applied to your situation in the past month.)**

	Not at all rewarding	Just a little rewarding	Somewhat rewarding	Very rewarding	NA
k. Your supervisor's respect for your abilities	1	2	3	4	0
l. Your supervisor's concern about the welfare of those under him/her	1	2	3	4	0
m. Your supervisor paying attention to what you have to say	1	2	3	4	0
n. Job security	1	2	3	4	0
o. The amount of support from co-workers	1	2	3	4	0
p. Your job offering good benefits, for example, paid sick leave	1	2	3	4	0

66. In your current JOB, in **the past month** how CONCERNED have you been about the following:

	Not at all concerned	Just a little concerned	Somewhat concerned	Very concerned
a. The job's dullness, monotony, lack of variety	1	2	3	4
b. The job's not using your skills	1	2	3	4
c. Having to do tasks you don't feel should be part of your job	1	2	3	4
d. Having to juggle conflicting tasks or duties	1	2	3	4
e. The income	1	2	3	4
f. Having too much to do	1	2	3	4
g. The job's taking too much out of you	1	2	3	4
h. Having to do things against your better judgment	1	2	3	4
i. People in jobs like yours being laid off or unemployed	1	2	3	4
j. Making less money than other people in your line of work	1	2	3	4
k. Making less money than you feel you deserve	1	2	3	4

66A. **In your current JOB, in the past month,** how CONCERNED have you been about: **(Please circle "0" if something has not applied to your situation in the past month.)**

	Not at all concerned	Just a little concerned	Somewhat concerned	Very concerned	NA
l. Lack of job security on this job	1	2	3	4	0
m. Your supervisor's lack of appreciation for your work	1	2	3	4	0
n. The possibility of unemployment	1	2	3	4	0
o. Your supervisor's having unrealistic expectations for your work	1	2	3	4	0
p. Not being able to get your own job done because of other people or red tape	1	2	3	4	0
q. Lack of support from your supervisor	1	2	3	4	0
r. Lack of support from co-workers	1	2	3	4	0
s. Lack of good benefits, for example, paid sick leave	1	2	3	4	0

67. Now, we'd like you to think about YOUR JOB AND YOUR FAMILY IN GENERAL, including your spouse or partner, each of your children, and your parents and your spouse's or partner's parents. For each statement below please circle the response indicating the extent to which you agree or disagree.

	Strongly disagree	Disagree	Agree	Strongly agree
a. The most important things that happen to me involve my family	1	2	3	4
b. I am very much personally involved with my family	1	2	3	4
c. Most of my interests are centered around my family	1	2	3	4
d. To me, my family is a very large part of who I am	1	2	3	4
e. The most important things that happen to me involve my present job	1	2	3	4
f. Most of my interests are centered around my job	1	2	3	4
g. I am very much involved in my job	1	2	3	4
h. To me, my job is only a small part of who I am	1	2	3	4

7

298

68. **Again, for each statement below, please circle the response indicating the extent to which you agree or disagree. When thinking about your family, please continue to include your spouse or partner, your child(ren) and your parents or parents-in-law.**

	Strongly disagree	Disagree	Neither agree nor disagree	Agree	Strongly agree
a. The demands of my work interfere with my home and family life	1	2	3	4	5
b. The amount of time my job takes up makes it difficult to fulfill family responsibilities	1	2	3	4	5
c. Things I want to do at home do not get done because of the demands my job puts on me	1	2	3	4	5
d. My job produces strain that makes it difficult to fulfill family duties	1	2	3	4	5
e. Due to my work-related duties, I have to make changes to my plans for family activities	1	2	3	4	5
f. The demands of my family or spouse/partner interfere with work-related activities	1	2	3	4	5
g. I have to put off doing things at work because of demands on my time at home	1	2	3	4	5
h. Things I want to do at work don't get done because of the demands of my family or spouse/partner	1	2	3	4	5
i. My home life interferes with my responsibilities at work, such as getting to work on time, accomplishing daily tasks, and working overtime	1	2	3	4	5
j. Family-related strain interferes with my ability to perform job-related duties	1	2	3	4	5
k. Having my family well cared for puts me in a good mood at work	1	2	3	4	5
l. I have had more positive feelings about myself at work because I have felt good about myself and my handling of family responsibilities	1	2	3	4	5
m. I have had greater confidence in myself at work because I have been able to handle family responsibilities well	1	2	3	4	5
n. Having a successful day at work puts me in a good mood to handle my family responsibilities	1	2	3	4	5
o. I have had greater confidence in my ability to handle family responsibilities because I have been able to handle my job responsibilities well	1	2	3	4	5
p. I have had more positive feelings about myself and my ability to handle my family responsibilities because I have felt good about myself at work	1	2	3	4	5
q. My family responsibilities provide me a needed break from work	1	2	3	4	5
r. My work provides me a needed break from my family responsibilities	1	2	3	4	5
s. Generally speaking, I am very satisfied with my family	1	2	3	4	5
t. I frequently think I would like to change my family situation	1	2	3	4	5
u. I am generally satisfied with the role I play in my family	1	2	3	4	5
v. I am generally satisfied with the degree to which I am managing my work and family responsibilities	1	2	3	4	5

68A. **For each statement below, please circle the response indicating the extent to which you agree or disagree.**

	Strongly disagree	Disagree	Neither agree nor disagree	Agree	Strongly agree
w. Generally speaking, I am very satisfied with my job	1	2	3	4	5
x. I frequently think of quitting my job	1	2	3	4	5
y. I am generally satisfied with the kind of work I do in my job	1	2	3	4	5
z. Most people in this job are very satisfied with the job	1	2	3	4	5
aa. People in this job often think of quitting	1	2	3	4	5

69. Thinking about the organization for which you are now working, please indicate the extent to which you agree or disagree with each statement. If you are self-employed skip to Question 70.

	Strongly disagree	Disagree	Neither agree nor disagree	Agree	Strongly agree
a. I am willing to put in a great deal of effort beyond that normally expected in order to help this organization be successful.	1	2	3	4	5
b. I talk up this organization to my friends as a great organization to work for.	1	2	3	4	5
c. I would accept almost any type of job assignment in order to keep working for this organization.	1	2	3	4	5
d. I find that my values and the organization's values are very similar.	1	2	3	4	5
e. I am proud to tell others that I am part of this organization.	1	2	3	4	5
f. This organization really inspires the very best in me in the way of job performance.	1	2	3	4	5
g. I am extremely glad that I chose this organization to work for over others I was considering at the time I joined.	1	2	3	4	5
h. I really care about the fate of this organization.	1	2	3	4	5
I. For me this is the best of all possible organizations for which to work.	1	2	3	4	5

70. The next questions concern how YOU feel or act in response to your many work and family duties. Please indicate how often each statement below describes how you feel or act.

	Never		Sometimes		Most or all of the time	NA
a. I try to realize I can't do it all, and that it's okay	1	2	3	4	5	
b. I get moral support and comfort from others	1	2	3	4	5	
c. I focus on the many good things I have	1	2	3	4	5	
d. I protect or set aside time for activities that are important to me	1	2	3	4	5	
e. I try to find humor in the situation	1	2	3	4	5	
f. I have back-up systems in case things don't happen as expected	1	2	3	4	5	
g. I lose track of what's important to me	1	2	3	4	5	
h. I limit my social activities	1	2	3	4	5	
i. I spend less time with my spouse or partner	1	2	3	4	5	0
j. I spend less time with other family members	1	2	3	4	5	
k. I attend activities separately from my spouse or partner because of conflicting schedules or responsibilities	1	2	3	4	5	0
l. I divide up household chores among family members	1	2	3	4	5	
m. I limit the number of my child(ren)'s activities that I attend	1	2	3	4	5	0
n. I lower my expectations of what should get done around the house	1	2	3	4	5	
o. I use a cell phone, pager, or voice messaging so that my family can reach me	1	2	3	4	5	
p. I wish others would be more supportive	1	2	3	4	5	
q. I limit my personal time for reading, exercise, or other leisure activities	1	2	3	4	5	
r. I plan my work hours around my child(ren)'s, parent(s), or spouse's or partner's schedule	1	2	3	4	5	
s. I plan to work at home so that I can be close to my family	1	2	3	4	5	
t. I have a beer, a glass of wine, or a drink.	1	2	3	4	5	
u. When necessary, I take time off from work to care for a parent or child	1	2	3	4	5	
v. I sometimes work long hours to avoid dealing with family responsibilities	1	2	3	4	5	
w. I prioritize and do the things that are most important and necessary	1	2	3	4	5	
x. I turn to my religious or spiritual beliefs	1	2	3	4	5	

9

300

71. Please indicate the extent to which your agree or disagree with each of the following statements.

I "cope" with the demands of work and family by:	Strongly disagree	Moderately disagree	Neither agree nor disagree	Moderately agree	Strongly agree	NA
a. Using modern equipment (e.g., microwave) to help out at home.	1	2	3	4	5	
b. Buying convenience foods which are easier to prepare at home.	1	2	3	4	5	
c. Leaving some things undone around the house (even though I would like to have them done).	1	2	3	4	5	
d. Specifically planning "family time together" into our schedules; planning family activities for all of us to do together.	1	2	3	4	5	
e. Hiring outside help to assist with our housekeeping and home maintenance.	1	2	3	4	5	
f. Overlooking the difficulties and focusing on the good things about our lifestyle.	1	2	3	4	5	
g. Having friends at work whom I can talk to about how I feel.	1	2	3	4	5	
h. Planning for time alone with my spouse.	1	2	3	4	5	0
i. Modifying my work schedule (e.g., reducing amount of time at work or working different hours).	1	2	3	4	5	
j. Relying on extended family members for financial help when needed.	1	2	3	4	5	
k. Planning work changes (e.g., transfer, promotion, shift change) around family needs.	1	2	3	4	5	
l. Cutting down on the amount of "outside activities" in which I can be involved.	1	2	3	4	5	
m. Limiting job involvement in order to have time for my family.	1	2	3	4	5	
n. Lowering my standards for "how well" household tasks must be done.	1	2	3	4	5	
o. Eliminating certain activities (home entertaining, volunteer work, etc.)	1	2	3	4	5	
p. Limiting my involvement on the job -- saying "no" to some of the things I could be doing.	1	2	3	4	5	

72. Please indicate the degree to which each statement below describes how you and your spouse or partner, AS A COUPLE, feel and act in response to your many work and family duties. (Circle 0 if you and your spouse/ partner are no longer together.)

	Never		Sometimes		Most or all of the time	NA
a. We work out who will have responsibility for particular family tasks	1	2	3	4	5	0
b. Together we decide changes in each other's work, such as work hours and job changes	1	2	3	4	5	0
c. We pick up the slack if the other is having a demanding time at work	1	2	3	4	5	0
d. We take time away just for us, without the kids or parent care responsibilities	1	2	3	4	5	0
e. We lean on and look to each other for moral support	1	2	3	4	5	0
f. We try to be understanding when the other is stressed	1	2	3	4	5	0

73. Because of your responsibilities for children or parents, in the past month, how many times have you had to, or chosen to: (Write "0" if none or circle NA if not applicable)

	Due to responsibilities for any of your **children**	NA	Due to responsibilities for any of your **parents or parents-in-law**	NA
a. Miss a day's work	_____ times	NA	_____ times	NA
b. Arrive late at work	_____ times	NA	_____ times	NA
c. Leave work early	_____ times	NA	_____ times	NA
d. Spend time at work on the telephone	_____ times	NA	_____ times	NA
e. Take time off during the work day	_____ times	NA	_____ times	NA

10

301

74. **In the past month**, how often have you worked less effectively because you were concerned or upset: (Circle 0 if you no longer have children at home or help out a parent.)

	Never	Seldom	Sometimes	Frequently	Most or all of the time	NA
a. About your child(ren)	1	2	3	4	5	0
b. About your parent(s)	1	2	3	4	5	0

75. **How comfortable are you talking with co-workers and with your supervisor at work about your responsibilities for children and parents?** (Circle 0 if you do not have co-workers or a supervisor.)

	Comfortable talking about **child(ren)**					Comfortable talking about **parent(s)**				
	Not at all	Just a little	Somewhat	Very	NA	Not at all	Just a little	Somewhat	Very	NA
a. Co-workers	1	2	3	4	0	1	2	3	4	0
b. Supervisor	1	2	3	4	0	1	2	3	4	0

76. **When a child or parent you are caring for needs assistance and you take time off from work, which ONE of the following is _most_ likely to make this possible? (Please circle only one response.)**

0 I am not able to take time off work
1 I use sick leave
2 I have flexible hours
3 I use emergency leave
4 I take a day off without pay

5 I use vacation or personal leave
6 I do my work at home
7 I never need to take time off for this reason
8 Other: _____
   _____

77. **Please indicate whether or not each of the following workplace supports is available to you through your employer. If YES, do you make use of this? Please skip to Question 79 if you are self-employed.**

	Don't know	No	Yes ---->	If YES: Do you use? No	Yes
a. Flexible work hours	8	0	1	0	1
b. Job-sharing	8	0	1	0	1
c. Option to work at home/telecommute	8	0	1	0	1
d. Unpaid leave to care for a family member	8	0	1	0	1
e. Personal Time Off or other paid leave which can be used to care for a family member	8	0	1	0	1
f. Family health care insurance	8	0	1	0	1
g. Pension/retirement plan	8	0	1	0	1
h. Program that allows workers to set aside pre-tax dollars to pay for child care	8	0	1	0	1
i. Program that allows workers to set aside pre-tax dollars to pay for care of a parent	8	0	1	0	1
j. Subsidy for child care	8	0	1	0	1
k. Subsidy for parent care	8	0	1	0	1
l. On-site child care center	8	0	1	0	1
m. On-site adult day care center	8	0	1	0	1
n. Resources and referral services for child care	8	0	1	0	1
o. Resources and referral services for elder care	8	0	1	0	1
p. On-site support groups on family-related issues	8	0	1	0	1
q. Seminars on work and family issues	8	0	1	0	1
r. Employee assistance program (EAP)	8	0	1	0	1
t. Wellness/fitness programs	8	0	1	0	1
u. Dental insurance	8	0	1	0	1
s. Other family-friendly benefits/programs (Specify:_____)	8	0	1	0	1

78. **What workplace supports or services do you _wish_ your employer offered?**

79. For each of the following types of technology, please indicate whether or not you currently have this technology. If you do have it, please note how helpful it is to you in managing your work and family responsibilities.

	Do you have?			If YES: How helpful is it?		
	No	Yes ----->		Not at all	Somewhat	Very
a. Voice mail/answering machine	0	1		1	2	3
b. Fax	0	1		1	2	3
c. Cellular phone	0	1		1	2	3
d. Beeper/Pager	0	1		1	2	3
e. Portable computer	0	1		1	2	3
f. Remote access to computer used for work	0	1		1	2	3
g. Internet/WWW access (for information, support)	0	1		1	2	3

80. To what extent does technology (like portable computers and voice mail) make it harder or easier for you to manage both your work and family responsibilities?

	Much Harder					Much Easier		Not Applicable
Technology makes it:	1	2	3	4	5	6	7	0

81. Because of your child or parent care responsibilities, in the past year, have you:

	No	Yes
a. Quit a job	0	1
b. Chosen a job that gives you more flexibility to meet your family demands	0	1
c. Refused to relocate	0	1
d. Refused or decided not to work toward a promotion	0	1
e. Refused or limited your travel	0	1
f. Had your parent(s) or parent(s)-in-law live with you so they can help you out	0	1
g. Had your parent(s) or parent(s)-in-law live with you to make it easier for you to help them	0	1
h. Participated in a support group for parents or for adult children	0	1
i. Worked reduced hours	0	1
j. Worked a different shift from your spouse or partner so that one adult is at home most of the time	0	1
k. Other (related to your work or family) _____	0	1

82. Please indicate which of the following have happened to you in the past year. During the past year, have you...

	No	Yes
a. Changed or left a job?	0	1
b. Changed your place of residence?	0	1
c. Been robbed or burglarized?	0	1
d. Become divorced or separated?	0	1
e. Had someone close to you either move in with you or leave your home?	0	1
f. Gotten married or had a marital reconciliation?	0	1
g. Had a family member or close friend who was seriously ill or injured?	0	1
h. Lost a parent through death?	0	1
i. Lost a child through death?	0	1
j. Lost a beloved family pet?	0	1
k. Experienced the death of some other family member or close friend?	0	1
l. Been seriously ill or injured yourself?	0	1
m. Been arrested or involved in a court case?	0	1
n. Had a decline in financial status?	0	1
p. Had a baby or adopted a child?	0	1
q. Has your spouse changed or left a job?	0	1
o. Other (Specify:_____)	0	1

12

303

83. **During the past few weeks did you ever feel . . .** No Yes
   a. Pleased about having accomplished something? 0 1
   b. That things were going your way? 0 1
   c. Proud because someone complimented you on something you had done? 0 1
   d. Particularly excited or interested in something? 0 1
   e. On top of the world? 0 1
   f. So restless that you couldn't sit long in a chair? 0 1
   g. Bored? 0 1
   h. Depressed or very unhappy? 0 1
   i. Very lonely or remote from other people? 0 1
   j. Upset because someone criticized you? 0 1

84. **Shown below are opposite pairs of words that may indicate how people feel overall about their life. Consider each of the word pairs and circle the number that best indicates how YOU feel about your life in general.**

   a. Boring   1 . . . . 2 . . . . 3 . . . . . 4 . . . . 5 . . . . . 6 7   Interesting
   b. Enjoyable   1 . . . . 2 . . . . 3 . . . . . 4 . . . . 5 . . . . . 6 7   Miserable
   c. Worthwhile   1 . . . . 2 . . . . 3 . . . . . 4 . . . . 5 . . . . . 6 7   Useless
   d. Lonely   1 . . . . 2 . . . . 3 . . . . . 4 . . . . 5 . . . . . 6 7   Friendly
   e. Empty   1 . . . . 2 . . . . 3 . . . . . 4 . . . . 5 . . . . . 6 7   Full
   f. Hopeful   1 . . . . 2 . . . . 3 . . . . . 4 . . . . 5 . . . . . 6 7   Discouraging
   g. Rewarding   1 . . . . 2 . . . . 3 . . . . . 4 . . . . 5 . . . . . 6 7   Disappointing
   h. Doesn't give me 1 . . . . 2 . . . . 3 . . . . . 4 . . . . 5 . . . . . 6 7   Brings out the
      much of a chance   best in me

85. Taking all things together, how would you say things are these days? Would you say that you are:

   1 very happy   2 pretty happy   3 not too happy

86. In general, how satisfying do you find the ways you're spending your life these days?

   1 completely satisfying   2 pretty satisfying   3 not very satisfying

87. **Below is a list of ways you might have felt or behaved. Please indicate how often you have felt this way during the past week by circling the appropriate number.**

During the past week:	Rarely or none of the time (less than 1 day)	Some or a little of the time (1-2 days)	Occasionally or a moderate amount of time (3-4 days)	Most of the time (5-7 days)
a. I was bothered by things that usually don't bother me	1	2	3	4
b. I did not feel like eating; my appetite was poor	1	2	3	4
c. I felt that I could not shake off the blues even with help from my family or friends	1	2	3	4
d. I felt that I was just as good as other people	1	2	3	4
e. I had trouble keeping my mind on what I was doing	1	2	3	4
f. I felt depressed	1	2	3	4
g. I felt that everything I did was an effort	1	2	3	4
h. I felt hopeful about the future	1	2	3	4
i. I thought my life had been a failure	1	2	3	4
j. I felt fearful	1	2	3	4
k. My sleep was restless	1	2	3	4
l. I was happy	1	2	3	4
m. I talked less than usual	1	2	3	4
n. I felt lonely	1	2	3	4
o. People were unfriendly	1	2	3	4
p. I enjoyed life	1	2	3	4
q. I had crying spells	1	2	3	4
r. I felt sad	1	2	3	4
s. I felt that people disliked me	1	2	3	4
t. I could not get "going"	1	2	3	4

13

88. Below are a number of characteristics that may or may not apply to you. Please circle the number next to each statement to indicate the extent to which you agree or disagree with each statement.

I see myself as someone who:	Disagree strongly	Disagree a little	Neither agree nor disagree	Agree a little	Agree strongly
a. Is depressed, blue	1	2	3	4	5
b. Is relaxed	1	2	3	4	5
c. Can be tense	1	2	3	4	5
d. Is emotionally stable, not easily upset	1	2	3	4	5
e. Worries a lot	1	2	3	4	5
f. Remains calm in tense situations	1	2	3	4	5
g. Gets nervous easily	1	2	3	4	5

These last questions are just the basics about you.

89. Your gender?   0 Male   1 Female

90. What would you say is your and your spouse's or partner's approximate combined household income before taxes? (If you and your spouse are no longer together, please write just your income.)

$_____ per year

91. Which of the following four statements best describes your ability to get along on your income?

1 We/I can't make ends meet
2 We/I have just enough, no more
3 We/I have enough, with a little extra sometimes
4 We/I always have money left over

92. How would you rate your overall health?

	Extremely poor	Poor	Fair	Good	Very good	Excellent	
	1	2	3	4	5	6	

93. How would you rate your spouse's or partner's overall health?

	Extremely poor	Poor	Fair	Good	Very good	Excellent	NA
	1	2	3	4	5	6	0

94. How would you rate your overall performance:

	Extremely poor	Poor	Fair	Good	Very good	Excellent	NA
a. At your work	1	2	3	4	5	6	0
b. As a spouse	1	2	3	4	5	6	0
c. As a parent	1	2	3	4	5	6	
d. As a caregiver to the parent or parent-in-law you're helping the most	1	2	3	4	5	6	0
e. In taking care of your own physical and mental health needs	1	2	3	4	5	6	

95. Thinking back to last year at about this time would you say your work and family situation has:

a. Improved   b. Worsened   c. Stayed the same

96. Why do you say this? (Please continue on back if necessary)

97. How would you say you are HANDLING your work and family situation now as compared to last year at about this time?

a. Better   b. Worse   c. About the same

98. Why do you say this? (Please continue on back if necessary)

99. How interesting or boring was this questionnaire?

Very boring	Pretty boring	Neither boring nor interesting	Pretty interesting	Very interesting
1	2	3	4	5

100. **Anything else you would like to add?**

THANK YOU FOR YOUR HELP!

Please return in the postage-paid envelope to:

Institute on Aging
Portland State University
P.O. Box 751
Portland, OR 97207-0751

306

C

Tables

TABLE 5.1
Paired Comparisons of Husbands' and Wives' Personal Characteristics

Scale/Item	M Husbands	M Wives	SD Husbands	SD Wives	n	p
Race (1 = White, 0 = other)	.95	.94	.22	.24	304	
Age	43.50	41.50	6.20	6.00	306	***
Education (years)	14.70	15.10	2.80	2.60	308	*
Mean gross annual household income	73,204	69,880	42,545	28,298	286	
Median household income	65,000	60,000				
Ability to get along on income (1 = *We can't make ends meet*, 4 = *Always have money left over*)	2.80	2.70	0.71	0.77	305	**
Negative affectivity (7 items; 1 = *disagree strongly*, 5 = *agree strongly*)	2.53	2.81	0.72	0.74	305	***
Family involvement (4 items; 1 = low, 4 = high)	3.49	3.71	0.51	0.41	308	***

*$p \le .05$; **$p \le .01$; ***$p \le .001$.

TABLE 5.2
Paired Comparisons of Husbands' and Wives' Spousal Role Characteristics

Scale/Item	M Husbands	M Wives	SD Husbands	SD Wives	n	p
Years together	17.90	17.90	6.60	6.60	305	
Previously married (0 = no, 1 = yes)	.18	.17	.38	.38	307	
Spousal role quality (overall)	1.68	1.42	1.14	1.25	308	***
Rewards (9 items; 1 = low, 4 = high)	3.38	3.26	0.60	0.65	308	***
Stressors (8 items; 1 = low, 4 = high)	1.70	1.84	0.69	0.71	308	***

*p ≤ .05; **p ≤ .01; *** p ≤ .001.

TABLE 5.3
Paired Comparisons of Husbands' and Wives' Child-Care Role Characteristics

Scale/Item	Means		SD		n	p
	Husbands	Wives	Husbands	Wives		
Number of children ≤18	1.84	1.84	0.78	0.77	309	
Children in household from prior relationship (0 = no, 1 = yes)	.08	.09	.28	.28	304	
Age of youngest child in household	10.40	10.40	5.02	4.99	309	
Have children not living in household (0 = no, 1 = yes)	.27	.27	.44	.45	301	
Child with special needs (0 = no, 1 = yes)	.12	.17	.33	.38	305	**
Satisfaction with child care (1 = low, 5 = high)	4.03	4.05	0.75	0.84	266	
Level of responsibility for child care (1 = low, 2 = medium, 3 = high)	1.55	2.54	0.54	0.51	300	***
Child-care role quality (overall)	1.77	1.73	0.80	0.83	309	
Rewards (8 items; 1 = low, 4 = high)	3.55	3.64	0.53	0.44	309	*
Stressors (13 items; 1 = low, 4 = high)	1.78	1.90	0.51	0.54	309	***

*p ≤ .05; **p ≤ .01; ***p ≤ .001.

311

TABLE 5.4
Paired Comparisons of Husbands' and Wives' Parent-Care Role Characteristics

Scale/Item	M		SD		n	p
	Husbands	Wives	Husbands	Wives		
No. of own living parents/stepparents	1.46	1.60	0.78	0.86	308	*
Couple's total no. of living parents/stepparents/in-laws	3.01	3.02	1.20	1.24	308	
No. of parents/in-laws helping	1.68	1.81	0.93	0.91	307	*
Weekly hours of parent care	7.46	9.78	10.99	11.68	281	**
The one parent respondent (R) is helping the most						
Relationship (0 = parent, 1 = parent-in-law)	.42	.31	.49	.46	297	*
Age of parent	72.75	71.83	8.74	8.87	285	**
Gender of parent (0 = male, 1 = female)	.71	.77	.45	.42	284	*
Marital status of parent (1 = married, 0 = not married)	.34	.36	.48	.48	306	
Relationship (0 = parent, 1 = parent-in-law)	.42	.31	.49	.46	297	*
Parent's income adequacy (1 = can't make ends meet, 4 = always has money left over)	3.06	2.98	0.90	0.95	288	
Living arrangements						
Parent and respondent live together (0 = no, 1 = yes)	.06	.06	.24	.24	303	
Parent lives independently (0 = no, 1 = yes)	.76	.69	.43	.46	303	**
Miles to parent	55.05	27.93	287.20	104.60	297	
Time to parent in minutes (truncated at 720)	38.43	31.19	105.47	70.20	302	

Scale/Item	M		SD		n	p
	Husbands	Wives	Husbands	Wives		
Care needs and help provided						
Weekly hours of care to this parent	5.10	6.78	6.83	7.28	266	***
Years helping parent	8.50	7.84	7.69	6.91	288	
Level of caregiving responsibility (1 = low/others main, 2 = Rs share equally with others, 3 = Rs main ones 4 = high/Rs only ones)	2.54	2.64	0.99	0.87	303	
Health of parent (1 = *extremely poor*, 6 = *excellent*)	3.27	3.25	1.07	1.14	304	
Amount of help needed with ADL (14 items, 0 = *none*, 3 = *totally dependent*; range = 0–42)	8.27	9.42	10.56	10.33	273	
No. of ADL Total R helps with (personal + instrumental, 0–14)	1.67	2.43	2.36	2.68	279	***
No. of personal ADL (PADL) R helps with (0–5)	0.16	0.24	0.61	0.74	282	
Specific PADL help R provides (0 = no, 1 = yes)						
Bathing	.02	.04	.16	.20	284	
Dressing	.02	.06	.16	.23	282	*
Transferring to chair, bed	.05	.08	.22	.27	283	
Toileting	.02	.03	.16	.18	283	
Eating/feeding	.04	.04	.185	.185	283	
No. of Instrumental ADL (IADL) R helps with (0–9)	1.51	2.19	1.99	2.33	279	***

(continued)

TABLE 5.4 *(continued)*

Scale/Item	M		SD		n	p
	Husbands	*Wives*	*Husbands*	*Wives*		
Specific IADL R helps with: (0 = no, 1 = yes)						
Shopping	.29	.37	.45	.48	282	*
Cooking	.06	.16	.24	.37	283	***
Housekeeping	.15	.27	.35	.45	282	***
Transportation	.40	.47	.49	.50	283	
Medications	.10	.18	.305	.38	281	**
Managing money	.19	.24	.39	.43	280	
Telephone use	.03	.04	.17	.19	281	
Laundry	.08	.15	.27	.36	281	***
Making care decisions	.21	.33	.41	.47	281	***
Quality of relationship with parent (4 items; 1 = low, 4 = high)	3.09	3.19	0.67	0.73	303	*
Amount of help parent provides						
Parent-care role quality (overall)	1.43	1.47	1.09	1.11	302	
Rewards (10 items; 1 = low, 4 = high)	2.91	3.12	0.84	0.80	302	***
Stressors (8 items; 1 = low, 4 = high)	1.48	1.65	0.54	0.54	304	***

*p ≤ .05; **p ≤ .01; ***p ≤ .001.

TABLE 5.5
Paired Comparisons of Husbands' and Wives' Work-Role Characteristics

Scale/Item	M		SD		n	p
	Husbands	Wives	Husbands	Wives		
Occupation (1 = professional/managerial/technical, 0 = other)	.37	.46	.48	.50	302	**
No. of employees in organization	23,704	7,759	116,238	52,505	258	*
No. of employees at worksite	420	266	1,696	1,103	285	*
Owns own business (0 = no, 1 = yes)	.15	.10	.36	.30	301	*
Years in current job	12.65	8.97	8.67	7.08	301	***
No. of hours worked per week	49.46	38.01	11.38	9.70	307	***
Hours preferred to work (1 = fewer, 2 = same, 3 = more)	1.52	1.48	0.59	0.57	305	
Shift (1 = days, 0 = other)	.77	.85	.42	.36	305	*
Standard full-time schedule (0 = no, 1 = yes)	.80	.59	.40	.49	300	***
Flexibility in work schedule to handle family responsibilities (1 = none, 4 = a lot)	2.98	3.13	0.84	0.84	306	*
Organization's responsiveness to Respondent's need to take time to deal with (1 = *not at all*, 5 = *extremely*)						
Planned family responsibilities	3.24	3.62	1.15	1.07	263	***
Unexpected family problems	3.58	3.71	1.13	1.11	265	

(continued)

TABLE 5.5 *(continued)*

Scale/Item	M		SD		n	p
	Husbands	*Wives*	*Husbands*	*Wives*		
Comfortable talking about responsibilities for (1 = *not at all*, 4 = *very*):						
Children						
With coworkers	2.77	3.23	1.03	0.86	257	***
With supervisor	2.45	2.76	1.12	1.12	229	**
Parents						
With coworkers	2.57	2.93	1.05	0.99	243	***
With supervisor	2.36	2.50	1.08	1.12	214	
Job involvement (4 items; 1 = low, 4 = high)	2.27	2.13	0.57	0.54	307	**
Job role quality (overall)	0.89	1.06	1.10	0.98	307	*
Rewards (16 items; 1 = low, 4 = high)	2.80	2.90	0.64	0.56	307	*
Stressors (19 items; 1 = low, 4 = high)	1.91	1.84	0.61	0.54	307	

*$p \leq .05$; **$p \leq .01$; ***$p \leq .001$.

TABLE 6.1

Paired Comparisons of Husbands' and Wives' Work–Family Fit, Well-Being, and Work Outcomes

Scale/Item	M		SD		n	p
	Husbands	Wives	Husbands	Wives		
Work–family fit						
Work-to-family conflict	3.11	2.99	0.94	0.98	308	
Family-to-work conflict	2.17	2.33	0.70	0.81	308	**
Work-to-family spillover	3.62	3.72	0.70	0.72	308	
Family-to-work spillover	3.83	4.02	0.65	0.63	308	***
Well-Being						
Depression	10.92	13.28	8.08	9.22	258	***
Life satisfaction	5.26	5.19	1.16	1.16	299	
Overall health	4.54	4.54	0.91	0.90	307	
Overall role performance (Composite)	4.38	4.41	0.65	0.60	307	
At work	4.93	5.00	0.73	0.74	307	
As a spouse	4.42	4.37	0.88	0.92	307	
As a parent	4.57	4.84	0.82	0.77	307	***
As caregiver to parent helping most	4.11	4.36	0.94	0.88	304	***
In taking care of own physical and mental health needs	3.85	3.49	1.08	1.12	306	***

(continued)

317

TABLE 6.1 (continued)

Scale/Item	M		SD		n	p
	Husbands	Wives	Husbands	Wives		
Work						
Job satisfaction	3.45	3.51	0.72	0.67	307	
Overall absence[a] composite	2.59	5.38	3.27	5.04	256	***
Days missed						
Because of children	0.32	0.87	0.70	1.34	264	***
Because of parents	0.16	0.49	0.63	1.33	226	***
Times arrived late[a]						
Because of children	0.69	1.90	1.76	3.49	259	***
Because of parents	0.15	0.32	0.68	1.28	222	
Times left early[a]						
Because of children	1.24	1.75	2.45	2.49	274	*
Because of parents	0.37	0.49	1.07	1.07	230	
Times spent time on phone[a]						
Because of children	2.90	4.82	5.31	6.89	271	***
Because of parents	1.56	2.73	3.28	4.31	244	***
No. of work accommodations made[b] *composite*	0.84	1.31	1.07	1.35	300	***
Quit a job[b]	0.01	0.02	0.10	0.15	298	
Chose a job that gave me[b] more flexibility to meet my family demands	0.08	0.24	0.27	0.43	299	***

Scale/Item	M		SD		n	p
	Husbands	Wives	Husbands	Wives		
Refused to relocate[b]	0.13	0.11	0.34	0.32	298	
Refused or decided not to[b] work toward a promotion	0.09	0.21	0.28	0.41	298	***
Refused or limited my travel[b]	0.23	0.27	0.42	0.45	298	
Had parents(-in-law) live with me so that they could help me out[b]	0.03	0.04	0.16	0.19	299	
Had parents(-in-law) live with me to make it easier for me to help them[b]	0.08	0.10	0.27	0.30	299	
Participated in a support group for parents or for adult children[b]	0.01	0.03	0.12	0.18	299	
Worked reduced hours[b]	0.17	0.31	0.37	0.46	298	***
Worked a different shift[b] from my spouse so that one adult is at home most of the time	0.13	0.15	0.33	0.35	299	
Poor work performance[a]	1.94	2.38	0.75	0.85	299	***
Because was concerned or upset about child(ren)[a]	2.01	2.47	0.89	0.92	303	***
Because was concerned or upset about parent(s)[a]	1.89	2.29	0.88	1.00	302	***

[a]Because of child- and/or parent-care responsibilities in the past month.   [b]Because of child- and/or parent-care responsibilities in the past year.

*$p \leq .05$; *$p \leq .01$; ***$p \leq .001$.

TABLE 6.2
Correlations Between Personal and Spousal Role Characteristics and Work–Family Fit

	Work-to-family conflict		Family-to-work conflict		Work-to-family spillover		Family-to-work spillover	
	Husbands	Wives	Husbands	Wives	Husbands	Wives	Husbands	Wives
Education (years)	-.08	.16**	.06	.14*	.11*	-.07	.05	-.08
Ability to get along on income	-.10	-.19**	-.08	-.08	.10	.08	.21**	.08
Negative affectivity	.19**	.26**	.19**	.23**	-.18**	-.15**	-.31**	-.20**
Spousal role quality	-.12*	-.23**	-.26**	-.18**	.18**	.20**	.29**	.17**

*p ≤ .05; **p ≤ .01; Ns ranged from 305–309.

TABLE 6.3
Correlations Between Personal and Spousal Role Characteristics and Well-Being

	Depression		Life satisfaction		Overall health		Overall role performance	
	Husbands	Wives	Husbands	Wives	Husbands	Wives	Husbands	Wives
Education (years)	-.13*	-.09	.18**	.16**	.22**	.11	.16**	-.05
Ability to get along on income	-.24**	-.31**	.22**	.19**	.27**	.15**	.28**	.22**
Negative affectivity	.62**	.57**	-.42**	-.32**	-.31**	-.36**	-.39**	-.33**
Spousal role quality	-.30**	-.38**	.33**	.26**	.13*	.09	.42**	.31**

* p ≤ .05; **p ≤ .01; Ns ranged from 275–308.

TABLE 6.4
Correlations Between Personal and Spousal Role Characteristics and Work Outcomes

	Job satisfaction		Overall absence		No. of work accommodations made		Poor work performance	
	Husbands	Wives	Husbands	Wives	Husbands	Wives	Husbands	Wives
Education (years)	.15**	.03	.18**	.03	-.07	-.10	.03	.08
Ability to get along on income	.12*	.10	-.03	-.15*	-.07	-.09	-.12*	-.15**
Negative affectivity	-.31**	-.18**	.01	.05	.09	.07	.24**	.28**
Spousal role quality	.12*	.08	-.03	-.03	-.03	-.11	-.13*	-.20**

*$p \leq .05$; **$p \leq .01$; Ns ranged from 274–308.

TABLE 6.5
Correlations Between Child-Care Role Characteristics and Work–Family Fit for Husbands and Wives

Child-care role characteristics	Work-to-family conflict		Family-to-work conflict		Work-to-family spillover		Family-to-work spillover	
	Husbands	Wives	Husbands	Wives	Husbands	Wives	Husbands	Wives
Number of children ≤ 18	-.01	.00	-.09	.02	-.04	-.07	.04	-.03
Child with special needs	.07	.10	-.04	.11	-.08	-.08	-.09	.04
Child-care role quality	-.17**	-.32**	-.19**	-.25**	.27**	.18**	.34**	.25**

*$p \leq .05$; **$p \leq .01$; Ns ranged from 306–309.

TABLE 6.6
Correlations Between Child-Care Role Characteristics and Well-Being for Husbands and Wives

Child-care role characteristics	Depression		Life satisfaction		Overall health		Overall role performance	
	Husbands	Wives	Husbands	Wives	Husbands	Wives	Husbands	Wives
No. children ≤18	-.01	-.02	.02	.04	-.04	.04	.03	.04
Child with special needs	.05	.10	-.04	-.03	.03	-.10	.05	-.05
Child-care role quality	-.24**	-.31**	.24**	.19**	.19**	.19**	.40**	.38**

**p ≤ .01; Ns ranged from 278–309.

TABLE 6.7
Correlations Between Child-Care Role Characteristics and Work Outcomes for Husbands and Wives

Child-care role characteristics	Job satisfaction		Overall absence		No. of work accommodations made		Poor work performance	
	Husbands	Wives	Husbands	Wives	Husbands	Wives	Husbands	Wives
No. children ≤18	.05	.01	.13*	.04	.02	.12*	-.01	-.05
Child with special needs	-.04	.06	.13*	.14*	.05	.06	.15**	.08
Child-care role quality	.16**	.11*	-.15*	-.10	-.09	-.09	-.28**	-.30**

*p ≤ .05; **p ≤ .01; Ns ranged from 274–308.

TABLE 6.8
Correlations Between Parent-Care Role Characteristics and Work–Family Fit for Husbands and Wives

Parent-care role characteristics	Work-to-family conflict		Family-to-work conflict		Work-to-family spillover		Family-to-work spillover	
	Husbands	Wives	Husbands	Wives	Husbands	Wives	Husbands	Wives
No. parents/in-laws helping	.04	.06	.06	.10	.01	.03	-.01	.00
No. ADL respondent helps with	-.03	.11*	.08	.12*	-.04	.06	.02	.03
Parent-care role quality	-.10	-.07	-.20**	-.09	.13*	.08	.18**	.12*

Note. ADL = activities of daily living; *p* ≤ .05; **p* ≤ .01; Ns ranged from 289–309.

TABLE 6.9
Correlations Between Parent-Care Role Characteristics and Well-Being for Husbands and Wives

Parent-care role characteristics	Depression		Life satisfaction		Overall health		Overall role performance	
	Husbands	Wives	Husbands	Wives	Husbands	Wives	Husbands	Wives
No. parents/in-laws helping	-.10	-.04	-.01	.10	.02	.01	.03	.02
No. ADL respondent helps with	.04	.03	.06	.00	-.08	-.11*	-.03	-.11
Parent-care role quality	-.22**	-.10	.18**	.10	.13*	.04	.23**	.16**

Note. ADL = activities of daily living; *p* ≤ .05; **p* ≤ .01; Ns ranged from 270–309.

TABLE 6.10

Correlations Between Parent-Care Role Characteristics and Work Outcomes for Husbands and Wives

Parent-care role characteristics	Job satisfaction		Overall absence		No. of work accommodations made		Poor work performance	
	Husbands	Wives	Husbands	Wives	Husbands	Wives	Husbands	Wives
No. parents/in-laws helping	.03	-.07	.00	.03	-.01	.04	.10*	.21**
Number of ADL respondent helps with	.01	-.05	.15**	.20**	.14*	.18**	.25**	.21**
Parent-care role quality	.19**	-.07	-.09	-.03	-.19**	-.07	-.10	-.07

Note. ADL = activities of daily living; *p ≤ .05; **p ≤ .01; Ns ranged from 263–308.

TABLE 6.11

Correlations Between Work Role Characteristics and Work–Family Fit for Husbands and Wives

Work role characteristics	Work-to-family conflict		Family-to-work conflict		Work-to-family spillover		Family-to-work spillover	
	Husbands	Wives	Husbands	Wives	Husbands	Wives	Husbands	Wives
No. hours worked per week	.34**	.34**	.08	.21**	.07	.09	.07	-.03
Flexibility in work schedule[a]	-.30**	-.19**	.10	-.10	.13*	.18**	.16**	.14*
Job role quality	-.35**	-.30**	-.11*	-.14*	.31**	.24**	.33**	.23**

*p ≤ .05; **p ≤ .01; [a]To handle family responsibilities; Ns ranged from 307–309.

TABLE 6.12
Correlations Between Work Role Characteristics and Well-Being for Husbands and Wives

Work role characteristics	Depression		Life satisfaction		Overall health		Overall role performance	
	Husbands	Wives	Husbands	Wives	Husbands	Wives	Husbands	Wives
No. hours worked per week	.01	-.02	.12*	.00	-.05	-.11	-.03	-.14*
Flexibility in work schedule[a]	-.06	-.17**	.13*	.14*	.06	.05	.09	.09
Job role quality	-.44**	-.28**	.39**	.27**	.21**	.14*	.30**	.22**

*p ≤ .05; **p ≤ .01; [a]To handle family responsibilities; Ns ranged from 278–309.

TABLE 6.13
Correlations Between Work Role Characteristics and Work Outcomes for Husbands and Wives

Work role characteristics	Job satisfaction		Overall absence		No. work accommodations made		Poor work performance	
	Husbands	Wives	Husbands	Wives	Husbands	Wives	Husbands	Wives
No. hours worked per week	.07	-.02	.04	.08	-.08	-.04	.09	.11
Flexibility in work schedule[a]	.27**	.30**	.24**	.06	.00	-.01	-.04	-.06
Job role quality	.67**	.60**	-.01	-.13	-.23**	-.12*	-.20**	-.15**

*p ≤ .05; **p ≤ .01; [a]To handle family responsibilities; Ns ranged from 277–308.

TABLE 6.14
Hierarchical Regression Analyses of the Relationship Between Role Characteristics and Work–Family Fit for Husbands and Wives

Scale/item	Work-to-family conflict		Family-to-work conflict		Work-to-family spillover		Family-to-work spillover	
	Husbands (n = 282)	Wives (n = 286)	Husbands (n = 282)	Wives (n = 286)	Husbands (n = 282)	Wives (n = 286)	Husbands (n = 282)	Wives (n = 286)
Education (years)	.02	.07	.02	.08	.09	-.02	.01	-.02
Ability to get along on income	-.04	-.03	.02	.01	-.05	-.02	.07	-.03
Negative affectivity	-.01	.14**	.05	.16**	-.03	-.05	-.11	-.10
Change in R^2, Step 1	**.04****	**.09*****	**.04****	**.07*****	**.04****	**.02**	**.10*****	**.04***
No. children ≤18	.04	.04	-.07	.04	-.03	-.06	.05	-.01
Child with special needs	-.01	.01	.01	.04	-.06	-.08	-.07	.10
No. parents/in-laws helping	.06	.01	.07	.05	.03	.06	.00	.03
No. ADL respondent helps with	-.06	.06	.03	.08	-.03	.11	.09	.06
No. hours worked per week	.39***	.30***	.11	.18**	.01	.10	.04	-.03
Flexibility in work schedule[a]	-.14*	-.03	.19**	-.01	.02	.09	.05	.03
Change in R^2, Step 2	**.19*****	**.12*****	**.03**	**.05***	**.03**	**.04***	**.02**	**.02**
Spousal role quality	-.07	-.13*	-.15*	-.12*	.10	.14*	.16**	.07
Child-care role quality	-.03	-.17**	-.12	-.11	.15*	.06	.18**	.19**
Parent-care role quality	-.05	.00	-.11	.00	.06	.07	.09	.08
Job role quality	-.29***	-.14*	-.13	-.02	.26***	.15*	.16*	.14*
Change in R^2, Step 3	**.07****	**.07*****	**.07*****	**.03***	**.10*****	**.05****	**.10*****	**.07*****
Total R^2	.30***	.28***	.15***	.15***	.17***	.12***	.23***	.12***

Note. Husbands: All standardized beta weights are from the third step of the regression analysis. ADL = Activities of daily living; [a]to handle family responsibilities; spillover refers to positive spillover; *p ≤ .05; **p ≤ .01; ***p ≤ .001.

TABLE 6.15

Hierarchical Regression Analyses of the Relationships Between Role Characteristics and Well-Being for Husbands and Wives

Scale/item	Depression		Life satisfaction		Overall health		Overall role performance	
	Husbands ($n = 263$)	Wives ($n = 257$)	Husbands ($n = 275$)	Wives ($n = 283$)	Husbands ($n = 281$)	Wives ($n = 286$)	Husbands ($n = 281$)	Wives ($n = 286$)
Education (years)	-.13**	-.09	.15**	.20***	.21***	.12*	.13**	.02
Ability to get along on income	-.06	-.12*	.07	.10	.19**	.08	.14**	.14*
Negative affectivity	.49***	.45***	-.25***	-.21***	-.24***	-.34***	-.16**	-.22***
Change in R^2 Step 1	**.41***	**.35***	**.20***	**.14***	**.19***	**.16***	**.20***	**.15***
No. children ≤18	.03	-.04	.02	.04	-.06	.07	.05	.07
Child with special needs	.09	.03	-.06	.01	.07	-.02	.09	.08
No. parents/in-laws helping	-.15***	-.11*	.03	.14*	.04	.05	.05	.07
No. ADL respondent helps with	-.04	-.06	.12*	.05	-.03	-.09	.07	-.06
No. hours worked per week	-.01	-.06	.11*	.01	-.03	-.05	-.03	-.10
Flexibility in work schedule[a]	.10	-.03	-.04	.01	-.00	-.03	-.03	-.06
Change in R^2, Step 2	**.04**	**.02**	**.04*	**.03**	**.01**	**.02**	**.02**	**.03**
Spousal role quality	-.16**	-.21***	.19***	.17**	.00	-.05	.27***	.14*
Child-care role quality	.04	-.13*	.03	.17**	.02	.11	.20***	.25***
Parent-care role quality	-.08	.03	.12*	.05	.08	-.08	.10	.04
Job role quality	-.24***	-.10	.21***	.18**	.05	.06	.09	.08
Change in R^2, Step 3	**.07***	**.08***	**.09***	**.07***	**.01**	**.02**	**.15***	**.10***
Total R^2	**.51***	**.45***	**.33***	**.24***	**.21***	**.20***	**.36***	**.27***

Note. All standardized beta weights are from the third step of the regression analysis. ADL = activities of daily living; [a]To handle family responsibilities; *$p \le .05$; **$p \le .01$; ***$p \le .001$.

327

TABLE 6.16
Hierarchical Regression Analyses of the Relationship Between Role Characteristics and Work for Husbands and Wives

Scale/item	Job satisfaction		Overall absence		No. work accommodations made		Poor work performance	
	Husbands (n = 282)	Wives (n = 286)	Husbands (n = 258)	Wives (n = 256)	Husbands (n = 278)	Wives (n = 284)	Husbands (n = 279)	Wives (n = 280)
Education (years)	.04	.10*	.16**	.11	-.05	-.09	.02	.05
Ability to get along on income	-.07	-.03	.05	-.10	.03	-.02	.02	-.05
Negative affectivity	-.09	-.09	-.05	.04	-.01	.03	.12	.20***
Change in R^2, Step 1	**.10***	**.04***	**.03***	**.04***	**.00**	**.02**	**.06***	**.10***
No. children ≤18	.01	-.00	.13*	.05	.04	.11	-.03	-.06
Child with special needs	-.01	.08	.14*	.09	.04	.03	.14*	-.03
No. parents/in-laws helping	.08	.00	.01	.04	-.03	.01	.07	.17**
No. ADL respondent helps with	.04	-.04	.13*	.18**	.10	.17**	.23***	.16**
No. hours worked per week	.02	.04	.08	.10	-.05	-.02	.12*	.09
Flexibility in work schedule[a]	-.02	.08	.31***	.25***	.12	.09	.08	.02
Change in R^2, Step 2	**.06****	**.11***	**.12***	**.09***	**.03**	**.05***	**.09***	**.08***
Spousal role quality	-.01	-.03	.02	-.03	.04	-.08	-.00	-.10
Child-care role quality	-.02	-.01	-.11	-.03	-.01	.00	-.18**	-.18**
Parent-care role quality	.10*	-.09	.01	-.04	-.14*	-.01	.06	.02
Job role quality	.65***	.57***	-.17*	-.18**	-.22**	-.13	-.14*	-.02
Change in R^2, Step 3	**.31***	**.25***	**.03**	**.03**	**.06****	**.02**	**.04****	**.04****
Total R^2	**.48***	**.40***	**.18***	**.16***	**.09****	**.09***	**.19***	**.22***

Note. All standardized beta weights are from the third step of the regression analysis. ADL = activities of daily living; [a]To handle family responsibilities; *$p \le .05$; **$p \le .01$; ***$p \le .001$.

328

TABLE 7.1
Paired Comparisons for Technology Availability and Usefulness in Managing Work and Family for Husbands and Wives

Comparison	M		SD		n	p
	Husbands	Wives	Husbands	Wives		
Availability[a]						
Voicemail/answering machine	.81	.84	.39	.37	300	
Fax	.40	.29	.49	.45	297	***
Cellular phone	.55	.56	.50	.50	299	
Beeper, pager	.30	.21	.46	.41	294	***
Portable computer	.23	.22	.42	.41	297	
Remote access to computer used for work	.24	.19	.43	.40	294	
Internet access	.44	.47	.50	.50	297	
Usefulness (when available)[b]						
Voicemail/answering machine	2.59	2.73	0.52	0.46	232	***
Fax	2.17	2.06	0.74	0.77	65	
Cellular phone	2.55	2.62	0.56	0.54	146	
Portable computer	2.00	2.29	0.86	0.69	31	
Remote access to computer used for work	2.43	2.35	0.66	0.65	23	
Internet access	2.23	2.24	0.68	0.72	106	

[a]0 = no, 1 = yes; [b]1 = not at all, 2 = somewhat, 3 = very useful; ***$p \le .001$.

TABLE 8.1
Coping Strategies Used by Husbands and Wives

Item	M		SD		n	p
	Husbands	Wives	Husbands	Wives		
I plan how I'm going to use my time and energy.	2.33	2.46	0.58	0.58	305	**
I reduce hours spent on certain tasks or demands.	2.04	2.10	0.45	0.45	305	
I involve and get help from other family members or friends to accomplish tasks or meet demands.	1.91	1.92	0.49	0.54	306	
I hire people who help me accomplish tasks or meet demands.	1.57	1.35	0.59	0.57	304	***
I stop doing things that are not absolutely necessary.	1.99	2.06	0.49	0.49	305	
I don't try to plan, I just take things as they come.	1.89	1.80	0.61	0.60	307	
I take on tasks if no one else is capable or available.	2.35	2.33	0.54	0.54	307	
I limit my volunteer work	2.34	2.32	.59	.59	301	
I try to realize that I can't do it all, and that it's okay.	2.23	2.17	0.57	0.55	306	
I get moral support and comfort from others.	2.19	2.23	0.51	0.54	304	
I feel guilty for not spending enough time with certain people or doing certain things.	2.12	2.28	.53	.55	306	***
I focus on the many good things I have.	2.34	2.40	0.57	0.56	304	
I recognize and accept that I may not be able to do my best.	1.92	2.00	0.51	0.54	305	

Item	M		SD		n	p
	Husbands	Wives	Husbands	Wives		
I protect and set aside time for activities that are important to me.	2.17	2.03	0.52	0.62	307	***
I try and find humor in the situation.	2.45	2.40	0.52	0.54	306	
I wish I could accept or ask for help from others.	1.95	2.05	0.47	0.47	304	***
I have back-up systems in case things don't happen as expected.	2.03	1.99	0.53	0.55	306	
I get help with my work from family members.	1.70	1.63	0.60	0.57	305	
I lose track of what's important to me.	1.68	1.81	0.58	0.56	304	**
I limit my social activities.	2.17	2.30	0.58	0.52	304	**
I avoid taking on new tasks if others are willing to do them.	1.98	2.05	0.55	0.60	305	
I spend less time with my spouse.	1.95	2.01	0.53	0.58	306	
I spend less time with other family members.	1.96	1.96	0.48	0.49	306	
I attend activities separately from spouse because of conflicting schedules or responsibilities.	1.88	2.07	0.52	0.57	305	***
I divide up household chores among family members.	2.09	1.96	0.62	0.59	307	**
I limit the number of my child(ren)'s activities that I attend.	1.58	1.50	0.61	0.59	300	
I lower my expectations about what should get done around the house.	1.96	2.15	0.56	0.60	305	***

(continued)

TABLE 8.1 (continued)

Item	M		SD		n	p
	Husbands	Wives	Husbands	Wives		
I use a cell phone, pager, voice messaging, so that my family can reach me.	1.98	1.94	0.86	0.88	305	
I wish others would be more supportive.	1.89	2.18	0.54	0.56	304	***
I limit my personal time for reading, exercise, or other leisure activities.	2.16	2.38	0.57	0.56	301	***
I plan my work hours around child(ren)'s, parent'(s), or spouse's schedule.	1.82	2.21	0.64	0.74	307	***
I plan to work at home so that I can be close to my family.	1.50	1.53	0.62	0.67	302	
When necessary, I take time off from work to care for a parent or child.	1.99	2.29	0.60	0.59	303	***
I sometimes work long hours to avoid dealing with family responsibilities.	1.20	1.15	0.47	0.38	304	
I help my spouse with his/her work.	1.74	1.55	0.54	0.62	305	***
I prioritize and do the things that are most necessary.	2.46	2.48	0.52	0.53	307	

Note. Responses were made on a 3-point scale on which 1 = never, 2 = sometimes, and 3 = most or all of the time; *$p \le .05$ **$p \le .01$; ***$p \le .001$.

TABLE 8.2

Coping Strategies Used by Husbands and Wives

Behavioral coping strategies that decrease social involvement

1. I limit my social activities.

2. I spend less time with my spouse or partner.

3. I spend less time with other family members.

Emotional coping strategies that increase emotional resources

1. I try to realize that I can't do it all, and that it's okay.

2. I focus on the many good things I have.

3. I get moral support and comfort from others.

4. I try to find humor in the situation.

Cognitive coping strategies that increase prioritizing

1. I protect or set aside time for activities that are important to me.

2. I lose track of what's important to me. (R)

Note. Items were rated on a response scale on which 1 = never, 2 = sometimes, 3 = most or all of the time. R = reverse scored.

TABLE 8.3

Paired Comparisons of Coping Strategies Used by Husbands and Wives

Coping strategies	M		SD		n	p
	Husbands	Wives	Husbands	Wives		
Behavioral: Decreasing social involvement	2.02	2.09	0.40	0.41	307	*
Emotional: Increasing emotional resources	2.30	2.30	0.34	0.36	307	
Cognitive: Increasing prioritization	2.25	2.11	0.43	0.48	307	***

$*p \leq .05; ***p \leq .001.$

TABLE 8.4
Correlations Between Coping Strategies and Outcomes for Husbands and Wives

Outcomes	Emotional: Increasing emotional resources		Behavioral: Decreasing social involvement		Cognitive: Increasing prioritization	
	Husbands	Wives	Husbands	Wives	Husbands	Wives
Work–family fit						
Work-to-family conflict	-.21**	-.10	.36**	.27*	-.20**	-.23**
Family-to-work conflict	-.16**	-.09	.27**	.20**	-.14*	-.19**
Work-to-family spillover	.19**	.21**	-.20**	-.10	.10	.12*
Family-to-work spillover	.25**	.34**	-.21**	-.21**	.16**	.30**
Well-being						
Depression	-.36**	-.31**	.34**	.28**	-.36**	-.33**
Life satisfaction	.34**	.41**	-.22**	-.32**	.24**	.39**
Overall health	.11	.19**	-.13*	-.15**	.22**	.18**
Overall role performance	.25**	.30**	-.342*	-.34**	.38**	.35**
Work						
Job satisfaction	.17**	.24**	-.16**	-.11	.13*	.33**
Overall absence	.02	.04	.06	-.01	-.07	-.07
No. work accommodations made[a]	-.05	-.10	.11	.20**	-.11	-.10
Poor work performance[b]	-.11	-.04	.28**	.11*	-.18**	-.12*

[a]Due to child- and/or parent-care responsibilities in the past year. [b]Due to child- and/or parent-care responsibilities in the past month; *Correlation is significant at the .05 level (2-tailed); **Correlation is significant at the .01 level (2-tailed).

TABLE 8.5
Hierarchical Regression Analyses of the Relationship Between Coping Strategies and Work–Family Fit for Husbands and Wives

Variable	Work-to-family conflict Husbands ($n = 298$)	Work-to-family conflict Wives ($n = 301$)	Family-to-work conflict Husbands ($n = 298$)	Family-to-work conflict Wives ($n = 301$)	Work-to-family spillover Husbands ($n = 297$)	Work-to-family spillover Wives ($n = 301$)	Family-to-work spillover Husbands ($n = 298$)	Family-to-work spillover Wives ($n = 301$)
Education (years)	-.03	.09	.04	.09	.09	-.03	-.01	-.03
Ability to get along on income	.02	-.05	.03	.01	-.02	-.02	.05	-.03
Negative affectivity	.03	.11	.06	.13*	-.02	-.03	-.07	-.06
Spousal role quality	.01	-.03	-.16**	-.04	.07	.10	.09	.03
Child-care role quality	-.06	-.18***	-.06	-.15**	.18***	.07	.17***	.14*
Parent-care role quality	-.03	.01	-.14*	-.01	.08	.04	.09	.06
Job role quality	-.27***	-.15**	-.01	-.02	.24***	.17**	.15**	.13*
Change in R^2, Step 1	**.13***	**.21***	**.11***	**.12***	**.16***	**.10***	**.23***	**.12***
Use of behavioral coping strategies	.17**	.19***	.11	.16**	-.01	-.08	-.05	-.08
Use of emotional coping strategies	.03	-.06	.01	-.05	.08	.10	.18***	.15**
Use of cognitive coping strategies	-.07	.01	-.08	.01	-.06	-.04	.07	.01
Change in R^2, Step 2	**.03**	**.03**	**.02**	**.02**	**.01**	**.01**	**.04***	**.03***
Total R^2	.17***	.24***	.13***	.15***	.17***	.11***	.27***	.15***

Note. All standardized beta weights are from the second step of the regression analysis; *$p \leq .05$; **$p \leq .01$; ***$p \leq .001$.

TABLE 8.6
Hierarchical Regression Analyses of the Relationship Between Coping Strategies and Well-Being for Husbands and Wives

	Depression		Life satisfaction		Overall health		Overall role performance	
	$(n = 277)$ Husbands	$(n = 270)$ Wives	$(n = 291)$ Husbands	$(n = 298)$ Wives	$(n = 297)$ Husbands	$(n = 301)$ Wives	$(n = 297)$ Husbands	$(n = 301)$ Wives
Education (years)	-.11*	-.11*	.12*	.18***	.22***	.12*	.15***	.01
Ability to get along on income	-.06	-.17***	.05	.07	.19***	.07	.09	.10
Negative affectivity	.45***	.38***	-.17***	-.14*	-.21***	-.32***	-.14**	-.13*
Spousal role quality	-.13**	-.18***	.14**	.14**	-.01	-.02	.22***	.11*
Child-care role quality	.04	-.06	.00	.03	.06	.10	.17***	.21***
Parent-care role quality	-.07	.02	.09	.04	.08	-.02	.10*	.06
Job role quality	-.17***	-.06	.16***	.15**	.03	.05	.03	.02
Change in R^2, Step 1	**.47***	**.44***	**.32***	**.22***	**.20***	**.17***	**.35***	**.26***
Use of behavioral coping strategies	.11*	.04	-.15***	-.05	-.06	.01	-.14**	-.11
Use of emotional coping strategies	-.06	-.08	.20***	.18***	.03	-.07	.07	.05
Use of cognitive coping strategies	-.01	-.12*	.08	.05	-.01	.14*	.10	.21***
Change in R^2, Step 2	**.01***	**.03**	**.07***	**.03**	**.00**	**.02**	**.04***	**.06***
Total R^2	**.48***	**.47***	**.39***	**.25***	**.21***	**.18***	**.39***	**.32***

Note. All standardized beta weights are from the second step of the regression analysis; *$p \leq .05$; **$p \leq .01$; ***$p \leq .001$.

TABLE 8.7

Hierarchical Regression Analyses of the Relationship Between Coping Strategies and Work for Husbands and Wives

Variable	Job satisfaction		Overall absence		No. work accommodations made		Poor work performance	
	(n = 298) Husbands	(n = 301) Wives	(n = 272) Husbands	(n = 270) Wives	(n = 294) Husbands	(n = 298) Wives	(n = 297) Husbands	(n = 301) Wives
Education (years)	.05	.07	.18**	.03	-.05	-.13*	.05	.03
Ability to get along on income	-.08	-.05	.02	-.14*	.00	-.03	-.01	-.06
Negative affectivity	-.06	-.12*	-.05	.01	-.01	.01	.16*	.17**
Spouse role quality	-.02	-.04	.03	.01	.07	-.06	.00	-.06
Child-care role quality	-.02	-.02	-.16*	-.05	-.01	-.04	-.19**	-.19**
Parent-care role quality	.12**	-.08	-.03	-.02	-.16**	-.05	.01	.01
Job role quality	.60***	.60***	-.01	-.11	-.15*	-.07	-.11	-.02
Change in R^2, Step 1	**.47***	**.38***	**.06***	**.05**	**.07****	**.04**	**.11***	**.16***
Use of behavioral coping strategies	.07	-.04	-.06	.00	.16**	.06	.02	.15*
Use of emotional coping strategies	.03	.01	.05	.07	-.03	.01	.06	.03
Use of cognitive coping strategies	.14**	-.04	-.11	-.03	.02	-.04	-.00	-.03
Change in R^2, Step 2	**.02***	**.00**	**.01**	**.00**	**.02**	**.01**	**.00**	**.02**
Total R^2	**.49***	**.38***	**.07***	**.05**	**.09****	**.05**	**.11***	**.18***

Note. All standardized beta weights are from the second step of the regression analysis; *$p \leq .05$; **$p \leq .01$; ***$p \leq .001$.

TABLE 9.1
Availability of Family-Friendly Workplace Supports as Reported by Husbands and Wives

Support type	M		SD		n	p
	Husbands	Wives	Husbands	Wives		
Alternative work arrangements						
Flexible work hours	.45	.49	.50	.50	262	
Job-sharing	.11	.17	.31	.38	262	**
Telecommuting	.10	.16	.30	.37	263	0
Dependent-care supports						
Unpaid leave	.49	.66	.50	.47	261	***
Personal time off/paid leave	.64	.68	.48	.47	262	
Family health insurance	.87	.73	.34	.44	262	***
Pretax dollars for child care	.33	.36	.47	.48	262	
Pretax dollars for elder care	.10	.13	.31	.34	262	
On-site child care	.04	.08	.19	.28	261	0
Resource/referral for child care	.12	.14	.33	.35	262	
Resource/referral for elder care	.08	.08	.27	.27	262	
On-site support groups	.11	.14	.31	.35	262	
Work and family seminars	.15	.25	.36	.44	261	

Note. Availability of supports was scored as follows: 0 = no, 1 = yes; *$p \le .05$; **$p \le .01$; ***$p \le .001$.

339

TABLE 9.2
Use of Family-Friendly Workplace Supports as Reported by Husbands and Wives

Support type	M		SD		n	p
	Husbands	Wives	Husbands	Wives		
Alternative work arrangements						
Flexible work hours	.33	.44	.47	.50	246	**
Job-sharing	.05	.08	.22	.27	246	
Telecommuting	.07	.12	.25	.33	246	0
Dependent care supports						
Unpaid leave	.12	.22	.32	.42	246	***
Personal time off/paid leave	.40	.51	.49	.50	246	**
Family health insurance	.72	.52	.45	.50	246	***
Pretax dollars for child care	.07	.09	.26	.28	246	
Pretax dollars for elder care	.01	.01	.09	.11	246	
On-site child care	.02	.01	.13	.11	246	
Resource/referral for child care	.01	.01	.11	.11	246	
Resource/referral for elder care	.01	.01	.11	.09	246	
On-site support groups	.02	.03	.13	.18	246	
Work and family seminars	.07	.17	.25	.38	246	***

Note. Use of supports was scored as follows: 0 = no, 1 = yes; *$p \leq .05$; **$p \leq .01$; ***$p \leq .001$.

TABLE 9.3
Paired Comparisons of Husbands and Wives on Composite Measures of Availability and Utilization of Work Supports

Work supports	M		SD		n	p
	Husbands	Wives	Husbands	Wives		
Availability of alternate work schedule	.22	.27	.26	.30	264	0
Availability of dependent-care support	.29	.33	.18	.20	263	0
Use of alternate work schedule	.15	.21	.23	.25	246	***
Use of dependent-care support	.14	.16	.11	.12	246	

*$p \leq .05$; ***$p \leq .001$.

TABLE 9.4
Hierarchical Linear Regression Analyses of the Relationship Between Workplace Supports and Work-Family Fit for Husbands and Wives

Variable	Work-to-family conflict		Family-to-work conflict		Work-to-family spillover		Family-to-work spillover	
	(n = 256) Husbands	(n = 273) Wives	(n = 256) Husbands	(n = 273) Wives	(n = 256) Husbands	(n = 273) Wives	(n = 256) Husbands	(n = 273) Wives
Education (years)	–.08	.09	.03	.07	.08	–.04	.02	–.05
Ability to get along on income	.01	–.08**	.04	–.03	–.04	–.03	.04	–.04
Negative affectivity	.00	.16	.08	.18***	–.01	–.07	–.10	–.11
Spousal role quality	–.01	–.10	–.19***	–.09	.09	.11	.16**	.04
Child-care role quality	–.04	–.22***	–.05	–.20***	.20***	.07	.21***	.16**
Parent-care role quality	–.01	.01	–.15**	–.01	.09	.06	.08	.08
Job role quality	–.38***	–.18***	–.13	–.06	.21***	.22***	.19***	.18***
Change in R^2 at Step 1	**.20*****	**.22*****	**.12*****	**.15*****	**.17*****	**.10*****	**.23*****	**.12*****
Alternate work schedule use	.12	.07	.18**	.06	.02	–.07	–.05	–.06
Dependent-care support use	–.10	.18***	–.05	.19***	.07	.01	.05	.11
Change in R^2 at Step 2	**.02**	**.04*****	**.03***	**.04*****	**.00**	**.00**	**.00**	**.01**
Total R^2	**.17*****	**.26*****	**.14*****	**.19*****	**.17*****	**.11*****	**.23*****	**.13*****

Note. All standardized beta weights are from the second step of the regression analysis; *$p \leq .05$; **$p \leq .01$; ***$p \leq .001$.

TABLE 9.5

Hierarchical Linear Regression Analyses of the Relationship Between Use of Workplace Supports and Well-Being for Husbands and Wives

Variable	Depression		Life satisfaction		Overall health		Overall role performance	
	Husbands (n = 239)	Wives (n = 245)	Husbands (n = 251)	Wives (n = 271)	Husbands (n = 255)	Wives (n = 273)	Husbands (n = 255)	Wives (n = 273)
Education (years)	-.13*	-.07	.12*	.13*	.22**	.12*	.15*	.03
Ability to get along on income	-.07	-.17**	.03	.07	.16*	.09	.08	.14**
Negative affectivity	.47**	.46***	-.24**	-.24**	-.24**	-.34**	-.22***	-.16***
Spousal role quality	-.15***	-.19***	.23**	.17*	.04	.01	.30***	.22**
Child-care role quality	.00	-.10	.06	.05	.05	.11	.18***	.24***
Parent-care role quality	-.08	.00	.08	.04	.06	-.10	.06	.07
Job role quality	-.17**	-.13*	.19***	.19***	.00	.09	.04	.07
Change in R^2 at Step 1	**.46***	**.47***	**.33***	**.22***	**.20***	**.20***	**.36***	**.29***
Alternate work Schedule use	-.06	.05	.11*	.00	.10	-.08	.07	-.07
Dependent-care support use	.01	-.07	-.05	.12*	.14*	-.02	.16***	.02
Change in R^2 at Step 2	**.00**	**.01**	**.01**	**.02**	**.03***	**.01**	**.03****	**.01**
Total R^2	**.47***	**.47***	**.34***	**.24***	**.23***	**.20***	**.39***	**.29***

Note. All standardized beta weights are from the second step of the regression analysis; *$p \le .05$; **$p \le .01$; ***$p \le .001$.

343

TABLE 9.6
Hierarchical Linear Regression Analyses of the Relationship Between Use of Workplace Supports and Work for Husbands and Wives

Variable	Job satisfaction		Overall absence		No. work accommodations made		Poor work performance	
	Husbands (n = 256)	Wives (n = 273)	Husbands (n = 233)	Wives (n = 244)	Husbands (n = 253)	Wives (n = 272)	Husbands (n = 253)	Wives (n = 267)
Education (years)	.05	.06	.12	-.02	-.09	-.17**	.03	-.01
Ability to get along on income	-.03	-.06	.04	-.17**	.05	-.07	-.01	-.08
Negative affectivity	-.11*	-.15***	-.02	.01	.05	-.02	.11	.21***
Spousal role quality	-.04	-.03	.01	.02	.02	-.09	.01	-.10
Child-care role quality	.02	-.05	-.17*	-.08	.01	-.06	-.17**	-.22***
Parent-care role quality	.10*	-.09	-.02	.03	-.19***	-.01	-.03	.00
Job role quality	.58***	.63***	-.05	-.16**	-.19**	-.13*	-.07	-.06
Change in R² at Step 1	**.46***	**.42***	**.05**	**.05**	**.07***	**.06***	**.07***	**.18***
Alternate work schedule use	.09	.03	.15*	.27***	.17**	.18***	.02	.08
Dependent-care support use	.01	.00	.09	.17	-.03	-.04	-.03	.162***
Change in R² at Step 2	**.01**	**.00**	**.03***	**.10***	**.02***	**.03***	**.00**	**.03***
Total R²	**.47***	**.42***	**.08***	**.15***	**.10***	**.10***	**.08***	**.21***

Note. All standardized beta weights are from the second step of the regression analysis; $*p \leq .05$; $**p \leq .01$; $***p \leq .001$.

TABLE 10.1
Means, Standard Deviations, and Paired Comparisons of Personal Characteristics, Role Demands, Role Quality, and Outcomes at Waves 1 and 2: Husbands

	Wave 1 M	Wave 2 M	Wave 1 SD	Wave 2 SD	n	p
Personal characteristics						
Education (years)	14.73		2.76		234	
Ability to get along on income	2.80	2.89	0.71	0.71	228	*
Negative affectivity	2.52	2.43	0.70	0.73	232	*
Role characteristics						
Child-care Role						
No. children ≤ 18 in household	1.82	1.67	0.76	0.78	234	***
Child with special needs	.11	0.08	0.32	0.28	224	
Parent-care role						
No. parents/in-laws helping	1.65	1.25	0.91	0.88	233	***
No. ADL respondent helps with	1.60	2.00	2.19	3.23	218	
Job role						
No. hours worked per week	49.34	48.73	10.21	10.34	224	
Flexibility in work schedule	2.96	2.91	0.82	0.85	223	
Role quality						
Spousal	1.66	1.60	1.16	1.25	231	
Child care	1.80	1.78	0.82	0.84	234	

(continued)

TABLE 10.1 (continued)

	Wave 1 M	Wave 2 M	Wave 1 SD	Wave 2 SD	n	p
Parent care	1.43	1.39	1.08	1.08	199	
Job	0.87	0.88	1.04	1.15	225	
Outcomes						
Work–family fit						
Work-to-family conflict	3.10	2.94	0.92	1.08	226	**
Family-to-work conflict	2.17	2.05	0.67	0.70	226	*
Positive work-to-family spillover	3.60	3.61	0.69	.78	225	
Positive family-to-work spillover	3.82	3.71	0.63	0.76	226	*
Well-being						
Depression	11.18	10.29	8.02	8.35	233	
Life satisfaction	5.20	4.93	1.19	1.22	228	***
Overall health	4.54	4.44	0.91	0.87	229	*
Overall role performance	4.36	4.37	0.63	0.66	229	
Work related						
Job satisfaction	3.47	3.51	0.69	0.76	225	
Overall absence	2.49	2.66	3.10	3.28	199	
Use of work accommodations	0.90	0.67	1.10	1.02	231	**
Poor work performance	1.92	1.94	0.73	0.77	223	

$*p \leq .05; **p \leq .01; ***p \leq .001.$

TABLE 10.2
Means, Standard Deviations, and Paired Comparisons of Personal Characteristics, Role Demands, Role Quality, and Outcomes at Waves 1 and 2: Wives

	Wave 1	Wave 2	Wave 1	Wave 2		
	M	M	SD	SD	n	p
Personal characteristics						
Education (years)	15.26		2.69		234	
Ability to get along on income	2.69	2.77	0.76	0.77	226	
Negative affectivity	2.78	2.68	0.75	0.69	230	**
Role characteristics						
Child-care role						
No. children ≤ 18 in household	1.81	1.68	0.75	0.79	234	***
Child with special needs	0.16	0.11	0.37	0.31	225	***
Parent-care role						
No. parents/in-laws helping	1.83	1.33	0.90	0.92	234	***
No. ADL respondent helps with	2.48	2.62	2.69	3.43	220	
Job role						
No. hours worked per week	37.74	37.95	9.41	9.59	225	
Flexibility in work schedule	3.13	3.17	0.83	0.72	225	
Role quality						
Spousal	1.40	1.30	1.26	1.34	232	
Child care	1.72	1.68	0.85	0.82	234	
Parent care	1.47	1.31	1.11	1.10	200	*

(continued)

TABLE 10.2 (continued)

	Wave 1 M	Wave 2 M	Wave 1 SD	Wave 2 SD	n	p
Job	1.06	1.11	0.98	1.01	225	
Outcomes						
Work–family fit						
Work-to-family conflict	2.95	2.75	1.01	1.06	224	***
Family-to-work conflict	2.29	2.08	0.82	0.81	224	***
Positive work-to-family spillover	3.71	3.75	0.73	0.71	223	
Positive family-to-work spillover	4.00	3.91	0.63	0.70	224	*
Well-being						
Depression	12.54	10.84	9.02	7.92	230	***
Life satisfaction	5.21	5.01	1.13	1.13	228	**
Overall health	4.59	4.55	0.88	0.93	232	
Overall role performance	4.42	4.46	0.61	0.65	232	
Work related						
Job satisfaction	3.51	3.57	0.67	0.74	224	
Overall absence	4.66	4.32	4.28	4.55	204	
Use of work accommodations	1.32	1.09	1.38	1.30	228	**
Poor work performance	2.32	2.32	0.86	0.87	219	

Note. ADL = activities of daily living; *$p \leq .05$; **$p \leq .01$; ***$p \leq .001$.

TABLE 10.3
Changes Experienced by Husbands and Wives in Role Demands and Role Quality Between Waves 1 and 2

Variable	Husbands (n = 234)				Wive (n = 234)			
	Increased	Decreased	Same	Missing	Increased	Decreased	Same	Missing
Role demands								
Child-care role								
No. children ≤18	1.3	15.8	82.9	0	2.6	15.0	82.4	0
Child with special needs	2.6	5.1	88	4.3	1.3	6.4	88.5	3.8
Parent-care role								
No. parents helping	10.3	35.9	53.4	.4	6.4	38.5	55.1	0
No. ADL respondent helps with	30.3	27.8	35.1	6.8	30.3	31.6	32.1	6.0
Job role								
No. hours worked	27.4	32.9	38.4	1.3	29.1	29.5	41.4	0
Flexibility in work schedule	18.8	21.8	54.7	4.7	20.5	19.7	56	3.8
Role quality								
Spousal	42.3	48.7	7.7	1.3	44.0	49.1	6	.9
Child care	47.9	48.7	3.4	0	44.4	53.4	2.2	0
Parent care	38.9	43.6	2.5	15.0	35.5	49.6	.4	14.5
Job	49.1	46.2	.9	3.8	47.4	48.3	.5	3.8

Note. All standardized beta weights are from the third step of the regression analysis. Flexibility in work schedule refers specifically to flexibility to handle family responsibilities. All table values are percentages. ADL = activities of daily living.

TABLE 10.4

Hierarchical Linear Regression Analyses of the Relationship Between Role Changes and Work–Family Fit for Husbands and Wives

Variable	Husbands (n = 168)	Wives (n = 175)	Husbands (n = 168)	Wives (n = 175)	Husbands (n = 168)	Wives (n = 174)	Husbands (n = 168)	Wives (n = 175)
Education (years)—Wave 1	-.16*	.21***	.04	.17**	.00	.00	-.06	.00
Ability to get along on income—Wave 1	.04	-.04	-.00	-.00	-.03	.11	.02	.18**
Negative affectivity—Wave 1	.22**	.11†	-.00	.05	.04	-.05	-.12	-.13*
Wave 1 dependent variable	-.33***	-.42***	-.48***	-.50***	-.47***	-.57***	-.39***	-.46***
Change in R^2 at Step 1	**.17***	**.26***	**.23***	**.27***	**.23***	**.32***	**.20***	**.21***
No. children ≤18 (change)	-.04	.03	-.08	.07	-.10	.11	.02	.01
Child with special needs (change)	-.06	-.05	.01	.10	.02	.03	-.07	-.06
No. parents/in-laws helping (change)	-.02	-.01	-.06	-.03	-.01	-.10	-.05	-.12†
No. ADL respondent helps with (change)	-.01	.07	-.13†	.07	.12	-.00	.03	-.02
No. hours worked per week (change)	.16*	.28***	-.03	.04	.04	-.05	-.01	.01
Flexibility in work schedule (change)	-.09	.01	.05	-.11	-.04	-.06	.15*	-.02

Variable	Husbands (n = 168)	Wives (n = 175)	Husbands (n = 168)	Wives (n = 175)	Husbands (n = 168)	Wives (n = 174)	Husbands (n = 168)	Wives (n = 175)
Change in R^2 at Step 2	.05	.08**	.02	.04	.03	.02	.04	.03
Spousal role quality (change)	-.03	-.14*	-.01	.01	.00	.13†	-.10	.20**
Child-care role quality (change)	-.05	-.04	.00	.11	.04	.03	.06	-.08
Parent-care role quality (change)	-.02	-.05	-.15*	-.10	.06	.16*	.09	.16*
Job role quality (change)	-.22**	-.22***	-.12†	.04	.10	.17**	-.02	.22***
Change in R^2 at Step 3	.05*	.07***	.03	.02	.01	.07***	.02	.11***
Total R^2	.27***	.42***	.28***	.33***	.27***	.42***	.26***	.34***

Note. All standardized beta weights are from the third step of the regression analysis. Flexibility in work schedule refers specifically to flexibility to handle family responsibilities. ADL = activities of daily living; †$p \le .10$; *$p \le .05$; **$p \le .01$; ***$p \le .001$.

TABLE 10.5
Hierarchical Linear Regression Analyses of the Relationship Between Role Changes and Well-Being for Husbands and Wives

Variable	Depression (change)		Life satisfaction (change)		Overall health (change)		Overall role performance (change)	
	Husbands (n = 157)	Wives (n = 157)	Husbands (n = 163)	Wives (n = 170)	Husbands (n = 164)	Wives (n = 173)	Husbands (n = 164)	Wives (n = 173)
Education (years)—Wave 1	.02	.05	.13†	.00	.06	.02	-.01	-.08
Ability to get along on income—Wave 1	-.06	-.06	-.07	.07	-.03	.03	.05	.02
Negative affectivity—Wave 1	.27**	.11	-.15†	-.09	-.10	-.06	-.10	.02
Wave 1 dependent variable	-.57***	-.58***	-.57***	-.51***	-.49***	-.36***	-.43***	-.31***
Change in R^2 at Step 1	**.20***	**.33***	**.29***	**.26***	**.20***	**.12***	**.16***	**.11***
No. children ≤18 (change)	.00	-.02	-.05	-.06	.05	-.04	-.02	.04
Child with special needs (change)	.08	.05	.08	.03	.00	-.01	.01	.10
No. parents/in-laws helping (change)	-.07	.04	.09	-.05	.10	-.08	.03	.01
No. ADL respondent helps with (change)	-.08	-.00	.03	.13†	.03	-.06	.10	-.01
No. hours worked per week (change)	.02	-.05	.10	-.04	.02	-.10	.06	-.09
Flexibility in work schedule (change)	-.12	-.02	-.00	.01	.10	-.04	.12	-.05

Variable	Depression (change)		Life satisfaction (change)		Overall health (change)		Overall role performance (change)	
	Husbands ($n = 157$)	Wives ($n = 157$)	Husbands ($n = 163$)	Wives ($n = 170$)	Husbands ($n = 164$)	Wives ($n = 173$)	Husbands ($n = 164$)	Wives ($n = 173$)
Change in R^2 at Step 2	.03	.01	.03	.02	.02	.02	.03	.02
Spousal role quality (change)	−.02	−.26***	.10	.17*	.01	.03	.16*	.24**
Child-care role quality (change)	.01	−.09	.01	.10	−.09	.10	−.00	.14†
Parent-care role quality (change)	−.03	−.10	.10	.21**	.11	.03	.20**	.05
Job role quality (change)	.01	−.08	.05	.06	.04	.00	.03	.08
Change in R^2 at Step 3	.00	.11***	.02	.09***	.02	.01	.06*	.10***
Total R^2	.23***	.46***	.34***	.38***	.24***	.15***	.25***	.22***

Note. All standardized beta weights are from the third step of the regression analysis. Flexibility in work schedule refers specifically to flexibility to handle family responsibilities. ADL = activities of daily living; †$p \le .10$; *$p \le .05$; **$p \le .01$; ***$p \le .001$.

TABLE 10.6
Hierarchical Linear Regression Analyses of the Relationship Between Role Changes and Work-Related Outcomes for Husbands and Wives

Variable	Job satisfaction (change)		Overall absence (change)		Use of work accommodations (change)		Poor work performance (change)	
	Husbands (n = 168)	Wives (n = 175)	Husbands (n = 145)	Wives (n = 153)	Husbands (n = 167)	Wives (n = 171)	Husbands (n = 166)	Wives (n = 171)
Education (years)—Wave 1	.03	-.12†	-.13†	.14†	.07	.06	.05	.08
Ability to get along on income—Wave 1	-.14*	.00	-.18*	.01	-.11†	-.04	-.02	-.06
Negative affectivity—Wave 1	-.07	.08	-.03	-.04	-.13*	-.17**	.05	.25***
Wave 1 dependent variable	-.34***	-.26***	-.47***	-.37***	-.61***	-.52***	-.55***	-.45***
Change in R^2 at Step 1	**.16***	**.17***	**.28***	**.16***	**.40***	**.33***	**.30***	**.23***
No. children ≤18 (change)	.02	-.06	.06	.05	.10	.03	-.09	-.04
Child with special needs (change)	-.01	-.04	.09	-.01	.00	-.03	-.06	-.03
No. parents/in-laws helping (change)	.08	-.07	.05	-.03	-.01	-.01	.05	-.02
No. ADL respondent helps with (change)	.07	-.04	-.03	-.04	-.01	-.04	.02	.24***
No. hours worked per week (change)	-.11	.05	.13†	.20*	.01	-.08	-.01	-.18**
Flexibility in work schedule (change)	.06	.10	.05	.22**	.05	.01	.06	-.09

Variable	Job satisfaction (change)		Overall absence (change)		Use of work accommodations (change)		Poor work performance (change)	
	Husbands (n = 168)	Wives (n = 175)	Husbands (n = 145)	Wives (n = 153)	Husbands (n = 167)	Wives (n = 171)	Husbands (n = 166)	Wives (n = 171)
Change in R² at Step 2	.06†	.04	.03	.07†	.02	.02	.02	.07*
Spousal role quality (change)	-.01	.09	.03	.07	-.12†	-.10	.14*	.13†
Child-care role quality (change)	.01	-.20**	.01	.04	.07	.14†	-.18*	-.21**
Parent-care role quality (change)	.02	.03	.07	-.06	-.12†	-.02	-.12†	.03
Job role quality (change)	.37***	.46***	.03	-.07	.01	.09	.00	.03
Change in R² at Step 3	.12***	.22***	.01	.01	.02	.03	.06*	.04†
Total R²	.34***	.43***	.31***	.24***	.44***	.37***	.37***	.33***

Note. All standardized beta weights are from the third step of the regression analysis. Flexibility in work schedule refers specifically to flexibility to handle family responsibilities. ADL = activities of daily living; †$p \leq .10$; *$p \leq .05$; **$p \leq .01$; ***$p \leq .001$.

Author Index

Subject Index